# Multi-level Reconciliation and Peacebuilding

This edited volume examines the group dynamics of social reconciliation in conflict-affected societies by adopting ideas developed in social psychology and the everyday peace discourse in peace and conflict studies.

The book revisits the intra- and inter-group dynamics of social reconciliation in conflict-affected societies, which have been largely marginalised in mainstream peacebuilding debates. By applying social psychological perspectives and the discourse of everyday peace, the chapters explore the everyday experience of community actors engaged in social and political reconciliation. The first part of the volume introduces conceptual and theoretical studies that focus on the pros and cons of state-level reconciliation and their outcomes, while presenting theoretical insights into dialogical processes upon which reconciliation studies can develop further. The second part presents a series of empirical case studies from around the world, which examine the process of social reconciliation at community levels through the lens of social psychology and discourse analysis.

This book will be of much interest to students of peacebuilding, conflict resolution, social psychology, discourse analysis and international relations in general.

**Kevin P. Clements** is Emeritus Professor at the University of Otago, New Zealand and the Director of Toda Peace Institute, Japan.

**SungYong Lee** is Associate Professor of the National Centre for Peace and Conflict Studies at the University of Otago, New Zealand.

## Routledge Studies in Peace and Conflict Resolution

The field of peace and conflict research has grown enormously as an academic pursuit in recent years, gaining credibility and relevance amongst policy-makers and in the international humanitarian and NGO sector. The Routledge Studies in Peace and Conflict Resolution series aims to provide an outlet for some of the most significant new work emerging from this academic community, and to establish itself as a leading platform for innovative work at the point where peace and conflict research impacts on international relations theory and processes.

Series Editors: Tom Woodhouse and Oliver Ramsbotham
*University of Bradford*

**Negotiating Intractable Conflicts**
Readiness theory revisited
*Amira Schiff*

**Political Expression and Conflict Transformation in Divided Societies**
Criminalising politics and politicising crime
*Daniel Kirkpatrick*

**Peace in International Relations**
*Oliver P. Richmond*

**Root Narrative Theory and Conflict Resolution**
Power, justice and values
*Solon Simmons*

**Healing and Peacebuilding After War**
Transforming trauma in Bosnia and Herzegovina
*Edited by Julianne Funk, Nancy Good and Marie E. Berry*

**Multi-level Reconciliation and Peacebuilding**
Stakeholder perspectives
*Edited by Kevin P. Clements and SungYong Lee*

For more information about this series, please visit: https://www.routledge.com/Routledge-Studies-in-Peace-and-Conflict-Resolution/book-series/RSPCR

# Multi-level Reconciliation and Peacebuilding

## Stakeholder Perspectives

**Edited by Kevin P. Clements and SungYong Lee**

Routledge
Taylor & Francis Group
LONDON AND NEW YORK

First published 2021
by Routledge
2 Park Square, Milton Park, Abingdon, Oxon OX14 4RN

and by Routledge
52 Vanderbilt Avenue, New York, NY 10017

*Routledge is an imprint of the Taylor & Francis Group, an informa business*



*British Library Cataloguing-in-Publication Data*
A catalogue record for this book is available from the British Library

*Library of Congress Cataloging-in-Publication Data*
A catalog record has been requested for this book

ISBN: 978-0-367-86231-2 (hbk)
ISBN: 978-1-003-01785-1 (ebk)

Typeset in Times New Roman
by Deanta Global Publishing Services, Chennai, India

# Contents

# Figures

# Tables

# Contributors

**Mohammed Abu-Nimer** is a Senior Advisor to KAICIID and a Professor at the School of International Service at American University. At the International Peace and Conflict Resolution programme, he served as Director of the Peacebuilding and Development Institute (1999–2013). He has conducted interreligious conflict resolution training and interfaith dialogue workshops in conflict areas around the world, including Palestine, Israel, Egypt, Chad, Niger, Iraq (Kurdistan), the Philippines (Mindanao) and Sri Lanka. He also founded the Salam Institute for Peace and Justice, an organisation that focuses on capacity-building, civic education and intrafaith and interfaith dialogue. In addition to his numerous articles and books, Dr Abu-Nimer is the co-founder and co-editor of *Journal of Peacebuilding and Development.*

**Kevin P. Clements** is Emeritus Professor and Foundation Chair of the National Centre for Peace and Conflict Studies at the Otago University, and Director of Toda Peace Institute, Japan. Prior to taking up these positions he was Foundation Director of the Australian Centre for Peace and Conflict Studies at the University of Queensland, Director of International Alert (London) and Lynch Professor and Director of the Institute for Conflict Analysis and Resolution at George Mason University. His career has been a combination of academic analysis and practice in the areas of peacebuilding and conflict transformation. He was the Secretary General of the International Peace Research Association and the Asia Pacific Peace Research Association. His most recent publications include *Toward a century of peace: A dialogue on the role of civil society in peacebuilding* (with Daisaku Ikeda, 2019, Abingdon, UK: Routledge) and *Identity, trust, and reconciliation in East Asia: Dealing with painful history to create a peaceful present* (2017, Cham, Switzerland: Palgrave Macmillan).

**Mari Fitzduff** is Professor Emerita at the Heller School for Social Policy and Management, Brandeis University. From 1990 to 1997, she served as chief executive of the Northern Ireland Community Relations Council, which was at the forefront in developing governmental policies and local community programs to tackle many decades of violent conflict. More recently she served as director of UNU/INCORE, a United Nations University centre and one of the world's leading organisations for international research on conflict. The centre was based at the University of Ulster, where she was Chair of Conflict Studies. Her many publications include *Community Conflict Skills: A Handbook for Anti-Sectarian Work* (1998, Community Conflict Skills Project); *Beyond Violence: Conflict Resolution Processes in Northern Ireland* (2002, Tokyo: UN University Press, won an American Library Association Notable Book award) and *NGOs at the Table* (co-edited with Cheyanne Church, 2004, Lanham: Rowman & Littlefield). She is also a co-editor of the three-volume series *The Psychology of War, Conflict Resolution* and *Peace*. In addition, she has edited *Public Policies for Shared Societies* which is concerned with optimal public policies for divided societies. Her current interest is in Conflict and Neuroscience and she has published an *Introduction to Neuroscience for Peacebuilders*.

**Damian Grenfell** works at RMIT University in Melbourne as an Associate Professor in the School of Global, Urban and Social Studies and Director of the Centre for Global Research. Through his work he has primarily focused on questions of social transformation in the wake of conflict, particularly in post-colonial states. As part of his work for RMIT, he has undertaken many research projects, particularly in Timor-Leste, with areas of focus being peace, reconciliation and conflict, gender (particularly gender-based violence), development and security. His recent publications appeared in Wallis, J. et al. (eds),2 *Hybridity on the ground in peacebuilding and development: Critical conversations* (2018, Canberra: Australian National University Press); Grenfell, D. and Warren, A. (eds), *Rethinking Humanitarian Intervention in the 21st Century* (2017, Edinburgh: Edinburgh University Press).

**J. M. Inton-Campbell** is a PhD Student at the National Centre for Peace and Conflict Studies at the University of Otago. I am currently researching how intergroup contact in an international development context between international volunteers and host-country counterparts influences intergroup relations across borders. A research framework based upon this work has been published in the *Journal of Peacebuilding and Development*. I completed an MA in Peace Studies at International Christian University as a Rotary Peace Fellow and is a Returned Peace Corps Volunteer (Morocco, 2012–2014).

**Mariska Kappmeier** is a Lecturer at the National Centre for Peace and Conflict Studies at the University of Otago. Her research focuses on intergroup conflict, identity and trust, addressing how intergroup conflicts can be overcome through quantified methods for trust building. Through her past research, she has developed the Intergroup Trust Model, which hypothesises that trust between groups is shaped by the five dimensions of competence, integrity, compassion, compatibility and security. Her articles and chapters appeared in *Journal of Social and Political Psychology*, *Peace and Conflict: Journal of Peace Psychology*, *Journal of Peacebuilding & Development* and J. Rothman (Ed.), *From Identity-Based Conflict to Identity-Based Cooperation* (2012, New York: Springer).

**SungYong Lee** is Associate Professor of the National Centre for Peace and Conflict Studies at the University of Otago. His areas of research expertise include third-party mediation in civil war peace negotiation, liberal peacebuilding and its alternatives and post-conflict reconstruction in Southeast Asia. His recent books include *Local Ownership in Asian Peacebuilding: Development of Local Peacebuilding Models* (2019, Basingstoke: Palgrave Macmillan), *International Peacebuilding: An Introduction* (with Alpaslan Özerdem, 2016, London and New York: Routledge) and *Local Ownership in International Peacebuilding* (with Alpaslan Özerdem, 2015, London and New York: Routledge).

**Caitlin Mollica** is a Lecturer with the School of Justice at Queensland University of Technology. Her research interests include youth, gender, transitional justice and human rights. Caitlin's primary research considers the engagement of young people with transitional justice and human rights practices. She has a PhD from Griffith University and an MA in Human Rights Studies from Columbia University. Her recent publications on reconciliation appeared in *Australian Journal of International Affairs* and *Pacific Review*.

**Raymond F. Paloutzian** is Professor Emeritus of Experimental and Social Psychology, and Fellow of the American Psychological Association and the Association for Psychological Science. He edited *The International Journal for the Psychology of Religion* for 18 years, and wrote at Westmont College, Stanford University, and University of Leuven. Paloutzian authored *Invitation to the Psychology of Religion* (3rd edn, 2017, New York: Guilford), co-edited *Forgiveness and Reconciliation* (2010, Cham: Springer), *Handbook of the Psychology of Religion and Spirituality* (2nd edn, 2013, Guilford), *Processes of Believing: The Acquisition, Maintenance and Change in Creditions* (2017, Cham: Springer) and *Assessing Spirituality in a Diverse World* (2020, Cham: Springer). He has given invited talks on "The Psychology of Religion in Global Perspective" in various countries around the world.

**Rachel Rafferty** works as a lecturer at the Department of Criminology and Social Sciences, University of Derby. She holds a PhD in Peace and Conflict Studies from the National Centre for Peace and Conflict Studies in the University of Otago. Her research investigates the ways that narratives can shape intergroup relations, with a particular focus on the political psychology of individuals living in post-conflict societies. Dr Rafferty's recent publications on reconciliation in Northern Ireland were published in *Peace and Conflict: Journal of Peace Psychology* and *Conflict Resolution Quarterly*.

**Zeynep Sagir** received her PhD in the Psychology of Religion from Istanbul University in May 2018 and is now Assistant Professor teaching Psychology at Firat University, Turkey. She has done extensive research with over 2,000

Syrian refugees in Turkey from the war in Syria, uniquely in part on the Syrian border in earshot of bombs. She almost immediately became viewed as a "refugee expert" and was highly sought after – she gave no less than four invited presentations before she got her degree. Her recent research has been on prejudice against refugees and lack of attention to disabled refugees. Of special concern in her research is the plight of refugee women.

**Chaiwat Satha-Anand** is Director and Founder of the Peace Information Center and Professor of Political Science at Thammasat University, Thailand. He is also Chairperson of the Strategic Nonviolence Commission in Thailand. Dr Satha-Anand is an expert on nonviolence theory and activism, and on Islam. For several years, he directed the International Peace Research Association's (IPRA) Commission on Nonviolence and serves on the Scientific Committee of the International University for Peoples' Initiative for Peace (IUPIP) in Rovereto, Italy. Dr Satha-Anand was the 2012 winner of the El-Hibri Peace Education Prize. His latest publications include *Nonviolence and Islamic Imperatives* (2017, Sparnas: Irene Publishing), *The Promise of Reconciliation? Examining Violent and Nonviolent Effects on Asian Conflicts* (2016, New Brunswick and London: Transaction Publishers), *Nonkilling Security and the State* (2013, Honolulu and Omaha: Center for Global Nonkilling), *Protecting the Sacred, Creating Peace in Asia-Pacific* (2013, New Brunswick and London: Transaction Publishers) and *Imagined Land?: The State and Southern Violence in Thailand* (2009, Tokyo, Japan: Sanrei Printing Co.).

**Ria Shibata** is a Research Fellow at the National Centre for Peace and Conflict Studies, University of Otago. Dr Shibata's research interests are in the areas of conflict resolution and reconciliation with a specific focus on identity, collective memory, victimhood and intractable conflicts. She is particularly interested in understanding how collective memory of historical trauma forms a group's identity and can become a major impediment to restoring damaged relationships between the perpetrator and the victim. Dr Shibata has also been trained in practical skills and strategies for conflict management and resolution through SIT's CONTACT program. Her recent publications on identity and reconciliation appeared in the *Journal of Peacebuilding and Development*, and Kevin Clements (ed.) *Identity, Trust, and Reconciliation in East Asia* (2018, Basingstoke: Palgrave Macmillan).

**F. LeRon Shults** is Professor at the Institute for Global Development and Social Planning at the University of Agder and scientific director of the Center for Modeling Social Systems at NORCE in Kristiansand, Norway. He has published 18 books and over 120 scientific articles and book chapters on topics related to religion, secularisation, computer modelling and the philosophy of science. Shults's most recent books are *Practicing Safe Sects: Religious Reproduction in Scientific and Philosophical Perspective* (2018, Leiden and Boston: Brill) and *Human Simulation: Perspectives, Insights, and Applications* (2019, Cham: Springer).

**Ervin Staub** is Professor Emeritus of Psychology at the University of Massachusetts, Amherst. He has been president of the International Society of Political Psychology as well as the Society for the Study of Peace, Conflict, and Violence. Dr Staub has published numerous articles and chapters on helping behaviour and altruism, the passivity of bystanders in the face of others' need, the development of caring and ways to reduce aggression in children. Included among his extensive writings are the influential *Psychology of Evil: The Origins of Genocide and Other Group Violence* (1994, Cambridge: Cambridge University Press) and *The Roots of Goodness and Resistance to Evil: Inclusive Caring, Moral Courage, Altruism Born of Suffering, Active Bystandership and Heroism* (2015, Oxford: Oxford University Press).

**Chiara Venanzetti** is currently enrolled as a PhD student at the National Centre for Peace and Conflict Studies, University of Otago. Her interest in social and political psychology has led her to deepen her knowledge about racism, political propaganda and intergroup trust, focusing on the immigrant communities in Italy. Chiara's other areas of interest include history and sociology (e.g., the rise of fascism, the Shoah, dehumanisation and deindividuation processes).

# Acknowledgements

First of all, we deeply appreciate all of our contributors to this volume, who worked with us diligently and patiently. We owe thanks to Tom Woodhouse and Oliver Ramsbotham, the editors of Routledge Studies in Peace and Conflict Resolution, as well as Andrew Humphrys (Senior Editor) and Bethany Lund-Yates (Editorial Assistant) of Routledge, for their support in the development of this volume. Special gratitude goes to Rosemary McBryde who edited the first draft of the manuscript. In the development of this book we benefitted greatly from the friendship and support of colleagues at the National Centre for Peace and Conflict Studies, University of Otago (New Zealand) and the editorial support from the Toda Peace Institute (Japan).

# Abbreviations

| | |
|---|---|
| **CAVR** | Commission for Reception, Truth and Reconciliation (Timor-Leste) |
| **CFA** | Ceasefire Agreement |
| **CNRT** | The National Council for Timorese Reconstruction, the (Timor-Leste) |
| **CRP** | Community Reconciliation Program, the (Timor-Leste) |
| **CVE** | Countering Violent Extremism |
| **ECCC** | Extraordinary Chambers in the Courts of Cambodia, the (Cambodia) |
| **GCC** | Grand Coalition for Change, the (the Solomon Islands) |
| **GRA** | Guadalcanal Revolutionary Army, the (the Solomon Islands) |
| **IFM** | Isatabu Freedom Movement, the (the Solomon Islands) |
| **IGT** | Inter-group Trust |
| **INTERFET** | International Force East Timor, the (Timor-Leste) |
| **IRD** | Interreligious Dialogue |
| **KR** | Khmer Rouge, the (Cambodia) |
| **LLRC** | Lessons Learnt and Reconciliation Commission, the (Sri Lanka) |
| **LTTE** | Liberation Tigers of Tamil Eelam, the (Sri Lanka) |
| **PRK** | People's Republic of Kampuchea, the (Cambodia) |
| **PVE** | Preventing Violent Extremism |
| **PVO** | Prosocial value orientation |
| **RAMSI** | Regional Assistance Mission to the Solomon Islands, the (the Solomon Islands) |
| **SICA** | Solomon Islands Christian Association, the |
| **TCM** | Trust and Conflict Map |
| **TMS** | Transcranial magnetic stimulation |
| **TRC** | Truth and Reconciliation Commission |
| **TRCT** | Truth for Reconciliation Commission of Thailand (Thailand) |
| **UNTAET** | United Nations Transitional Authority for East Timor, the (Timor-Leste) |
| **vmPFC** | Ventromedial prefrontal cortex |

# 1 Introduction

*Kevin P. Clements and SungYong Lee*

> Reconciliation requires changes of heart and spirit, as well as social and economic change. It requires symbolic as well as practical action.

This axiomatic statement of Malcolm Fraser (2003) reinforces the importance of a holistic approach to reconciliation in conflict-affected societies. From an individual's inner trauma to residual grievances between different identity groups, there are multi-layered and inter-connected factors that generate and intensify victimhood and seemingly irreconcilable divisions between different social actors. If we are to build mutuality across boundaries of difference and attend to diverse broken relationships, it is critical that we think in a systemic and multidimensional way so that we can see that things which are apart are in fact connected and work to ensure social healing at micro, meso and macro levels of analysis and action. Such a holistic approach to reconciliation is particularly needed in the societies that have experienced mass violence between different identity groups. But what do we really know about how to implement such holistic measures in post-conflict peacebuilding processes?

Although academic studies on reconciliation have a long history, it is only since the mid-1990s that reconciliation has been extensively discussed in the context of post-conflict peacebuilding (Kelman 2008; Bar-Tal and Bennink 2004). The relative success of the Truth and Reconciliation Commission (TRC) in post-apartheid South Africa drew keen attention from many post-war societies about how to bring about consolidated peace and reconciliation between former warring parties. Since then, "social reconciliation" quickly emerged as a central element in peacebuilding processes (Lerche 2000: 61) and a range of programmes for "assisting antagonists to put their pasts of violence and estrangement behind them" have been implemented. Academic debates on the nature and functions of reconciliation in conflict-affected societies have been developed in academic disciplines like Peace and Conflict Studies, Politics, International Studies, Psychology, Human Geography, Sociology and the like.[1] Through such research, the complexity and multidimensionality of reconciliation have been clarified and examined. Reconciliation requires deep psychological, sociological, theological and philosophical insights and actions at multiple levels (national, societal, communal levels). This chapter argues that the practice of peacebuilding should come up with holistic, contextualised and systematic approaches to reconciliation.

Nevertheless, despite renewed attention to reconciliation in contemporary peacebuilding programmes, its community-level dimensions remain under-theorised and under-researched. Instead, most attention was given to different reconciliation mechanisms that are mainly relevant to state or inter-state institutions (e.g., Alfonsin 1993; Lederach 1997; Amnesty International 1998; Rigby 2001). For instance, state peacebuilding agencies considered truth-telling, reparation to victims and prosecution of the perpetrators as the primary resources for promoting reconciliation, through organisations such as the TRC, international tribunals for war crimes, reparations for victims, sites and practices of remembrance and educational measures that have been adopted in most reconciliation programmes. TRCs especially were considered the single most important institution and some 40 peacebuilding processes have applied this mode of reconciliation over the past decades. A large number of humanitarian agencies and peacebuilding organisations nowadays incorporate social reconciliation programmes into their portfolios and Western donor agencies have adopted reconciliation as one of four key areas for funding (Smith 2004; Bloomfield 2006). In addition to these institutions, peacebuilding actors also pay attention to the roles of security, political, economic and governance structures in supporting good conditions for reconciliation (Bloomfield 2003; Bar-Tal and Bennink 2004; Guthrey 2015; Breen Smyth 2007; Rotberg and Thompson 2000; Bockers et al. 2011).

The limitations of such state-centric institutional approaches to social reconciliation, however, became obvious in the late 1990s. Some studies argued that economic and political institutions may play a supplementary role, but cannot offer sufficient conditions for reconciliation; others clarified that these institutions may work in "democratic" countries, but not in nondemocratic states (Lederach 1997, 1998; Simpson 1997; Kriesberg 1998; Lipschutz 1998; Wilmer 1998; Arnson 1999; Arthur 1999; Breuneis 2016: 9; Lie et al. 2007). Moreover, from a broader perspective, it was found that the domination of Western models of peacebuilding creates many barriers to the promotion of sustainable and consolidated peace in conflict-affected areas. Notwithstanding the findings and suggestions, the forms of major practice for reconciliation have not changed much and are still based upon state-centric assumptions (Hameiri 2010; Charbonneau and Parent 2012).

In the light of this bias, recent peacebuilding practice regarding reconciliation has been supplemented by and integrated into a wider range of research on reconciliation in general. *Multi-Level Reconciliation and Peacebuilding* offers a different perspective on ways in which conflict-affected areas can think about reconciliation in holistic terms. This edited volume aims to illuminate the intra- and intergroup dynamics of reconciliation that emerged in the post-conflict peacebuilding process, by focusing attention on social, psychological and bottom-up practices of reconciliation.

Under the overarching question of "How do people rebuild and define the relations with former harm-doers in their everyday lives?," 12 chapters investigate more specific questions from conceptual, theoretical and practical perspectives.

Each chapter reflects on the cognitive and psychological aspects of reconciliation at the inter-personal and intergroup levels in *conflict-affected societies*. In terms of the topic areas, this volume examines various aspects of reconciliation at individual, interpersonal and intergroup levels, as well as their implications in laying the groundwork and creating ripe conditions for top-level mechanisms for reconciliation (such as TRCs) to take place.

## Social psychology and the discourse of everyday peace

In developing the core analytical frameworks of this project, the literature on reconciliation developed in social psychology and the "everyday peace" discourse in peace and conflict studies offers particularly useful references, although the perspectives in the contributing chapters are not restricted to these research areas only.

First, the studies developed in social psychology offer a foundation for understanding how people understand reconciliation with their former enemies and react to the practice aimed at facilitating reconciliation. Conventional studies on reconciliation in this discipline have illuminated the roles of "psychological ingredients (…) to discuss the very different context that applies in a post-violence society emerging from a sustained war or an oppressive regime" (Bloomfield 2006: 10).

At the individual level, healing and forgiveness, among other aspects, have attracted keen academic attention. The importance of psychological healing of the victims has been emphasised as the first step toward reconciliation, enabling victims to cope with trauma with a sense of dignity (Volkan 2006, 2008; Parent 2011; Hamber 2009; Staub 2003; Charbonneau and Parent 2012). Nevertheless, healing in the aftermath of chronic violence and material deprivation tends to be a lengthy and non-linear process (Parent 2011), and is marked by various procedures and outcomes depending on the individuals, groups and communities (Galappatti 2003; Kandowitz and Riak 2008). Hence, any attempt to come up with a universally applicable prescription for healing is likely to end up in failure.

While forgiveness can be a powerful foundation for post-war reconciliation, it should be understood and dealt with in a very nuanced way through victims' individual self-experience. Victims' willingness to forgive and change depends on the level of acknowledgement, expression of regret, the people to be forgiven, the existence of bystanders and the like (Enright 2001; McCullough et al. 2000; Massey and Abu-Baker 2009). Moreover, positive inter-personal relationships and high awareness of group membership are identified as effective sources of forgiveness (Hewstone 1996; Hewstone et al. 2000). Hence, institutional or normative pressure on victims to forgive, without considering individuals' own challenges, is likely to generate negative consequences (Govier 2002).

At the social level, studies examined the psychological dimensions that penetrate the societal fabric. In these studies, reconciliation involves "modifying motivations, beliefs, and attitudes of the majority" (Bar-Tal and Bennink 2004: 11) which are related to subjective factors such as "misperceptions, mistrust, and frustrated basic needs" (Fisher 1999: 85). In order to develop a common psychological framework in which different social groups can accept coexistence with others, studies have investigated the social psychological consequences of reconciliation programmes like restorative justice, truth-telling and amnesia (Riek et al. 2008).

Recent studies have attempted to integrate social psychology perspectives into the post-conflict peacebuilding contexts. Significant studies include Ilai Along and Daniel Bar-Tal's *The Role of Trust in Conflict Resolution: The Israeli-Palestinian Case and Beyond* (2016) and Bruno Charbonneau and Genevieve Parent's *Peacebuilding, Memory and Reconciliation: Bridging top-down and bottom-up approaches* (2012). A few journals, such as *Political Psychology* and *Peace and Conflict: Journal of Peace Psychology*, have attempted to bridge the discussions in these silos. There are also a significant number of studies that aim to reflect bottom-up approaches and psychological aspects of the "reconciliation in post-war settings" (i.e., Brouneus 2016; Montiel and Christie 2003; Riek et al. 2008).

Second, this volume adopts "everyday peace" discourse as a core framework in order to acknowledge and examine the existence (or nonexistence) of reconciliatory elements embedded in people's daily living. The discourse on everyday peace has recently emerged to offer an alternative perspective to the mainstream liberal peace agenda. In these studies, everyday denotes "a set of micro-processes of practices in a constant interaction driven by the agency of ordinary people in concrete circumstances" (Chandler 2015: 43). Although detailed foci vary, the studies adopting "everyday" approaches by and large pursue locally based, non-prescriptive, reflexive (open to change) approaches to peacebuilding that can be safeguarded against elite capture (Mac Ginty 2013). In particular, studies by people such as James Scott and Michel de Certeau lay a solid foundation for the studies.

This discourse was adopted by Peace and Conflict Studies to address the limitations of institutionally oriented debates on peacebuilding. Indeed, it is risky when such mainstream peacebuilding practice disregards the significance of less visible practices of peacebuilding carried out by local populations in their everyday life. The avenues of people's livelihood such as "local agency, rights, needs, custom and kinship" provide important context to decision-making, promote active peacebuilding (Richmond 2010) and attempt to "accurately reflect the on-the-ground situation in a textured way that is meaningful to local communities" (Mac Ginty 2013).

The values and utilities of the everyday peace have been explained from conceptual, theoretical and practical perspectives. Practically, such everyday approaches enable peacebuilders to reflect "the complexity and fluidity of social practices" and "the spatial dispersal of 'communities' with networked connections" (Chandler 2015: 42) in their practice. Moreover, peacebuilding programmes can find strategies to overcome unrealistic notions of linear process or sequential time and accurately see the complex reality (Castañeda 2009; Mac Ginty 2008). From a normative perspective, such everyday forms of peacebuilding can constitute more *emancipatory* and *bottom-up* approaches, placing locals at the centre of peacebuilding (Chandler 2015; Bräuchler 2015; Richmond and Mitchell 2012;

Mac Ginty 2014; Berents and McEvoy-Levy 2015; Felix da Costa and Karlsrud 2012; Tadjbakhsh 2011).

Nevertheless, the examination of people's everyday practice of social reconciliation has not yet attracted academic attention. Recently, a small number of empirical studies began to pay attention to everyday avenues for reconciliation. While some studies look at the roles of indigenous resources/leadership in the process of reconciliation (Qurtuby 2012/2013; Baines 2007; Power 2005), others examine the strategies or processes underpinning how local communities utilise everyday resources for reconciliation (Berents 2014; Heitmeyer 2009). Compared to the overall academic contention over the framework, the reflection of everyday framework on the practice of reconciliation is still at an early stage.

*Multi-Level Reconciliation and Peacebuilding* aims to contribute to the ongoing development of peacebuilding discourse, by illuminating the dynamics of reconciliation that occur outside of state-centric institutions. The research foci in psychological dimensions and community residents' everyday life illuminate the complex process of intra-individual, inter-personal and intergroup dynamics of promoting reconciliation, which has largely been discarded in the mainstream peacebuilding literature. In particular, the social psychology perspectives enable the researcher to understand how individuals and groups cope with reconciliation issues in the aftermath of massive violence, as well as how such perceptions transform over time. Moreover, everyday discourse helps people acknowledge and examine people's daily practice as forms and procedures for social reconciliation.

Reconciliation in this volume denotes the processes promoting the psychological, cultural or structural foundations of peaceful relationships between (former) antagonists. In this definition, reconciliation is understood more as a process than an outcome. In fact, conventional studies have clarified the distinct nature of reconciliation as "process" and "outcome." When reconciliation is defined as outcome, reconciliation is usually set as an end state that people pursue. For instance, some studies present a maximalist view like "re-establishing harmony and cooperation between antagonists" (Fisher 1999: 83) while others attempt to establish a more modest threshold which aims for "the establishment of a civilized political dialogue and an adequate sharing of power" (Huyse 2003: 19). Taking a step further, there are studies that acknowledge and analyse different levels of reconciliation from non-violent coexistence to empathetic mutual acceptance (McGrew 2011).

While this volume does incorporate these views for examining progress with efforts for reconciliation, its central definition of reconciliation emphasises the dynamic, adaptive and non-linear, and multiple approaches that aim to change and redefine the relationship between antagonistic persons or groups (Lederach 2001; Kriesberg 1998). From this perspective, the process of reconciliation should be appreciated as meaningful as an ongoing endeavour for gradual transformation, even where it does not bring about immediately positive outcomes, and the forms and procedures are highly contextualised and difficult to generalise.

## Objectives and outline of the book

The authors in this book are all, in their own way, endeavouring to grapple with the central question – how do people rebuild and define relations with former harm-doers in their everyday lives? – so that shared visions might engage political realities to construct harmonious and peaceful relations. It is unashamedly constructivist in orientation so that it can understand the cumulative, multilevel, open-ended and continuous interactive processes that either generate shared understandings and common perceptions of problems or generate misunderstandings, misperceptions and division.

To achieve this objective, this volume comprises two distinct sections. In Part I, "Reconciliation: Concepts and Approaches," chapters explore key conceptual and theoretical issues in the reconciliation literature at individual and intergroup levels. The main topics for investigation reflect on the contemporary academic approaches to reconciliation, roles of religion and culture, inter-religious reconciliation, bystandership in the facilitation of reconciliation, and intergenerational narrative inheritance. Most authors of Part I are the researchers who have conducted extensive research on reconciliation and trust-building as leading scholars in the field. Based on their long-term experience and academic reflection, these chapters will revisit the limitations of the conventional approaches to reconciliation and present the thematic/theoretical lines that require more rigorous academic consideration.

In contemporary peacebuilding practice, there is a very pressing need for states, civil society actors and the private sector to think of reconciliation as a process that both addresses past grievances and the ongoing sources of existential threat that affect most conflict-afflicted communities. Considering this, Kevin P. Clements in Chapter 2 proposes a few new directions for promoting future reconciliation processes, paying particular attention to three critical pre-requisites: (1) To extend the boundaries of, and work towards, a politics of compassion; (2) to adopt non-violence as an imperative for peaceful interaction; and (3) to engage in honest and truthful facilitated dialogue. All of these qualities hinge on developing positive and suppressing negative views of the other, especially those who might wish to harm us or have harmed us in the past. The chapter concludes that, to promote new pathways to reconciliation in a world of fear and despair, we should give more weight to the transformative power of love, courage and hopefulness.

Chapter 3, written by Mari Fitzduff, proposes to develop Behavioural Peacebuilding by bringing the lessons from the emerging fields of behavioural sciences into the promotion of reconciliation. Her argument is that current peacebuilding practice can be improved by understanding the complexity and predictability of human nature and its neural legacies, and how behavioural science might be applied. Specifically, it explains the tension between two aspects of our brain – the "emotional" and "reasoning" minds – that play important roles in determining people's approaches to reconciliation. Moreover, people's attitudes to the out-groups are influenced by their physiological and psychological awareness of possible negative eventualities pertaining to the issues coming out from the engagement with the group. Our beliefs in many cases appear to be determined not by "truth," but by our own physical and psychological predispositions, our needs for beliefs or moral values and the cultural context in which we live. This chapter introduces a significant number of intrapersonal dynamics that can be reflected in future practice for promoting reconciliation at individual and group levels.

In Chapter 4, Mohammed Abu-Nimer focuses on the role that inter-religious dialogue can play in supporting personal, community, national and international reconciliation processes. While religions share common values of peace, reconciliation, mercy, love and respect for human dignity, the implementation and transmission of these values into sustainable structures to regulate people's lives have been extremely limited, especially in wider social systems. Seeking ways to develop a more effective practice for inter-religious dialogue, this chapter introduces key principles of facilitation that are related to trust-building, mutual learning, the nature of communication channels, risk-taking, dealing with challenging agendas and mobilising actions. It also highlights major obstacles that have prevented effective promotion of inter-religious dialogues in many places, which include a lack of institutional commitment, theological obstruction of dialogical, policy-makers' involvement, and being stuck in the loop of CVE/PVE (counter-violence extremism).

Chaiwat Satha-Anand's Chapter 5 proposes the concept of *reconciliation culture* as a key resource for promoting social reconciliation in conflict societies and, among others, singles out forgiveness as a central element to measure the reconciliation culture. It then examines how forgiveness is understood and incorporated into the processes for social reconciliation in three Theravada Buddhist countries: Thailand, Sri Lanka and Cambodia. The concept and practices of forgiveness in these countries are less pronounced in the reconciliation projects born out of societies with mainly Buddhist culture due to the influence of the non-human karmic law at work. Individual or collective action is not governed by human intentionality, but by *karma* – the cosmic order of actions and their effects. In this regard, the chances for explicit expression of forgiveness is less likely to happen, which may affect the dynamics of promoting reconciliation culture in these Buddhist societies.

Ervin Staub's Chapter 6 is an autobiographical essay that derives many insights from the author's life-long journey of utilizing psychological principles to promote social reconciliation. The chapter first describes some of the author's research on caring, helping, active bystandership and the origins of genocide and collective violence, as a background to interventions in real-world settings aimed to create positive change. They include working with teachers to create classrooms that promote caring and helping; training police to prevent or stop unnecessary harmful actions by fellow officers, and similarly, students in schools to prevent harmful actions; promoting reconciliation, using trainings and workshops, and educational radio programs in Rwanda, Burundi and the Congo; working to improve Dutch–Muslim relations in Amsterdam after violence; and a number of other projects. In these projects, information and participants' experiences combined to create "experiential understanding." Evaluation studies showed positive effects. These projects and their evaluation show that research- and theory-based interventions can be effective. An initial motivation for this work was the author's early childhood experience during the Holocaust in Hungary and receiving help from bystanders.

Chapter 7 tackles the roles of trust in promoting reconciliation and peace in conflict-affected societies. It proposes three sets of conceptual models to understand the nature of trust within and between conflict-affected societies. The Trust and Conflict Map and the Trust–Conflict Helix are presented as conceptual tools to visualise the interdependent relationship between trust and multi-layered conflict themes. Moreover, the Intergroup Trust Model is proposed as a unique tool capable of mapping weaknesses and strengths in the relationship between two hostile parties, allowing interveners to detect favourable points of entry for reconciliation and approaches for building intergroup trust in order to break the vicious cycle of conflict, paving the way toward an effective and lasting peacebuilding. Then, by using data collected from Moldova-Transdniestria to try and understand a frozen peace two decades after open violence, this chapter demonstrates how these conceptual models can be applied in the empirical examination and emphasises the importance of trust-building in the promotion of reconciliation.

Part II, "Reconciliation in Practice," examines the social dynamics relevant to reconciliation in six conflict-affected areas: Timor-Leste, Solomon Islands, Cambodia, Japan, South Korea, Northern Ireland and Turkey. These empirical studies will highlight different aspects related to reconciliation at individual and community levels, such as healing, memory, silence and narratives. Moreover, parts of the discussions in these case studies will be linked to the thematic/theoretical discussions presented in Part I.

Damian Grenfell's Chapter 8 examines the reconciliation between survivors and the dead in Timor-Leste. In Timor-Leste one of the most important social relationships is that between the still-living and the ancestral spirits of family members. Spirits are very commonly understood as actants with power to determine the well-being of the still-living, including the ability to cause illness, misfortune and even death if they are not adequately venerated. Peace, then, this chapter argues, is determined for many people by an ability to reconcile with the dead, a point that is particularly relevant in the aftermath of war, given so many have been killed, gone missing and have died in horrific and unnatural circumstances. The chapter explains how such life attitudes are reflected in local communities' everyday life by using an example of the recovery of graves in Lolotoe. It then calls for the transformation of the conventional approaches to reconciliation, such as the Commission for Reception, Truth and Reconciliation (CAVR), to promote a shift in three aspects: The emphasis on the still-living, the secular nature of that approach to reconciliation and how the nation is scaled.

Chapter 9 is a case study on the adaptive and responsive nature of reconciliation processes in the context of the Solomon Islands Truth and Reconciliation Commission (TRC) process. TRCs have a history of adapting the lessons learnt from previous TRCs in a way that balances "best practice" with the on-the-ground reconciliation interests of the local community. This is evident in the increased consideration given to inter-personal reconciliation during the Solomon Islands TRC process. The author argues that the move away from TRC processes focused pre-dominantly on political reconciliation has produced practices that are more inclusive of a diverse range of voices and thus more mindful of the importance of meaningful community engagement for the maintenance of sustainable peace.

In Chapter 10, SungYong Lee examines the reconstruction of relationships between the perpetrators and victims occurring in people's daily lives. In many peacebuilding processes, a majority of the population is marginalised from politically oriented mechanisms for social reconciliation. The processes for building a social relationship at local communities usually developed independently from such institutional mechanisms. In order to systematically examine this local process, this study proposes a typology of post-war relationship building at community levels: Physical revenge, concealed antagonism, commitment to move on, tolerance and dehumanisation. It then examines the complex motivations of victims to develop each type of relationship-building. For this purpose, the author conducted 22 interviews with the victims of the Khmer Rouge violence in two provinces in Cambodia. Finally, it will highlight the forms of agency that community residents form and utilise for developing *everyday peace*.

Ria Shibata's Chapter 11 expands the scope of the analysis to inter-state relations between Japan and South Korea over the historical disputes, especially focusing on collective intergenerational narrative inheritance. Conflicts that are protracted are often rooted in memories of historical violence. Accepting collective intergenerational responsibility for injustices of the past is a crucial component in advancing reconciliation between the transgressor and the transgressed. Collective memory of violent trauma can be transmitted via narratives in official textbooks, mass media, rituals and commemorations, popular cultural products and through individual sharing of stories. Japan has often been criticised for downplaying information about its wartime atrocities like the Nanjing Massacre and coercion of "comfort women" in its official discourse. This chapter examines how current generations of Japanese "remember" the past war and how exposure to narratives focusing on Japanese people's wartime victimisation may affect their willingness to accept the nation's responsibility to redress past mistakes and may thus become an obstacle to Japan's reconciliation with its neighbours in East Asia – namely China and South Korea.

Chapter 12, written by Rachel Rafferty, deals with the representations of victimhood and reconciliation in the narratives of local peacebuilders in Northern Ireland. In the aftermath of violent conflict, sustainable peace cannot be achieved by institutional reforms alone; reconciliation entails a qualitative change in how former adversaries perceive and interact with one another. Civil society actors in post-conflict societies have an important role to play in achieving this, but often the goal of reconciliation lacks legitimacy in their eyes. A particular barrier to legitimising reconciliation is provided by the continued circulation of collective narratives that focus on in-group experiences of victimhood as a rationale for continued mistrust and hostility towards the out-group. This chapter examines an exception: The case of a group of local actors in a post-conflict society who are strongly in favour of reconciliation. Based on a study of the life history narratives of local peacebuilders in Northern Ireland, this chapter explores how these local peacebuilders represent conflict-related victimhood in ways that support them to view reconciliation as a legitimate, and necessary, goal for their society. Implications for addressing collective narratives at the individual and institutional levels in post-conflict peacebuilding practice are discussed.

Chapter 13 develops a model for promoting reconciliation by integrating the lessons from psychological research on the relative roles of forgiving and reconciliation and the events in history in which direct adversaries cooperated to defeat a powerful common enemy. Especially, it adopts the lessons from the experience of Syrian refugees in Turkey as an example relevant to reconciliation at the community level, and the collaboration of the Western democracies (UK and US) with the Soviet Union during World War II as an example of inter-state reconciliation. Reflecting on the lessons from these examples, the authors propose computational modelling of the process of reconciling in which success depends on taking steps of an acceptable size, small enough not to violate the expectations of the adversary, while all sides share the same superordinate values and confront a common enemy – whether a human or non-human existential threat.

Finally, the concluding chapter summarises the discussions that appeared in these chapters, by integrating them under four concurrent themes. First, the dynamics of post-conflict reconciliation are primarily about the ways in which individuals, groups and nations deal with suffering, pain and trauma. Second, reconciliation is ultimately a question of how to heal and fix broken relationships, which involves not only the interplay between scales of the local and national, but also even between the living and the dead. Third, although their positive roles are undeniably important, the limit of the elite-level political systems' roles is clear, and more bottom-up processes for supplementing the limit should be explored. Accordingly, to promote effective post-conflict reconciliation, more analytical and political attention should be directed to understanding *bottom-up* strategies for reconciliation at inter-personal or intergroup levels. Finally, a number of chapters acknowledge the importance of dialogue in promoting reconciliation and present proposals for engaging in more meaningful dialogue.

## Note

1 To learn more about how these disciplines develop debates on reconciliation, see: Malley-Morrison, K., Mercurio, A., and Twose, G. (eds.) (2013). *International Handbook of Peace and Reconciliation*. New York: Springer-Verlag New York; Trimikliniotis, N. (2013). Sociology of reconciliation: Learning from comparing violent conflicts and reconciliation processes. *Current Sociology*, 61(2), 244–264; Keim, W., (2011). The concept of 'ethic of reconciliation' and the disciplines. *Current Sociology*, 59(5), 595–599; Leach, F., & Dunne, M. (eds.) (2007). *Education, Conflict and Reconciliation: International Perspectives*. Oxford: Peter Lang; Brouneus, K. (2003). *Reconciliation – Theory and Practice for Development Cooperation*. Stockholm: SIDA.

## References


Al Qurtuby, S. (2012/2013). Reconciliation from below: Indonesia's religious conflict and grassroots agency for peace. *The Canadian Journal of Peace and Conflict Studies*, *44/45*(2/1), 135–162.

Alfonsin, R. (1993). Never again in Argentina. *Journal of Democracy*, *4*(1), 15–19.

Along, I., & Bar-Tal, D. (2016). *The Role of Trust in Conflict Resolution: The Israeli-Palestinian Case and Beyond*. Cham: Springer.

Amnesty International (1998). *Guatemala: all the truth, justice for all (AMR 34/02/98) (AMR 34/02/98)*. Retrieved from https://www.amnesty.org/en/documents/AMR34/002/1998/en/

Arnson, C. J. (1999). Conclusion: Lessons learned in comparative perspective. In C. J. Arnson (Ed.), *Comparative peace processes in Latin America* (pp. 447–463). Stanford, CA: Stanford University Press.

Arthur, P. (1999). The Anglo-Irish peace process: Obstacles to reconciliation. In R. L. Rothstein (Ed.), *After the peace: resistance and reconciliation* (pp. 85–109). Boulder, CO: Lynne Rienner.

Baines, E. K. (2007). The haunting of Alice: Local approaches to justice and reconciliation in Northern Uganda. *The International Journal of Transitional Justice*, *1*(1), 91–114.

Bar-Tal, D., & Bennink, G. H. (2004). The nature of reconciliation as an outcome and as a process. In Y. Bar-Siman-Tov (Ed.), *From conflict resolution to reconciliation* (pp. 11–49).Oxford: Oxford University Press.

Berents, H. (2014). 'It's about finding a way': Children. Sites of opportunity, and building everyday peace in Colombia. *International Journal of Children's Rights*, *22*, 361–384.

Berents, H., & McEvoy-Levy, S. (2015). Theorising youth and everyday peace (building). *Peacebuilding*, *3*(2), 115–125.

Bloomfield, D. (2003). Reconciliation: An introduction. In D. Bloomfield, T. Barnes & L. Huyse (Eds.), *Reconciliation after violent conflict: a handbook* (pp. 1–18). Stockholm: International IDEA.

Bloomfield, D. (2006). *On good terms: Clarifying reconciliation*. Berlin: Berghof Research Center for Constructive Conflict Management.

Bockers, E., Stammel, N., & Knaevelsrud, C. (2011). Reconciliation in Cambodia: Thirty years after the terror of the Khmer Rouge regime. *Torture*, *21*(2), 71–83.

Brāuchler, B. (2015). *The cultural dimension of peace: Decentralization and reconciliation in Indonesia*. Basingstoke: Palgrave Macmillan.

Breen Smyth, M. (2007). *Truth recovery and justice after conflict: Managing violent pasts*. Abingdon: Routledge.

Brounéus, K. (2016). *Truth for peace?: Exploring the links between the Solomon Islands' TRC process and people's attitudes towards peace*. Dunedin: National Centre for Peace and Conflict Studies, University of Otago.

Castañeda, C. (2009). How liberal peacebuilding may be failing sierra leone. *Review of African Political Economy*, *36*(120), 235–251.

Chandler, D. (2015). Resilience and the 'everyday': Beyond the paradox of 'liberal peace'. *Review of International Studies*, *41*(1), 27–48.

Charbonneau, B., & Parent, G. (2012). *Peacebuilding, memory and reconciliation: bridging top-down and bottom-up approaches*. London: Routledge.

Enright, R. D. (2001). *Forgiveness is a choice: A step-by-step process for resolving anger and restoring hope*. Washington, DC: American Psychological Association.

Felix da Costa, D., & Karlsrud, J. (2012). Contestualising libeal peacebuilding for local circumstances: unmiss and local peacebuilding in South Sudan. *Journal of Peacebuilding & Development* 7(2), 53–66.

Fisher, R. J. (1999). Social-psychological processes in interactive conflict analysis and reconciliation. In Ho-won Jeong (Ed.), *Conflict resolution: dynamics, process and structure* (pp. 81–104). Aldershot: Ashgate.

Fraser, M. (2003). Speech on National Sorry Day 2003 (Great Hall of Parliament, Canberra, 26 May 2003). Retrieved from: https://archives.unimelb.edu.au/explore/collections/malcolmfraser/resources/postparliamentspeeches/national-sorry-day-2003

Galappatti, A. (2003). What is a psychosocial intervention? Mapping the field of Sri Lanka. *Intervention, 1*(2), 3–17.

Govier, T. (2002). *Forgiveness and revenge*. London: Routledge.

Guthrey, H. (2015). *Victim healing and truth commissions: Transforming pain through voice in the Solomon Islands and Timor-Leste*. Switzerland: Springer International.

Hamber, B. (2009). *Transforming societies after political violence: Truth, reconciliation, and mental health*. New York: Springer.

Hameiri, S. (2010). *Regulating statehood: State building and the transformation of the global order*. New York: Palgrave Macmillan.

Heitmeyer, C. (2009). 'There is peace here': Managing communal relations in a town in central Gujarat. *Journal of South Asian Development, 4*(1), 103–120.

Hewstone, M. (1996). Contact and categorization: Social psychological interventions to change intergroup relations. In N. Macrae, M. Hewstone & C. Stangor (Eds.), *Foundations of stereotypes and stereotyping* (pp. 323–368). New York: Guilford.

Hewstone, M., Voci, A., Cairns, E., Judd, C., & McClernon, F. (2000). *Intergroup contact in a divided society: Changing group beliefs in Northern Ireland*. Paper presented at the Society of Experimental Social Psychology meetings. Atlanta, GA.

Huyse, L. (2003). The process of reconciliation. In D. Bloomfield, T. Barnes & L. Huyse (Eds.), *Reconciliation after violent conflict: A handbook* (pp. 19–33). Stockholm: International IDEA.

Kandowitz, R., & Riak, A. (2008). Critical Links between peacebuilding and trauma healing: A holistic framework for fostering community development. In B. Hart (Ed.), *Peacebuilding in traumatized societies* (pp. 3–27). Lanham: University Press of America.

Kelman, H. (2008). Chapter 1. Reconciliation from a social-psychological perspective. In A. Nadler, T. E. Malloy & J. D. Fisher (Eds.), *The social psychology of intergroup reconciliation* (pp. 15–32). Oxford: Oxford University Press.

Kriesberg, L. (1998). Coexistence and the reconciliation of communal conflicts. In E. Weiner (Ed.), *The handbook of interethnic coexistence* (pp. 182–198). New York: The Continuum Publishing Company.

Lederach, J. P. (1997). *Building peace: Sustainable reconciliation in divided societies*. Washington, DC: United States Institute of Peace Press.

Lederach, J. P. (1998). Beyond violence: Building sustainable peace. In E. Weiner (Ed.), *The handbook of interethnic coexistence* (pp. 236–245). New York: Continuum.

Lederach, J. P. (2001). Civil society and reconciliation. In C. A. Crocker, F. O. Hampson & P. Aall (Eds.), *Turbulent peace: The challenges of managing international conflict* (pp. 841–854). Washington, DC: UNITED STATES institute of peace.

Lerche, C. (2000). Peace building through reconciliation. *International Journal of Peace Studies, 5*(2), 61–76.

Lie, T. G., Binningsbo, H. M., & Gates, S. (2007). *Post-conflict justice and sustainable peace*. Post-Conflict Transitions Working Paper No. 5, World Bank Policy Research Working Paper 4191.

Lipschutz, R. D. (1998). Beyond the neoliberal peace: From conflict resolution to social reconciliation. *Social Justice: A Journal of Crime, Conflict and World Order*, *25*(4), 5–19.

Mac Ginty, R. (2008). Indigenous peace-making versus the liberal peace. *Cooperation and Conflict*, *43*(2): 139–163.

Mac Ginty, R. (2013). Indicators +: A proposal for everyday peace indicators. *Evaluation and Program Planning*, *36*(1), 56–63.

Mac Ginty, R. (2014). Everyday peace: Bottom-up and local agency in conflict-affected societies. *Security Dialogue*, *45*(6), 548–564.

Massey, R., & Abu-Baker, K. (2009). Chapter 2. A systemic framework for forgiveness, reconciliation, and peace: Interconnecting psychological and social processes. In A. Kalayjian & R. F. Paloutzian (Eds.), *Forgiveness and reconciliation*. Berlin: Springer Science + Business Media.

McCullough, M. E., Pargament, K. I., & Thoresen, C. E. (2000). The psychology of forgivenenss: History, conceptual issues, and overview. In M. E. McCullough, K. I. Pargament, & C. E. Thoresen (Eds.), *Forgiveness: Theory, research, and practice* (pp. 1-14). New York: Guilford.

McGrew, L. (2011). *Victims and perpetrators living together, apart* [Doctoral Thesis]. Coventry University.

Montiel, C., & Christie, D. (2003). Liberation movement during democratic transition: Positioning with the changing state. In F. M. Moghaddam, R. Harre & N. Lee (Eds.), *Global conflict resolution through positioning analysis* (pp. 155–172). New York: Springer.

Parent, G. (2011). Peacebuilding, healing, reconciliation: An analysis of unseen connections for peace. *International Peacekeeping*, *18*(4), 379–395.

Power, M. (2005). Building communities in a post-conflict society: Churches and peace-building initiatives in Northern Ireland since 1994. *The European Legacy*, *10*(1), 55–68.

Richmond, O. (2010). Resistance and the post-liberal peace. *Millennium: Journal of International Studies*, *38*(3), 665–692.

Richmond, O., & Mitchell, A. (2012). *Hybrid forms of peace: From everyday agency to post-liberalism*. Basingstoke: Palgrave Macmillan.

Riek, B. M., Gaertner, S. L., Dovidio, J. F., Brewer, M. B., Mania, E. W., & Lamoreaux, M. J. (2008). A social-psychological approach to postconflict reconciliation. In A. Nadler, T. E. Malloy, & J. D. Fisher (Eds.), *The social psychology of intergroup reconciliation* (pp. 255–273). Oxford University Press.

Rigby, A. (2001). *Justice and reconciliation: After the violence*. Boulder: Lynne Rienner Publishers.

Rotberg, R. I., & Thompson, D. (2000). *Truth v. justice: The morality of truth commissions*. Princeton: Princeton University Press.

Simpson, G. (1997). Reconstruction and reconciliation: Emerging from transition. *Development in Practice*, *7*(4), 475–478.

Smith, D. (2004). *Towards a strategic framework for Peacebuilding: Getting their act together: Overview report of the joint Utstein study of peacebuilding*. Oslo: Royal Norwegian Ministry of Foreign Affairs.

Staub, E. (2003). *The psychology of good and evil: Why children, adults, and groups help and harm others*. Cambridge: Cambridge University Press.

Tadjbakhsh, S. (2011). Introduction: Liberal peace in dispute. In S. Tadjbakhsh (Ed.), *Rethinking the liberal peace: External models and local alternatives* (pp. 1–16). London: Routledge.

Volkan, V. D. (2006). *Killing in the name of identity: A study of bloody conflict*. Charlottesville: Pitchstone Publishing.

Volkan, V. D. (2008). Trauma, identity, and search for a solution in Cyprus. *Insight Turkey*, *10*(4), 95–110.

Wilmer, F. (1998). The social construction of conflict reconciliation in the former Yugoslavia. *Social Justice: A Journal of Crime, Conflict and World Order*, *25*(4), 90–113.

# Part I

# Reconciliation

## Concepts and approaches

# 2 Promoting reconciliation

## Going back to basics

*Kevin P. Clements*

## Introduction

Although the number of efforts to promote post-conflict reconciliation has rapidly increased over the past decades, the achievements are limited when we focus on their quality and durability. Many post-conflict reconciliatory processes (especially in post-colonial societies) are directed towards the protection of Western interests and security and fail to acknowledge the central point, which is that most people in the world live in daily existential terror in terms of food, housing, clothing, safe water supplies and the right kinds of medicines to deal with preventable diseases. There is a very pressing need, therefore, for states, civil society actors and the private sector to think of reconciliation as a process that addresses both past grievances and the ongoing sources of existential threat that affect most conflict-afflicted communities.

But the central problem remains. How can peace researchers, practitioners and policymakers promote and consolidate peace and enhance reconciliation in deeply divided societies? How can they move beyond state-centric models for social reconciliation towards processes that deal with community and societal brokenness and the centrality of healing processes at the interpersonal and intergroup levels, and how can this be done in grossly unequal and unjust systems? So, what are some of the pre-requisites for multilevel healing and peacebuilding? This chapter will attempt to address these questions by integrating some key themes of my work from the past 20 years.

## To extend the boundaries of, and work towards, a politics of compassion

By and large, most of us do not work very hard on expanding our individual capacity for compassion. I am aware that I belong to a group which is white, comparatively wealthy and often powerful, and therefore these comments speak from my personal perspective. The challenge that we wealthy, white and powerful people face is how to make a loving and creative sense of suffering. What are our responsibilities for the suffering of self and others? How do we witness it creatively? How do we embrace it so that we might be softened and transformed by it? With those who are suffering, how do we discern creative possibility? How in the face of polarisation and division do we stand for union and reunion of self with the other and self with the world? As Benjamin Barber (2007) mentions, (i) we are increasingly governed by impulse; (ii) feeling dominates thinking; (iii) me dominates us; (iv) now dominates later; (v) egoism dominates altruism; (vi) entitlement dominates responsibility; (vii) individualism dominates community; and (viii) private dominates public. In this context we are happy to do harm to one another as long as our privilege, power, wealth, status and property are safeguarded.

In an interdependent world, it is becoming clearer each day, however, that we can no longer afford to have narrow circles of compassion. Narrow circles of compassion are effectively narrow circles of responsibility. Who is included and who excluded from such circles – whether these be kin and friendship, community, national or regional circles – is an important determinant of who we are willing to care for and who we are willing to be empathetic towards. Those of us who are middle class, for example, do not normally have circles that stretch downward. We do not, by and large, feel responsibility for, or in times of suffering and death, grieve for, the poor, the homeless or the voiceless. On the contrary, we idolise and obituarise the wealthy and successful. So, a pre-requisite for more inclusive thinking and for promoting more dialogical processes for grappling with the world's problems, and certainly a pre-requisite for multilevel reconciliation, is an enlargement of our boundaries of compassion and empathy.

When we do this, we are able to advance ideas of species identity – or what it means to be human – rather than narrow xenophobic notions of national identity. One of the important elements of this is a clear understanding of the social psychological meaning of recognition. The need for acknowledgement and recognition is fundamental to life itself. An unacknowledged, unrecognised life is one that is likely to be *nasty, solitary, brutish and short*. Mutual acknowledgement and norms of recognition, therefore, are a precondition for life and fruitful conversation. They also underpin that very intentional conversation that we call human dialogue. Non-acknowledgement breeds frustration, anger and deep animosity. Direct challenges to identity and the self are worse, however, and generate even deeper senses of despair and humiliation. Both community and society flow from actions which generate commitment and a mutuality of respect between disparate individuals and groups. These are fundamental to the generation of peaceful relationships.

Expanding these circles of compassion is a pre-requisite for developing true reconciliation in divided societies and for developing an inclusive community. The challenge is, how do we extend the boundaries of compassion? While the detailed procedures vary according to the contexts in which reconciliation is promoted, the first step towards it is to properly acknowledge the inter-relatedness of all individuals and groups in society. In an interdependent world we can no longer afford to have narrow circles of compassion. Who are we willing to grieve for? We do not normally mourn for the deaths of those who are not our kith and kin, nor for the poor, homeless or voiceless. We certainly do not mourn for the lost generations of Aborigines, Maori or indigenous peoples of North America.

It is critical that we enlarge the boundaries of compassion and empathy in order to advance species identity – what it means to be human – rather than narrow xenophobic notions of national identity.

### *To adopt a real historical sense*

The inter-connectedness is not only between the people in the same era, but between peoples across generations in history. This awareness is particularly important in imagining true reconciliation between new migrants (colonisers) and indigenous peoples. However, we on many occasions ignore this and behave like ahistorical beings. Let's consider the countries that are dominated by European migrants like, for example, Australia. How do we (people of all races, cultures and languages) imagine Australia – in terms of its geography, culture, politics and community? We, "white fellows," by and large imagine Australia in terms of a relatively small strip of "civilised" capital cities that perch precariously on the edge of a fairly intimidating and unforgiving continent. We imagine it in terms of its urban icons, the Opera House, the South Bank Complex, its wealth, its minerals; we imagine it in terms of migratory waves beginning from colonisation; and we imagine it in Northern, largely European, terms. This inhibits our capacity to think expansively, inclusively and peacefully about who we are, where we are and what we are to be. We rarely begin our "imaginings" with the traditional owners of the land and certainly do not wish to end with the traditional owners of the land.

We exist in a very precarious present which does not create conditions that are conducive to reconciliation. The absence of any real historical sense means that there is no need to say sorry. There is no need to apologise for violations of individual and collective rights, and security is given more value than liberty. We are trapped in worlds of deceit and manipulation where the grand gesture is given more value than the slow process.

This precarious present does not take account of 50,000 years of civilisation or even a medium- to long-term historical perspective. It is important that we live at least in what my friend Elise Boulding calls a 200-year present (Boulding et al. 2016). That is a present that acknowledges that there is someone with us today who was born one hundred years ago and thus brings 100 years of life, living experience and wisdom to bear on the present moment. There will also be someone else born today who will live one hundred years from now. This means that our decisions have to survive for at least 100 years. We are a long way from this aspiration as well. On the contrary we are caught in a paralysing present which seems fearful and frightening precisely because we are not well-rooted in history and have no clarity about the future we wish to see realised.

### *To focus on violence structure*

True peace and reconciliation require a separation of persons from problems and deep analytical awareness of the structures of violent conflict. Promotion of reconciliation and other types of good peacebuilding need to begin with holistic analyses of conflict systems.

This approach will enable individuals involved in conflict resolution and the promotion of reconciliation to manage their interpersonal emotions by focusing on a contextual analysis of the sources of the conflict and the actors that need to be brought into peacebuilding and reconciliatory processes. For instance, it is important for analysts and interveners to understand the structural sources of conflict and have answers to some basic questions such as:

1. How many parties and how many issues are involved in the particular conflict?
2. Is the conflict a simple two-party single-issue conflict or a multiparty multi-issue conflict, and how likely is it that these different parties are going to respond to positive and negative incentives that will bring them into fruitful dialogue with one another?

These structural elements seem simple but it is important to understand them before any actor begins working with the protagonists on the design of an intervention process; they are even more important in the design and delivery of reconciliatory processes. In these intervention processes, one of the important questions that have to be confronted is who is best placed to make a positive contribution to generating an environment conducive to collaborative and non-violent problem-solving? Through the consideration of these points, interveners and researchers can have deeper understandings of the historical and current contexts for violence, analyses based on best case assumptions and scenarios, and a willingness to build mutual respect across deep political division. Good conflict analysis should also be identifying connectors capable of responding to dividers and different actors capable of playing complementary roles in these challenging peacebuilding tasks.

### *To set a vision of redemptive history with new moral imagination*

To deal with the paralysing present we must engage in what I call *redemptive history*. It is vital that we become actively engaged with and understand history in all its violence and complexity in order to establish benchmarks and criteria for human improvement and betterment. This is vital to understanding what human beings are capable of doing and what they are capable of becoming. This is not just a question of studying history to learn from its mistakes but rather interrogating the past in order not to reproduce the institutions or processes that have resulted in oppression or widespread inhumanity between peoples.

In the process of developing redemptive history, people should be proactive in promoting new moral imagination. John Paul Lederach (2005) has been addressing some of these issues and argues that moral imagination requires four things:

1. The capacity to imagine ourselves in an inclusive and expandable web of relationships

2. The ability to sustain a problem-solving curiosity that embraces complexity without reliance on dualistic polarity – either/or decision-making
3. A fundamental belief in, and pursuit of, the creative act, and
4. Courage and acceptance of the risks in peacebuilding

All of these qualities are critical to discerning ways in which violent or potentially violent situations can be transformed into non-violent ones. Imagining ourselves in an inclusive and expandable web of relationships, for example, demands some awareness of responsibilities and obligations but Lederach sharpens this basic notion of inclusiveness, by asking us to imagine ourselves in a web of relationships that might include people who wish to harm us. Reflecting on the ways in which we are connected to such people and how we wish to relate to them is crucial to discovering the strengths and weaknesses of a variety of non-violent options. But reflecting on these persons/groups in relationship with us forces us to think much more creatively about basic norms of reciprocity and what is most likely to generate virtuous rather than vicious cycles of behaviour.

Similarly, thinking in non-dualistic ways about complex social phenomena helps us transcend narrow dichotomous categories and is much more likely to generate a deeper awareness of how social and political dynamics are playing themselves out in different situations. Both of these criteria are crucial to effective peacebuilding.

In such a new pathway for developing human history, it is vital to ensure that *human dignity* remains at the heart of our endeavour. We accord persons dignity by assuming that they are good and that they share the human qualities we ascribe to ourselves. This is a pre-requisite for social reconciliation, as well as other kinds of social and political transformation. If we do not make this assumption, the possibility for positive change is very slight indeed. Equally important is to *place the weakest at the heart of our approaches*. States do not exist to serve the interests of the rich and the powerful. These groups can look after themselves. We need to emphasise a radical preference for sharing the material fruits of the economy with the poor, marginalised and vulnerable. As Nelson Mandela put it in his final speech to the South African parliament: "The common good ultimately translates into a deep concern for those that suffer want and deprivation of any kind" (Mandela 2004).

## To adopt non-violence as an imperative for peaceful interaction

Actions for reconciliation rest on a radical commitment to patient, non-violent options and the design of processes that advance the capacities of individuals to recognise each other's common humanity. It was Bruno Bettelheim who said that "[v]iolence is the behaviour of someone incapable of imagining other solutions to the problem at hand" (cited in Lederach 2011: 5). Gandhi said "I object to violence because when it appears to do good, the good is only temporary; the evil it does is permanent" (Gandhi 2002). Both of these individuals understood intuitively and experientially that the transformation of violent relationships is a marathon and not a sprint. It requires patience, humility and a rigorous adherence to processes that are reversible and do no harm. True reconciliation, therefore is more likely to flow from non-violent than violent struggle. It comes from attempting to live life in the spirit of love, truth and peace, and with a deep reverence for all life. These beliefs give rise to a strong commitment to equality, justice, compassion and a desire to treat each person as a holy place. While the language might seem quaint, these are good values for those of us seeking to develop some radical alternatives to living lives in the spirit of enmity, hostility, untruth and revenge.

French philosopher Emmanuel Levinas's work was oriented toward controlling those who individually and collectively attempt to totalise, tyrannise, delegitimise and destroy those they could not face or tolerate. In setting the ethical frameworks for advocating non-violence (1988, 1989), he presents a case for welfare and non-violence from which it is possible to identify criteria for determining whether different types of actions will generate fear and anxiety or confidence and peace. Through a focus on exposing the roots of violence, racism, sexism and classism, he was interested in identifying ways of preventing such pathologies in the future (see Burggraeve 2002).

For Levinas, ethics is essentially, "a struggle to keep fear and anxiety from turning into murderous action" (Levinas 1988: 34). He therefore wanted to understand the deepest sources of human fear and an awareness of how these might be addressed. To do this, he wished to eliminate any possible justification either for causing harm to others or for killing those who are doing no harm. Levinas knew that it was not possible to prevent all human aggression and conflict; rather, his aim was to develop a methodology and framework for engaging the "Other" in order to minimise the effectiveness of aggression and make it the bluntest of all instruments for realising human potential and serving the common good.

Levinas was profoundly aware of the universal vulnerability of all human beings and this underpinned his development of an ethics of responsibility. Levinas suggests that every human being on the planet grapples with a triple vulnerability: physical, psychological and moral.

First, there is a permanent physical vulnerability; death is a certainty for us all and may come at any time. Levinas sees our sense of mortality, this universal fate, as an extremely important equaliser; our response to this certainty will have an important impact on whether or not we are disposed to non-violence or violence. He believed that an acknowledgement of our mortality, individually and collectively, could give rise to a softening of our demands on one another as we all confront death. In this reflective process he suggests that we need others to help us live and to die.

Related psychological research suggests that enhanced salience of our own mortality provokes positive and negative motivations, attitudes and behaviour. More specifically, terror management theory argues that mortality salience will generate increased focus on what brings us value and esteem, such as a heightened in-group solidarity versus out-group derogation, and an expansion of concern for close personal relationships (Greenberg et al. 2008; see also Becker 1973).

While Levinas may agree with these propositions, he was generally more interested in mortality as a spur to thinking about ways of enhancing life, such that confronting mortality generates broader concerns about meaning, value, specialness and our particular place in the world.

In response to psychological research on mortality salience, Levinas would likely ask how we define our boundaries of care and responsibility. If we have a wide definition, with some idea of species identity, for example, Levinas argues that an awareness of physical or mortal vulnerability should engender an openness to thinking more profoundly about relational obligations across boundaries such as national difference. If we have narrow conceptions of identity centred on kin and locality, and a strong sense of group identification, then our salience of mortal vulnerability may generate a less generous response (Staub 2021; Vollhardt et al. 2009).

Second, Levinas addresses the vulnerability that has to do with living in the company of or alongside others – what he calls a psychological vulnerability. Other people, he argues, simply because they are Other, constitute a psychological threat. As Albert Schweitzer put it, "I am life that wills to live, in the midst of life that wills to live" (Schweitzer 1965: 26). The other may take advantage of us at any moment, and this existentially unsettling idea may lead us all too easily to become wary of others instead of trusting them. The struggle with psychological vulnerability in our social relationships is, therefore, critical to determining the extent to which we forego an ethics of fear in favour of an ethics of care. If a paranoid disposition toward others is adopted and we assuage that with deterrent threat and capacity for coercion, the behavioural outcomes generated will be very different than if we have a more optimistic disposition toward others and look for ways in which we can at least coexist, or more optimally develop strong and sustained relationships with others (see Kramer and Messick 1998, for a related argument).

Third, and most importantly, Levinas identifies what he calls our moral vulnerability. In the eyes of the Other, I too am the Other; I am potentially threatened by the Other and at the same time, constitute a threat to the Other. Each individual must decide what kind of relationship they wish to have with others, and in particular, those who are strangers. The decision we make is based on the awareness of our moral vulnerability, or our capacity to do harm to others, and this is absolutely critical to the evolution of Levinas' sociological ethic. He writes: "As a threat to others I am here in the world with no right to exist; if I cannot claim to be harmless, how can I claim any right to be here?" (Levinas 1989: 80). This capacity to harm others represents an underlying challenge to all interpersonal, intergroup and international relationships.

Levinas concludes that being intentional about addressing the ways in which we individually and collectively constitute a threat to others is the only solution to this moral vulnerability. He devises an elegant solution that underpins all relational ethics. The only way that individuals and collectivities can establish their harmlessness to others, in his view, is to accept unconditional (and unlimited) responsibility to and for the Other. The way we do that, at a minimum, is by accepting a responsibility not to kill the Other and more optimally, by accepting responsibility for the welfare of the Other. Individuals, groups and institutions must enable this by considering much more extensively and intentionally the sorts of social, economic and political relationships which will create a peaceable community and guarantee its continuity through time. This is a compelling sociological argument for a deepening of relationships and for paying more attention to the quality and "sanctity" of the intersubjective.

Rational choice theorists, on the other hand, argue that not prioritising individual welfare and maximisation of resources for one's self is irrational. However, it seems equally irrational not to care about the welfare of others and the welfare of the community – whatever we choose as our definition of the boundaries of that community – when thinking about building sustainable peace. Here, it is also important to note that there are selfish as well as altruistic reasons for doing so. Because human beings are equal in their sense of vulnerability, Levinas argues they can only be truly safe in relationships where their selfish interests give way to the interests of the Other and vice versa. Moreover, this imperative of unconditional responsibility for the Other does not have to be justified by any social contract, political system or special relationship between me and the Other (Lesser 1996: 149). It is an argument that assumes an acceptance of responsibility, where the only expectation of return is that most precious return of all – human trust. Accepting responsibility for the welfare of others creates the only solid basis for a peaceful community and for addressing Levinas' triple vulnerabilities of human existence. As such, the case for an ethics of responsibility is predicated on deep reciprocity, thereby providing a compelling social psychological and political rationale for an ethic of non-violence.

Levinas argues that assumption of responsibility to and for the Other is sufficient to give meaning and shape to life. This is contrary to terror management theorists who argue that mortality salience generates higher levels of selfishness (Becker 1973; Greenberg et al. 2008), If, as Becker (1973) claims, people deal with death, in part, through a quest for personal "heroism," then Levinas is also right in that the heroism that is most rewarded in many societies is altruistic. This heroism flows from service to others rather than being generated in opposition to others. Furthermore, the service-oriented heroism that builds sustainable peace is communitarian rather than military. The real heroes are those who subordinate self when promoting and building resilient and inclusive relationships. They create communities of inclusion and possibility rather than exclusion and fear. For peacebuilders, therefore, the challenge is to illuminate the heroic actions that build social relationships, rather than those that destroy. Perhaps one reason why feminists have been so prominent in developing relational ethics and the ethics of care is that, in most communities of the world, women "heroically" sacrifice self to ensure the wellbeing of families, neighbourhoods and communities (Boulding 2000).

These arguments, which Levinas advances in relation to dyadic relationships, are then extrapolated to much more complex relationships, including triads, groups and institutions. As complexities are added to social relationships, especially when there are major discrepancies of power, privilege and prestige, all sorts of other issues come into play. Therefore, the ethics of care and responsibility are based on some degree of equality of power, privilege and opportunity; thus, the promotion of equality is a fundamental contribution to peacefulness.

## To engage in honest and truthful dialogue

Deep and appreciative dialogue is critical to peacebuilding and reconciliation. However, to engage in truthful dialogue in practice is much easier said than done. There are a number of guidelines for dialogical steps towards reconciliation. First, it should be noted that dialogue for reconciliation needs to flow from deep contextual analysis. As John Paul Lederach (1997) proposes, that place called reconciliation is where there is a meeting of truth, justice, peace and compassion. There can be no reconciliation without all four of these qualities. True reconciliation involves a deep recognition of past wrongs; a request for forgiveness; the expression of apology and contrition; a willingness to make reparation; and a desire to celebrate differences. These all demand deep listening skills, appreciative dialogue, a willingness to think beyond simplistic dualities, high levels of love, hope and courage and a capacity to see things in their wholeness, and interdependence. Only by taking this holistic view will we be able to see our part in the sources of suffering and be able to discern our part in their solution.

Most of the conversations that generate harmony are spontaneous and normal features of "sociation." Sometimes, however, people get stuck and cannot talk with each other spontaneously. They lose their ability to attend to and listen to others because of different kinds of verbal and background noise. An inability to communicate effectively, however, sooner or later results in deep misperception, division and, in fragile environments, violence. When this happens, there is a need to become much more intentional about what kinds of conversations or dialogue will begin restoring peaceful relationships.

When individuals or groups get stuck in this way and realise that they have problems, they probably need the help of others, "third party intervenors," to help them break the impasse in which they find themselves.

In the first place, conflict analysts are likely to propose some kind of facilitated dialogue. The social-psychological pre-requisites for successful dialogue are as follows.

(i) A safe catalytic space. This is a space within which both parties (or all parties if there are more than two) feel comfortable. They should not feel too comfortable though, or nothing catalytic will happen. Safe spaces, as the name implies, are places within which actors can vent concerns without fear. It's a space for costing the conflict and it's a space within which impasse-breaking possibilities can be explored. The third party guarantees the personal and relational safety of all the participants. The intervener enables individuals to take risks that they might otherwise be unwilling to take. As we shall see later this is a pre-requisite for courageous peacemaking.

(ii) An invitation to the parties to converse with each other. This invitation can be given by the intervener or by the parties themselves, through conciliatory gestures, signalling a desire to talk or to engage in dialogue in order to transform antagonistic relationships into cooperative ones.
(iii) An orientation to collaborative problem-solving. Productive dialogue rests on a willingness to engage in collaborative problem-solving – both with allies and with putative enemies. Thus. interveners have to model the benefits of non-zero-sum decision-making and the costs of the alternatives.
(iv) A delight in social encounter for its own sake. Although this is a quality that can be neither prescribed nor taught to those who have no inclination to see the satisfactions that flow from good relationships, it is important that there be some participants who derive enjoyment from "social encounters" for their own sake.
(v) Acknowledgement of the "eternal" in the other, a "reverence for life." This quality is not one that can be forced on others, but it flows from an enhancement of empathetic awareness. It grows as one's circle of compassion grows and as one becomes more deeply aware of the essential interdependence of life. It too creates very positive dispositions towards collaborative problem-solving.
(vi) Deep listening skills and a willingness to engage in non-judgemental listening. This quality is absolutely critical to good dialogue. Without listening to the presenting and underlying problems, it is difficult for individual actors to discern areas of commonality and areas of difference. Without such a capacity it is also difficult to understand what is critical and what non-critical to hostile parties.
(vii) A reflective capacity that helps the parties understand themselves and each other more deeply and intimately. This quality is intimately connected to listening qualities. The more one listens to others and attends to their underlying needs and interests, the more one is inclined to adopt a reflective and reflexive stance in relation to them and the more likely it is that antagonistic parties will engage in de-escalating dynamics.
(viii) An option-generating capacity. This capacity is also vital to effective problem-solving. Having identified the issues at stake, it is always important that there be some actors who are adept and skilled at generating creative options. It is also important that they, and/or others, are able to implement the options that are generated. This role should not be underestimated in any conflict transformation process. It is often the creative opportunistic response to what appears to be an impossible impasse which unfreezes stuck relationships.

## Conclusion

To promote such a new pathway in a world of despair, we should not underestimate the critical power of hopefulness. True reconciliatory processes require a measure of hopefulness in a cynical world so that intervenors and antagonists might be an inspiration to others. We have to analyse and understand ways in which mistrust can be replaced with trust in order to generate confidence between peoples and better conditions for peaceful transactions. If we operate from worst-case assumptions or adopt paranoid dispositions (as many leaders are wont to do) we will never be able to generate the right sorts of conciliatory gestures to break cycles of violence or generate creative options. Reconciliation is a process, a coming together, an encounter between justice, peace, truth and compassion. None of these values/qualities will emerge spontaneously. Individuals and groups have to be predisposed towards truth-telling, reparation, equality, justice, compassion and a commitment to restore relationships where they are broken. This requires changes in individual attitudes and behaviour but it also requires attention to the deeper structural and cultural sources of violence and non-violence. Peacebuilding and reconciliation processes, therefore, are, as has been pointed out in many places in this book, multilevel, multidimensional and relationally transformative.

## References

Barber, B. (2007). *Consumed: How markets corrupt children, infantilize adults and swallow citizens whole*. New York: W.W. Norton & Company.

Becker, E. (1973). *The denial of death (Vol. 1)*. New York: The Free Press.

Boulding, E. (2000). *Cultures of peace: The hidden side of history* (1 ed.). Syracuse, NY: Syracuse University Press.

Boulding, R., Clements, K. P., Morrison, M. L., & Yodsampa, A. S. (2016). Elise Boulding's legacy to the twenty-first century: Reflections on her contributions to understanding conflict and peace. *Negotiation and Conflict Management Research, 9*(4), 274–291.

Burggraeve, R. (2002). *The wisdom of love in the service of love: Emmanuel Levinas on justice peace and human rights*. Milwaukee, WI: Marquette University Press.

Gandhi, M. (2002). *The essential Gandhi: An anthology of his writings on his life, work, and ideas* L. Fischer (Ed.). New York: Vintage Books.

Greenberg, J., Solomon, S., & Arndt, J. (2008). A basic but uniquely human motivation: terror management. In G. W. Shah & Y. James (Eds.), *Handbook of motivation science* (1st ed., pp. 114–134). New York: Guilford Press.

Kramer, R. M., & Messick, D. M. (1998). Getting by with a little help from our enemies: Collective paranoia and its role in intergroup relations. In C. Sedikides & J. Schopler (Eds.), *Intergroup cognition and intergroup behavior* (pp. 233–255). Mahwah, NJ: Erlbaum.

Lederach, J. P. (1997). *Building peace: Sustainable reconciliation in divided studies*. Washington, DC: United States Institute of Peace Press

Lederach, J. P. (2005). *The moral imagination: The art and soul of building peace*. New York: Oxford University Press.

Lederach, J. P. (2011). *The poetic unfolding of the human spirit*. Kalamazu, MI: Fetzer Institute.

Lesser, A. H. (1996). Levinas and the Jewish ideal of the sage. In S. Hand (Ed.), *Facing the other: The ethics of Emmanual Levinas* (pp. 141–152). London: Curzon Press.

Levinas, E. (1988). *Existence and existents* (Reprinted with minor corrections. ed.). Dordrecht: Kluwer Publishers.

Levinas, E. (1989). Ethics as first philosophy. In S. Hand (Ed.), *The Levinas reader* (pp. 75–87). Oxford: Blackwell.

Mandela, N. (2004). Address by Nelson Mandela during a joint sitting of Parliament to mark 10 years of democracy in South Africa, Cape Town. Retrieved from http://www.mandela.gov.za/mandela_speeches/2004/040510_democracy.htm

Schweitzer, A. (1965). *The teaching of reverence for life*. London: Peter Owen.

Staub, E. (2021). Preventing violence and promoting active bystandership and peace and conflict. In K. Clements & S. Lee (Eds.), *Multi-level reconciliation and Peacebuilding*. London: Routledge.

Vollhardt, J., Migacheva, K., & Tropp, L. R. (2009). Social cohesion and tolerance for group differences. In J. De Rivera (Ed.), *Handbook on building cultures of peace* (pp. 139–152). New York: Springer.

genopolitics, political physiology, behavioural genetics, social neuroscience and cognitive neuroscience, etc. Their work includes the study of genetic, hormonal and neural attitudinal tendencies, as well as the social environmental factors that influence such tendencies. Such studies have been substantially enabled by new methodologies of investigation such as genetic and hormonal testing, fMRI and electroencephalography, which have the huge advantage of enabling more objective data, rather than the self-assessment reports and group observations that were once par for the course in the social sciences.

Over the last decade, such a behavioural approach has recently revolutionised the study of e.g. economics, in the form of a new sub-field called behavioural economics, which is now espoused by many governments, and by the World Bank (2015) in its efforts tackle seemingly intractable social and economic world problems. Social media companies such as Google, Facebook and Twitter are also using behavioural approaches as part of their business strategies (Dooley 2011). Now even governmental policy units are using such an approach e.g. some years ago, the UK government set up a public policy "Nudge" unit (Behavioural Insights Team) based on the behavioural sciences to help shape public policy. The Australian government (Benedictus 2013) is also using such approaches to modify their policy development strategies.

All of these institutes are working on the assumption that by drawing on insights from the behavioural sciences, and in particular the social neurosciences, new kinds of interventions can be generated. Such approaches have either validated or enhanced our understanding about previously little understood human and social factors which shape our relationships with each other, both individually and collectively in groups.

Many of the findings of these new disciplines are vitally relevant to the work of peacebuilding, but as yet we in the peacebuilding field have not yet really begun to investigate whether or not some of these new understandings may help us to better address some of the many challenges that we face in our work. This chapter is an attempt to outline some of these understandings, and what they might mean for how we refocus our reconciliation work.

I am aware that in so focusing, I am facing at least three major challenges. The first is that focusing on biosciences may turn the spotlight away from structural and societal issues that are unfair, and that exclude and oppress certain groups, and which make their use of violence understandable, if not justified. However, on the contrary, based on my research (Fitzduff 2013; Fitzduff and Stout 2006; Fitzduff 2017), it is clear that an understanding of such psychosocial/neural factors will be ineffective in the long term if structural issues are not addressed. *The reality is that it is often our social and political contexts that will decide whether we as human beings function to the best of our human nature, or to the worst.* Wars start not because of our biological natures, but because our bio-predispositions come into play through manipulation and violence within a situation where people often feel unequal and excluded. Most of our recent and current wars have come about because of issues of inequality or exclusion; these include wars in Syria, Iraq, Sri Lanka, Philippines, Vietnam, Ukraine, Northern Ireland, Cameroon and Egypt.

# 3 Behavioural peacebuilding

## Ensuring sustainable reconciliation

*Mari Fitzduff*

### Introduction

For decades, like many in our field, I have been struggling with questions that are core to the field of peacebuilding. Questions such as the capacity of most groups and nations to believe that the violence they inflict is justified – and the violence of their enemy is not. How to explain the power of fundamentalist ideologies to possess the minds and hearts of people, often beyond their own lives, as well as that of many others. I have even, on occasion, found myself feeling cynical about the belief that "of course everyone wants peace, don't they?," as was once said to me by a gentle and intelligent professor and President yes – Prime Minster from the Republic of Ireland.

I have now come to believe that many of the tenets we hold about how to prevent and bring an end to conflicts often do not add up, nor do they explain the many seeming irrationalities and inconsistencies that seem to be part and parcel of our wars. Through my work as a social psychologist, I have long been aware of issues like the effect of horizontal inequalities on a community's grievances, the importance of group belonging, and the ubiquitous role of seemingly endless enmities and intolerance in shaping our conflict histories. I have also lived and worked for many years in many countries on long and difficult tasks of reconciliation, which I define as moving the resolution of conflict from the use of violence, to the alternative use of e.g. politics, law, and/or social-economic development to resolve differences.

It has been through a relatively new science – or a combination of other sciences –s that I have come to see more and more of the confusions I have faced in a different light. These were the processes associated with emerging ideas about the ways in which our bodies and brains have been physically and mentally shaped by the exigencies of our evolution. I have learned a new appreciation of the fact that this shaping may have left us with many legacies which appear to help foment and maintain the existence of societal and national violence.

Such sciences, often called the behavioural sciences, involve fresh efforts to incorporate *more realistic notions of human nature* into their ideas than those normally espoused by the classical rational theories of the field. They draw much of their material from the work of political psychology, social biopsychology,

If such contexts had been handled differently, the individual and group differences noted in this research might just be part of the normal grist of a society that is both blessed and challenged with different and often competing approaches to the social issues that are the norm in most peaceful societies.

The second challenge is the fact that the legacy of scientific racism, that is, the use of scientific techniques and hypotheses to support or justify presumptions of racial inferiority, or superiority, is still with us. Many within our various fields were, and still are, rightly horrified about the abuse of genetic and social data that was the legacy of the 19th and 20th centuries, and to a certain extent is still with us today, although less frequently openly justified. However, none of the research that follows will give any sway or ballast to anyone interested in eliciting such differences for reasons of discrimination. Alas, the contrary is true – we are all of us indicted for the instincts and the confusion that we often bring to bear on our conflicts.

The third challenge is the fact that much of the research that I write about in this paper is very tentative. The advantages of neuroscience have been much touted for their ability to look under the hood of our brains, and help us to see some of the mechanisms and processes that can help to create and perpetuate conflict. However, the reality is that many of the mechanisms that are used to measure our conscious and unconscious thoughts and behaviour, such as fMRI neuroimaging, are still in their infancy. Therefore, much of what is contained within this chapter will inevitably change as the research continues to multiply.

We also need to remember that most of the research outlined in this chapter has been conducted predominantly by and on what are called WEIRD people i.e. Western, Educated, Industrialised, Rich and Democratic. Such a limitation in terms of constituencies studied brings its own significant cultural biases (Heinrich et al. 2009).

A few other caveats: I am adopting a non-judgemental approach to the differences that appear to be evident between human beings and their neural architectures. As the research shows, people and groups *are* different in the way they think and process information, the kinds of emotions they bring to bear upon decisions, the needs they have to belong to a group, what they prioritise as values, the importance of ideology in their lives, the way they identify enemies, the way they see facts, what they remember and forget, their fear and suspicions of out-groups and their need for leaders. These differences are neither good, nor bad. They just are – and they exist possibly because somewhere along the line of our past, such differences, and a mix of such differences, have been critical for individual and group evolutionary survival. What is important is that we understand these differences and take them into account in our reconciliation work.

## The Rider and the Elephant: Who is in charge of us?

Who is in charge of our minds and our emotions? Where do our ideas and attitudes come from? Most of us think they come from the rational part of our brains – the part that we use through reasoning and argument to clarify what we are thinking, and to decide what should be our next best course of action. In fact, our influence over our thoughts, our emotions and our actions is much weaker than we assume.

Our brains have many activity centres which have different functions, are connected by chemical impulses and are often at war with each other. There are two regions of the brain that are important for peacebuilders to understand: The part of our brain that processes our automatic/intuitive impulses and the part that deals with our conscious/reasoned processes. The first is the size of an almond and is called the amygdala. It deals with our senses, our memories and our emotions such as pleasure or fear. Its processes are automatic, sometimes called intuitive or implicit processes, and are impulsive or instinctive in nature – which means that we often have little choice about feeling them. This part of our brain is often called the old, or "lizard" brain. It is the deepest part of the brain and is reckoned to be at least 60–200 million years old. It records memories of behaviours which have produced feelings of good or bad experiences in our lifetimes, and in those of our ancestors. It exerts a very strong influence on our choices, often at an unconscious level. Those of us who have bad tempers, or road rage, or difficulty in restraining our eating, or other appetites, or who have been present in a situation of active war or genocide, can understand its power. The other important section of the brain which peacebuilders need to understand is the prefrontal cortex which concerns itself with conscious/rational processes, and is the part that contributes to more analytic, logical and thoughtful responses to a situation. It is considered to be the "new" brain and is deemed responsible for the development of human language, for abstract thought, for our imaginations, for reasoning and for consciousness. The amygdala conveys our feelings to the frontal cortex, the brain region that controls thinking and planning and such feelings then affect our rational processes.

However, few of us realise the tension there is between these two aspects of our brain. These "emotional" and "reasoning" minds coexist uneasily. This challenge has been well captured by Haidt (2001) in his analogy of the Elephant and the Rider, where our emotional side is the Elephant and our rational, reasonable side is the Rider. The Rider is perched atop the Elephant, and seems to be the leader, but her/his/their control is precarious because the Rider is so small and so new relative to the much older and deeper Elephant. Any time the Elephant and the Rider disagree about which direction to go, the amygdala/Elephant part of our brain is likely to win, unless we are able to bring our prefrontal cortex/reasoning strongly to bear upon our decisions.

The amygdala is particularly likely to come to the fore if we are under stress, as is normal in most conflict contexts. This makes it more likely for our emotions to bypass our thinking cortex and to return to thinking and acting according to the "older" brain drives. The predominance of intuitive/emotive thinking versus cognitive reasoning, or "fast versus slow thinking" as it has been termed recently (Kahneman 2012), is particularly evident and automatic in situations where fear is a factor. Such amygdala feelings come not only from current situations of conflict, but in many cases have been generated and fostered by many decades of conflict, and are often the product of many generation's histories of emotions.

Many of us fail to understand how precarious is the conscious/rational side of our brains, until we find ourselves in a context that unleashes the forces of our amygdala. We are all of us, no matter how well educated, subject to the strength of such emotions. Where our families, communities and ourselves feel under stress, fear and group processes often overtake our emotions. These emotions can be extremely hard to control, particularly at group level. It has been suggested by Greene (2012) that the human brain is like a dual mode camera with both automatic settings and a manual mode. The "automatic" settings are for emotions, and the "manual" mode is for reasoning. Nowhere are such forces as evident as in the many contexts of conflict in which peacebuilders work.

## Brains differ

Our brains differ in terms of how we are affected by our amygdala, or our cortex. Functional magnetic resonance imaging or functional MRI (fMRI) is a technology that measures brain activity by detecting associated changes in blood flow. fMRI scans have shown that there are differences in genetics and in our biology that influence the differences in our attitudes and beliefs. Some people show bigger grey matter volume in the amygdala, the structure that performs a primary role in the processing and memory of emotions. Others show a bigger grey matter volume in the anterior cingulate cortex, the structure of the brain associated with rational/logical thinking, with monitoring uncertainty and with handling conflicting information. At one end of the spectrum, people, usually called traditionalists or conservatives in the literature, more often use their amygdala, the part of the brain associated with the body's fight-or-flight system, when making decisions. They appear to have a genetically greater sensitivity to fear and uncertainty, and these differences can be observed from birth. They respond much more quickly to sudden noises and threatening visual images (Carraro et al. 2011). The degree to which individuals are physiologically responsive to such threats appears to indicate the degree to which they advocate policies that protect the existing social structure from both external out-groups and internal norm-violator threats. Fearful people tend to be more conservative. They have a greater need for order, structure and certainty in their lives, resist change more often and are less open to risk-taking. Researchers have shown that they are usually more supportive of policies that provide them with a sense of security; hence their greater backing for military spending, capital punishment, patriotism and tougher laws on immigration (Hatemi and Mc Dermott 2011; Somit and Peterson 2011). Such people also report greater physiological levels of disgust when faced with bugs, or blood, and in relation to such issues as gay marriage and abortion. They usually value "purity" and order and are known to devote high levels of attention to norm violations. While the predisposition to experience greater fear has a genetic component, what exactly people will fear, or towards which out-group they will harbour suspicions, will of course differ depending on their environment, their culture and their social contexts.

On the other end of the amygdala–cortex continuum, there are people who are genetically more open to new things, and to new experiences – these are often termed "liberals." fMRI scans have shown that they can better tolerate uncertainty and cognitive complexity, take risks more often and have wider and more diverse friendships. They often exhibit stronger preferences for social change and equality when compared with traditionalists. When faced with a conflict, liberals are more likely than conservatives to be more flexible and to alter their habitual response when cues indicate it is necessary (Mooney 2012). There is speculation in the literature that, for evolutionary purposes, it may have proved useful to have such varied types of individuals in a society to ensure the best survival responses to different sets of societal and group challenges. It appears however that conservatism has been the majority norm throughout history, and that the growth in liberalism may be viewed as an evolutionary luxury that is increasingly afforded only by the fact that many societies today are becoming less deadly.

Twin studies seem to bear out the contention that social and political perspectives are genetically shaped. In 2005, a US twin study examined the attitudes of identical twins regarding 28 different social and political issues such as capitalism, trade unions, X-rated movies, abortion, school prayer, divorce, property taxes and the draft. Researchers compared them to non-identical twins, and it was estimated that genetic factors accounted for 53% of the variance (Alford et al. 2005). In a later study using facial electromyography (EMG) and skin conductance, those who had a high startle response i.e. a largely unconscious defensive response to sudden or threatening stimuli, such as sudden noise or sharp movement were more likely to take conservative positions such as supporting capital punishment, defence spending, patriotism and the Iraq war, while individuals with a lower startle response were more likely to take liberal positions on issues such as supporting foreign aid, gun control, lenient immigration policies and pacifism (Oxley et al. 2008).

Many later studies have confirmed this link between genetics and attitudes. Hatemi et al. (2014) undertook a study of over 12,000 twin pairs, ascertained from nine different studies, conducted in five democracies, to ascertain the effect of genes on social and political attitudes such as left–right attitudes, right-wing authoritarianism, life values, economic egalitarianism, individualism vs collectivism and freedom vs equality. The studies were conducted in five countries – Denmark, Australia, Sweden, Hungary and the US – and were carried out over the course of three decades between 1980–2011. They found that genetic factors account for a significant amount of the variance in individual differences in ideology across time, location, measures and populations.

Thus it seems that people who support greater military spending, harsher punishment for criminals and more restrictive immigration are not doing so just because they are ignorant or angry about such issues, but because they are more physiologically and psychologically aware of possible negative eventualities pertaining to such issues. It seems that a more conservative ideology, with its emphasis on tradition, hierarchy and maintenance of the status quo, provides a better match than liberal or progressive ideology for those who feel a greater need to reduce uncertainty and threat. Thus, it makes sense that conservatives are more likely to support public policies that would mitigate the dangers they see ahead, in part because their brain patterns lead them to be more cognisant than liberals of such impending dangers.

However, it is important to remember, that people fall along a continuum of such characteristics, and also that *people are predisposed, but not predestined* to become more "conservative" or more "liberal." How much our genetics influence our attitudes and behaviour is still a major research question. The suggestions range from 40% to 53%. While it is suggested that genetic predispositions can be altered, effecting such change has been likened to turning a supertanker – such change takes considerable effort and time. However, it is also important to note that certain environments, such as that post-9/11, may be so powerful that they elicit a common response in humans that leaves little room for genetic differences to manifest. A study of survivors who were highly impacted by the 9/11 attack on the New York World Trade Center found that three times as many of them reported becoming more politically conservative in the 18 months following the attack (Bonanno and Jost 2006).

Such categorisations have a long history that extends way before the invention of magnetic resonance imaging and hormonal testing. Thomas Jefferson has been noted as one of the first "neuro-politicians," and indeed one who was open about his own preferred bias. The president was convinced that the hardened Federalists he opposed "were suffering from damaged brains, and diseased minds, which rendered them incapable of supporting healthy social growth." He suggested that they were "nervous persons, whose languid [nerve] fibres have more analogy with a passive than active state of things" (Salon Staff 2013). Jefferson of course did not have the advantage of fMRI scans capable of confirming or otherwise his viewpoint. But the fact that there are now fMRI scanners that can test, describe and predict how we will think and feel about an issue or an out-group, must give us pause for our reconciliation work, and challenge us as to how we can use this knowledge to make our work more effective.

## Us and them: Who is my neighbour in today's world?

Human beings have spent most of their lives in relatively small groups, assisted by their hormones. Experiments have shown that bonding within groups is assisted by a rise in the level of oxytocin which appears to provide a "glue" between people. The change in the hormone oxytocin during social interactions can be measured. If it is present in abundance it can make you demonstrably more generous, trusting and compassionate towards your neighbours, or otherwise. This hormone increases a sense of belonging and of connectedness to a group, and positively rewards cooperation. For example, spraying oxytocin into people's noses makes them more likely to cooperate in a version of the conflict resolution game called the "Prisoner's Dilemma" (Chappelow 2019; De Dreu et al. 2011). Oxytocin is important for the inhibition of the brain regions such as the amygdala, and it thus reduces the fear of social betrayal in humans. The genetic basis for oxytocin production and receptivity has been identified, and there are indications that their levels may be inherited. It is believed that the hormone may have had an evolutionary function in that high levels of oxytocin, which have been found to correlate with different levels of cooperation, and it may have enabled some groups to thrive better than others. However, while oxytocin can increase levels of cooperation within a group, it can also promote ethnocentric behaviour. It can increase our suspicion and rejection of "others" outside the group or the tribe, and it makes people *less* likely to cooperate with members of an out-group (Baumgarthner et al. 2008). This has led to the suggestion that *biologically, humans have evolved for cooperation but only with some people, and not with others*, and for some researchers to suggest our brains are wired for tribalism. There are also findings that suggest that out-group biases such as race bias may be a fear "prepared" by evolution and not purely contextual, as elements of the amygdala appear to be responsible for, and associated with, implicit, as opposed to explicit, attitudes towards racial outgroups (Liu et al. 2015).

Our attitude towards out-groups is also affected by what scientists call "mirror neurons." Brain imaging experiments using fMRI have shown that the human inferior frontal cortex and superior parietal lobe are active when the person both performs an action, and also sees another individual performing an action. It has been suggested that these brain regions contain mirror neurons which appear to be linked to our capacity for empathy, the emotion which enables us to better understand other peoples' intentions, feelings and emotions and allows us to see the world from another's point of view (Gallese et al. 2007). Before the discovery of mirror neurons, scientists generally believed that it was through the use of our cognitive thought processes that we interpreted and predicted other people's behaviour. Now, however, many have come to believe that we actually understand others not by thinking, but by feeling through the "mirror" neurons in the affective brain circuits. These circuits are automatically mobilised when we feel our own pain, and also feel the pain of (some) others. This ability to empathetically perceive and respond to the affective states of another emerges as early as two years of age. It is a universally hard-wired response, although its expression varies according to cultural contexts. Of interest to note is that the part of the brain that controls empathy appears to be bigger in women, who show enhanced empathetic ability when compared to males (Moore et al. 2014).

It is suggested that empathetic responses towards one's group may have served an adaptive evolutionary function. When the context is one of perceived conflict with another group, the brain appears to switch off the empathetic neuron almost completely and actively resists emotional connection with the perceived "other" group. This would have helped foster the aggressive instincts that were crucial in tribes fighting to survive. Sociological studies have already shown that high levels of integration or "bonding" within a group seems to reduce a group's capacity to develop "bridging" and cooperation, between differing identity groups (Putnam 2000), and this is confirmed by the research on mirror neurons.

The power of contact and dialogue in increasing empathy and reconciliation has been examined using fMRI imaging, which can measure such changes. While dialogue appears to have positive effects, such effects are highly influenced by the social and political perspectives of groups in relation to each other's perceived status. Positive empathy towards opposing groups improves most among members of the disempowered groups, such as Palestinians and Mexicans, who told their own stories, and were listened to by the group that they perceived to be more powerful. On the other hand, groups that were perceived to be dominant groups, such as the Israelis and the US Americans, increased their empathy by listening to the stories of the groups who perceived themselves to be excluded or oppressed (Bruneau and Saxe 2012).

It therefore seems that the form of dialogue most effective in soliciting empathy differs according to the perceived power asymmetries between the groups. These findings illustrate the need to address, or promise to address, structural societal differences as a complement to dialogue strategies for reconciliation.

Why do our brains exhibit such differing hormonal and neural responses to our own group and to other groups? Without doubt, the apparently selective nature of group survival has been a keen factor in societal conflicts and wars. The categorisation of out-groups into enemies or friends, part of our group or not part of our group, is a universal trait that takes place in all societies and nations. Such identification of the enemy will obviously differ and change from context to context, but has ever been part of our history, as have been the changes in such categorisations. People from Ireland and Italy were not considered "white" by most 19th-century Americans, and it took a US court to decide in 1909 that Armenians were part of the "white" race. Even what appears to be the smallest of differences such as those between Sunni or Shia, or Catholic or Protestant, or French or English speakers can provide a framework for violent and often deadly conflict. While religion and ideologies often bind a group together, they are only one framework for the development of group boundaries. Almost any form of group relationships, such as gangs, cults or paramilitarism can suffice. Such racial, religious, ethnic and language categorisations at community, regional, national and international level are grist for the mill of most of the wars around the world today and are easily utilised by leaders for their own gain.

Leaders are assisted in this by our predisposed tendencies to be suspicious of out-groups. In addition, devotion to leaders may have developed to facilitate cooperation in large groups. Our leaders are often selected because of emotional choices. A lot of this appears to be part of our evolutionary history. Being social animals, we are perhaps "programmed" to try to lead, and to be led, to have faith in hierarchies, because of our desire to conform and be protected. Studies by Milgram (1974) illustrate our tendency to "blindly" carry out the orders of an authority, even when it means administering painful electric shocks and potentially harming an innocent victim.

We usually choose our leaders because of our gut instincts, rather than through an analysis of their characters or strategies. We often prefer our leaders to speak with certainty about issues about which we are concerned – often irrespective of the substance of their arguments. (Murray and Schmitz 2011). Leaders who express hesitation, or even endorse the value of consultation, can be anathema to us. Our need for our leaders is for them to be clear and strong, particularly if we are afraid (Fitzduff 2017). Once people have adopted a leader, even new negative information about that leader can often lead people to intensify rather than lessen their support for him/her/them.

Once again, it is important to remember that such tendencies can be mitigated. One of the most important conclusions from neuroscience research is that the human brain, throughout life, is predisposed to be physically moulded, in ongoing ways, by human interactions in contexts that provide for social learning, and the rewiring of neural pathways. The memory parts of the brains of both taxi drivers and waitresses have been shown to grow bigger because of the increased activity necessitated by their work focus. Buddhist monks who practise compassion meditation have been shown to modulate their amygdala, the part of the brain that is involved with the experiencing of emotions, during their practice. People living in more market-focused societies tend to be more altruistic and tolerant to strangers, and more adept at cooperating with them. This suggests that although our brains are wired for tribalism, they can (eventually?) be rewired to relate to wider groups through experience, and contexts and institutions that facilitate tolerance. Whether we can totally eradicate this tendency appears doubtful.

## Facts versus fake facts

In 2015, researchers from the University of York and the University of California, Los Angeles, decided to study the effect of transcranial magnetic stimulation (TMS) – a non-invasive procedure that uses a metal coil to send pulses to the brain – to see how it affected their subjects' approach to social problems (Holbrook et al. 2016). All the participants were politically moderate college undergraduates and were pre-screened to make sure that they held religious convictions before beginning the experiment. As part of the process participants were asked to rate their belief in the devil, demons, hell, God, angels and heaven. The participants also read two essays ostensibly written by recent immigrants. One essay was extremely complimentary toward the US, and the other essay was extremely critical of the US.

The findings revealed that people in whom the targeted brain region was temporarily shut down by TMS reported 32.8% less belief in God, angels or heaven. They were also 28.5% more positive in their feelings toward an immigrant who criticised their country. Thus, by activating certain regions of the brain, researchers were able to change prejudicial beliefs, and even beliefs in God.

In another exercise, ten patients with bilateral damage to the ventromedial prefrontal cortex (vmPFC), ten other patients with damage to areas outside the vmPFC, and 16 medical comparison patients, who had experienced life-threatening, but non-neurological medical events, completed a series of scales measuring authoritarianism, religious fundamentalism and specific religious beliefs (Asp et al. 2012). The degree of authoritarianism and religious fundamentalism expressed by those with damage to the vmPFC was significantly higher than the norm for such values. In addition, patients with damage to the vmPFC themselves reported that their levels of fundamentalism had risen after brain injury.

It seems then that it is far from clear-cut why we believe what we believe. Because it is true? Rarely, it appears. Our beliefs in many cases appear to be what is called "motivated reasoning" i.e. it is determined not by "truth," but by our own physical predispositions, our emotions, our needs for beliefs, or moral values and the cultural context in which we live. In other words, beliefs often come first from our social environment – and we mainly rationalise what our gut (and fears) tell us.

Experiments have shown the interdependence of genetic, social and environmental factors in the development of our beliefs and moralities. Researchers have used genome-wide linkage analysis, an examination of the many common genetic variants in different individuals, in order to identify chromosomal regions associated with social and political attitudes along the "liberalism/conservatism" scale. In 2010 a study implicated a gene known as DRD4 in the development of general social/political orientation. The DRD4 gene encodes a receptor molecule for a neurotransmitter called dopamine. Those with a variant of DRD4 called 7R, and also a large network of acquired friends, tended to be more liberal (Settle et al. 2010). The researchers speculated that the interaction of that tendency, with its attendant exposure to lots of different ideas held by lots of different people might push an individual in a liberal direction. Later research has found a further 11 genes, different varieties of which might be responsible for inclining people towards liberal or conservative beliefs. These included genes involved in the regulation of three neurotransmitters – dopamine, glutamate and serotonin – and also G-protein-coupled receptors, which react to a wide variety of stimulants. Many other studies have shown that biology and psychology are inextricably linked. Our memories too are also notoriously faulty – they often reframe and edit events so as to create a story that will fit our current beliefs, and current context, conflating the past and present to suggest a story to us that suits what we need to believe today (Steinfurth et al. 2014).

While our personalities may be different in terms of our fear levels, the substance of our beliefs is usually determined by our context. Our views as part of a group are rarely based on cognitive processing; they are often a case of groupthink – views that are based on group needs, rather than based on fact-checking. They are what Haidt (2003) calls "groupish" which means that we usually approve of what we think or are told is good for our group. While beliefs often successfully serve to bind us more closely to each other, and thus ensure our group survival, they unfortunately often blind us to the points of view of other groups. In Haidt's term, morality "binds and blinds" – it binds us to the group and blinds us to the point of view of outsiders.

Once group beliefs are sacrosanct, the members of a group often lose their ability (and their freedom) to think rationally about them. This is helped by the fact that, once our views have been formed, we have a tendency to see and find evidence in support of already existing beliefs, and ignore evidence that challenges them. fMRI studies have shown that, when faced with logical contradictions to their deeply held beliefs, people often feel negative emotions, but there is no increase in the dorsolateral cortex, the part of their brain which is used for reasoning (Westen et al., 2006). Most of us do all that we can to protect our group beliefs by watching media sources such as Fox News, or certain programmes on MSNBC, or by reading for example, *The New York Times* or *The Washington Times*, or *The Times* or *The Guardian*, *Haaretz* or *The Jerusalem Post*, which serve to solidify what we believe. Of course, most of us may be unaware of such biased choices, and refuse to acknowledge this. Conflicting groups watching the same media coverage of their differences all think it is biased against them (Perloff 2015). When asked to choose between accepting the views of an expert (on a subject such as global warming) and being a good member of a tribe, the latter is often more important for some people/groups. Those of us who have tried to have theological, moral or social discussions with religious or social fundamentalists have usually found how unsuccessful such an exchange process can be. For many people, moral reasoning is often generated only after a belief has been assumed instinctively. We often lie even to ourselves because it appears that self-deception is an assistive process that enables us to more convincingly deceive others (Ariely 2012). This also means that we suffer from attribution bias, the tendency to attribute different causes and justifications for our own beliefs and actions than to those of others. When bad things happen, it is always their fault, not ours, their violence is terrorism, ours is justified by security needs.

While systems of belief, and the shared nature of values, can foster great courage and group altruism, it seems that such altruism is often of a parochial nature, and associated with a particular ideological or territorial group rather than a global one. How such group altruism can fare in the increasing diversity of all our societies, and within an increasingly globalised world is a major question for the peacebuilders of today.

The upshot of such precariousness between emotion and reasoning is that for change to happen, people need to be *both* emotionally and rationally engaged in reconciliation work. It is not enough for people to intellectually understand that they should take actions that can end a conflict.

## What consequences do the behavioural sciences have for our reconciliation work?

*We should recognise that anger and fear are closely related.* We need to remember that anger is often a consolidation of feelings of fear into action. It is therefore often more useful to ask ourselves and others what people or groups are afraid of, rather than what they are angry about. A better understanding of the feelings behind their arguments, rather than just the facts, may suggest different approaches that may be more productive.

*Accept that most people are conservative*, for good evolutionary reasons, and their reasons for not changing are often "rational" when understood within their own framework – if not in yours. It is usually the more conservative people who are the majority. Valuing and understanding such conservatism, and the fears and emotion behind it, is important in order to strategise for effective change.

*We should not base peacebuilding strategies solely on processes that depend upon the power of reason.* We also need to provide emotional experiences that can diminish the fear between groups. This may mean enlisting and using community leaders, religious leaders and political leaders aligned in some ways through trust to those who are most resistant to change. A dismissal of "facts" is often as much due to a lack of trust in the sources and the filters through which we learn about facts, as it is to intelligence.

*Provide alternative roles for people who have espoused violence.* Remember that some people have often found an exciting and meaningful role in their war-related activities. Opportunities for continuing such meaning in differing ways is essential if a post-conflict society is to be sustainable.

*Help people to understand their own, often unconscious, feelings of bias.* Biases can be elicited easily from almost everyone using dialogue techniques (see Fitzduff and Williams 2019). Having to face up to such biases is a humbling process. We all, however, need to remember that while we may not be responsible for such initial feelings, which are often a product of our human nature, and our social context, we are very much responsible for what we do to others as a result of those feelings.

*Increase oxytocin and trust levels between opposing parties.* Such processes can be increased by gestures such as gift-giving, meal-sharing, alcohol, where such is culturally permitted (just a modicum – too much can make us belligerent!), positive physical gestures, expressions of understanding and appreciation, sharing of family stories and group singing. (Note that none, or almost none of these are mentioned in the mediator's guidebooks, but fMRI and hormonal testing indicate that perhaps they should be.)

*Remember that people usually believe what they say.* People need to recognise that their opponents are not necessarily uninformed or unintelligent but rather that, at a very basic level, they often interpret the world differently. Thus the "truths" felt at e.g. Trump and (some) other leaders' rallies will matter far more to their supporters than those expounded in newspapers, by other politicians or by academics. Fact-checking is often useless, as seeming "errors" often exist because they serve a psychological need on the part of an individual or group. Understanding the feelings and needs behind apparently irrational ideas is important if changes are to happen.

*Encourage perspective taking.* The power of increasing empathy and cooperation through perspective shifting – changing the way people understand and think about other groups by cognitively and emotionally standing in their shoes – has been examined using fMRI imaging. It shows that encouraging perspective shifting through meeting and talking can, if done effectively, actually alter the neural circuits concerned with identity differences. However, such sharing cannot ignore histories of perceived inequalities or its effect will be temporary and limited.

*Create new groups for people to belong to.* People need to belong somewhere. It makes it easier for them to adjust to change if there are institutions that are open to people who are willing to effect change. Without such institutions, new perceptions can quickly die in the face of societal change and the danger of personal isolation.

*Do single identity/within* group work prior to work between groups. Bringing differing groups to increase understanding can be counter-productive if groups have not had a chance to manage their own differences. If groups have not had a chance to deal with such differences, they are likely to assume a narrower collective stance about their beliefs and objectives when they find themselves in intergroup situations.

*Encourage moderates to speak first in group work.* The first person to speak in an intergroup process of reconciliation will usually set the tone of the dialogues that follow. Encouraging group moderates to speak first in an intergroup process can set a more open tone for the later conversation. It can also relieve concerns about betrayal on the part of those participants who are fearful of being seen as more tolerant, and therefore excluded by the group.

*Use the media to increase an understanding of different perspectives.* Media, including social media, are often the only practical sources for opposing groups to hear from each other. Constructively using such tools – such as the work by Search for Common Grounds media programmes (www.sfcg.org/our-media/) – can help diminish ignorance and dehumanisation.

*Undertake effective contact work.* Contact work, despite usually being well-intentioned, is often of no avail unless it can include political, military or community leaders who can affect the institutions of society. Such contact work needs to include such important change-makers as soon as possible if it is to be authoritative and successful.

*Constructively deal with the past.* Collective memories of the past need to be reviewed and teased out together with opposing groups so that the differences in remembering such perspectives can be shared and the feelings, as opposed to just the "facts" behind such memories, can be understood. One can argue with another person's facts, but not their feelings.

*Remember to work with diasporas.* Because the nature of their belonging is often insecure, diaspora communities are often the last to be open to the compromises necessary for peacebuilding. This can delay a peace agreement unless prior work is done with them on the necessities for the way forward, and an emotional preparation for such.

*Where possible create sustainable institutions that promote understanding between groups.* Schools, universities, workplaces, youth groups, sports groups, civil service and government groups, as well as cultural and religious institutions can all play an important part in increasing understanding and bridging social, national, global and religious divides. Often such understanding can be best facilitated by long-term cooperative work between groups where their identities are known and salient.

*Recognise that groups/tribes often have distinctive moral and/or religious commitments* that other groups do not recognise as authoritative. It is important to elicit these in order to be able to help groups to negotiate with an understanding, and a use of such values and commitments where possible.

*Avoid horizontal inequalities*. Horizontal inequalities are those that occur on an identity basis, that is, people are poor/excluded/mistreated because of their identity (Stewart 2008). Recent evidence shows that the main factor in developing internal conflicts is horizontal inequalities based on issues of identity and involving issues of fairness and equality. Thus, there is a vital need to ensure that peacebuilding processes address, or promise to address, societal inequities and exclusion. Little empathy between perceived victims and oppressor groups can be achieved without such promises.

## Conclusion

My hope is that a greater appreciation of how our physical and mental predispositions, as well as environmental influences, can affect our human behaviour, can strengthen our reconciliation work. The upshot of the precariousness between emotion and reasoning is that for change to happen, people need to be *both* emotionally and rationally engaged in reconciliation work. Many of us in the field have filing cabinets full of possible "rational" approaches to all of the conflicts in which we are working. However, for people to actually approach that filing cabinet, and its possible solutions, they also need to be emotionally motivated to do so, which is often a harder process to manufacture than any reasoning in favour of particular solutions. Time and again we see groups continue fighting well beyond much apparent reasonable gain for all involved. Peace agreements fall apart because, although the cognitive skills of those involved have crafted clever political and social compromises, the lack of the necessary emotions and will to process such agreements dilutes their capacity for success.

I believe that it is better to understand both our complexity and our predictability as individuals and social beings rather than remain in ignorance of such. Such learning, if used wisely, can build on a greater understanding of the realities of human nature, and its neural legacies, rather than ignoring them. It may help us, and the groups we work with, to understand better and relate more empathetically, more realistically and more compassionately to conflicted groups who behave as they do often at such significant cost to themselves and others, and thus assist us to craft more effective reconciliation strategies for the many challenges ahead of us in the decades to come.

## References

Alford, J. R., Funk, C., & Hibbing, J. R. (2005). Are political orientations genetically transmitted? *American Political Science Review*, *99*(2), 153–167.

Ariely, D. (2012). *The (honest) truth about dishonesty: How we lie to everyone-especially ourselves*. New York: Harper Perennial.

Asp, E., Ramchandran, K., & Tranel, D. (2012). Authoritarianism, religious fundamentalism, and the human prefrontal cortex. *Neuropsychology*, *26*(4), 414–421.

Baumgartner, T., Heinrichs, M., Vonlanthen, A., Fischbacher, U., & Fehr, E. (2008). Oxytocin shapes the neural circuitry of trust and trust adaptation in humans. *Neuron*, *58*(4), 639–650.

Benedictus, L. (2013). The nudge unit – Has it worked so far? *The Guardian*. Retrieved from http://www.theguardian.com/politics/2013/may/02/nudge-unit-has-it-worked

Bonanno, G., & Jost, J. (2006). Conservative shift among high-exposure survivors of the September 11th terrorist attacks. Retrieved from https://pdfs.semanticscholar.org/6259/7854c763c76c13ac93cb5ed7ccd93c9ada5c.pdf

Bruneau, E., & Saxe, R. (2012). The power of being heard: The benefits of 'perspective-giving' in the context of intergroup conflict. *Journal of Experimental Social Psychology*, *48*(4), 855–866.

Carraro, L., Castelli, L., & Macchiella, C. (2011). The automatic conservative: Ideology-based attentional asymmetries in the processing of valenced information. *PLOS ONE*, *6*(11), e26456.

Chappelow, J. (2019). Prisoner's dilemma. Investopedia. Retrieved from https://www.investopedia.com/terms/p/prisoners-dilemma.asp

Christov-Moore, L., Simpson, E., Ferrari, P., Grigaityte, K., Iacoboni, M., & Ferrari, P. F. (2014). Empathy: Gender effects in brain and behaviour. *Neuroscience and Biobehavioural Review*, *46*(4), 604–627.

De Dreu, C. K., Greer, L., Van Kleef, G. A., Shalvi, S., & Handgraaf, M. J. (2011). Oxytocin promotes human ethnocentrism. *Proceedings of the National Academy of Sciences*, *108*(4), 1262–1266.

Dooley, R. (2011). *Brainfluence, 100. Ways to Persuade and Convince Consumers with Neuromarketing*. Hoboken, NJ: Wiley.

Fitzduff, M. (2013). *Public policies in shared societies*. Basingstoke: Palgrave Macmillan.

Fitzduff, M. (2017). *Why irrational politics appeals: Understanding the allure of trump*. Westport, CT: Praeger.

Fitzduff, M., & Stout, C. (Eds.) (2006). *The psychology of resolving global conflicts: From war to peace*. Westport, CT: Praeger Security International.

Fitzduff, M., & Williams, S. (2019). *Dialogue in divided societies: Skills for working with groups in conflict*. Siem Reap: Center for Peace and Conflict Studies.

Gallese, V., Eagle, M. N., & Migone, P. (2007). Intentional attunement: Mirror neurons and the neural underpinnings of interpersonal relations. *Journal of the American Psychoanalytic Association*, *55*(1), 131–176.

Greene, J. (2012). *Moral tribes: Emotion, reason and the gap between us and them*. London: Atlantic Books.

Haidt, J. (2001). The emotional dog and its rationalist tail: A social intuitionist approach to moral judgement. *Psychological Review*, *108*(4), 814–834.

Haidt, J. (2003). *The righteous mind: Why good people are divided by politics and religion*. London: Penguin Publishing.

Hatemi, P., & McDermott, R. (2011). *Man is by nature a political animal: Evolution, biology, and politics*. Chicago, IL: University of Chicago Press.

Hatemi, P., Medland, S., & Martin, N. G. (2014). Genetic influences on political ideologies: Twin analyses of 19 measures of political ideologies from five democracies and genome-wide findings from three populations. *Behavioural Genetics*, *44*(3), 282–294.

Henrich, J., Heine, S. J., & Norenzayan, A. (2009). The weirdest people in the world: How representative are experimental findings from American University students?, what do we really know about human psychology? Retrieved from http://www2.psych.ubc.ca/~henrich/pdfs/Weird_People_BBS_final02.pdf

Holbrook, C., Izuma, K., Deblieck, C., Fesslert, D., & Iacoboni, M. (2016). Neuromodulation of group prejudice and religious belief. *Social Cognitive and Affective Neuroscience*, *11*(3), 387–394.

Kahneman, D. (2012). *Thinking fast and slow*. London: Penguin Publishing.

Liu, Y., Lin, W., Xu, P., Luo, D., & Luo, Y. (2015). Neural basis of disgust perception in racial prejudice. *Human Brain Mapping*, *36*(12). doi: 10.1002/hbm.23010

Milgram, S. (1974). *Obedience to authority: An experimental view*. New York: Harper Collins.

Mooney, C. (2012). *The Republican brain: The science of why they deny science--And reality*. Chichester: Wiley Press.

Murray, G., & Schmitz, D. (2011). Caveman politics: Evolutionary leadership preferences and physical stature. *Social Science Quarterly*, *92*(5), 1215–1235.

Oxley, D. R., Smith, K. B., Alford, J. R., Hibbing, M. V., Miller, J. L., Scalora, M., ... Hibbing, J. R. (2008). Political attitudes vary with physiological traits. *Science*, *321*(5896), 1667–1670.

Perloff, Richard M. (2015). A three-decade retrospective on the hostile media effect. *Mass Communication and Society*, *18*(6), 701–729.

Putnam, R. (2000). *Bowling alone: The collapse and revival of American Community*. New York: Simon & Schuster.

Salon Staff (2013). Is being liberal a choice? *Salon*, March 6. Retrieved from https://www.salon.com/2013/03/06/is_being_liberal_a_choice/

Settle, J., Dawes, C., Fowler, J., & Fowler, J. H. (2010). Friendships moderate an association between a dopamine gene variant and political ideology. *The Journal of Politics*, *72*(4), 1189–1198.

Somit, A., & Peterson, S. (2011). *Biology and politics: The cutting edge*. Bingley: Emerald Publishing.

Steinfurth, E. C., Kanen, J. W., Raio, C. M., Clem, R. L., Huganir, R. L., & Phelps, E. A. (2014). Young and old Pavlovian fear memories can be modified with extinction training during reconsolidation in humans. *Learning and Memory*, *21*(7), 338–341.

Stewart, F. (Ed.) (2008) *Horizontal inequalities and conflict understanding group violence in multiethnic societies*. Basingstoke: Palgrave Macmillan.

Westen, D., Blagov, P. S., Harenski, K., Kilts, C., & Hamann, S. (2006). Neural bases of motivated reasoning: An fMRI study of emotional constraints on partisan political judgment in the 2004 U.S. Presidential election. *Journal of Cognitive Neuroscience*, *18*(11), 1947–1958.

World Bank (2015). *World Bank development report 2015: Mind, society, and behavior*. Washington, DC: World Bank.

# 4 Interreligious dialogue and the path to reconciliation

*Mohammed Abu-Nimer*

## Introduction

> When I met someone from the other side, I discovered how little I knew about their faith, nation and culture.

The path to reconciliation has many steps. Conflict parties and their constituencies experience them in different ways and at a different pace. Nevertheless, meeting the other and understanding their perspective is a necessary condition for mutual reconciliation to occur. Dialogue platforms are effective spaces to achieve such a level of understanding. I have heard the above-mentioned statement or a variation from hundreds of courageous participants in dialogue encounters. For a person to admit to this level of ignorance of the other, he or she must have experienced a powerful encounter, one so powerful that it made him/her re-examine deep-seated assumptions and misperceptions of the other side and of him/herself.

The dialogue is a platform that allows participants to look at themselves through the other. A dialogical encounter, contrary to what many people think or describe, is not meeting the other. It is meeting oneself and confronting one's own negative images and biases of the other. These are often real obstacles that block the reconciliation process. In dialogue, we need the other to show us what we think and feel. The other becomes the mirror in which we examine our own feelings and ask risky questions that we would not ask if we were not forced to meet the other in a trusting environment. Such self-questioning is crucial for the reconciliation process. Without such questioning, an Israeli participant will not understand the plight of a Palestinian refugee who lives a few miles away from his hometown. Similarly, a Palestinian will not understand the Israeli's resistance to reconciliation without realising that he/she does not know the other side. Both have to respond to the question: Why did I not know about their plight?

Reconciliation processes require dialogical spaces that contain certain dynamics to facilitate a painful process of self-discovery which has been prohibited or blocked (intentionally or unintentionally) by social agencies. The blocking of such reconciliation processes is certainly not done intentionally by most socialisation agencies. Society with all its agencies has conspired against its members to prohibit and prevent everyone, especially children, from dialogically meeting the other and imagining a reconciled relationship. Thus, the norms and skills of posing self-critical questions regarding the other (enemy, different religion or culture) are often lacking. In fact, it can be highly dangerous to publicly speak about the perspective of reconciliation with the other faith groups or their truth, especially when there is an ongoing conflict with such groups. Being accused of betrayal or treason is just one of the potential consequences that a daring person can face from his/her own community (or even family). For example, if an Azeri[1] citizen speaks about the Armenian perspective on the Nagorno-Karabakh War[2] and subsequent clashes, it can be at the cost of their own career, if not their citizenship.

## Faith, dialogue and reconciliation

To reconcile is to accept the assumption that the other has a different point of view and narrative, and such difference requires its own space and right to exist alongside one's own. Resistance to reconciliation among faith-based constituencies stems from the fact that most, if not all, religious doctrines claim certain exclusive truths. The membership in each faith has requirements, duties and privileges. The degree of critical self-examination varies between, and even within, members of the same faith group. Nevertheless, theological interpretations have been constructed in a way that allows for the possibility of reconciliation with other faiths. However, such hermeneutics is neither necessarily mainstreamed nor dominant in most faith groups. On the contrary, those who believe and promote interfaith and/or intrafaith dialogue often find themselves on the margins of their own faith group. They face many challenges from within (Gerrard and Abu-Nimer 2018).

Engaging in a dialogical process for reconciliation requires that the follower accepts certain assumptions, some of which might contradict his/her own faith group's theological interpretations. The conditions for an effective dialogical process that may contribute to reconciliation include, but are not limited to, six key elements briefly discussed in the following.

First, it is critical to assume that *trust can be built or rebuilt in other faith group members*. Trust is necessary to build a relationship based on honesty and transparency. In conflict areas, especially in contexts in which religious identities have been manipulated by the various sides to justify violence in the name of protecting one's own faith group, it becomes highly challenging to take the risk of trusting members of the other faith. In a context like the Israeli-Palestinian conflict, misperceptions and stereotypes are deeply ingrained in the collective mind and psyche of the three Abrahamic groups. Thus, during the early stage of the first reconciliation encounter, participants often admit to the following negative images: "Muslims cannot be trusted, they always side with each other in situations of violence; that is what their faith tells them. Don't you know about their brotherhood pact?!," "Jews will always stick together no matter what you do with them." "Christians only buy from each other. They cannot be trusted." Such statements are not exclusive to this region, in that Buddhist, Muslim, Hindu and Christian participants in Sri Lanka also exchange such views when they meet for the first time.

The second principle is rooted in the notion that we are all here in the reconciliation encounter for the *purpose of learning* about each other. Within most faith groups, learning about other religions is done through one's own clergy and religious agencies. In fact, there are whole systems or structures within faith groups that have evolved to specialise in teaching children and adults about the other faith groups and their religions. In Islam, for example, Da'awa (spreading the word of Allah), which consists of comparing Islamic teaching to the teachings of other faith groups, is very central in persuading the individual to adopt the path of Islam. Similarly, the Evangelical missionary tradition has a practice that compares Protestant teachings to Catholic teachings, or to other faiths like Judaism or Buddhism (Omar 2009; Woodberry 2009). Even in faith groups that do not adopt conversion as part of their belief systems, the religious institutions provide their followers with answers to the question of who other faith groups are, and why *ours* is better or the best path. Engaging in the reconciliation process necessitates a secure space for learning and unpacking the dogmatic style and content of one's own group, which is a highly challenging practice. In the dialogical encounter, the participant finds himself/herself facing the following dilemmas: How do I deal with the information that was given to me about the other faith groups by my religious authorities? Who is right and who is wrong when the information is contradictory? Who has deceived me? Once the principle of learning through the encounter is adopted by the religious participant, the pressure of defending one's own story as was told by the rabbi, imam, priest or Buddhist monk is relieved. The participant begins exploring the possibilities of new sources of information about their own faiths and other faith groups.

The third principle for promoting dialogue for reconciliation is that the *interaction has to take place through proper communication channels* that allow the religious and cultural meanings and codes to be accurately interpreted. This means, for example, that Muslim participants have to fully listen and be able to articulate clearly their own perceptions of their Islamic spiritual and religious identity, especially those aspects that block them from reconciliation. In most cases, participants arrive to the encounter with a default communication system that is based on inter- and intrareligious defensive and offensive strategies to sustain separation.

In an encounter when a Christian participant describes his perception of Islam and Muslims, on many occasions, the Muslim participants immediately assume the role of the traditional teacher who needs to "set the record straight" and make sure that the other speaker knows the "correct version of Islam." This dynamic repeats itself when the Muslim describes Christianity or Judaism. Due to the negative historical collective memory and current interreligious conflict dynamics, the need to defend one's own side is deeply ingrained in the follower's mind. Thus, open communication is rarely deployed or utilised in the encounter. Reconciliation facilitators are certainly needed, at least in the initial encounters, to ensure that the old and default negative communication patterns are broken and at least partially replaced with new and jointly agreed communication methods.

The new form of interreligious listening allows, for example, the Jewish participant to verify whether the message stated by the Muslim indeed meant what she/he understood. This verification process takes place throughout the encounter by posing questions such as: "When you said … did you mean to say this …?" or "this is what I understood from your message … is this what you meant to say?" Although such statements or open questions seem simple, they are very effective tools to prevent the person from blindly using his/her own religious framework to understand and communicate with the other.

*Symmetry* is another principle that ensures the effectiveness of the dialogue for the reconciliation process. In the reality that exists outside the reconciliation process, individuals or members of different faith groups are rarely in a symmetrical relationship with each other. The fact that they belong to different ethnic or national groups has placed them in asymmetrical power relations. For example, Sri Lankan Muslim clergy, as members of the minority in a Buddhist dominant majority state, will always feel under-represented and less influential than their counterpart, the Buddhist clergy. Similarly, a member of the Christian clergy in the Egyptian context will experience the same feeling of asymmetrical relations when he/she is in the presence of a member of the Muslim clergy from al-Azhar[3] who belongs to the dominant Muslim majority. Such asymmetrical relations are reflected in daily social and cultural interactions. However, the dialogical process for reconciliation is based on the assumption that all members of the group are equal and have the same rights to expression and action. No priority is given to members of the dominant faith group in society; on the contrary, often facilitators compensate for the external asymmetrical relations by empowering the faith minority groups throughout the process. For example, one such method of empowerment would be providing the minority faith group with their own independent and safe space to practise their own rituals and develop their own separate path for engagement with the dominant faith group.

Symmetry is crucial for the dialogical reconciliation process as it affects issues of justice and grievance, which are the heart of reconciliation. Faith groups will not feel comfortable if the outside reality is reproduced within the encounter design and gives privileges to the dominant faith groups. For example, in the Philippines during an interfaith dialogue between Christians and Muslims, the location and venue of the meeting was often decided or determined by the Christian groups and their agencies who organised the meeting. The site in many cases was a church or related property. A number of Muslim participants expressed frustration and demanded a change of venue or to at least have a meeting within Muslim territories. The language of the encounter is another manifestation of the asymmetric relationship. When Arabic-speaking participants in an Arab–European encounter were told that they could not speak their own language and no translation was available, English was utilised as a common language for the encounter. Providing such participants with the opportunity and space to feel equal to their counterparts is essential in nurturing dignity and respect in the dialogue for reconciliation context.

Obviously, the dialogical encounter cannot fully escape the interreligious asymmetric relations in the outside reality. As stated by Abu-Nimer and Lazarus in capturing the asymmetric relations in the Israeli–Palestinian conflict and its implication for the encounter:

> The 'toll' of the conflict is not equally distributed among the participants, nor is it only psychological. Israelis and Palestinians live in a reality of asymmetric power relations, in which most Israelis are born with access to rights, resources, and opportunities that are denied or severely curtailed for most Palestinians. Many Palestinian participants struggle during encounters with what they experience as over-psychologizing the relationship, or blurring the differences between Israeli life in a society enforcing an occupation and Palestinian life under occupation. Psychosocial approaches encourage participants to articulate and recognize their separate and unequal social realities. Such recognition is an essential step for participants on both sides to understand each other's distinct, but equally real and equally human, fears and needs, the different ways in which both groups perpetuate the dynamics of conflict, and the different ways in which people on each side pay 'the price of no peace.'
>
> (Abu-Nimer and Lazarus 2007)

However, the organisers of the dialogue can be intentional in shifting the dynamics and in constructing an environment that allows the minority faith group to feel more empowered and the dominant majority to experience a dynamic of genuine equality. When the participant from the dominant faith group experiences and accepts the possibility of equal and symmetrical relations, their theological framework changes in a way that allows them to hold on to the newly constructed view of the other. One such example occurred when Sunni Muslim participants from a dominant faith group in a second dialogical encounter in Pakistan began articulating Qura'nic and hadith sayings to support their newly constructed view of the Shia and other minority groups who attended a dialogical encounter.

Organisers of interfaith dialogue have the opportunity to construct and design their encounters with a number of symmetrical conditions within each encounter's design and process. A decision to do so will affect their choices regarding the type of participants they select, the venue and location, the language to be utilised, food to be served, games to be played, projects to be initiated and so on. The fact that many religious institutions avoid such symmetry in encounters often reflects the level of commitment to genuine dialogical encounters versus symbolic or ritualistic encounters that replicate the dominant subordinate interreligious dynamics existing in reality.

The fourth principle for dialogical reconciliatory process is related to the ability of the participants to *take risks* through the interreligious dialogue, as the participants need to feel that they can go beyond a point where they feel safe or comfortable while participating in the process. Taking risks is an important step for each participant in the reconciliation process. If the participant does not take any risk in the interaction with other faith groups, he/she is not able to learn beyond his/her comfort zone. Educational and learning theories have already empirically established the principle that the zone of learning expands when the learner dares to ask questions and take risks in pursuing new information from other sources. The reconciliation zone certainly stretches beyond the typical comfort zone of the participants who come from different sides of the conflict.

Thus, for a Muslim participant to learn more about Christianity in a dialogical process, he/she needs to dare to challenge the theological grounding of the Holy Trinity and compare and contrast it with his/her own Islamic theological interpretations. Similarly, the Christian needs to ask daring questions about the notion of Jihad in Islam and be able to listen to the Muslim participants in articulating the spiritual and religious meaning of Jihad in his/her own faith. In addition, both have to pose the question "how does this different understanding affect my willingness to reconcile with this group?" In dialogue for reconciliation, taking risks is not only related to raising challenging theological questions or critically examining your own faith interpretation and narrative, but it can extend to posing questions about the religious identity and its boundaries as it is manifested in reality. For example, a Christian European participant in a dialogical setting with Muslim and Jewish Europeans can explore ways in which the European Christian institution's culture has benefitted his/her life in comparison to other religious minorities in the European context. Exploring these privileges related to religious identity can be risky for such participants. The realisation that, as a Christian in a European context, you do not have to worry about the legitimacy of or accessibility to your rituals might lead to a new awareness or need for action.

In many encounters that do not encourage risk-taking through the process of the dialogue, participants tend to remain in their comfort zone and recycle the same information and knowledge or awareness that they have had prior to the encounter. A genuine dialogical encounter will not only be focused on ritualistic presentation of the faith groups, but will go beyond that. It will allow participants to pose questions that otherwise are not possible to raise in day-to-day life or interreligious interaction.

A fifth principle for reconciliation through dialogue is *the ability to engage with the other and with one's own faith group members* and discuss difficult theological and non-theological issues. Participants and organisers often, intentionally or unintentionally, avoid dealing with difficult issues because of their fear of experiencing discomfort and pain. Moreover, others argue that it is better to focus on the commonalities and avoid differences. In dialogue, avoiding the difficult issues reduces the possibility of genuine reconciliation that builds a deep and sustained trusting relationship. If such an approach is adopted and participants remain on the surface or in the polite stages of interaction, their relationship will also be temporary or will not build enough resilience to withstand the political or security crisis. Thus, the outcome is temporary management of the issues and no reconciliation. In fact, many dialogue groups have collapsed once violence escalated within or between their groups due to the lack of trust and lack of commitment.

Tackling the hard issues means that the dialoguers in interreligious encounters have allowed themselves to venture into disputed areas that in the past had generated, and will continue to generate, distrust and suspicion between members of the faith groups. For example, Muslim and European dialogue for reconciliation has to include issues such as historical crusade campaigns, colonialism, Palestinian issues and Islamophobia. These are examples of challenging themes that have to be addressed in order to reach a level of trust and sense of honesty in the discussion. On a theological level, issues such as: a) recognition of the Holy Trinity as a fundamental difference between Islam, Judaism and Christianity; b) recognition of Islam as a faith or religion by the Christian and Jewish religious institutions; c) the concept of jihad in Islam; d) sexual orientations in all religions; e) gender roles are issues that need to be raised and explored. When the dialogue deliberately avoids these controversial issues and focuses exclusively on the interreligious theological commonalities such as peace, forgiveness, justice, prayers, fasting or charity, the dialogue space becomes less risky, less vulnerable, and more comfortable for its members maintaining their negative perceptions of the others too.

Obviously delving into the difficult issues needs to be done in a gradual and professional way. In addition, it needs to be built on the phase of exploring interpersonal and intercultural commonalities. However, the process should not stop with these commonalities. Critical thinking and critical self-reflection emerge from the dialogue for reconciliation process that confronts the differences and controversial issues. In fact, the respect for diversity deepens when members of different faith groups realise that there are inherent contradictions and differences that the dialogue cannot bridge and these ought to be accepted and respected as part of the relationship. Taking such an approach may produce a stronger belief in religious diversity and pluralism and thus constitute a stronger foundation for a sustained reconciled relationship.

Dialogue for reconciliation is also based on *the principle of action*. The interreligious encounter is limited in its effect or success when it remains at an abstract level and participants are not able to commit to any sort of joint or unilateral action to illustrate their commitment to reconciliation. Such a process or dynamic is often cited as a limitation of many interreligious dialogues. To walk the walk is an expectation that is often shared by participants in the initial interreligious dialogue. Members of the different faith groups join the encounter because they are frustrated by their reality and the type of relationship their community has with the other faith groups. Thus, they want to change. They want a new form of relationship. However, they soon realise that the members differ in their capacity, willingness and awareness of what they can do and what needs to be done. Thus, the interreligious dialogue becomes a platform for exploring what can be done both together and separately to respond to the challenges facing the faith groups.

A common paradox within interreligious dialogue is the dynamics or interplay between members of the minority faith groups. Their attitude towards the process of reconciliation is often associated with their limited access to power or lack of capacity to influence processes and structures of the conflict. They often join the dialogue in order to change the dominant political, social and cultural structures, which impose certain limitations on their religious rights and aspirations. On the other hand, members of the dominant faith group often join the dialogue to learn about other faiths; discover commonalities; and in many cases, partially relieve themselves from the burden of guilt of being labelled as members of the dominant (oppressive or privileged) group (Abu-Nimer 1999). It is the desire to reconcile but without taking individual or collective responsibility or actions for such a process. This tension between Muslims and Christians in the European context is reflected in Muslim minority groups' demands, expectations of and advocacy for the dialogue outcomes to be policy-oriented, namely to change European states' regulations regarding, for example, the production of halal meat, circumcision or religious education. Conversely, at the starting point of the dialogue, dominant faith majority members (Christians or secular participants) do not necessarily see this as a problem or obstacle that urgently needs to be changed.

Regardless of the nature of the action that has been agreed upon by the members within the encounter, it is essential that such action be jointly designed and implemented by the various faith groups. The joint action produced by the interreligious encounter is the glue that binds the interfaith group together and advances the chances to create sustained dialogue for reconciliation. There are many conditions that determine or shape the nature of the joint action which the interreligious dialogue group produces. Some of these include: Power symmetry dynamics between the faith groups; the duration of the encounter (short- or long-term engagement); the availability of a professional third party facilitator for the encounter; the degree of threat and obstacle generated by the context of the encounter (low level of violence versus high level of religiously motivated violence); engagement or non-engagement of the policy-makers in the process. Unfortunately, the scope of this chapter does not allow further exploration of these conditions and possible ways to reduce their negative effect on interreligious dialogue for reconciliation. Nevertheless, as an organiser of interreligious dialogue, it is important to be aware that such internal and external conditions can shape the level of success and alter the motivation and wider impact of the dialogue for reconciliation experience.

The six principles of interreligious dialogue outlined above are obviously also applicable to other forms of reconciliation meetings. In addition, this is not an exhaustive list of principles that can enhance interreligious dialogue; however, they are central in shaping the process, design and outcome towards a genuine reconciliation process. Having explored the principles for interreligious dialogical encounters, we can move now to the remaining questions of this chapter that focus on the limitations of interreligious dialogue for reconciliation from an institutional perspective.

## Obstacles in institutionalising interreligious dialogical for reconciliation

As stated above, research and practice of dialogue have identified many principles and conditions for effective encounters. There is no shortage of theoretical frameworks or guidelines to articulate the process and dynamics of a positive encounter (Bohm 1996; Schoem and Hurtado 2001; Smock 2001; Grundmann 2015). Despite this reality, the field of Interreligious Dialogue (IRD) for reconciliation is still in its infancy as a professional field. There are internal and external factors that affect the development of this field as an effective form of interreligious interaction. The following are a few of the central factors:[4]

*Religious agencies lack institutional commitment to interreligious dialogue*: There is no doubt that in the past two decades, there has been a significant increase in the interest and willingness of policy-makers and religious actors and agencies to engage in dialogue (Little 2007; Gerard and Abu-Nimer 2018). Nevertheless, these engagements remain either on the symbolic level or serve as *lip service* to appease policy-makers who are pursuing the engagement of religious agencies to counter violent extremism. As a result, there is no deep commitment or vision to pursue a reconciled state of relationship. In most cases, crisis management has been the primary motivation to support or ask for dialogue.

In most conflict areas, especially in the southern hemisphere, government and security agencies have included engagement with religious authorities as part of their strategies to counter terrorism and violent extremism. Thus, religious agencies have to respond to the pressure of the governed agencies to show that they are moderate or open enough to accommodate a certain level of religious diversity. Thus, muftis and patriarchs are invited by government agencies and intergovernmental organisations to participate in and even initiate programmes with a focus on dialogue, tolerance and religious freedom.[5] However, the measures proposed by these agencies rarely take into account the structural or cultural factors that block reconciliation and transformation of the conflict relationships.

Despite this fast growth in the number of meetings and projects for religious freedom, interreligious dialogue and religious pluralism and diversity, the formal and traditional religious authorities and their institutions have not made a clear institutional shift in their structure to ensure that IRD and the culture of religious encounter is an integral part of their theological and operational structures. Indeed, there are designated individuals in the Islamic, Jewish, Buddhist, Hindu and Christian religious institutions; however, these individuals and their centres or departments rarely have the necessary human or financial resources to further the significance of interreligious encounters institutionally. For example, compare how much such institutions spend on missionary work or internal theological education versus how much is being spent on interreligious dialogue for reconciliation.

Most religious institutions have compartmentalised their IRD work or have designated one individual whose mission is to persuade the various religious associations in his faith group to adopt IRD as a priority or plan of action. Regardless of whether IRD is confined within a small unit in the religious authority structure or designated to one person, it remains marginalised in comparison to the priorities of religious institutions as whole. Thus, when such individuals are removed or simply die of old age, it takes a long period of time to select another person or to resume the IRD engagement in these institutions. Sustained institutional IRD is still missing in most religious authority structures.

*Theological obstruction of dialogical*: In most religious institutions, the production of new knowledge and new leadership is done through their system of theological seminaries and other higher education systems. A brief examination of at least 40 Christian and Muslim religious seminaries' curricula and syllabi indicated very few of them have included IRD or the art of interreligious encounter in their formal system. In fact, there is no single one of these institutions which introduced the concept of reconciliation as part of its formal or informal curricula. Thousands of Christian and Muslim religious scholars have graduated from seminaries and Sharia colleges without receiving any education about the need for interreligious dialogue and reconciliation. The concept of the interreligious dialogical is strange to them. In fact, many graduates have been socialised to debate and defend the faith in every interaction they have with the other faith groups.[6] How can such graduates educate for religious pluralism and spread a culture of dialogue if they themselves did not receive the basic skills in dialogue? Integrating the concept of IRD in these theological seminaries could be a major contributor to the spread of culture dialogue in such a context.

*Constructive engagement of policy-makers*: In most parts of the world the majority of religious institutions are under the political authority or are governed by laws and regulations. Such reality is an opportunity to expand the engagement of policy-makers with religious authorities to strengthen the field of IRD in such institutions. If they are interested, government and policy-makers can intentionally support dialogue and religious diversity programmes in formal education systems as well. In many parts of the world, especially in conflict areas, the engagement of policy-makers with religious institutions and actors is often negative and manipulative. Such intervention is often identified as one of the obstacles to reconciliation. Politicians engage with religion to gain wider electoral support and policy-makers' appeal to religious authority to support certain policies and assist them in disseminating them to the grassroots and their communities. The manipulation of religious leaders affects their credibility and capacity to preach positive and reconciliatory messages in the society. Thus, it weakens their ability to call for an encounter with the other faith groups or their capacity to call for joint action with other faith groups to advance justice and equality.

*Getting stuck in the countering violent extremism and preventing violent extremism (CVE/PVE) loop*: In many instances where the engagement between religious agencies and policy-makers is well established, the context is limited to either countering violent extremism and/or preventing violent extremism. These approaches bring with them several challenges that extend beyond the issue of the potential loss of legitimacy for religious leaders and agencies within their own communities. They risk damaging the ability to build trust among certain groups within the dialogue because of the potential reinforcement that both the CVE and PVE narratives have for Islamophobia. Thus, they foster an approach of "defensive Islam" particularly for Muslim countries or institutions that develop programmes and projects aimed at joining policy-makers and religious agencies.

These approaches also remain locked in securitisation, which makes it difficult to detach programmes and projects from terrorism, fundamentally preventing the ability to develop a meaningful encounter (Abu-Nimer 2017). The reconciliation process needs both policy-makers and religious agencies to go beyond the securitisation approach and utilise models of intervention that aim to address the root causes of the violent conflicts.

## Conclusion

Reconciling conflicts is an old quest, as old as human conflict interaction. It is not a new topic that we are discovering in the 21st century. In human history, societies and people have struggled to construct social systems that facilitate peaceful contacts between people with different desires and opinions. There have always been a voice and a trace of knowledge and experience that pointed human beings towards dialogue and reconciliation with the other. Such a thread is also manifested in every faith group. Religions share common values of peace, reconciliation, mercy, love and respect for human dignity. Unfortunately, the implementation and transmission of these values into sustainable structures to regulate people's lives have been extremely limited, especially in wider social systems. Most, if not all, children are deprived of the possibility of living in dialogical cooperative systems; instead they are well-trained in the competitive culture.

This chapter articulated basic principles that can be integrated into the interreligious encounter to maximise its impact in transforming misperception and distrust in other faiths into a more dialogical relationship. Overcoming the limitations and obstacles by adopting these principles in society is not only the responsibility of the religious institutions and their structures, but also of policy-makers.

A strong culture of dialogical encounter is an effective social and psychological immunisation tool with which any society or agency can equip its members to prevent religious-based violence, to enhance its capacity to constructively resolve its conflicts peacefully. A society that has integrated a culture of dialogical encounters within its system grants its members safe spaces to explore creative ways to solve problems, and to respect diversity and view such diversity as a source of strength as opposed to source of disunity and fragmentation.

Obviously, there are good practices in the field of IRD that can be utilised as best practice models and effective templates to advance the culture of dialogical encounters. These experiences need to be celebrated and recognised by religious authorities and policy-makers as well. Such a shift in the priorities of these institutions requires a deeper examination of their role in spreading and sustaining the current structures of violence that regulate the lives of most humans. Constructively shifting and transforming these structures of violence cannot be done without a well-developed framework for dialogical encounter.

These systems have been tested repeatedly throughout history. The COVID-19 reality in 2020 is the latest example in which human cultural practices are put to the test in responding to stress, scarcity and threat. If a reconciliatory framework is adopted by the policy-makers, religious leaders, and other influential persons, many human lives will be saved and a stronger culture of cooperation can emerge. We have seen examples of human solidarity and compassion on grass root, local, national, and global levels. These are glimpses of hope to counter the unilateral and competitive behaviours adopted by certain major world leaders. The global responses to this crisis will certainly affect the capacity to act in a reconciliatory manner.

## Notes

1 A Turkic ethnic group primarily in one of the regions of Azerbaijan.
2 The civil conflict between the two main ethnic groups of Armenians and Azeris in the region of Nagorno-Karabakh, with the involvement of Azerbaijan and Armenian governments.
3 An Islamic institute in Cairo, Egypt that has a long tradition of teaching and doing research on Sunni theology and Sharia law.
4 Examples and evidence to support the analysis presented in the following section is based on the author's engagement with KAICIID's interreligious encounter programmes between 2013–2019, in four main regions: Central African Republic (CAR), Nigeria, Myanmar and the Arab region. Other examples are derived from a series of interfaith training conducted within the Interreligious Fellowship programme which has trained over 250 fellows from the five major faith groups (Christianity, Judaism, Islam, Buddhism and Hinduism).
5 Recently the US government convened its second annual Ministerial meeting focusing on religious freedom and religious pluralism with over 100 governments represented and approximately 1,000 civil society and FBO groups. In addition, most European Union countries have appointed a special envoy for religious freedom. These specialised ambassadors for religious freedom are spreading the message that dialogue encounter is also an effective tool to expand the space for religious freedom.
6 The examples shared above are based on a series of consultations the author conducted with Muslim and Christian theological seminaries in the Arab region between 2016–2019.

## References

Abu-Nimer, M. (1999). *Dialogue, conflict resolution, and change: Arab-Jewish encounters in Israel*. New York: SUNY Press.

Abu-Nimer, M. (2017). *Alternative approaches to transforming violence extremism: The case of Islamic Peace and interreligious Peacebuilding*. The Berghof Handbook. Retrieved from https://www.berghof-foundation.org/fileadmin/redaktion/Publications/Handbook/Dialogue_Chapters/dialogue13_Abu-Nimer_lead.pdf

Abu-Nimer, M., & Lazarus, N. (2007). The peacebuilder's paradox and the dynamics of dialogue: Psychosocial approaches to Israeli/Palestinian peacebuilding. In J. Kuriansky (Ed.), *Beyond bullets and bombs: Grassroots peacebuilding between Palestinians and Israelis* (pp. 19–32). Westport, CT: Praeger Publishing.

Bohm, D. (1996). *On dialogue*. London: Routledge.

Gerrard, M., & Abu-Nimer, M. (Eds.) (2018). *Making peace with faith: The challenges of religion and peacebuilding*. Lanham, MD: Rowman and Littlefield Publishing Group.

Grundmann, C. H. (Eds.) (2015). *Interreligious dialogue: An anthology of voices bridging cultural and religious divides*. Winona, MN: Anselm Academic.

Little, D. (2007). *Peacemakers in action: Profiles of religion in conflict resolution.* Cambridge: Cambridge University Press.

Omar, Abul Rashid (2009). The right to religious conversion: Between apostasy and proselytization. In M. Abu-Nimer & D. Augsburger (Eds.), *Peace-building by, between, and beyond Muslims and evangelical Christians* (pp. 179–195). Lexington Books.

Schoem, D., & Hurtado, S. (2001). *Intergroup dialogue: Deliberative democracy in school college, community ad workplace.* Ann Arbor, MI: University of Michigan Press.

Smock, D. R. (Ed.) (2001). *Interfaith dialogue and peacebuilding.* Washington, DC: USIP Press.

Woodberry, Dudley (2009). Toward mutual respectful witness. In M. Abu-Nimer & D. Augsburger (Eds.), *Peace-building by, between, and beyond Muslims and evangelical Christians* (pp. 203–215). Lanham, MD: Lexington Books.

# 5 Towards reconciliation culture(s) in Asian Buddhist societies?

*Chaiwat Satha-Anand*

## Introduction

The deadly conflict in Southern Thailand has raged on for the last 15 years since a resumption of violence in January 2004. According to Deep South Watch Database, from January 2004 until June 2019, there have been 20,323 violent incidents claiming 6,997 lives and wounding 13,143 people (Jitpiromsri 2019). The conflict has been between the Thai Bangkok-based government and Malay Muslim insurgents. Victims have included fighters and civilians on both sides: Malay Muslims who are the majority in the area and the Buddhist minority.

Early into this deadly conflict in 2005, the Thai government appointed the National Reconciliation Commission (NRC) headed by the former prime minister Anand Panyarachun. The NRC's objectives were to find ways to ensure that the Malay Muslim majority and the Buddhist minority could live together in peace as Thai citizens. The NRC submitted its final report, *Overcoming Violence with the Power of Reconciliation*, to the government on 5 June 2006. Unfortunately, this report came at a time when Thailand was undergoing acute political conflict at all levels. The government of then-Prime Minister Thaksin Shinnawatra paid little attention to it, and three months later was ousted in the 2006 coup d'état which plunged the country deeper into political conflict which has continued until the present.

Though the report was applauded by some from the international diplomatic community (US Department of State 2006), it was excluded from Priscilla Hayner's list of 40 truth commissions covering the period from 1974 to 2009, perhaps because Southern Thailand violence has very little to do with transitional justice (Hayner 2010). Duncan McCargo critically concluded that it was a "flawed response to the Southern conflict," primarily because of its emphasis on issues of justice while relegating the issue of governance, especially in terms of how power is organised, as "off-limits" due to a variety of cultural and historical reasons (McCargo 2010). As a commissioner of NRC and the technical director responsible for drafting the report, I wrote a response that it was a "difficult reconciliation." This is not only because it was created in the midst of deadly conflict, but also the fact that the report employs the health metaphor, namely diagnosis–prognosis–therapy, and the methodology of differentiating the world into layers, agency–structure–culture, while separating causes of deadly conflict from justifications. Both the metaphor and the methodology were clearly influenced by Johan Galtung's tradition of critical peace research (Satha-Anand 2010).

While such academic criticism was not unexpected, the most surprising criticism came much earlier from the local Buddhist Sangha[1] in Pattani. On 20 October 2005, they called for the dissolution of the NRC. The commission was accused of creating disunity and disrupting the integrity of the Thai security sector. In an interview with the Thai press, the provincial head of the Pattani Sangha, who issued the call, explained that after monks were killed inside Buddhist temples, the local Sangha felt that the NRC was biased in favour of the Malay Muslim insurgents and the Muslim majority population, without recognising the suffering of local Buddhists and the monks. Apart from criticising the state for its lack of continuity in problem-solving, the monk remarked:

> I think the use of violence in response to the insurgents depends on judgment. Though I would love to see reconciliatory approach, but the Deep South problem is like iron, how could throwing water on (hot) iron relinquish problem of violence?
>
> (Prachathai 2005: n.p.)

My NRC experience prompts me to ask this question: How is it possible that the very first call for the dissolution of the then-only commission designed to find ways to peacefully engender reconciliation in Thailand – a Buddhist society – came from local Buddhist monks? I wonder if there was something much deeper at work that made reconciliation works so very difficult in a country with such a strong Buddhist influence. Is it possible to raise a question that though Thai society and culture is primarily Buddhist, and that Buddhism is generally considered a "peaceful religion" (Galtung 1988), it lacks some kind of reconciliation culture necessary for the reconciliation process to be easily accepted? To deal with this question, it is important to examine the concept of *reconciliation culture*.

Inspired by culture-based concepts that influence the study of peace and security, namely peace culture(s) and strategic culture(s), this chapter is an attempt to argue that for reconciliation efforts to be meaningful in a society, some kind of reconciliation culture needs to be identified. The chapter relies on reconciliation experiences in three Buddhist societies with different degrees of deadly conflict: Cambodia with its genocidal past, Sri Lanka with its civil war experiences and Thailand with its mixture of continuing ethnic insurgency in the South and violent suppression of Bangkok street protesters almost a decade ago which has left an indelible mark on the national psyche. After reviewing the concept of reconciliation culture, inspired by peace and strategic culture with a strong emphasis on the notion of "forgiveness," traces of "reconciliation culture" as reflected in the presence of "forgiveness" in three official commission reports will be examined. The reports are from Truth for Reconciliation Commission of Thailand (TRCT, Thailand), the Lessons Learnt and Reconciliation Commission (LLRC,

Sri Lanka), and the Extraordinary Chambers in the Courts of Cambodia (ECCC, Cambodia). Finally, the question of how reconciliation culture could be identified in these Asian Buddhist contexts will be briefly addressed.

## Reconciliation culture?

In a 1977 report titled *The Soviet Strategic Culture: Implications for Limited Nuclear Options*, Jack Snyder defined "strategic culture," a novel concept at the time, as the "sum total of ideals, conditional emotional responses, and patterns of habitual behaviour that members of the national strategic community have acquired through instruction or imitation and share with each other with regard to nuclear strategy." The endurance of such modes of thinking qualifies them as manifestations of a "culture" rather than mere policy. Strategic culture is believed to be ingrained in our "irrational" mental strata, forming a code of conduct strong enough to resist changes coming from outside sources (Al-Rodhan 2015). To avoid confusion arising from conflating culture as ideas with the behaviour through which those ideas manifest, some redefine the concept as "consisting of common ideas regarding strategy that exist across populations." Disconnecting strategic culture from behaviour "forces us to confront these challenges directly in the context of efforts to understand the different ways that patterns of ideas may produce patterned behavior" (Lock 2017: n.p.). This recent development within strategic culture discourse resonates well with what peace researchers have done earlier.

Almost three decades ago, the late peace researcher Elise Boulding discussed the importance of peace culture. She pointed out that the term "peace culture" is

> a culture that promotes peaceableness. Such a culture would include lifeways, patterns of belief, values and behaviour that foster peace-building and accompanying institutional arrangements that promote well-being, equality, stewardship and equitable sharing of the earth's resources, security for humankind whether as individuals, families, identity groups or nation states, without the need to resort to violence.
>
> (Boulding 1992: 107)

Importantly, she maintains that peace culture per se cannot be found anywhere. Nor does an all-embracing peace culture exist, because the term is but a construct referring to "a cluster of attributes" that enable peacemaking behaviour to take place in a society (Boulding 1992: 108).

In the context of the present discussion, I wonder what could be those "deeply held beliefs, lifeways, and values" that legitimise reconciliation in societies that have gone through deadly conflict? Moreover, if the idea of reconciliation, not unlike transitional justice, is believed to be spreading from place to place like a "justice cascade" through "norm entrepreneurs" (Sikkink 2011), then it seems to make sense to raise the issue of how reconciliation projects move across different geopolitical/social terrains. Along a similar line of thought, can one conceptualise a "reconciliation culture" where reconciliatory practices will be legitimised and enable a society to accept the reconciliation project more easily? It might be useful to ground the effort to answer this question in concrete contexts.

Reviewing a large number of studies covering more than 25 countries, Siwach Sripokangkul (2017) concludes that there are at least six conditions necessary for any successful reconciliation projects. They are regime change and (establishment of) truth commissions, truth revealed, accountability (of perpetrators), healing, security sector reform and opening up space for memory. Culture is curiously absent from this list, however.

Looking at issues of justice and reconciliation in Southeast Asia and beyond, Ehito Kimura raises the question: What kinds of factors would influence the practice and success of the reconciliation project? Using examples from Indonesia, Timor Leste and Cambodia, Kimura maintains that internal factors in a society are more crucial to reconciliation than external ones. His "internal factors" include: The natures of the state (regime type, domestic politics and type of transition), nature of society (culture and social capital) and the character of conflict (scale of violence and conflict type) (Kimura 2016: 20).

Kimura points out that cultural argument for restorative justice often suggests a discomfort with "Western" traditions because they are "overly legal" and have "little appeal" to Asian people who could be uncomfortable with reconciliation initiatives that involve facing one's offender or victim and/or trying to remember the past rather than to "forget" it (Kimura 2016: 16). Cultural practices in Indonesia, namely *peusijeuk* and *Islah*, are used to illustrate his points. *Peusijeuk* (to cool down) is a ritual to show that harmony and peace has been restored to a community after deadly conflict in Aceh. It involves pouring sacred water over yellow rice or powder as a way to bless those who have reconciled. *Islah* (to repair broken social ties) was used to achieve reconciliation between the Indonesian soldiers and the victims of the Tanjong Priok massacre in 1980s. Several military officers involved in the massacre went to the community mosque to initiate *Islah* directly. These cultural practices need to be cautiously approached, because while *Islah* could be a way for the military to avoid accountability in the context of an ongoing trial, *peusijeuk* displaced legal action put in place to resolve conflict between the Indonesian military and Acehnese ex-combatants (Kimura 2016: 17).

But here I want to make a distinction between a "culture of reconciliation" and "reconciliation culture." Both *Islah* and *Peusijeuk* are ritualistic practices, and there are many such practices that could be considered part of a "culture of reconciliation." Reconciliation culture, on the other hand, is a reified concept depicting some forces within a society that are responsible for justifying those cultural practices that are considered reconciliatory. Drawing from critical peace research, not unlike Galtung's use of civilisations as units of analysis in pursuit of solutions to global belligerence (Satha-Anand 1992: 145), I am treating culture as the deepest layer of explanatory factor that can help us understand how reconciliation works. There could be a lifeway or pattern of belief that legitimises reconciliation and makes it easier for a society to accept it than a society without such belief. By introducing this notion of reconciliation culture, I could perhaps be accused of essentialising culture. But then arguably this could be in line with what Gayatri Chakravorty Spivak terms "strategic essentialism," since I am not interested in cultural practices per se, but more in the forces of culture(s), understood as a variable within the human process that is responsible for the working of reconciliation in a society (see Tangseefa 2006).

To address the issue of reconciliation culture as deeply held beliefs means one has to examine religious values such as forgiveness. As Boulding (1992) has argued, religion is the seed of the relevant cultural themes since it is the belief system that legitimises the totality of a society's projects that constitute the macrosocietal reality.

Though forgiveness does have its limitations (Eisikovits 2004), here I choose forgiveness as the religious value that best mirrors reconciliation culture for the following reasons. First, in a South African survey conducted in 2003, the former research director of the South African Truth and Reconciliation Commission, Charles Villa-Vicencio, found that there was a substantial association between reconciliation and forgiveness. It must be noted that Villa-Vicencio did warn that reconciliation ought not to be too closely tied to a theology of forgiveness (van Antwerpen 2008). But I am interested in forgiveness as a culture with a relationship to religions' deep culture in a society, not as a theology. Second, one way to construe the relationship between reconciliation and forgiveness is to raise two basic questions: Whose reconciliation? and Which rationality? The second question in particular addresses the competing rationalities between the "secular" and the "religious" which inform different understandings of reconciliation's appropriate articulations and aims. As such, I would argue that forgiveness is primarily informed by religious rationality (van Antwerpen 2008). Third, if reconciliation has to deal with "the worst of human condition" because it is an effort to "repair the brokenness of relationships and life itself" (Lederach 2005: 160), then forgiveness is arguably central to such an endeavour, since it is known to help avert the harms of revenge, and releases one from resentment, as encouraged by world religions (Minow 2019). Fourth, it transcends the complexity of conflicts, especially ethnic and group conflicts where atrocities appear on both sides which make it difficult to speak of clear victims and perpetrators (Eisikovits 2004). Fifth, as a result, if reconciliation aims for the restoration of human relationships damaged by violence in order for a wounded society to move into its chosen future, then forgiveness is crucial for any reconciliation project (Tutu 1999).

It is certainly important to recognise the ways in which forgiveness is closely related to Christianity, and that it is informing the mode of reconciliation as being practiced in truth commissions around the world (Eisikovits 2004), as well as critically underscoring forgiveness' political nature (Satha-Anand 1998). The degree to which the reconciliation projects as generally practised are or are not meaningful depends on how they interact with the reconciliation culture of a particular society. Here I am interested in what this may mean, especially if the society is non-Christian, as the three reconciliation projects in three Buddhist societies – Thailand, Sri Lanka and Cambodia – will demonstrate next.

## Forgiveness in three reconciliation reports: A brief methodological note

This research paper looks at three reconciliation reports in three Buddhist societies with past violence. There are three methodological issues that need to be elucidated. First, these three countries are countries with a clear Buddhist majority: more than 90% in Cambodia and Thailand, and 70% in Sri Lanka. They all practise Theravada Buddhism, a branch of Buddhism claimed to be oldest and practiced mainly in the Southeast Asian countries, with the exception of Sri Lanka. Buddhist culture(s) is strong in these societies. To identify them as Buddhist, however, does not mean that other cultural influences such as Hinduism are absent. Judging from rituals and practices, it could be seen that Buddhism is officially recognised and most pronounced for its cultural influences in all three societies. Second, these three countries went through different degrees of violence, from the most horrible genocide claiming more than a million lives in Cambodia in the late 1970s, to civil war between the Sri Lankan government and the Tamil insurgents that killed more than a hundred thousand and violent suppression of protesters in Thailand with less than a hundred killed and close to 2,000 wounded. It goes without saying that these different types of past violence with various degrees of intensity impact upon the three societies differently. The ways in which these societies call on their cultures, primarily influenced by Buddhism, to respond to their tragic experiences would help elucidate how reconciliation works in these contexts. Third, I choose the word forgiveness as a marker of reconciliation culture, as it appears in the three official reconciliation reports. Though identifying the word is not much of a problem, since I will be using the English translation of the official reports, and therefore local language complications can be avoided, the problem lies with the reports selected as sites of data used here.

For example, in the case of both Thailand and Sri Lanka, there is more than one reconciliation report. In addition, the document I will use for Cambodia is not exactly a "reconciliation" report, but court material. Relying on the significance of their names (Satha-Anand 2018b), the Truth for Reconciliation Commission of Thailand (TRCT) is chosen because its name clearly shows that the truth it pursues is for reconciliation, while the Lessons Learnt and Reconciliation Commission (LRCC) is included because of its emphasis on lessons learned so that violence can be avoided in the future. Though the Extraordinary Chambers in the Courts of Cambodia (ECCC) is a court, it has several features resembling a reconciliation project. In its trials, public participation was very high. In some instances, victims confronted defenders in the trials with the truth of the atrocities which occurred, because victims were granted the right to participate directly in the trials. A total of 4,222 victims were admitted as "civil parties," not as witnesses. More importantly, to underscore the fact that justice is not revenge, ECCC excludes the death penalty in meeting the UN standards (Jenner 2018). An ECCC spokesperson claimed that "The tribunal facilitates reconciliation and at the same time provides an opportunities (sic) for Cambodians to come to terms with their history" (Maguire 2018). As a result, a part of the ECCC document will be used here in place of the reconciliation report.

### *Forgiveness in three reconciliation reports*

1. Forgiveness in the TRCT report, Thailand 2012

From April to May 2010, the "Red Shirts" movement mobilised their protest, not only in Bangkok but in the provinces, especially in the north and northeast. Then they moved to Bangkok with a demand to dissolve the House and call for a new national election, since they considered the Abhisit Vejjajiva government to be without any legitimacy. The government tried to negotiate with the Red Shirts protesters but when the effort failed, violence began. Facing the threat of government repression, some protest leaders said on stage: "If you (the military) seize power, our people will burn the whole country. … Bangkok will become a sea of fire" (Satha-Anand 2018a: 250–251).

The Red Shirts' protest, however, was by and large nonviolent. Some actions were common nonviolent resistance techniques, such as demonstrations occupying the streets with tens of thousands of people. Others were "problematic" nonviolent actions, such as when human blood collected from approximately 70,000 donors were splashed at the private home of the Prime Minister in March 2010 (Satha-Anand 2018a). The protest ended in violence with 94 killed (six of these were women and the youngest was 12), and 1,400 people wounded. Most of those killed were protesters. Bangkok was engulfed in flames, especially in business districts; some believe the fire was started by the protesters, while others claim that the fire was started by unknown parties after the protest was called off when most of the leaders were under police custody.

In July 2010, then Prime Minister Abhisit Vejjajiva established the Truth for Reconciliation Commission of Thailand (TRCT), a quasi-judicial commission with a core mission of fact-finding on the bloodshed during April and May 2010. On 17 September 2012, the TRCT issued a long-awaited report on the violence. The 2012 TRCT report was criticised for blaming the violence on the actions of unknown elements while failing to address the legal transgression of the security forces. In producing a weak outcome with unconvincing explanations, it was criticised for failing to promote reconciliation and thereby contributed to further polarisation in the already divided society that has lasted until the present day (McCargo and Thabchumpon 2014).

In the 377 pages of the TRCT report in English, the word forgiveness appears five times. First, twice with identical wordings, it proposes that the government helps Thai society understand amnesty and forgiveness as a short-term measure (TRCT 2012: 299, 366). Second, the TRCT conducted a statement-taking project with victims of violence so that they might voice their feelings, rage, grievance and frustration, with representatives of TRCT listening in all sessions. The TRCT believed that these sessions would enable victims to communicate among themselves as well as with the larger public which "may lead to apology and forgiveness which is a form of healing" (TRCT 2012: 28). Third, the TRCT suggests that in order not to undermine the dignity of the people, restoration should be carried out in the "dimension of apology," and that the money used for these monthly payments as an expression of apology should appear in the government's annual budget for those affected. Such action could lead "to true forgiveness." (TRCT 2012: 18, fn. 22) Fourth, perhaps most importantly, the TRCT recommends that money should be paid ex gratia and "it is not necessary to prove who was at fault – no fault liability." This is because "the aim of restorative justice is to bring about reconciliation and forgiveness so that people can live together peacefully and happily, more than to prove wrong-doing and punish offenders" (TRCT 2012: 254).

From the text, the TRCT thinks of forgiveness as a "short-term measure," not as a value that would serve as the soil for fertile reconciliation, yet it believes that in pursuit of restorative justice, forgiveness is far more significant than finding facts about the wrongdoers and punishing them. In addition, forgiveness is seen more as a condition by which people could live together in peace without concern for past wrongs. Apart from recognising forgiveness' healing power, it seems to believe that "true forgiveness" comes from clever bureaucratic mechanisms especially in terms of how compensation could be distributed.

2. Forgiveness in the LRCC Report, Sri Lanka 2011

Sri Lanka is a multicultural society of more than 20 million people with a predominantly Buddhist Sinhalese population of 75%, while 15% are Tamils with the majority of them Hindu (11%). After independence from the British in 1948, Sinhalese nationalism was on the rise with the passing of xenophobic laws such as the Ceylon Citizenship Act in 1948, which remained in force until 2003, and denied citizenship to the disadvantaged Indian Tamils. Such policies have resulted in mounting ethnic tension which later gave rise to the Tamil separatist movement determined to create a self-governing Tamil state in Northern Sri Lanka. With the creation of the Liberation Tigers of Tamil Eelam (LTTE) in the 1970s, brutal violence raged on. The Mahinda Rajapaksa government which came to power in 2005 launched a military offensive on the LTTE which ended with a military victory for the Sri Lankan government in May 2009. The United Nations estimated that it claimed some 100,000 lives over the course of 26 years of civil war, with approximately 40,000 killed in 2009 alone (Bentrovato and Nissanka 2018).

In May 2010, the Sri Lanka President established the Commission of Inquiry on Lessons Learnt and Reconciliation, commonly known as the Lessons Learnt and Reconciliation Commission (LLRC). It was tasked with an inquiry into and report on the facts and circumstances which led to the failure of the Ceasefire Agreement (CFA), which was signed on 22 February 2002, and the sequence of events that followed up to the Sri Lankans' military victory on 19 May 2009. LLRC submitted its report in November 2011.

Critics point out that LLRC's recommendations would not facilitate ethnic reconciliation in the country, not only because it made reconciliation its secondary objective, but more importantly, in justifying civilian casualties, it cleared Sri Lankan civilian and military leadership of committing a crime against humanity, as suggested by the UN expert panel in 2011. LLRC is seen as an instrument of the then-Sri Lankan government to mitigate international criticisms and make "all of its observations and recommendations firmly standing within the position of the regime in power" (Keethaponcalan 2016: 96).

In its 407-page report, forgiveness appears three times. First, proposing a role for religion in reconciliation under the arc of interfaith activities, several delegations emphasised the fact that Sri Lanka is enriched with the traditions of four world religions: Buddhism, Hinduism, Islam and Christianity (LRCC 2011: 316). In order to prevent the emergence of future conflicts, forgiveness and tolerance should be the common language of spirituality. Accountability for serious violations of human rights could be pursued but not in terms of punishment, because merely punishing another person alone does not bring about reconciliation (LRCC 2011: 317).

Second, forgiveness appears twice in two passages with exactly the same wording, on sections related to the "need for political consensus" (LRCC 2011: 323, 387). Pointing out that the tragedy could have been avoided had the two sides acted in the national interest and forged consensus on the fate of the Tamils among them, the passage reads in part:

> The process of reconciliation requires a full acknowledgement of the tragedy of the conflict and a collective act of contrition by the political leaders and civil society, of both Sinhala and Tamil communities .... A collective act of contrition ... would come only if they are ready to make a profound moral self-appraisal in the light of the human tragedy that has occurred. Seeds of reconciliation can take root only if there is forgiveness and compassion .... Religious leaders and civil society should work towards it and emphasize the healing impact it would have on the entire process of reconciliation.

There are two important points regarding forgiveness/reconciliation from the LLRC text. First, in articulating the need for political consensus, the LRCC recognises the power of forgiveness in terms of its healing impact and considers it one of the two conditions necessary for the "seeds of reconciliation" to take root other than compassion. But that is only possible when "both" conflicting parties can make "a profound moral appraisal" in light of the "human tragedy." Second, in the context of interfaith activities, the delegate who proposed this was not a Buddhist, but a bishop of the Methodist Church on behalf of the Congress of Religions before the LLRC at Colombo on 24 September 2010 (LRCC 2011: 317).

3. Forgiveness in the ECCC report, Case 001, Cambodia 2005–2012

After the American withdrawal from Indochina, the Khmer Rouge ruled supreme in Cambodia from 1975 to 1979. The regime imposed a communist ideal with unprecedented harshness. Khmer genocide targeted ethnic minorities as well as class-based groups and religious personnel. The Muslim Cham, Buddhist monks and the middle-class, as well as educated people, were put to death, among many others. More than 1.7 million people lost their lives. Most were murdered by the Khmer Rouge while others died of hunger and illness due to a severe lack of medical facilities (e.g., Chalk and Jonassohn 1990). The brutal regime ended with the Vietnamese invasion in 1979, but the Khmer Rouge rule, in alliance with King Sihanouk and backed by the US, continued until 1998 when global politics shifted and the Khmer Rouge became obsolete (Rungswasdisab 2004).

Prime Minister Hun Sen established the Extraordinary Chambers in the Courts of Cambodia (ECCC) in April 2005 with a treaty between the UN and the Cambodian government. Unlike the International Criminal Tribunals for the former Yugoslavia and Rwanda, which were created either by the UN Security Council or by a treaty and stood apart from national court systems, the ECCC is by and large a Cambodian national court. While drawing its subject matter from both international criminal law and the Cambodian national legal system, the majority of judges have all been Cambodians (Scheffer 2015).

The ECCC is extraordinary for the Cambodian state's decision to prosecute only the leadership of Khmer Rouge in the name of reconciliation. In September 2009, when a prosecutor formally recommended that five more suspects be investigated for crimes against humanity, Prime Minister Hun Sen, who has ruled Cambodia from 1997 until now, said: "I would like to tell you that if you prosecute (more leaders) without thinking beforehand about national reconciliation and peace, and if war breaks out again and kills 20,000 or 30,000 people, who will be responsible?" (Cheang 2009).

The five leaders considered to be most responsible for the genocide were: Former Khmer Rouge head of state Khieu Samphan and former chairman of the Democratic Kampuchea National Assembly Nuon Chea who were charged with crimes against humanity; Kaing Guek Eav, better known as "Duch," the commander of the atrocious Tuol Sleng prison; former foreign minister Ieng Sary; and former minister of social affairs Ieng Thirith. Only the first three stood trial in ECCC through to the end, because Ieng Sary died during the trial, while his wife Ieng Thirith was considered unfit to stand trial due to her mental condition.

Here I want to focus only on Case 001, not only because of the heinous crimes Duch committed while in command of Tuol Sleng, nor the complex character that he is (Hinton 2016), but also because of the way he offered his defence in court which is most relevant to the discussion on forgiveness as reflecting reconciliation culture. Unlike other leaders, Duch appealed his case but it was overturned by the Supreme Court. He was finally subjected to life imprisonment, the maximum punishment under Cambodian law, died while serving in prinson in 2020. In the 15-page transcript of statements he gave to ECCC at various trials, forgiveness appears ten times.

Duch's asking for forgiveness features differently in his testimony. First, though he accepted that his crimes against his victims were unforgivable, he pleaded to them to leave the door open for him to ask for forgiveness (ECCC 2009: 3). This point he repeated again in his final statement made on 30 March

2011 when he said: "I still maintain my position to ask for forgiveness for the soul (sic) of the victims of 12,273 people who lost their lives at S-21, and for the families of those victims to accept my apology and forgiveness" (2009: 15).

Second, for him forgiveness was the "value I set for my life" and there was nothing else he could do (2009: 5). Third, forgiveness is his consolation. He offered prayer for forgiveness from the victims, from his parents, and from the entire nation (ECCC 2009: 5). Fourth, he asked forgiveness from a former victim in person when a document was found after his earlier denial in this case. Fifth, in relation to the "crimes of smashing people," he defended himself saying that the order came from "upper echelons." Though he protested sometimes, he considered the burden was his and therefore asked for forgiveness from the souls of those who died (2009: 5). Importantly, when he returned to the site of atrocity, he said:

> I recalled the lives of children who were killed and might have been killed in a particularly disgusting way like smashing them against a tree .... I had to kneel down and pray for forgiveness from those souls. As a Christian, too, I had to pray for their lost souls. I went there with such feeling and whatever I did there I did it with profound feeling.
>
> (2009: 13)

Forgiveness was clearly prominent in Duch's short court testimony, far more than in the two much longer reports mentioned earlier. Though he admitted that his crime is unforgiveable, he relentlessly asked for forgiveness from his victims. Left with nothing else he could do, he said that forgiveness is his only consolation. Forgiveness, for him, reflects his deepest feeling of remorse. Importantly, it was the "value he set for his life." With that value, he "knelt down and prayed for forgiveness" from his victims. This emphasis on the power and importance of forgiveness is based on his religious value. Duch is not a Buddhist. Long before his ECCC trials, he converted to Christianity in 1996, a year after he was stabbed and his wife was killed in a robbery (Hinton 2016). If forgiveness is said to be "at the religious, theological and ethical core of the Christian tradition" (Eisikovits 2004), then is this a reason why Duch as a Christian was so relentless in pursuing the path of forgiveness?

## Reconciliation culture in three Buddhist societies

Comparing the places and weight of forgiveness in these three reports, it could be seen that forgiveness was much less pronounced in the Thai and Sri Lankan reports than in Duch's testimony as found in ECCC. When the term appears in those reports at all, it was there primarily as being instrumental in pursuit of some other goals, but not as the fundamental value itself in the Thai case. When forgiveness was pointed out to be a crucial condition for the seeds of reconciliation to take root in a suffering society in the case of Sri Lanka, it was proposed by a Christian bishop.

Reframing the question of "weak presence of forgiveness" as a lack of strong reconciliation culture, I would ask: What is it about Theravada Buddhism which makes it difficult to forgive, and thereby weakens reconciliation projects in societies informed by its cultural influences? To answer this question, it is instructive to ponder Buddhist culture on the subject.

In the Buddha's lifetime, his nemesis, Devadatta, who authored the first schism in Buddhism with his more ascetic doctrine, including strict vegetarianism, publicly attempted to unseat him from his position as the leader of the Order. Devadatta later planned to kill the Buddha, first by using soldiers on loan from another king to shoot at the Buddha with arrows, then by rolling a huge stone from the Vultures' Peak, injuring the Buddha's foot. Lastly, he sent the elephant Nalagiri to kill the Buddha. But the elephant yielded to the Buddha's power of compassion. At the end of his life, Devadatta desired to see the Buddha, presumably to ask for forgiveness, but along the way he was finally swallowed by the earth down to hell (Satha-Anand 2014).

I would argue that in Buddhism, it is more difficult to forgive because an individual's or collective action is not governed by human intentionality, but by *karma*, the cosmic order of actions and their effects. Devadatta was not successful in meeting the Buddha. In fact, forgiveness did not take place in this case since Devadatta was dramatically swallowed by the earth before he could even meet the Buddha. His karma made it impossible for him to appear before the Buddha. In this sense, forgiveness seems beyond the reach of even someone such as the Enlightened One (Satha-Anand 2014). Since it is this non-human law of karma, maybe not completely unbreakable but very difficult to break, that binds people to one another, it tends to lock one inside the stream of karmic forces that can only be loosened, but not entirely salvaged by one's forgiveness.

A case of a victim unable to utter the word forgiveness may illustrate how one is locked inside the stream of karmic forces. Savuth Penn, a survivor who lost most of his family during the Cambodian genocide, writes:

> For those four years of living under the inhumane treatment of an insane Khmer Rouge government, every day seemed like months, months seemed like years and years seemed like centuries. Time seemed to be at a standstill. … The only things I learned were hatred and revenge for my father (sic) and sisters' deaths. Even after seventeen years, I'm not so sure I can say the word *forgive*, but I surely will never forget what the Khmer Rouge did to my family and their own Khmer people.
>
> (Penn 1997: 43–49)

There are five important words in Savuth Penn's horror account: Time, hatred, revenge, forgetting and forgiveness. The way these words connect to reveal his dark world is extremely important to understanding how reconciliation requires some kind of deep cultural value to make it work. For Penn, time stood still, locking the survivor in the imaginary of the irreversible past of horror. The still time refuses to allow the mind to forget the horror. As a result, the mind was occupied by hatred and desire for revenge. These combined forces make it difficult for the word forgiveness to come out of him.

Looking back at the three reports discussed above, when forgiveness appears or features meaningfully, it did not come from those who were Buddhists, but from those influenced by Christian culture. Taken together, I would argue that the relatively weak presence of forgiveness in these reconciliation reports coming out of the three primarily Buddhist societies reflects a weak reconciliation culture, which is in turn a condition, among others, responsible for their rather unsuccessful reconciliation projects.

## Conclusion: Seeking the elegant essence?

John Paul Lederach once raised a curious question about reconciliation, namely: "What if reconciliation were more like a creative artistic process than a linear formula of cumulative activities aimed at producing a result?" (Lederach 2005: 159). He believes that when reconciliation is framed as an intellectually complex process, it creates "so much noise and distraction that the essence is missed" (2005: 160). This is perhaps why the book's epilogue, written in the form of a conversation, begins with the question asked by a reader: "How do I make the moral imagination appear?" Responses to the reader's question come from various sources. I find that the most striking is from the haiku master who laughed when he/she gave the response: "When overwhelmed by complexity, seek the elegant essence that holds it together" (2005: 179).

The haiku master's response resonates well with the notion of reconciliation culture examined in this chapter. Facing the horror of past violence, reconciliation projects that emerge must be complex. To avoid being overwhelmed by such complexity resulting from the past, the surrounding circumstances, and the powers at work, the advice is to seek something that holds it together. The essence that holds the reconciliation projects together that I seek is reconciliation culture. The "essence" found here may be weak, and more importantly, far from elegant, but it is there. Yet while the concept and practice of forgiveness is less pronounced in the reconciliation projects born out of societies with mainly Buddhist culture due to the influence of the non-human karmic law at work, the fact that it did find its place in the reports at all indicates that there is indeed some space for it in the reconciliation culture that is Buddhist.

Thinking through the haiku master's response, two important and related questions should be raised: "Why did the master laugh?" and "where could the elegant essence be found?" The master might laugh because to find the "elegant essence," one needs to look for it in the right place. It is laughably futile to search for forgiveness that mirrors reconciliation culture in the wrong place. The right place for the "elegant essence" that is reconciliation culture in these Buddhist societies should be found in Buddhists' everyday life. For ordinary Theravada Buddhists, there are primarily two occasions when forgiveness is called for: Before a person becomes a monk, and before his or her death. Both are cases of complete life transformation: Leaving the old life and moving into the new one of monkhood with a completely different set of life-governing rules, and death with its own mystery.

If forgiveness does exist in ordinary Buddhists' lives when the time for life-changing experiences arrive, and if reconciliation projects in Buddhist societies are not unlike collective life-changing experiences, then it means that reconciliation culture conducive to meaningful reconciliation projects in Buddhist societies can be identified and fostered.

## Note

1 Sangha denotes a Buddhist order or community that usually consists of professional priests (monks, nuns) but occasionally includes lay leaders.

## References

Al-Rodhan, N. (2015). Strategic culture and pragmatic national interest. *Global Policy*, 22 July 2015. Retrieved from https://www.globalpolicyjournal.com/blog/22/07/2015/strategic-culture-and-pragmatic-national-interest

Bentrovato, D., and Nissanka, M. (2018). Teaching peace in the midst of civil war: Tensions between global and local discourses in Sri Lankan civics textbooks. *Global Change, Peace and Security*, *30*(3), 353–372.

Boulding, E. (1992). The concept of peace culture. In Eide, A., Rupesinghe, K., Wiberg, H., Ghai, D., Ghai, Y., Westendorff, D., Boulding, E., Satha-Anand, C. (Eds.), *Peace and conflict issues after the Cold War* (pp. 107–133). Paris: UNESCO.

Chalk, F., & Jonassohn, K. (1990). *The history and sociology of genocide: Analysis and case studies* (pp. 398–407). New Haven, CT: Yale University Press.

Cheang, S. (2009). Prosecutor wants 5 more Khmer Rouge investigated. *The San Diego Union Tribune*, 8 September 2009. Retrieved from https://www.sandiegouniontribune.com/sdut-cambodia-khmer-rouge-tribunal-090809-2009sep08-story.html

Eisikovits, N. (2004). Forget forgiveness: On the benefits of sympathy for political Reconciliation. *Theoria*, *52*(1), 31–63.

Extraordinary Chambers in the Courts of Cambodia (ECCC) (2009). *Compilation of statements of apology made by Kaing Guek Eav alias Duch during the proceedings*, Phnom Penh: ECCC.

Galtung, J. (1988). *Buddhism, a quest for unity and peace*. Honolulu, HI: Dae Won Sa Buddhist Temple.

Hayner, P. (2010). *Unspeakable truths: Transnational justice and the challenge of Truth Commissions*. London: Routledge.

Hinton, A. L. (2016). *Man or monster?: The trial of a Khmer Rouge torturer*. Durham, NC: Duke University Press.

Jenner, R. (2018). ECCC, great Cambodian achievement. *Khmer Times*, 19 November 2018.

Jitpiromsri, S. (2019). Algorithms of 15-year violence variation in the Southern Border/Patani (16 August 2019). Retrieved from https://www.the101.world/algorithm-of-violence-in-deep-south/

Keethaponcalan, S. I. (2016). Violence, nonviolence, and ethnic reconciliation in post-war Sri Lanka. In C. Satha-Anand & O. Urbain (Eds.), *The promise of reconciliation?*

*Examining violent and nonviolent effects on Asian conflicts* (pp. 87–102). New Brunswick, NJ: Transaction Publishers.

Kimura, E. (2016). Justice and reconciliation in Southeast Asia and beyond. In C. Satha-Anand & O. Urbain (Eds.), *The promise of reconciliation? Examining violent and nonviolent effects on Asian conflicts* (pp. 11–21). New Brunswick, NJ: Transaction Publishers.

Lederach, J. P. (2005). *The moral imagination: The art and soul of building peace*. Oxford: Oxford University Press.

Lock, E. (2017). Strategic culture theory: What, why, and how. In Thompson, W. & Dalton, R. (Eds.), *Oxford research encyclopedia: Groups and identities, history and politics, world politics*. Oxford: Oxford University Press (Online Publication).

LRCC (2011). *Report of the commission of inquiry on lessons learnt and reconciliation of Sri Lanka*. Colombo: LRCC.

Maguire, P. (2018). The Khmer Rouge trials: The good, the bad, and the ugly. *The Diplomat*, 14 November 2018.

McCargo, D. (2010). Thailand's national reconciliation commission: A flawed response to the Southern Conflict. *Global Change, Peace and Security*, *22*(1), 75–91.

McCargo, D., & Thabchumpon, N. (2014). Wreck/conciliation?: The politics of truth commissions in Thailand. *Journal of East Asian Studies*, *14*(3), 377–404.

Minow, M. (2019). Do alternative justice mechanisms deserve recognition in international criminal law? Truth Commissions, amnesties, and complementarity at the International Criminal Court. *Harvard International Law Journal*, *60*(1), 1–45.

Penn, S. (1997). The dark years of my life. In D. Pran, (Eds.), *Children of Cambodia's killing fields: Memoirs by survivors* (pp. 43–49). Chiang Mai: Silkworm Books.

Prachathai (2005). *A special interview with the "Pattani Provincial Sangha Head" and the call to dissolve the NRC (23 October 2005, News article in Thai)*.

Rungswasdisab, P. (2004). Thailand's response to the Cambodian genocide. In S. E. Cook (Ed.), *Genocide in Cambodia and Rwanda: New perspectives* (pp. 79–126). New Haven, CT: Yale Center for International and Area Studies, Genocides Studies Program.

Satha-Anand, C. (1992). Towards a peace culture in Asia. In Eide, A., Rupesinghe, K., Wiberg, H., Ghai, D., Ghai, Y., Westendorff, D., Boulding, E., & Satha-Anand, C., (Eds.), *Peace and conflict issues after the Cold War* (pp.135–159). Paris: UNESCO.

Satha-Anand, C. (1998). The politics of forgiveness. In R. Herr & J. Zimmerman (Eds.), *Transforming violence: Linking local and global peacemaking* (pp. 68–78). Scotdale, PA. Herald Press.

Satha-Anand, C. (2010). Difficult reconciliation?: Southern Thailand and the influence of Galtung's peace research. In J. Johansen & J. Jones (Eds.), *Experiments with peace: Celebrating peace on Johan Galtung's 80th birthday* (pp. 305–314). Cape Town: Pambazuka Press.

Satha-Anand, C., ed. (2014). Forgiveness in Southeast Asia: Political necessity and sacred justifications. In *Essays on the Three Prophets: Nonviolence, Murder, and Forgiveness*, (pp. 85–86). Dunedin: Dunedin Abrahamic Interfaith Group, University of Otago.

Satha-Anand, C. (2018a). Repression engendering creative nonviolent action in Thailand. In L. R. Kurtz & L. A. Smithey (Eds.), *The paradox of repression and nonviolent movements* (pp. 242–269). Syracuse, NY: Syracuse University Press.

Satha-Anand, C. (2018b). Celestial axe: On the politics of naming. *CSEAS Newsletter*, *76* (Spring/Summer 2018), 15–25.

Scheffer, D. (2015). What has been ‘extraordinary’ about international justice in Cambodia?, address at the William & Mary Law School Williamsburg, Virginia (25 February 2015). Retrieved from www.cambodiatribunal.org

Sikkink, K. (2011). *The justice cascade: How human rights prosecution are changing world politics*. New York: W.W. Norton & Company.

Sripokangkul, S. (2017). *On reconciliation*. Khon Khaen: Khon Khaen University Printing House, a Publication in Thai.

Tangseefa, D. (2006). Taking flight in condemned grounds: Forcibly displaced Karens & the Thai-Burmese in-between spaces. *Alternatives: Global, Local, Political*, *31*(4), 405–429.

TRCT. (2012). *Final report of truth for Reconciliation Commission of Thailand (TRCT) July 2010 –July 2012*. Bangkok: Truth for Reconciliation Commission of Thailand (TRCT).

Tutu, D. M. (1999). *No future without forgiveness*. New York: Image Book.

US Department of State (Office of the Spokesman). (2006). Thailand: Report by the National Reconciliation Commission. Retrieved from https://2001-2009.state.gov/r/pa/prs/ps/2006/68193.htm

Van Antwerpen, J. (2008). Reconciliation reconsidered: Religion, secularism, and the language of transition. In W. Kymlicka & B. Bashir (Eds.), *The politics of reconciliation in multicultural societies* (pp. 25–47). Oxford: Oxford University Press.

# 6 Preventing violence and promoting active bystandership and peace

## My life in research and applications[1]

*Ervin Staub*

I spent almost all of my professional life, starting in the mid-1960s, studying the roots of goodness (helping, caring about other people's welfare, moral courage and active bystandership) and the roots of evil (the influences leading to genocide and mass killing, and, to a lesser extent, violent conflict and terrorism). I also engaged in activities both to increase caring, helping and active bystandership, and to prevent harm and violence and promote reconciliation after great violence.

This article is primarily about the applications of research and theory, mainly my own but also others', to real-world settings. It originates from a talk I gave at the National Summit on Violence in November 2016 at the American Psychological Association offices in Washington, D.C. The editor of this journal was present and invited me to write an article describing the "interventions" my associates and I have conducted in varied settings, my experiences along the way and the lessons I learned, in the hope that it would help others doing similar work. He suggested that I could do this in an autobiographical manner.

I begin by considering the roots in my early experience of my lifelong commitment to such work. Next, I briefly describe some of my research and theory, which guided the applications. The applications range from working with teachers to create classrooms in which children learn to be caring and helpful; to making proposals to the city administration of Amsterdam to improve Dutch–Muslim relations after violence between the groups there; to working with police to create active bystandership – officers acting to prevent or stop the use of unnecessary force or other unlawful actions by fellow officers; to training students in schools to be active bystanders who prevent or stop bullying of fellow students; to promoting healing and reconciliation in Rwanda after the genocide of 1994 to improve lives and prevent further violence, and the extension of this work from Rwanda to Burundi and the Congo. I also write about formulating some lectures to groups – for example, in Belgrade during the violence in Bosnia – to have an educational impact relevant to prevention. Another aspect of my autobiographical approach will be to describe in each case how my engagement came about – working with police, working in Rwanda and so on.

## The origins of my motivation: Early experiences with evil and goodness

The original impetus for my engagement in research on "goodness" and "evil" came from my earliest experiences. I was a 6-year-old Jewish boy in Hungary at the worst of times, during the Holocaust. At that time, I experienced evil, but was also the recipient of goodness. Once I began this work, my motivation and engagement evolved further. As my own and others' research shows, people learn by doing and change as a result of their own actions, both in negative and positive directions (Staub 1989a, 2015).

Hungary started to pass anti-Semitic laws in 1920, and at the time of World War II was a voluntary ally of Germany. Still, there was no killing of Jews through the spring of 1944. Then the Germans found out that the Hungarian ruler had reached out to the allies in the hope of a creating a separate peace. They responded by occupying Hungary in March 1944. I happened to be on a main street of Budapest when the Germans arrived. Maria, a woman who worked for my family, and I were pushing my baby sister in a carriage when we heard the roar, and then saw the German tanks rolling into the city. In the summer of 1944, Adolf Eichmann, 50 SS members, and about 200,000 Hungarian police, gendarmes and volunteers gathered the Jewish population from the countryside, about 450,000 people, packed them into wagons and sent them to Auschwitz, where most of them were immediately killed (Braham 1997, 2014). The Jews of Budapest were to be next.

Raoul Wallenberg, a Swede, a relatively poor member of a rich and distinguished family, was a partner of a Hungarian Jew in Sweden in an export–import firm. He agreed to come to Hungary to try to save lives. As a neutral country, Sweden had some influence. He was appointed a diplomat and, in Hungary, created a "protective pass" that said that the bearer would become a Swedish citizen after the war, and during the war was under the protection of Sweden. My father and uncle were in forced labour camps. My mother and aunt stood in line in front of the Swedish embassy and succeeded in getting these documents for us. The Hungarian government agreed to respect a limited number of them, but Wallenberg created many more.

He bought up apartment houses in Budapest and had the people with these letters of protection move in there. As I later learned, he was totally invested in saving lives, running next to and on the top of trains crowded with Jews to be taken away while being shot at, trying to hand letters of protection to people. The Nazis also tried to kill him in a car "accident." The Soviet army, as it liberated Budapest in early 1945, made him disappear. There is speculation but no real knowledge about why the Soviets took him into custody. My belief is that Wallenberg had developed some influence in Budapest, and the Soviets did not want to have anyone around who might interfere with their plans for Hungary. He apparently died in a prison in Moscow, probably in 1947.

In the second half of 1944, Hungarian Nazis, the Arrow Cross, were gathering Jews in the streets of Budapest, taking them to the Danube, sometimes tying several people together, shooting some, and pushing them all into the river. They often raided the "protected houses," taking people away because they did not have a protective pass, or for other – to us, unclear – reasons.

Rather than abandoning us, Maria, the Christian woman who worked for my family, came with us to the protected house. She prepared dough, took it to a bakery in a baby carriage, and then brought the bread back. Once Arrow Cross members stopped her, made her stand against the wall with her hands up for hours, and threatened to kill her for helping Jews. An Arrow Cross member who knew her arrived and told the others to let her go.

She continued helping, baking bread and also procuring other food, as before. She also took a copy of a letter of protection to my father in the countryside, asking someone standing inside their camp's barbed wire fence to call him, and handed him the letter. Although it was probably useless to him, it may have given him confidence. He escaped during a stopover in Budapest as his group was taken to Germany. He was its only survivor.

He came to our "protected house." One day I saw a group of black-uniformed men marching down the street. I shouted, "They are coming!" My mother told my father to sit in the corner of the room, pushed an armchair over him and threw a blanket over the chair. The black-uniformed Hungarian Nazis thoroughly searched the small apartment, but did not find him. I was 6 years old at the time. I have vivid memories of what happened, can see the men looking in drawers and closets, but not the feelings I had at the time. But these experiences gave me models of acting on others' and one's own behalf, and, I think, showed me that it is possible to act effectively.

After the war, Hungary was under Communist rule. In October 1956, there was a revolution. The Communists did not allow people to leave the country, but now the borders were less guarded. I was 18 years old and escaped with a close friend of my age and his two years older brother, three weeks after Soviet troops put down the revolt. My parents were too old (55 and 60) and too impacted by their traumatic lives during the Holocaust – and also during the Communist era, when the small clothing store they restarted after the war was nationalised – for the adventure of escape and starting a new life. My 13 year old sister was too young to take along. She later became ill. I saw them all again for the first time ten years later, after I became a US citizen, which made it safer to return, and had my first job and could afford to travel. I then continued to go to Hungary, even after my parents and sister died, visiting Maria. I was with her when she died in January 1991.

I lived in Vienna for close to three years, with my friends, much of the time in a house set up for Hungarian refugee students by a Danish organisation, studying at universities for part of this time. Then in 1959, I received a visa to the United States. My friends decided to stay in Vienna. I ended up in Minnesota and managed to get into the university, where I studied psychology. I went to graduate school at Stanford University. All this time, I thought little about the Holocaust and issues of goodness and evil. I was doing research with Walter Mischel on delay of gratification, and taking courses with Al Bandura, Eleanor Maccoby and Leon Festinger, and with Arnold Lazarus, a visiting professor who was an early cognitive behaviour therapist.

During my second year at Stanford, I became a tennis partner and friend of another visiting professor, Perry London. He and a couple of his associates conducted the first study of rescuers, European Christians who endangered themselves to save the lives of Jews during the Holocaust. They had important initial findings (London 1970) but could not continue their research because no one would fund it. They were told, in 1962 to 1963, that too much time had passed to learn reliably about the motivation and characteristics of rescuers. It took quite a while for people to have enough emotional distance from the horrors of the Holocaust to seriously study it. As the Holocaust received more public attention, social scientists returned to the study of rescuers, with important studies appearing beginning in the 1980s (Fogelman 1994; Oliner and Oliner 1988; Tec 1986).

## My research on helping and positive bystandership

The conversations with Perry London inspired me to begin to study positive behaviour. With the empirical orientation I received at Stanford, I wanted to do this experimentally, in a measurable way. In my first job at Harvard University starting in 1965, I began to do research on children's sharing behaviour (Staub and Noerenberg 1981; Staub and Sherk 1970). Then, inspired by Latane and Darley's (1970) studies of bystander behaviour, I did a series of studies of children and adults helping (or not helping) when they heard a crash and sounds of distress from an adjoining room. I also studied emergency helping with other designs. I will briefly review a few results here that are especially relevant to my later work, in part by applying principles derived from them to real-world situations.

In one study with children (Staub 1970b), helping increased from kindergarten to first grade, and then to second grade; remained at about the same level in fourth grade; and then sharply decreased in sixth grade to about the level of kindergarteners. As we saw this surprising decline in helping, we began to ask children about the reasons for their actions. They said things like, "I thought I was not supposed to stop working on my task" and "I did not think I was allowed to go into the other room." It seemed that children learned conventional rules of behaviour but not that, under certain circumstances, caring or moral principles override them.

To explore this further, I conducted a study in which seventh graders were working on a drawing (Staub 1971). Some were told nothing (no information), others were told not to go into the adjoining room because someone else was working there on a task (prohibition) and some were told they could go into the adjoining room if they needed more drawing pencils (permission condition). While working on their drawing, children heard a crash and sounds of distress from the adjoining room. Children in the first two groups helped with exactly the same frequency, a little over 25%. Children in the permission condition helped almost 90% of the time. It seems that no information functioned as a prohibition, as with sixth graders in the previous study. Following conventional rules, which would be specific to a group's culture, may be an inhibitor of helping by adults as well. Among police, such a rule seems to be "Support your fellow officer no matter what he or she is doing," including the use of unnecessary force.

In the study of helping varying with children's age (Staub 1970b), we also explored whether children show the "bystander effect": Latane and Darley (1970) had shown that the presence of other bystanders makes it less likely that any one bystander helps. We had children hear the distress sounds from the adjoining room either alone or in pairs and found that kindergarteners and first graders did not show this effect. When they heard distress sounds in pairs, they began to talk about it and joined together in action. But this disappeared by second grade. Perhaps this change is also the result of environmental influence, children learning to hide their reactions in public, or learning to feel less responsible when another child is present.

In another study, the helpful example of an adult made it more likely that children helped, as did warm interactions compared with neutral interactions with an adult (Staub 1970a). There is a good amount of research showing that parental warmth, especially when combined with appropriate guidance, contributes to positive behaviour (Eisenberg et al. 2015; Eisenberg et al. 2006; Staub 1979). In one study, when children interacted with a warm adult, they remembered more the positive behaviour of diorama figures; when they engaged with an indifferent adult, they remembered more the diorama figures' negative actions (Yarrow and Scott 1972).

Some people try to avoid information about the need to help. In one study, a confederate, one of my students at Harvard, collapsed on a quiet street in Cambridge when someone was approaching either on the same side or the other side of the street. Helping was less when the bystander passed on the other side. But some people approaching on the other side immediately rushed over. Others hesitated and, while they did so, sometimes new passers-by arrived and helped. A phenomenon that emerged was that some passers-by looked away after a single glance, never looking back, and some of them turned off the street at the next corner (Staub and Baer 1974). In my later work, I found that avoiding information, presumably to lessen feelings of responsibility or guilt for inaction, happens in various settings, such as with bystanders inside and outside a country in the course of increasing hostility and violence (Staub 1989a, 2011). As a result, I have defined bystanders as people who are in a position to know what is happening and in a position to take action (Staub 2005).

Witnesses have substantial power to influence events. In one of my studies, what a confederate said in response to sounds of distress from another room greatly influenced helping by another person, the study participant. The frequency of help was lowest, about 25%, when the confederate said that the sounds may be from another study and, at any rate, were irrelevant to them. When the confederate said in response to the crash and distress sounds, "That sounds bad, maybe we should do something; you go into the other room and I'll find the person in charge," and left the room through another door, every participant went into the room where the sounds came from (Staub 1974, Section VII). A witness defining the meaning of events and appropriate behaviour appears to have powerful influence.

Both circumstances and personality matter in helping. Both can be a source of responsibility to help. The research by Latane and Darley (1970) on the bystander effect showed a situational influence. The presence of other bystanders made it less likely that any one bystander helped. Also, in a study with kindergarteners and first graders who were working on a drawing, the adult, before leaving the room, said, "Someone else is working in the other room; if anything happens, you are in charge." First graders who received this message were more likely to help than those who did not (Staub 1970a).

In a series of studies, my students and I assessed what I have called prosocial value orientation (PVO). It has three primary elements: A positive view of human nature, concern about others' welfare and, most important, feelings of and belief in one's responsibility to help others. Weeks later, we put each participant into a situation where there was a need to help someone either in physical or psychological distress. In the study with physical distress (Staub 1974), a person working alone on a task heard groaning from an adjoining room. If the study participant did not go into that room, the distressed person came into their room. This person, saying that he had a stomach ailment, offered several opportunities to help, graded in the effort required (Staub 1974). Participants with a stronger PVO helped earlier and expended more effort.

I conducted this first study on the relationship between the personal disposition PVO and helping at Harvard. My students and I conducted further studies on this after I moved to the University of Massachusetts at Amherst in 1971. In a study of psychological distress, a study participant and a confederate were working separately on the same task. The material they worked with described a distress situation. In response, the confederate talked about something that happened to her, expressing more or less severe psychological distress (Feinberg 1978; see Staub 1978, 1980). Greater PVO was again associated with more helping when the person was in greater distress. Helping in this case meant primarily stopping work and attending to the distressed person.

In these studies, we measured PVO by a combination of tests that we factor analysed, which provided a strong summary measure. I then developed a test specifically to measure it, in response to a request by the magazine *Psychology Today* to publish a test on values and helping (Staub 1989b). Over 7,000 people returned the completed questionnaire. PVO was strongly associated with varied forms of self-reported helping, including subtle indicators like the time that has passed since you last helped. The association was even stronger with a combination of PVO and belief in one's capacity to improve others' welfare (intended as a measure of competence). Items with just feelings of responsibility to help and competence were also strongly associated with helping (an article on this study was already in galleys to be published in *Psychology Today*, when the magazine stopped publication for several years, but see Staub 2003).

In further research, working with children in Amherst schools, I explored how children can become more caring and helpful as they are guided to engage in helpful behaviour and "learn by doing," change as a result of their own actions (Staub 1979, 2015). The anthropologists Whiting and Whiting (1975) found in their study of six cultures that in groups in which children have responsibilities that contribute to the welfare of the group, such as tending animals or taking care of younger siblings, they are more helpful. In societies in which they do not have such responsibilities, they are more egoistic, seeking and accepting help. Children were least helpful in the one US city they studied, in the Northeast, in which their only responsibility was to take care of their room.

Because there may be other aspects of societies that contribute to the differences in helpfulness, I conducted a series of experiments to assess learning by doing in children. Fifth and sixth graders were taught to make toys, received materials and spent four 40-min periods making toys for poor hospitalised children. This increased later helping. What Hoffman (2000) called "induction," pointing out to children the negative consequences of their behaviour on other people, contributes to the development of empathy in young children (Yarrow and Waxler 1976). I assumed that pointing out positive consequences would also have beneficial effects. In some conditions, the positive reactions of children who received the toys were described to participants, which increased later helping. In another study, fifth and sixth graders taught second and third graders, which led to more later helping by the teachers. This was more the case when the interactions were positive. In each case, these positive results were found compared with control conditions with similar activities that did not benefit anyone.

The children who engaged in helpful behaviour later helped more, for example, by assembling photos and stories cut out of magazines or written down by them, and then creating packages of them for poor hospitalised children (Staub 1979; see also Staub 2015). Studying genocide, I later found that learning by doing and evolution is also a central characteristic of societies moving toward great violence (Staub 1989a).

## Studying the roots of violence, primarily by groups

After a decade-and-a-half study of the roots of positive behaviour and ways to increase it, I was emotionally ready to look at the dark side: The roots of violence between groups, especially genocide and mass killing. I also thought that my prior work had relevance: For example, I assumed and found that bystanders relinquishing responsibility contributes to genocide. I was concerned that by moving from experimental research on positive behaviour to doing research in the way necessary to study genocide as a societal process, I would become an outsider, given the strong methodological focus in academic psychology at that time on experimental research. But my motivation at this point was strong. A somewhat rare, overt reaction to this shift was at a lecture I gave at the University of Trier, in Germany, in1987. I was invited to talk about my research on altruism. I asked if I could instead talk about the roots of genocide. One of the first questions after my talk was whether it was psychologically challenging for me to give up experimental research to study genocide.

In addition to turning, around 1980, to this new field of study and the new approach it required, starting at the end of the 1980s I increasingly engaged in projects outside the university that aimed to bring about change. My colleagues in social and personality psychology and in the Department of Psychology in general did not indicate any problem with my shift. A few seemed to appreciate this new direction in my work. I published three books between 1978 and 1980, began to study genocide and mass violence after that and for a while I published less, because I was working hard on research in this new field and my first book on this topic, *The Roots of Evil: The Origins of Genocide and Other Group Violence* (hereafter, *The Roots of Evil*; Staub 1989a). I remember that my yearly personnel committee evaluation had suffered during this period.

I worked with graduate students who approached me, but I felt inhibited in attracting graduate students because my work was so different from what they envisioned when they applied for our programme in social and personality psychology. I was also concerned about their job prospects. This changed the last years of my university career, because with the help of anonymous donors, I was able to start a doctoral programme in the psychology of peace and violence. This attracted outstanding graduate students who entered the programme deeply interested in the issues I was engaged with. When they received their doctoral degrees, they found good jobs.

My family was also affected by my shift in research. I had books lying about with dead people on the cover. Whenever they noticed a programme about violence on TV, not fictional but real, my sons, Adrian and Daniel, would call to me saying, "Dad, there is something related to your work on TV!"

Two more events during my visit at the University of Trier are especially relevant to the study of group violence. One was another question – at this University in Germany, a professor of education asked, "But is there not something wrong with the Jews, given that they were always persecuted in the course of history," showing the persistence of devaluation. In Ancient Rome, it was Christians who were thrown to the lions. Later the Church identifying the Jews as Christ-killers and focusing on converting them, led to intense discrimination and a long history of persecution. Another event was a meeting with a group of Germans who were at least teenagers at the time Hitler came to power, which I asked my hosts to arrange. In talking about their lives under Hitler, the people in this group again and again returned to talking about the satisfactions of life at the time, sitting around campfires, singing songs. It took time and effort for them to recover memories of the very public persecution of Jews (Staub 1989a).

My approach to the study of genocide and mass violence was to analyse the history and group relations in societies in which genocide or mass killing has been perpetrated, applying knowledge gained from psychological research and theory. Then I developed a conception to explain the roots of such violence and applied it to new instances. I studied the Holocaust, the genocide of the Armenians, the autogenocide (killing of Khmer by Khmer) and genocide against minorities in Cambodia, and a mass killing, the disappearances in Argentina (Staub 1989a). Later I studied the genocide in Rwanda (Staub 1999, 2011) and, in less depth, the mass killing in Bosnia (Staub 1996b). To explore the applicability of principles I identified, I also studied the intractable violent conflict between Israelis and Palestinians, and both Palestinian and Al Qaeda terrorism (Staub 2011). Along the way, I increasingly worked on developing an understanding of how groups may reconcile after (or before) extreme violence, and the prevention of such violence (Staub 2011, 2014, 2015).

The starting points for great violence between groups such as genocide and mass killing are a combination of a number of instigating conditions (Staub 1989a; see also Staub 2011). A primary one is difficult life conditions in a society, such as economic decline, great political disorganisation and rapid, large-scale social change. Another primary influence is persistent and intense group conflict. These all frustrate core psychological needs for security, positive identity, the capacity to influence events, connections to other people and understanding the world and one's own place in it. The basic human needs theory that I developed (Staub 1989a, 2003, 2015) is a derivative of, but also different from, Maslow's (1971) theory of human needs.

The frustration of basic needs results in psychological and social processes, such as scapegoating some group for one's life problems, and creating (destructive) ideologies. The latter are visions of a better future and way of life for the group, which become destructive as they identify enemies who stand in the way of their fulfilment. These visions can be quite varied, ranging from nationalism, a frequent one, to a combination of nationalism (expansion of Lebensraum or life space/territory), racial superiority and submission to a supreme leader, which was the Nazi ideology, to total social equality, the ideology of the Khmer Rouge. The Khmer Rouge identified groups of people as enemies who they believed would not be willing to contribute to or live in a society of equality. This included intellectuals. Hostile actions against the scapegoat or ideological enemy can start an evolution of increasing violence – steps along a continuum of destruction. In the course of this evolution, individuals change, the standards of behaviour toward a target group change, and institutions are created to serve persecution and violence (Staub 1989a, 2011).

Experimental research also shows such evolution. For example, Buss (1966) found that "teachers" who were to punish learners for mistakes on a task progressively increased the level of shocks they administered. A study by Bandura, Underwood, and Fromson (1975) showed that overhearing the derogation of some people leads to more intense punitive responses to them, and that this effect appears increasingly over trials.

The existence of certain cultural and political characteristics of a society makes such evolution more likely. Of central importance is a history of division between subgroups and the devaluation of some group, usually a minority. They tend to become the scapegoat and identified as the ideological enemy. Harm done to this group is justified, at least in part, by increasing devaluation of the group and also by its necessity for fulfilling the ideology. Another cultural element is past victimisation or other great group trauma. This creates insecurity and makes the world look dangerous. The group then responds intensely to real or perceived threats, which can lead to unnecessary "defensive" violence (Staub 1996a, 2011). Another contributor is the absence of pluralism, due to culture and excessive respect for authority, or an autocratic system. In societies that perpetrate mass violence, there is usually a strongly hierarchical social system, with obedience to adults stressed in child-rearing, and to leaders in adults' behaviour. The absence of pluralism and overly strong respect for authority make active bystandership to resist the evolution of hostility and violence less likely. Leaders who propagate scapegoating, destructive ideologies and violence, their followers and also passive bystanders have important roles in the unfolding of the processes that lead to violence.

Prevention requires active, constructive responses to the instigating conditions, both by people within the country (e.g., Roosevelt's work programmes during the depression), and outsiders who can provide support and material help. It requires generating constructive psychological and social responses, such as resisting scapegoating, and generating a constructive, inclusive ideology. It requires addressing the cultural characteristics that make violence more likely. Humanising previously devalued groups and healing from past group victimisation and other trauma, and from the persistent psychological and cultural wounds that result from them, are among important processes of prevention. Prevention requires active bystanders, both to resist the influences that lead to violence and to promote positive processes (Staub 2011, 2015).

Understanding both the influences that lead to extreme violence and avenues to prevention contributes to healing from past trauma (see the section on "Reconciliation and the prevention of violence") and may lead people to engage as active bystanders. Reconciliation, the development of more positive attitudes toward each other by all parties, also requires deep, meaningful contact (Deutsch et al. 2014; Pettigrew and Tropp 2006). It requires identifying and working together for shared goals. It requires the creation of a shared history in place of the conflicting histories of the past, or at least understanding and some acceptance of other groups having their own views of the past (Staub 2011, 2014).

## Applying research and theory I: Working with teachers to create classrooms that promote caring and helping

Scientists, including research psychologists, have traditionally been interested in causation, relationships, and principles that describe reality. That has also been an interest for me, but from the start, I was also concerned about how we can create change and how we can improve the human condition. Even research I described that identified causation, for example, the influences that lead to mass violence, embodies the potential for creating change, by addressing those conditions. Some other research I have described was specifically about creating change, for example, engaging children to help others, thereby increasing their later helping. Given both my research on helping and violence for several decades, and my underlying motivation, I was ready and eager when opportunities arose to bring about change, and I sometimes looked for them. This orientation is consistent with, and might even be considered a central aspect of, peace psychology.

At some point, I began to receive invitations to give lectures or workshops with teachers, occasionally parents, and sometimes whole schools on the origins of caring and helping in children. In some cases, these were in part to address ongoing issues. For example, in a high school in New Jersey, there was a basketball rivalry with another school, and during or after each game, there were fights. As part of talking about caring and helping, I addressed the issue of "us and them," and how easily such divisions arise and can prevent caring and helping and lead to hostility and violence.

After the school shooting at Columbine on 20 April 1999, I was asked to assess positive and negative (bullying) interactions among students in a whole school district. We also assessed the frequency of active bystandership by students (very low) and how students felt about their lives in school. Even more than those who received many negative behaviours directed at them, students who were excluded (received both few positive and negative behaviours) felt bad about their lives at school. Bullied students who received active bystandership and students who acted as bystanders felt better about their school lives (Staub et al. 2003; Staub and Spielman 2003). In a one-day event, we then reported and discussed our research findings with the staff.

My engagements with teachers became more regular when Facing History and Ourselves invited me to do sessions in their summer teacher training programmes, which I did for over ten years, starting around 1991. Facing History is an organisation that provides materials and training to teachers to use the Holocaust as a lens on how human cruelty comes about. The information guides students to see the role of individual human beings as passive bystanders, or their potential to prevent violence as active, caring, and courageous bystanders. Their work and mine had both similar substance and similar aims. But my job in this context was not to talk about violence and genocide. Instead, I engaged with teachers about the origins of prosocial behaviour in children and proposed and discussed creating classrooms that provide children with experiences that generate caring and helping, and make violence less likely (see Staub 2003, for a design of such classrooms).

Briefly, the central elements of what I had to say was that warmth, affection and nurturance by parents, teachers and peers create positive connections to human beings. This has to be accompanied by guidance in values, and rules derived from values, at least in part provided by reasoning and explanation. The guidance has to be effective in moving children to act on essential values and rules (what Baumrind (1975) called firm control), but not harsh. The example of models is important. Guiding children to engage in helpful behaviour, inside the classroom or outside of it, is an important way for developing caring and helping (Staub 1979, 2015). Creating positive connections among children belonging to different groups, for example, through joint projects, including cooperative learning techniques (Aronson et al. 1978), is important for developing caring across group lines.

These principles derive from laboratory research (see Eisenberg et al. 2006, 2015; Pettigrew and Tropp 2006; Staub 1979, 2005, 2015). In addition, a large-scale study of heroic rescuers in Europe during the Holocaust showed that they grew up in families that practised such child rearing. They also had one parent who was a humanitarian model. Moreover, many of these families did not draw a sharp line between ingroup and outgroup, for example, in Poland between Catholics, the main religious group, and others. They engaged with others, including Jews (Oliner and Oliner 1988).

The teachers and I discussed being open to the cultural difference among children from varied backgrounds; creating opportunities for children to be helpful, so that they learn by doing; and finding ways for all children to experience being special – if not in academics, then by taking care of plants, having roles in plays or in other ways. The teachers talked about relevant experiences. One teacher selected a student who had behaviour problems to write on the blackboard the plans for the day every morning. Having this responsibility and special role changed the student's behaviour. Another teacher described a collection in the school for a charitable cause. A student who previously stole something was extremely eager to go around the classrooms to collect the donations. Despite others' hesitation, the teacher selected him and reported a clear beneficial effect on the student.

One lesson I learnt in this context, which I applied in my other work, was that engaging participants in trainings and workshops to contribute their expertise is of great benefit. Many have special, relevant knowledge. Many teachers have much more direct experience with students than academic researchers. Being an active part of training and combining ideas motivates everyone. A second, related lesson was that weaving together research findings and knowledge based on them as well as knowledge based on practical experience leads to the best outcomes.

## Applying research and theory II: Trainings in active bystandership – the police and schools

In 1989, I published *The Roots of Evil*, which was widely reviewed, including by some public media. Perhaps due to this exposure, a journalist from the Los Angeles Times called me after the Rodney King incident in March 1991, and asked me how such events come about.

In that incident, Rodney King did not stop his car when a police officer tried to flag him down. The officer, and then more police cars, chased him. When they finally stopped him and pulled him out of his car, a number of police officers beat him while he was lying on the ground, with 17 officers standing around watching. Although this was before cell phones, someone filmed this and sent it to a TV station, and it went viral around the world.

My comments were published in a front-page article (Scott 1991). I was then invited to speak at a one-day event addressing police violence, organised by Warren Christopher, later President Clinton's Secretary of State (Staub 1992, 2001). After that, the California Peace Officers Standards and Training, the organisation responsible for all police training in the state, invited me to develop a training for police academies to reduce the use of unnecessary force.

The training focused on developing active bystandership by police. The foundation for the training included my earlier work, for example, on the power of bystanders to influence others, as well as others' work, for example, on the inhibitors of active bystandership (Latane and Darley 1970). Officers were to engage when their fellow officers got unnecessarily heated in an interaction. Entering into the interaction, taking over the engagement with a civilian or acting to stop it when a fellow officer engaged in harmful or violent behaviour were all part of the training.

Acting seemingly contrary to a fellow officer is in opposition to traditional police culture. Therefore, the training had to work on culture change. It had to transform the meaning of good teamwork, so that an officer preventing or stopping a fellow officer from harming an innocent civilian is seen as good teamwork and real loyalty. The training had to include superior officers, who potentially could punish active bystanders. Their support was essential for active bystandership to take hold. It was to use videos of role-plays of interventions as well as actual role-playing in order to develop new skills and behaviour strategies.

I delivered the training late summer in 1992 to a committee charged with addressing the conditions that led to the Rodney King event, consisting of community leaders and representatives as well police officers. After a two-day meeting, the group reached a series of positive recommendations (without me in the room), one of which was that "The subject of intervention should be taught to all levels of police officers (Basic course through Executive Development)" (Staub 1992; see also Staub 2015). However, the group decided to use their internal staff for the application of the training to courses in the police academies, and I do not know how they applied it.

But I do know what the police in New Orleans have been doing. In 2014, Mary Howell, an attorney in New Orleans who knew about my work, managed to have training in active bystandership included in a consent decree signed by New Orleans and its police department with the justice department, agreeing to changes in police training. New Orleans has a tragic history of violence by police against community members. Mary Howell is a civil rights attorney who, because there were no criminal prosecutions of violent police officers, brought many civil suits against the police and the city. Very recently, people she represented whose relatives were killed by police during and right after Hurricane Katrina finally received a substantial settlement from the city and a very rare apology from the mayor (Litten 2017). Despite this history, she now closely works with the police on their EPIC (Ethical Policing Is Courageous) programme, the name for the active bystandership project. This is another lesson: Adversarial relations can be conducted in a manner that makes later collaboration possible. This was perhaps made more possible by the consent decree and a new police chief.

The police department was obligated, but also fully committed itself, to train officers in active bystandership. Starting with the training that I developed for California and working with consultants like me, as well as others, they created their own version of the training. By September 2017, most officers had received initial training. Their version, in addition to protecting members of the community, stressed, more than my original programme, the benefits to police officers and their families. Stopping a fellow officer from harmful and illegal conduct prevents the possible criminal prosecution of that officer as well as of the passive bystander (Aronie and Lopez 2017). Creating ethical policing also avoids the psychological strain of being part of a corrupt system and keeping quiet while some officers act illegally. Being part of such systems may contribute to the high incidence of alcohol and drug abuse and suicide among police.

The leaders in the New Orleans police department are totally committed to this programme. The police chief, Michael Harrison, said at a meeting with the judge overseeing the programme, which Mary Howell attended, that he wears his EPIC pin (which participants receive at the end of their training) all the time "as a sign of a contract he has made with his officers ... if anyone sees him about to do something wrong, he is asking them to intervene ... regardless of rank ... and that is what the pin signifies" (M. Howell, personal communication, 24 May 2017).

One remaining challenge is evaluation. A formal evaluation in New Orleans has not been possible, because as part of the consent decree, other changes have also been introduced to police training. In response to articles about the training in active bystandership in *The New York Times* (Robertson 2016) and elsewhere (Aronie and Lopez 2017), a large number of police departments want to use the training, which would make evaluation possible. A conference to introduce them to it took place in April 2018.

But anecdotal reports by police and community members are coming in. As one New Orleans commander described an event at a demonstration, "Promonument protestors were screaming insults at the police ... when officers saw a fellow officer about to lose it, (I) saw them step in, put their hands on his shoulder, tell him to step back to cool off" (M. Howell, personal communication, 24 May 2017). Jonathan Aronie, the court-appointed administrator of the court order, reported,

> A sergeant told me ... one of her officers had an incident a day or two after she took EPIC training. She was involved in an arrest of a very resistant subject. The subject spit in her face. She did not strike back, although she conceded she came close to doing so. She confided in the sergeant following the incident, 'I had to EPIC myself. I'm not sure I would have been able to resist if I hadn't just had EPIC training.'
>
> (J. Aronie, personal communication, 23 July 2017)

This relates to an effect of the training I have also observed in the training of students (see below). Training in active bystandership, which includes discussion of the impact on people who are harmed and the motivations of harm-doers, even without intervention, can reduce the likelihood of harmful actions. Mary Howell keeps herself deeply informed about police-related events in New Orleans, and she also wrote, "To my knowledge we didn't have any real incidents of police over-reaction – with one exception early on but that was quickly addressed" (M. Howell, personal communication, 24 May 2017).

Evaluation was possible in another Training of Active Bystanders that my associates and I developed to prevent or stop harassment, intimidation and bullying of fellow students in schools. The curriculum for the training elaborated, to a greater degree, elements that are part of the other trainings as well: Understanding why someone would engage in unjustified harmful behaviour; understanding the inhibitors of active bystandership, such as diffusion of responsibility, pluralistic ignorance, potential costs and devaluation of those who need help; skills in intervening in the least forceful manner that may be effective; using, among other techniques, role-playing (extensively used in the training in New Orleans); and engaging other bystanders as allies (for details of the training, see Staub 2015, Chapter 16; for the complete curriculum, see www.ervinstaub.com).

Eighth and tenth grade students and adults were trained to be trainers. Then student–adult pairs trained over 600 eighth and tenth graders in two schools in adjoining cities. In many of the sessions, there was an observer to assess, for later feedback, the extent to which the training followed the design.

An evaluation study compared the frequency of negative behaviour before, and about six months after the end of the training, with such behaviour by students in two comparable schools in neighbouring cities. There was a 20% decrease in negative behaviour by students who were trained compared with students who were not. In addition, anecdotal reports indicated other positive effects. For example, students reported to administrators a student who talked about engaging in violence in the school, and the students attributed this active bystandership to the training. The effects of being trainers, which may have been even greater, were only studied in interviews, in qualitative evaluation. One of a number of informative comments was, "I used to do such things (bullying) and never thought about its effects on the other person" (Staub 2015, Chapter 16).

One lesson is that studying both student and adult trainers, and police trainers, would be valuable. Teaching others seemed to have positive effects, possibly an example of learning by doing, as in my studies described earlier (Staub 1979, 2015). In this instance, not only the positive action of teaching, but also its content would have contributed to positive changes in trainers.

Another lesson is the importance of positive participation by leaders. In the Stanford Prison study, there were cameras in the "jail" set up in the basement of the Stanford psychology department, and Professor Zimbardo, the Superintendent, and his assistants observed the guards' abusive behaviour, without taking any action (Staub 2007a; Zimbardo 2007). This allows the evolution of increasingly abusive behaviour. The opposite can also be true: Superiors can guide the evolution of positive action. They must be part of any efforts at system change, as they have been in New Orleans. A third lesson for creating culture and behaviour change is the engagement of community stakeholders. In New Orleans, community members have been involved, and police officers were part of designing the training and leading trainings. In our school programme, before we began, we had extensive meetings with the superintendents of the two school systems, principals and relevant staff members. Knowledgeable outsiders as advisors and local stakeholders will ideally work together.

## Applying research and theory III: Reconciliation and the prevention of Violence – Rwanda, Burundi and the Congo

Sometime in 1995, a man who had read *The Roots of Evil*, and was part of a small organisation in Washington DC, the Friends of Raoul Wallenberg, was traveling through our area and asked me to lunch. He persuaded me to organise a conference with the "Friends," which took place in Sweden in 1997, called "Options for the Prevention of Genocide." Our experience at this conference inspired me and my associate, Laurie Anne Pearlman, to go to Rwanda.

I invited Charles Murigande to the conference in Sweden. He was the government official in Rwanda who, in 1995, invited me to Rwanda to a conference that considered how the country could move on after the genocide of 1994. I was in India at the time at a small conference with, and for, the Dalai Lama and could not go. But our conference was already in preparation and I invited the Dalai Lama to it. He accepted, which led to a set of complex events. My role for, and in, the conference was to develop its substantive content and agenda and invite people; the role of the 'Friends' was to find a venue, generate funding and also to invite people. At first, everyone was pleased that the Dalai Lama would come. But at a planning meeting with one of the Friends, he told me that they had disinvited the Dalai Lama.

A main funding source was going to be the Wallenberg family, who are sometimes referred to as the "Swedish Rockefellers." They had substantial business interests in China, and because China is extremely hostile to the Dalai Lama, the decision was made to disinvite him. This action was understandable given possible business consequences for the Wallenbergs, but also ironic, given the history of Raoul Wallenberg, as well as unacceptable to me. We engaged in a process, supported by outside "bystanders" who encouraged us. In the end, with apologies, we invited the Dalai Lama again. He came and gave an inspiring talk. The importance of speaking out, discussion and support by outside parties for resolving a conflict was evident in this process.

For a long time in Rwanda, the Tutsis were dominant. After World War I, the Belgians ruled Rwanda, and they elevated the Tutsis to rule on their behalf, which they did in an oppressive manner. In 1959, there was a Hutu uprising, and since then, the majority Hutus (85% of a population of about 8 million) had ruled the country, with occasional violence against Tutsis, some of which amounted to mass killing. In 1990, a Tutsi rebel group entered from Uganda and began to fight the government army. There was a peace process and peace accords in 1993. In April 1994, the Rwandan President's plane was shot down, and a genocide began, in which about 700,000 Tutsis and 50,000 Hutus – mostly those regarded as political opponents – were killed by the army and Hutu militias, called the Interahamwe (Des Forges 1999). Much of the killing was done with machetes, person to person. Charles Murigande deeply affected everyone at the conference with his description of the terrible events in the genocide.

Our participants at the conference in Sweden engaged with several instances of group violence, which we discussed in small groups, using background materials my students and I had prepared. At the end of the conference, we asked participants, again meeting in small groups, to commit themselves to work for the prevention of violence, in the United States or other places.

Charles Murigande invited me and Laurie Anne Pearlman, a clinical psychologist (who has also been my life partner since 1992) specialising in research on and treatment of trauma (e.g., Pearlman and Caringi 2009; Pearlman and Saakvitne 1995), to come to Rwanda to help with healing and reconciliation. During the discussion in our small group, she and I committed ourselves to do so. On returning home, serendipity entered. Two different psychologists sent me information about a call for proposals on forgiveness by the John Templeton Foundation. We applied for and received a grant on Healing, Forgiveness, and Reconciliation in Rwanda.

Our work in Rwanda – which began in January 1999, expanded to Burundi and the Congo, and is still ongoing in all three countries – probably would not have happened without the active bystandership of a prominent social psychologist, David Myers. He was a member of the final panel at the John Templeton Foundation that was to select the proposals to be funded. He knew we had applied, and he knew my work, as he had written in his textbooks about it. He was surprised when he did not see our proposal in the final group. He asked to look at it and found a clerical (computational) error. When it was corrected, ours was among the top proposals.

Before we first went to Rwanda, we organised a meeting in Boston with Rwandans living in the Boston area, and with experts on Rwanda, to inform ourselves about Rwandan culture. We gained valuable information, but also information about the culture that was no longer valid after the genocide, such as people not talking about their feelings to anyone except intimate family members. The intensity of pain was so great that many Tutsis, members of the victim group, would tell us about their losses immediately upon meeting us. This was the case with taxi drivers, with a young man we met on a dark night on an empty street on the day of our arrival as we walked from one hotel to another and even with high-level government officials once we had even a limited relationship to them.

We arrived in Rwanda early in January 1999. I am almost foolhardy in terms of my limited anxiety about physical danger. But I had intense nightmares the night before we started on our trip. There was still violence in Rwanda, as perpetrators who had escaped to Zaire (now the Democratic Republic of the Congo) made incursions into northern Rwanda, and they were killing Tutsis while the Tutsi government fought them. Friends and colleagues in the United States were telling us not to go because of the danger. And the collaborator whom Charles Murigande had recommended to us was not communicating, so we did not know whether he would meet us at the airport or whether we would have a hotel room. All of this, added to my personal history, might explain the nightmares.

Arriving in Rwanda, we experienced people as still deeply traumatised. Many seemed frozen – the expressions on their faces, the way they moved or remained motionless for long periods of time. Because outsiders were only allowed to work in the country in collaboration with a local organisation, our collaborator (who was at the airport when we arrived and had reserved a hotel room) introduced us to the director of an organisation with which we were initially to collaborate. One day, we travelled with him and his wife in their small truck, with two boys in the open back of the truck. They were the sons of the director's sister, who was a Tutsi, killed by her Hutu husband during the genocide. Such terrible things were not uncommon during the genocide, with even parents in mixed marriages killing their own children.

We intended to set up a free-standing intervention and its evaluation, but within 48 hours changed our plans. We realised that to have lasting impact, we would have to work through local institutions. In the next couple of days, we visited eight of them. We invited them to a one-day meeting to discuss what we had to offer. We were perhaps the first Western individuals, rather than staff of large organisations such as Catholic Relief Services, who came after the genocide to help. We were usually very warmly welcomed. But in one group, a widows' group, the director needed to be certain that we cared and understood their situation. This was a very rare occasion when I mentioned that I was also the survivor of a genocide.

At the meeting in the morning, we presented what we had to offer, which included information about the influences that lead to genocide, and understanding trauma and healing. These were the topics of most intense interest, and in the afternoon we discussed them in greater detail. We worked with these organisations, all of which worked with groups in the community, to set up a training or workshop for their staff in the summer.

During this first visit we also met with government officials. We were invited to one of the first activities of the newly established National Unity and Reconciliation Commission. They held meetings around the country to ask people what they would require for reconciliation. We went to a meeting for women in Kigali, who came in large numbers, colourfully dressed for the occasion. Many of them were widows; among the things they said included that in the genocide, their husbands were killed and their property and livelihood were destroyed. They needed material support to care for their children and be able to send them to school (which, at that time, required fees; since then, the government has made schooling free).

Beginning that summer and continuing for the next nine years, we conducted training and workshops with varied groups on our trips to Rwanda two to three times a year. In addition to the staff of the eight organisations, we had workshops for community leaders, members of the media, national leaders – government ministers, advisors of the president, members of the Supreme Court and parliament – as well as the staff of the Unity and Reconciliation Commission, which also helped us to arrange training.

In the first workshop, we offered information about the origins of genocide, as I briefly described it earlier. Rwandans had a deep need to understand how what happened to them could happen. But we also believed that survivors coming to see that the genocide is the outcome of understandable human processes, even if this outcome was terrible, would change their perception of perpetrators as simply evil. This would make it more possible for them to reconcile and to act to prevent future violence. We also thought that understanding would help reduce the shame of members of the perpetrator group (there were no actual perpetrators in our trainings), and perhaps the guilt of some of them, just enough that they would be able to engage constructively with members of the victim group, and express their group's and perhaps their own responsibility as bystanders, as well as their regret. We also discussed in this first long – nine days – workshop the traumatic impact of the violence, on survivors, perpetrators and passive bystanders. We gave lectures and engaged in discussion in our large group, and participants did many things in small groups, whose members reported back to the large group for further discussion. We did role-plays, which Rwandans seem to enjoy and do very well. In small groups, participants also discussed what happened to them during the genocide.

We had both informal evaluation, at the end of each day and after the last day, and a formal evaluation study. In the informal evaluation, participants said things like, "so this was not God's punishment of us" and "If we know how such violence comes about, we can act to prevent it." For the study, our Rwandan staff, now including two research assistants, organised community groups. There were three conditions: Treatment groups, which were led by participants in our training; treatment control groups, led by people from the same organisations who did not participate in our workshop; and no treatment control, who only participated in assessments. In the treatment groups, our participant-leaders used an integration of the approach in our seminar and their customary approach, which we worked on in the workshop. There were several subgroups in each of our conditions, for example, those whose leaders included a religious orientation and those who did not.

We assessed these groups on a variety of dimensions three times: before any treatment, immediately after, and two months after the end of treatment. There was significant decrease in trauma symptoms, increase in understanding genocide, increase in the acceptance of the other group (e.g., "I can work with them for the sake of our children") and in conditional forgiveness ("I can forgive them if they acknowledge what they did") in the treatment group from before the treatment to two months afterward compared with the other two groups. There were no differences immediately after the treatment. Their experience in the treatment group most likely reactivated participants' experience of the genocide, and the effects appeared once these emotional reactions subsided (Staub 2005; see also Staub 2011).

In subsequent workshops, we also included information about reconciliation, and engaged more with approaches to healing. Having discussed conditions that could reduce as well as increase violence in a group, we divided national leaders into small groups and asked them to consider legislation they had just introduced or planned to introduce, and evaluate the extent to which it might help prevent or contribute to violence. In the media group, we asked them to write news reports in ways that would not incite, but, when possible, help prevent violence – for example, by decreasing the division between "us" and "them" and the devaluation of "them" (Staub 2011; Staub and Pearlman 2006).

We were encouraged by many people, including the national leaders we trained, to expand the reach of our work. We invited George Weiss, a producer of film and TV who lived in Amsterdam, to join us in Rwanda to produce educational radio programmes. Over time, he created an organisation, La Benevolencija Humanitarian Tools Foundation, for this work.

We developed informational programmes and a radio drama. We spent many hours in Kigali, sitting with the staff hired for the project, working out the details of our prototype radio drama Musekeweya (New Dawn). We created a storyline, its central element being conflict and violence between two neighbouring villages. There is a famine, and people from the poorer village, led by an angry leader and his followers, attack the better-off village, which later retaliates in a counterattack. There are also positive active bystanders in both villages. There is a Romeo and Juliet story between the sister of the bad leader and a young man in the other village, both of them constructive bystanders. We created communication messages – brief statements of the central principles we wanted to communicate about the origins of violence, trauma, reconciliation and prevention. Some examples are as follows (Staub and Pearlman 2009, Table 1):

> Life problems in a society frustrate basic needs and can lead to scapegoating and destructive ideologies
>
> Genocide evolves as individuals and groups change as a result of their actions
>
> Devaluation increases the likelihood of violence, while humanisation decreases it
>
> The healing of psychological wounds helps people live more satisfying lives and makes unnecessary defensive violence less likely
>
> Passivity facilitates the evolution of harmdoing whereas actions by people inhibit it

Rwandan writers, initially led by Western producers, later by Rwandans, wrote weekly episodes, with the educational content guided by the communication messages. The radio drama began to broadcast in May 2004, and it is still ongoing. The fictional villages over the years moved to reconciliation, and then joined to prevent new violence by others in the region. The episodes were translated into English, and Laurie Pearlman and I initially read and commented on the educational content, on the basis of which the episodes were revised as necessary. In 2006, radio dramas were introduced into Burundi, and then in the eastern part of the DRC. After a few years, the new storyline was created every couple of years by groups that included local stakeholders. We also created informational programmes about the origins of genocide, justice and other matters. Sometime in 2005, two of my then-students, Johanna Vollhardt and Rezarta Bilali, and then Adin Thayer, joined us in providing feedback on the educational content of the episodes. Later, Johanna and Rezarta did further evaluation research in both Rwanda and the Congo (Bilali and Vollhardt 2013, 2015), and Adin continues to participate in storyline workshops and training the staff in educational content.

We, the initiators, over the last five years or so, increasingly took a back seat. The project, led by George Weiss, is continuing to thrive.

A complex but extensive evaluation study of the radio drama in Rwanda found a variety of positive effects after the first year. There were six treatment groups around the country, whose members listened to Musekeweya (Paluck 2009; Staub and Pearlman 2009; see also Staub 2011). Members of six control groups listened to an alternative radio drama. Participants in the control group agreed not to listen to the weekly broadcasts of Musekeweya; in exchange, at the end of the year, they would receive cassettes of all the broadcasts and a cassette recorder. Members of all groups received these. The evaluation study found that members of the control groups lacked crucial knowledge, indicating that they had not listened to the programmes.

Those who listened to the radio drama expressed more empathy for varied groups – victims, survivors, perpetrators, bystanders, leaders. They said they would communicate what they believe to others, and did so, by saying the same thing both to an individual interviewer and in a focus group, for example, about the level of mistrust in their community. Those in the control condition did not. They admitted, for example, distrust to the interviewer, but not in the focus group. Those who listened to Musekeweya participated more in reconciliation activities, engaging with people in the other group, whereas those in the control group mainly advocated reconciliation.

After the end of the study, there was a party in each of the 12 groups, during which they received the tapes and cassettes. During the party, in an unobtrusive measure seemingly not part of the project, they were to decide who would hold these materials. In all six control groups, one person suggested that they give them to the village leader, and this was immediately accepted. Such a suggestion was also made in each of the six treatment groups, but others disagreed, the group discussed it, and decided that a member of the group would hold it for the group. This indicated that in this very "authority-oriented" (Staub 1989a, 2011) country, the study accomplished one of our aims: To lessen the influence of authorities.

In working there, we almost inevitably became involved in ideological-political issues that are relevant to healing and reconciliation. From the time the Tutsi rebels invaded the country, and now as Tutsis rule the country, they propagated an ideology of unity: "There are no Tutsis and Hutus – these divisions have caused our conflict and the genocide – we are all Rwandans." This became so intensely held by them that when, in our training of leaders, we talked about divisions between groups, they said, about seven years after the genocide, "But we have no groups in Rwanda." It was only after long discussion that they came to the view that perhaps there are no biologically different groups, but there are social differences and negative attitudes of Tutsis and Hutus toward each other (Staub and Pearlman 2006).

The government has strongly disapproved and even punished people talking about Tutsis and Hutus, under laws against "divisionism" and "genocidal ideology." But people in Rwanda continued to see each other, and identified each other, at least to us outsiders, as Hutu and Tutsi. Instead of attempting to impose a single identity, propagating a dual identity (Dovidio et al. 2009) e.g., Hutu–Rwandan is likely to work better.

An ideology of unity is seemingly constructive, but from our psychological perspective, the way it was used seemed a hindrance to reconciliation. The government position made it impossible for Tutsis and Hutus to engage with and discuss their differences and issues. When I said that to the editor of the major newspaper there in an interview, he said he could not write that – his prime minister would not like it. I suggested that he identify me as responsible for saying it, and he did publish it. In various ways, this policy has continued. In addition, although there have been several justice processes with the perpetrators of the genocide, there has been no mention in the country and no discussion of the killing of large numbers of Hutus. This is also a barrier to reconciliation. Also, the government has not allowed a serious challenge in the election of the President – Paul Kagame has been elected to a third term – or, in general, any challenge to Tutsi political rule.

Still, the actual long-term effects of these government policies provide an experiment. Perhaps persistent peace, combined with Rwanda's substantial economic advance, and efforts to create equal educational and economic opportunities – to various degrees at work in Rwanda – will change attitudes by Hutus and Tutsis toward each other, even under political oppression.

There are a variety of lessons from this work. It is essential to show and feel respect for the experience and knowledge of local people. One gains from their understanding of the culture and their experience of, and perspective on, the issues. This was one reason that, in our first workshop, we worked on integrating our perspective and the approaches participants used with groups. But it is also essential for an outsider to form his or her own judgement and use his or her knowledge. For example, it was widely believed by people that the genocide was the result of ignorance and bad leaders. This was also propagated by government leaders, presumably so that people would not fear the possibility of recurring genocide, now that they had "good leaders." Our presentation and discussion of the influences leading to genocide showed that this simple view was partly incorrect (ignorance) and partly insufficient (yes, bad leaders are problematic, but the origins of genocide are much more complex). Another lesson was that even when a group or government wants reconciliation, psychological and political processes may lead to counterproductive policies.

Cultural differences can be challenging, and it is important to understand what is the result of the culture and what is purely personal. Rwandans tend to be intelligent and hardworking. But they tended to tell us, perhaps because we were regarded as people with authority, what they thought we wanted to hear. Questioning you is a nearly superhuman effort for them, except for leaders. Our first Rwandan associate was repeatedly not at his phone at agreed-upon times; another associate was more than once an hour late to meetings. Neither of this is unusual. But interestingly, in our workshops, participants arrived on time, even if they came from far away. There are also different expectations in interpersonal realms. When someone told us about a challenging matter, we tended to empathise; they wanted advice, as specific as possible.

## Applying research and theory IV: Preventing violence and promoting positive relations between the Dutch and Muslims in Amsterdam

In 2004, Theo van Gogh, a Dutch film director and TV personality, and Hirshi Ali, a Somali woman who was then a member of the Dutch parliament and a committed activist for the rights of Muslim women, prepared a TV programme about women in Islam. The programme began with the image of the naked back of a woman, with text on it from the Koran. Enraged by the programme, a Muslim man killed van Gogh and left a note threatening Hirshi Ali. This was followed, in this peaceful country, by hundreds of attacks on Muslim schools, mosques and churches.

The mayor of Amsterdam, where these events took place, organised a conference on how to address Dutch–Muslim relations in the city. I was invited to speak, and then invited to make proposals to the city government on how to improve Dutch–Muslim relations and thereby prevent future violence. The intermediary who proposed my involvement was Jerome de Lange. During the first few years of our radio programmes, he was the First Secretary at the Dutch embassy in Kigali. A Dutch grant to Radio La Benevolencija, whose main office is located in Amsterdam, provided partial support for our programmes.

I met with the mayor's Chief of Staff and her staff in a mutual informational meeting and interviewed some other people. Some people were really scared. A professor of education asked me, "Are we all in danger?" I also read a great deal of material about Dutch–Muslim relations in the Netherlands, including yearly reports of a government agency and research articles. The Dutch staff of La Benevolencija helped me gather information. I made a presentation of my understanding of the situation and thoughts about addressing it to members of the city government and some other influential people in the city. Soon afterward, I provided them with a written report of my proposals and the rationale for them, based on my understanding of the situation, relevant research and my prior work. Later, I turned this into an article (Staub 2007b).

I made 11 proposals, each followed by extensive discussion of relevant research and applied experience that provide the basis for the proposal.

De Lange noted an important lesson: That members of the city government whom I had not directly engaged along the way were sceptical at first. However, once they had heard my talk and had the written proposals, they supported their implementation, according to de Lange, "because of its in-depth analysis of the origins of hostility and violence and concrete proposals for action" (2007: 252). In working with local groups, it is highly desirable for an outsider proposing interventions to bring everyone into the discussion of the problems and their solutions. If local stakeholders feel excluded, they may sabotage the work. In Rwanda, after the first year or two, the ongoing storyline of the radio drama has been developed every two years by groups consisting of both staff and local stakeholders.

I will list those proposals that Jerome de Lange (2007) specifically mentioned in a follow-up article to mine, describing actions the city government took to implement the proposals. Actions to promote positive relations are usually relevant to several principles.

Proposal 1: Humanising the "other" is essential to overcome devaluation and the danger of violence

Proposal 2: The Dutch and Muslim leaders and communities should engage in dialogue aimed at creating a constructive, inclusive ideology that includes mutual understanding, accommodation and a shared vision of a good society to which all groups can contribute and help create

Proposal 7: It is important to foster deep contact (significant engagement) between people across group lines as an avenue to overcoming devaluative stereotypes and hostility

Except for one or two small enclaves in the city, where there was interaction among young people, the ethnic Dutch population of Amsterdam (and the Netherlands) and its Muslim population had very little contact with each other. As a result of housing patterns, with groups living in separate areas, schools were segregated. Most of the information Muslims had about the Dutch came from TV, including free sexual practices that are deeply contrary to the values of Islam. They also experienced discrimination – real and perceived. The Dutch, in turn, were affected by roving groups of mostly teenage Muslims who harassed store owners and passers-by, by their resentment of social and financial support for Muslims and their stereotype of Muslim criminal behaviour (Staub 2007b).

The city government instituted several practices to promote connection between members of the groups. It established a study center that was to provide information about Muslims to non-Muslims. During Ramadan, the government organised a festival, with "many meetings and debates about Islam in the Netherlands (…) and Muslim families inviting non-Muslims to share dinner with them after sunset" (de Lange 2007: 253). During the year, days of dialogue were organised. In addition, "children of migrants interviewed their parents about their background and migration story," which were shared on the internet and publications (de Lange 2007: 253). A "soap" series was in production on local TV, somewhat similar in conception to our educational radio drama in Rwanda. To combat segregation, meetings were set up between children in so-called Black (Muslim) and White (non-Muslim) schools, with the project called "Welcome to My Neighbourhood" being extended to more areas of the city.

These activities were also relevant to several of my other proposals, such as Proposal 6:

> Proposal 6: Promoting active, positive bystandership by all segments of the population – leaders, the media, community organisations, individual citizens – makes the evolution of hostility and violence less likely. Every person, or organisation, can be active in fostering constructive engagement by others.

In addition to the activities described above, billboards around the city encouraged young Muslims to call a special organisation set up to combat discrimination when they witness it. The police received special training to be aware of discrimination.

Proposal 10 noted that it is crucial to develop inclusive caring in children as an aspect of long-term peacebuilding. This means caring that extends beyond the boundaries of their own group, however that group is defined, and specifically caring about members of other groups in their society, including previously hostile groups. In addition, especially for children who are members of groups that have suffered from victimisation and other trauma, it is important to facilitate "altruism born of suffering" (Staub 2005, 2011; Staub and Vollhardt 2008). Further, an "organisation has been set up to give advice to school personnel who are confronted with polarisation and radicalisation in their classes" (de Lange 2007: 254). The various activities and organisations the city has created are also relevant to Proposal 3, to facilitate psychological healing to prevent the negative consequences of painful past experiences.

This project shows the potential of cooperation between authorities and "experts." It shows the active bystandership of city leaders in responding to difficult events. They initiated my involvement and used information based on scholarship and experience as they took significant actions to improve relations between groups. But what if leaders have no motivation, or initiative, or understanding of how to access, and then use, information relevant to a situation that requires action? Perhaps psychology organisations, such as the American Psychological Association, American Psychological Society, Society for the Psychological Study of Social Issues or International Society for Political Psychology, or the Peace Psychology Division of APA, should establish task forces, which can reach out to authorities in difficult times and offer such service.

## It is not all roses: Cold cuts in Hungary

After the collapse of the Soviet Union, which also meant freedom for the East European countries that it had dominated, there was a lot of antagonism between people in the media on the left and right in Hungary. Someone approached me with the idea to go there and attempt to bring them together, some form of conflict resolution between the two sides.

I went to Hungary and had many individual meetings with TV and print journalists and producers on both sides, including leading personalities. I discussed with them the issue of the divisions in the media – their differences as well as antagonism. I proposed a meeting of media people on the left and right. Each person I talked to agreed.

I rented a hall and arranged for high-quality cold cuts and salads to be brought in. At the appointed time, everyone on the left, the people I talked to and others they contacted, had arrived. One person on the right showed up. I learned afterward that one of the influential people on the right decided the day of the meeting not to come, and initiated a phone chain discouraging others from coming. The one person who came did not get the message.

This was my earliest direct engagement with groups in conflict. In the general mood of disappointment, it did not occur to me to have a discussion with the people who came about strategies to improve the relationship between the groups.

I think they saw the people in the media on the right like Democratic members of Congress came to see Republican members during the Obama years – there was no way to move them. Still, a discussion, even if starting with bitterness, might have turned constructive. One lesson for me is to reinforce, again and again, people's positive intentions – and in this case, not assume that once they agree to come to such a meeting, it is a done deal. Another is to be ready to try even for the smallest possible gain – in this case, working with the one group that came on strategies of overcoming hostility. And perhaps a more general one – be ready for all contingencies.

## Applying research and theory V: Aiming to create change through lectures and as an expert witness

In some of my lectures, I aimed to promote change in conflict and post-conflict situations. This was the case with a lecture on the origins of hostility and violence that I gave to about 500 people in Belgrade, very soon after NATO first bombed Serb positions to stop attacks on the Bosnian capital, Sarajevo, which had been under a long siege.

I was invited to Belgrade to give a talk on my research on the roots of caring and helping, but my hosts also arranged this second lecture. There was consecutive translation, after every few sentences. I started by saying, "I will talk about the origins of hostility and violence between groups, but I will not apply it to the circumstances in the former Yugoslavia. I am inviting you, the audience, to do the application to your situation." I have used this approach before – for example, in Israel – and found it effective. In Rwanda also, after talking about the influences leading to genocide, we asked participants in trainings to apply it to their own situation.

After my talk, there was pandemonium in the room. People were shouting at each other – especially members of two groups on different sides of the room. As my translator told me, some of them were shouting, "We did not know what our people were doing!" Others were shouting that one could get it from CNN (which, at that time, did not transmit to Serbia but could be picked up from neighbouring countries). Some people shouted that CNN lies. The intense "discussion" on this and other topics by a substantial number of people went on for some time.

I was then interviewed by a journalist who asked, "So do you support the NATO bombing?" I was concerned. I read in the paper that there was one (or more – I did not remember) murder of someone who publicly opposed Serb actions. But after hesitating, I said "yes." Serbs were attacking Bosnian Muslims, committing atrocities, and there seemed no other way to stop it.

After more substantial NATO bombings, the Serb leader, Slobodan Milošević, entered into negotiations, leading to the Dayton Agreement, which ended the fighting. Milošević was then ousted by huge non-violent demonstrations by students and workers, who blocked the streets of Belgrade. Still later, he was tried in The Hague, and died in prison before his trial ended.

I had educational aims in other lectures as well. I gave the opening talk at the international conference in 2004 that initiated the tenth anniversary memorialisation of the Rwandan genocide (followed by a talk by President Paul Kagame). I discussed the influences that lead to genocide and mentioned how victimised groups tend to respond to new threat with the use of force, even when this is unnecessary. Between World War I and 1959, when there was a Hutu uprising, under Belgian overrule, Tutsis treated Hutus very badly (Des Forges 1999; Mamdani 2001). When I interviewed, in prison, the woman who was the justice minister during the genocide, the first thing she said was that the reason for the genocide was slavery – meaning the slavery of Hutus under Tutsi rule.

My primary purpose in talking at the conference about formerly victimised groups at times engaging in unnecessary "defensive" violence was to help Tutsis consider that their own victimisation in the genocide might increase the possibility that they would harm others. I did this in part because Rwanda under Tutsi rule has become a militarily powerful country. The military killed many Hutus civilians in the Congo, when they invaded there to stop former génocidaires from attacking into Rwanda. But the next day, Mrs Kagame approached me and asked, "So are we responsible for creating the genocide?" My response was, and is, that past victimisation does make harmdoing more likely, but far from inevitable. Individuals and groups still have choices. Subsequent Hutu governments could have worked on improving relations between Tutsis and Hutus, but mostly they oppressed and at times killed Tutsis.

Furthermore, it is seemingly always a variety of influences that combine in leading to extreme group violence. In Rwanda, these included economic decline due to the substantial drop in the international markets of the prices of Rwanda's primary exports, tin and coffee; for the first time, new political parties were allowed, and many were created, leading to substantial political chaos; the strengthening of anti-Tutsi "Hutu Power" ideology; the civil war; and more (Des Forges 1999; Mamdani 2001; Staub 1999, 2011). Moreover, some individuals and groups that have been victimised develop "altruism born of suffering," turning their suffering into caring about and helping others. This requires healing and support from others (Staub 2005, 2011; Staub and Vollhardt 2008).

I gave many lectures over the years, and all had, of course, educational aims, but the aims were usually not as focused on bringing about behaviour change as the work I have described in this article. The way that I structured the talk in Belgrade, I hoped to generate active bystandership, and in Rwanda, to prevent harmdoing by the Tutsi government. But the series of talks I gave, for example, at yearly conferences arranged by the State Department on the prevention of genocide had a less focused aim: the hope that the US government would seriously attend to prevention. Although President Obama created, in 2011, an Atrocity Prevention Board, this is still an unfulfilled hope.

Another attempt on my part to create change using information was my participation in one of the Abu Ghraib trials as an expert witness. I agreed to be a defence witness because I wanted to show the military tribunal that the guards who abused prisoners acted as part of, and were influenced by, the system. I was asked to be a witness for Sgt Javal Davis, the only African-American defendant. The charges included stamping on detainees' hands and bare feet as they were lying in a pile on the ground assembled by the guards, including him, and jumping on that pile of detainees. He was also charged with being a passive bystander to others' actions. Actions by other guards included hitting a prisoner with a metal bar, forcing prisoners to strip and masturbate, ordering a pair of detainees to simulate fellatio, placing a leash around the neck of a detainee, having dogs attack prisoners, holding the dogs back in the last moment and more.

Sergeant Davis had already pled guilty, so the only issue was the sentence he would receive. In the room where the proceedings took place were the judge, two prosecutors, a military and a civilian defence counsel and the members of varied ranks of the military tribunal sitting in two rows. In the audience, on the side, were Sergeant Davis's parents, his estranged wife and his young child and a good number of other people, including military personnel who were part of the court system.

The abuse of the prisoners at Abu Ghraib was outrageous. But trying nine guards, without judicial procedures against those who exerted systematic influence leading to their actions, was just as outrageous (Denner 2005; Hersh 2009). My aim was to provide information about the context that led to their actions.

Attacks and attempted uprisings in some parts of the prison created frustration and anger among the guards. Investigators, whose job was to get information and confessions from the prisoners, told the guards to soften them up for their interrogation. Such "requests" were initiated and approved by the Secretary of Defense, Donald Rumsfeld. Superior officers witnessed abusive behaviour, for example, prisoners marched through a compound naked and put in a cell naked. They did nothing, treating it as normal. Violence usually evolves, becoming more intense over time, unless there are constraining forces. Superior officers not setting and enforcing standards of appropriate conduct allows a system of violence to develop, as we have also seen with the police – and as it has happened in the Stanford Prison Study (Staub 2007a).

One of the guards was identified as an instigator and leader, Cpl Charles Graner – he received a ten-year prison sentence. It has been found in other instances, ranging from the Stanford Prison Study to terrorist groups, that one aggressive person, without control by superiors or other parties, can influence others – and even a whole system. The US military who served as guards in Abu Ghraib had no training as prison guards, which may have made it easier for standards to shift. However, Charles Graner was a prison guard in the United States before he joined the military, with a number of accusations against him for brutality. He also had a number of documented instances of abuse of his estranged wife, with court orders to stay away from her. There was also evidence of his prejudice against African-American inmates in the United States. Prejudice against Iraqis by American soldiers in constant interaction with a difficult prison population also likely played a role in the abuse.

Sergeant Davis's sentence was a reduction in rank, six months in prison, and a bad-conduct discharge. Prison sentences ranged from ten years to six months.

Only one defendant received no prison sentence, Spc. Megan Ambuhl, whose rank was reduced to private and who lost half a month's pay.

I cannot assess the influence of my testimony on the members of the tribunal. But some military people in the audience came up to me after the trial and said that my testimony gave them a new understanding of the behaviour of the guards.

## Final comments: Information and experience

I have stressed all along developing positive connections to people in the settings one works in. Local people not only facilitate the work, but especially in far away and culturally unfamiliar settings, positive connections to them help with understanding the culture, and make the work rewarding, rather than excessively challenging. Such connections also increase the likelihood that the work will fit the culture and be sustainable. Connections to both the people one works with and associates with also help inhibit or reduce vicarious trauma, the effect of substantial exposure to others' trauma (Pearlman and Caringi 2009; Pearlman and Saakvitne 1995). Moreover, in Rwanda, it is presumably because of relationships with some high-level officials that we have been allowed to broadcast programmes that are at odds with both the authority orientation of the culture and an authority-oriented government.

The positive effects of our interventions, a number of them evident in evaluation studies, show the value of developing interventions based on research and theory. In the interventions I described, we provided information in the context of or in relation to people's actual experience, which made it likely that it would generate what I have called "experiential understanding" (Staub 2006). In Rwanda, we asked participants to discuss whether, and in what way, the information about the origins of genocide applied to their experience of the genocide there. The educational content in radio dramas was directly relevant to listeners' experience. In the training of active bystanders, information joined with police or students engaging in or witnessing harmful behaviour. In the case of students, information sometimes also joined with students being victims of harmful behaviour. Role-plays also connect information with at least "as if" experience. The information I provided in Amsterdam was connected to the circumstances there at that time. The joining of information and experience is likely to lead to deeper and more durable knowledge. As we found in the work described in this article, it contributes to behaviour change.

I found, in my early research, the power of the joining of information and experience. In one study, we provided information to people about the properties of electric shocks, which reduced both their physiological and experiential impact when they subsequently received shocks (Staub and Kellett 1972). In another, I provided information about snakes and their behaviour, which added to the influence of progressively exposing individuals to a snake in reducing phobia (Staub 1968).

This early research related to fear and its elimination was inspired by the courses of Arnold Lazarus at Stanford. In retrospect, it is highly likely that it was also influenced by my early life experience during the Holocaust and under Communism. So was a study on self-control, in which people who administered electric shocks to themselves had much lower heart rate and galvanic skin responses than participants paired with them who received the same intensity shocks, but had no control (Staub et al. 1971). (In neither of my shock studies did we administer strong shocks to people.) Early in my career, wanting to be a real scientist, I avoided thinking about connections between my life and work – which later became completely obvious. It seems that all the work I have done was in part shaped by my life experiences. I wonder to what extent the work of other psychologists and social scientists is influenced by life experience. I know that people who study genocides usually have a personal connection, through family or at least group membership.

The issue of culture is relevant to all the work we have done. Cultural characteristics combine with societal conditions as starting points for group violence. Police culture makes change in police behaviour challenging. Children learning what I have referred to as rules of conventional behaviour interferes with helping. Environmental conditions are much less likely to create harmful actions if culture promotes positive relations and attitudes toward others. It is both the culture of a society and that of a family that can imbue children with caring and responsibility both for people in and outside their group.

In Rwanda – and Burundi and the Congo – it certainly was our intention to generate culture change – to help people understand and to lessen devaluation of the other, lessen the intense authority orientation of people, and to help with healing and make it less likely that the genocide becomes a "chosen trauma" (Staub 2011; Volkan 2004) that defines identity. Proponents of dynamical systems theory (Vallacher et al. 2010) suggest that culture change can take substantial time to manifest itself. Given the Rwandan governmental system, which, while moving people toward equality, is politically and socially oppressive, it is difficult to judge the current state of the culture. Hopefully, when the system becomes more open, or when conditions make active bystandership essential, whatever cultural changes we have contributed to will manifest themselves.

Relevant to culture change is the role in American psychology of the kind of research and interventions I have described. The field of social psychology and psychology in general has begun to shift, becoming more engaged with issues relevant to group violence and prevention, such as collective victimhood and the experience of inclusive (being open to seeing others also as victims) versus exclusive victimhood (Noor et al. 2017), conflict narratives, forgiveness and more. There have been significant interventions and applications of psychology by peace psychologists, for example, working to reunite child soldiers with their communities (Wessells 2009). There is recent interest in interventions by social psychologists, as indicated by symposia on the topic at conferences, and some interventions like work with police on subtle prejudice. But significant interventions that aim toward sustainable change related to conflict (i.e., preventing violence and promoting positive intergroup relations) and their impact evaluations in real-world contexts seem rare (for a more extended discussion, see Bilali and Staub 2017).

There has been a long history of research on contact between groups to overcome negative attitudes, but contact is often of limited duration or nature, and its effects are mostly evaluated immediately after it took place. But sometimes researchers use naturally occurring situations, such as a three-week-long summer camp in Maine that brings together youth in conflict situations – Israeli, Palestinian, Serb, Croat and Bosnian – which had powerful immediate effects, but also positive effects two to four years later, for example, fearing the outgroup less (Worchel and Coutant 2008). A project in Sri Lanka with Sinhalese and Tamil youth combined contact and peace education. A year later, participants expressed more empathy for the other group and donated more money for poor children in the other group (Malhotra and Liyanage 2005). Hopefully, applying knowledge to create change in the realm of conflict and evaluating its impact will expand further.

Finally, I have not written about the emotional experience of being in and working in settings where people have been greatly victimised and deeply traumatised. Inevitably, we were deeply affected by such suffering, by the stories we were told, by the visible, palpable pain of people. Empathy is natural, inevitable and necessary. But in a world of suffering, for me, being actively engaged in trying to help was redemptive. I believe that not only for me but also my associates, what made it possible not to be overwhelmed by the pain was, first, our ongoing efforts to help, balancing empathy and compassion with a focus on what felt like our meaningful and hopefully significant work, and second, connections to associates and the people we worked with.

## Note

1 This chapter is the reproduction of the author's article published in *Peace and Conflict: Journal of Peace Psychology* (Vol. 24 No 1, 2018), 95-111. This article received the 2018 Otto Klineberg International and Intercultural Relations Award of the Society for the Psychological Study of Social issues (SPSSI).

## References

Aronie, J., & Lopez, C. E. (2017). Keeping each other safe: An assessment of the use of peer intervention programs to prevent police officer mistakes and misconduct, using New Orleans' EPIC program as a potential national model. *Police Quarterly*, *20*(3), 295–321.

Aronson, E., Stephan, C., Sikes, J., Blaney, N., & Snapp, M. (1978). *The jigsaw classroom*. Beverly Hills, CA: Sage.

Bandura, A., Underwood, B., & Fromson, M. E. (1975). Disinhibition of aggression through diffusion of responsibility and dehumanization of victims. *Journal of Research in Personality*, *9*(4), 253–269.

Baumrind, D. (1975). *Early socialization and the discipline controversy*. Morristown, NJ: General Learning Press.

Bilali, R., & Staub, E. (2017). Interventions in real world setting: Using media to overcome prejudice and promote intergroup reconciliation in Central Africa. In C. G. Sibley &

F. K. Barlow (Eds.), *The Cambridge handbook of the psychology of prejudice* (pp. 607–631). New York: Cambridge University Press.

Bilali, R., & Vollhardt, J. R. (2013). Priming effects of a reconciliation radio drama on historical perspective-taking in the aftermath of mass violence in Rwanda. *Journal of Experimental Social Psychology*, *49*(1), 144–151.

Bilali, R., & Vollhardt, J. R. (2015). Do mass media interventions effectively promote peace in contexts of ongoing violence? Evidence from Eastern Democratic Republic of Congo. *Peace and Conflict: Journal of Peace Psychology*, *21*(4), 604–620.

Braham, R. L. (1997). A népirtás politikája: A holocaust Magyarországon - 2. bo″v. és átd. *Kiad [The politics of genocide: The Holocaust in Hungary]*. Budapest, Hungary: Belvárosi Kvk.

Braham, R. L. (2014, March 22). The assault on the historical memory of the Holocaust. *Hungarian Spectrum*. https://hungarianspectrum.org/2014/03/22/randolph-l-braham-the-assault-on-the-historical-memory-of-the-holocaust/

Buss, A. H. (1966). The effect of harm on subsequent aggression. *Journal of Experimental Research in Personality*, *1*, 249–255.

de Lange, J. (2007). The impact of the Staub model on policy making in Amsterdam regarding polarization and radicalization. *Peace and Conflict: Journal of Peace Psychology*, *13*(3), 361–364.

Denner, M. (2005). *Torture and truth: America, Abu Ghraib, and the war on terror*. New York: New York Review of Books.

Des Forges, A. (1999). *Leave none to tell the story: Genocide in Rwanda*. New York: Human Rights Watch.

Deutsch, M., Coleman, P., & Marcus, E. C. (2014). *The handbook of conflict resolution: Theory and practice* (3rd ed.). San Francisco, CA: Jossey-Bass.

Dovidio, J. F., Gaertner, S. L., & Saguy, T. (2009). Commonality and the complexity of "we": Social attitudes and social change. *Personality and Social Psychology Review*, *13*(1), 3–20.

Eisenberg, N., Eggum-Wilkens, N. D., & Spinrad, T. L. (2015). The development of prosocial behavior. In D. A. Schroeder & W. G. Graziano (Eds.), *The Oxford handbook of prosocial behavior* (pp.114–137). New York: Oxford University Press.

Eisenberg, N., Fabes, R. A., & Spinrad, T. L. (2006). Prosocial development. In W. Damon (Ed.), *Handbook of child psychology: Vol. 3. Social, emotional, and personality development* (5th ed., pp. 646–718). New York: Wiley.

Feinberg, J. K. (1978). *Anatomy of a helping situation: Some personality and situational determinants of helping in a conflict situation involving another's psychological distress* [Doctoral Dissertation]. University of Massachusetts, Amherst, Amherst, MA.

Fogelman, E. (1994). *Conscience and courage: Rescuers of Jews during the Holocaust*. New York: Anchor Books.

Hersh, S. M. (2009). *Chain of command: The road from 9/11 to Abu Ghraib*. New York: Harper Collins.

Hoffman, M. L. (2000). *Empathy and moral development*. New York: Cambridge University Press.

Latane, B., & Darley, J. (1970). *The unresponsive bystander: Why doesn't he help?* New York: Appleton-Crofts.

Litten, K. (2017, February 20). With NOPD settlement complete, families still struggle for forgiveness. *Times-Picayune*. Retrieved from http://www.nola.com/politics/index.ssf/2016/12/families_danzinger_katrina_bru.html

London, P. (1970). The rescuers: Motivational hypotheses about Christians who saved Jews from the Nazis. In J. Macaulay & L. Berkowitz (Eds.), *Altruism and helping behavior* (pp. 241–250). New York: Academic Press.

Malhotra, D., & Liyanage, S. (2005). Long-term effects of peace workshops in conflicts. *Journal of Conflict Resolution, 49*(6), 908–924.

Mamdani, M. (2001). *When victims become killers: Colonialism, nativism, and the genocide in Rwanda*. Princeton, NJ: Princeton University Press.

Maslow, A. H. (1971). *The farther reaches of human nature*. New York: Viking Noor.

Oliner, S. B., & Oliner, P. (1988). *The altruistic personality: Rescuers of Jews in Nazi Europe*. New York: Free Press.

Paluck, E. L. (2009). Reducing intergroup prejudice and conflict using the media: A field experiment in Rwanda. *Journal of Personality and Social Psychology, 96*(3), 574–587.

Pearlman, L. A., & Caringi, J. (2009). Living and working self-reflectively to address vicarious trauma. In C. A. Courtois & J. D. Ford (Eds.), *Treating complex traumatic stress disorders: An evidence-based guide* (pp. 202–224). New York: Guilford Press.

Pearlman, L. A., & Saakvitne, K. W. (1995). *Trauma and the therapist: Countertransference and vicarious traumatization in psychotherapy with incest survivors*. New York: Norton.

Pettigrew, T. F., & Tropp, L. R. (2006). A meta-analytic test of intergroup contact theory. *Journal of Personality and Social Psychology, 90*(5), 751–783.

Robertson, C. (2016, August 29). With eye on reform, New Orleans is training officers to police one another. *New York Times* (p. A9). Retrieved from http://mobile.nytimes.com/2016/08/29/us/anew-orleansprogram-teaches-officers-to-police-each-other.html

Scott, J. (1991, March 28). Violence born of the group: The beating of Rodney G. King follows patterns observed by researchers. Police, the military and other embattled entities are especially susceptible. *Los Angeles Times*. https://www.latimes.com/archives/la-xpm-1991-03-28-mn-1329-story.html

Staub, E. (1968). The reduction of a specific fear by information combined with exposure to the feared stimulus. *Proceedings, 76th Annual Convention of the American Psychological Association, 3*, 535–537.

Staub, E. (1970a). A child in distress: The effects of focusing responsibility on children on their attempts to help. *Developmental Psychology, 2*(1), 152–153.

Staub, E. (1970b). A child in distress: The influence of age and number of witnesses on children's attempts to help. *Journal of Personality and Social Psychology, 14*(2), 130–140.

Staub, E. (1971). Helping a person in distress: The influence of implicit and explicit "rules" of conduct on children and adults. *Journal of Personality and Social Psychology, 17*(2), 137–144.

Staub, E. (1974). Helping a distressed person: Social, personality, and stimulus determinants. In L. Berkowitz (Ed.), *Advances in experimental social psychology* (pp. 293–342). New York: Academic Press.

Staub, E. (1978). *Positive social behavior and morality: Personal and social influences (Vol. 1)*. New York: Academic Press.

Staub, E. (1979). *Positive social behavior and morality: Socialization and development (Vol. 2)*. New York: Academic Press.

Staub, E. (Eds.). (1980). Social and prosocial behavior: Personal and situational influences and their interactions. In *Personality: Basic aspects and current research* (pp. 237–294). Englewood Cliffs, NJ: Prentice Hall.

Staub, E. (1989a). *The roots of evil: The origins of genocide and other group violence*. New York: Cambridge University Press.

Staub, E. (1989b). What are your values and goals? *Psychology Today*, 46–49.

Staub, E. (1992). Understanding and preventing police violence. *Center Review*, *6*, 1–7. [Publication of the Center of Psychology and Social Change: An Affiliate of the Harvard Medical School, Cambridge, MA].

Staub, E. (1996a). Breaking the cycle of violence: Helping victims of genocidal violence heal. *Journal of Personal and Interpersonal Loss*, *1*(2), 191–197.

Staub, E. (1996b). Cultural-societal roots of violence. The examples of genocidal violence and of contemporary youth violence in the United States. *American Psychologist*, *51*(2), 117–132.

Staub, E. (1999). The origins and prevention of genocide, mass killing and other collective violence. *Peace and Conflict: Journal of Peace Psychology*, *5*(4), 303–336.

Staub, E. (2001). Understanding and preventing police violence. In S. Epstein & M. Amir (Eds.), *Policing, security, and democracy* (pp. 221–231). Huntsville, TX: Office of Criminal Justice Press.

Staub, E. (2003). *The psychology of good and evil: Why children, adults and groups help and harm others*. New York: Cambridge University Press.

Staub, E. (2005). The roots of goodness: The fulfillment of basic human needs and the development of caring, helping and nonaggression, inclusive caring, moral courage, active bystandership, and altruism born of suffering. In G. Carlo & C. Edwards (Eds.), *Moral motivation through the life span: Theory, research, applications. Nebraska Symposium on Motivation*. Lincoln, NE: Nebraska University Press.

Staub, E. (2006). Reconciliation after genocide, mass killing or intractable conflict: Understanding the roots of violence, psychological recovery and steps toward a general theory. *Political Psychology*, *27*(6), 867–894.

Staub, E. (2007a, August). Evil: Understanding bad situations and systems, but also personality and group dynamics. [Review of the book The Lucifer effect: Understanding how good people turn evil by P. Zimbardo]. *Psychcritiques 52*, n. p.

Staub, E. (2007b). Preventing violence and terrorism and promoting positive relations between Dutch and Muslim communities in Amsterdam. *Peace and Conflict: Journal of Peace Psychology*, *13*(3), 333–360.

Staub, E. (2011). *Overcoming evil: Genocide, violent conflict, and terrorism*. New York: Oxford University Press.

Staub, E. (2014). Reconciliation between groups: Preventing (new) violence and improving lives. In M. Deutsch, P. T. Coleman & E. L. Marcus (Eds.), *The handbook of conflict resolution: Theory and practice* (3rd ed., pp. 971–998). San Francisco, CA: Jossey-Bass.

Staub, E. (2015). *The roots of goodness and resistance to evil: Inclusive caring, moral courage, altruism born of suffering, active bystandership and heroism*. New York: Oxford University Press.

Staub, E., & Baer, R. S., Jr. (1974). Stimulus characteristics of a sufferer and difficulty of escape as determinants of helping. *Journal of Personality and Social Psychology*, *30*(2), 279–285.

Staub, E., Fellner, D., Barry, J., & Morange, K. (2003). Passive and active bystandership across grades in response to students bullying other students. In E. Staub (Ed.), *The psychology of good and evil: Why children, adults and groups help and harm others* (pp. 240–244). New York: Cambridge University Press.

Staub, E., & Kellett, D. S. (1972). Increasing pain tolerance by information about aversive stimuli. *Journal of Personality and Social Psychology*, *21*(2), 198–203.

Staub, E., & Noerenberg, H. (1981). Property rights, deservingness, reciprocity and friendship: The transactional character of children's sharing behavior. *Journal of Personality and Social Psychology*, *40*(2), 271–289.

Staub, E., & Pearlman, L. A. (2006). Advancing healing and reconciliation. In L. Barbanel & R. Sternberg (Eds.), *Psychological interventions in times of crisis* (pp. 213–244). New York: Springer-Verlag.

Staub, E., & Pearlman, L. A. (2009). Reducing intergroup prejudice and conflict: A commentary. *Journal of Personality and Social Psychology*, *96*(3), 588–593.

Staub, E., Pearlman, L. A., Gubin, A., & Hagengimana, A. (2005). Healing, reconciliation, forgiving and the prevention of violence after genocide or mass killing: An intervention and its experimental evaluation in Rwanda. *Journal of Social and Clinical Psychology*, *24*(3), 297–334.

Staub, E., & Sherk, L. (1970). Need for approval, children's sharing behavior and reciprocity in sharing. *Child Development*, *41*(1), 243–253.

Staub, E., & Spielman, D. (2003). Students' experience of bullying and other aspects of their lives in middle school in Belchertown. In E. Staub (Ed.), *The psychology of good and evil: Why children, adults and groups help and harm others* (pp. 227–240). New York: Cambridge University Press.

Staub, E., Tursky, B., & Schwartz, G. E. (1971). Self-control and predictability: Their effects on reactions to aversive stimulation. *Journal of Personality and Social Psychology*, *18*(2), 157–162.

Staub, E., & Vollhardt, J. (2008). Altruism born of suffering: The roots of caring and helping after experiences of personal and political victimization. *American Journal of Orthopsychiatry*, *78*(3), 267–280.

Tec, N. (1986). *When light pierced the darkness: Christian rescue of Jews in Nazi-occupied Poland*. New York: Oxford University Press.

Vallacher, R. R., Coleman, P. T., Nowak, A., & Bui-Wrzosinska, L. (2010). Rethinking intractable conflict: The perspective of dynamical systems. *American Psychologist*, *65*(4), 262–278.

Volkan, V. (2004). *Blind trust: Large groups and their leaders in times of crisis and terror*. Charlottesville, VA: Pitchstone.

Vollhardt, M., Mari, S., & Nadler, A. (2017). The social psychology of collective victimhood. *European Journal of Social Psychology*, *47*(2), 121–134.

Wessells, M. (2009). *Child soldiers: From violence to protection*. Cambridge, MA: Harvard University Press.

Whiting, B. B., & Whiting, J. W. M. (1975). *Children of six cultures: A psychocultural analysis*. Cambridge, MA: Harvard University Press.

Worchel, S., & Coutant, D. K. (2008). Between conflict and reconciliation: Toward a theory of peaceful coexistence. In A. Nadler, T. Malloy & J. D. Fisher (Eds.), *Social psychology of intergroup reconciliation* (pp. 423–446). New York: Oxford University Press.

Yarrow, M. R., & Scott, P. M. (1972). Imitation of nurturant and nonnurturant models. *Journal of Personality and Social Psychology*, *8*, 240–261.

Yarrow, M. R., & Waxler, C. Z. (1976). Dimensions and correlates of prosocial behavior in young children. *Child Development*, *47*(1), 118–125.

Zimbardo, P. (2007). *The Lucifer effect: Understanding how good people turn evil*. New York: Random House.

# 7 No peace without trust

## The trust and conflict map as a tool for reconciliation

*Mariska Kappmeier, Chiara Venanzetti and J. M. Inton-Campbell*

### Introduction

How can people envision a future together with a former enemy after experiencing a violent conflict? Consider the *de facto* division of Moldova-Transdniestria, which has persisted for decades, despite daily violence having long ceased and some measure of stability emerging between the groups. As they attempt to find a way to live side by side, how do communities like these relate to each other when narratives of violence remain so vivid in their collective memories?

Following violence, reconciliation requires a change in the relationship between the two parties, a shift from deliberate aggression and hostility to greater tolerance and peaceful coexistence. But how can such a radical change occur? Reconciliation focuses on restoring and restructuring a damaged relationship (Lederach 2001). Or as Staub (2006: 868) frames it: "Reconciliation means that victims and perpetrators, or members of hostile groups, do not see the past as defining the future, as simply a continuation of the past … [To] see the possibility of a constructive relationship." It is difficult, however, to foster the transformation of relationships under the complex circumstances of intergroup conflict, as antagonism is embedded in the fibres of society and hostilities manifest across many contexts (e.g. education, mass media, language). Even when change occurs, this may remain fragile and hard to capture, presenting a challenge for interveners and stakeholders who need a precise understanding of those factors that characterise the tangle of conflict themes and undercurrents in a post-conflict society.

In this chapter, we propose the Trust and Conflict Map as a tool for assessing the interdependent relationship between trust and the multilayered themes of conflict. We first problematise the lack of focus on trust in existing approaches to conflict assessment. Then, rooted in the empirical case study of the frozen conflict between Moldova and Transdniestria, we explore the obstacles to building strong trust relations more than two decades after open violence has ended. Lastly, we discuss how the cycle of trust relations is interwoven with social conditions and visualise it using a Trust-Conflict DNA helix model, which can be used to inform reconciliation efforts interventions at the civil society and community level of analysis.

## The missing key: Trust

Reconciliation is a process that must engage all levels of society, which demands building relationships with real people in real situations. This requires understanding the deeper psychological and subjective aspects of people's experiences, an understanding of how groups can relate to each other (Lederach 2001) and furthermore, building a positive relationship with a former enemy, trust playing a vital role in this relationship (Kappmeier and Mercy 2019).

"There is no peace without trust" is a quote often attributed to Albert Einstein, tapping into an understanding that it is trust (or lack thereof) that defines relationships. Trust can be defined as "a group's willingness to become vulnerable to the behavior and actions of an outgroup, where the outgroup's actions are outside of one's control and the outgroup is perceived to be of questionable character" (Kappmeier 2016: 135). Given that in intergroup conflict, the past interactions are mostly hostile and antagonistic between groups, it is indeed challenging for groups to make themselves vulnerable towards each other and to trust that they will not exploit such vulnerability. Kelman (2005) describes this vicious cycle as: "parties cannot enter into a peace process without some degree of mutual trust, but they cannot build trust without entering into a peace process" (2005: 641). It is only through interactions with each other that groups can learn that their trust will not be exploited (Cakal and Petrović 2017). However, this can come at a costly expense if trust is put blindly in another's hands.

Since reconciliation needs to reach all fibres of society, multiple relationships need to be changed, and multiple types of trust need to be built. For example, often reconciliation projects rely on people-to-people projects, where members from former conflicts parties are working together on a joint project. In such a context, trust can be eroded by the perception that the other lacks the skill to do meaningful work on the project – a lack of *competence-based trust*. Or worse, trust can be eroded by the concern that the other continues to have inherently malign intentions towards one group, based on a negative predisposition – a lack of *integrity-based trust*. The latter refers to the fundamental attribution error that individuals and groups explain their own behaviour through context, but the behaviour of others through predisposition (Vollhardt and Bilali 2008) and tends to be particular persistent in long-lasting, identity-based conflict (Bar-Tal and Alon 2016). This brief reflection highlights one important characteristic of trust: Trust is not a uniform construct, but it consist of different types of trust (Connelly et al. 2015; Levine and Schweitzer 2015). For instance, trust based on perceptions of competence is different than trust based on perceptions of integrity. We build on this theoretical tradition and use the multidimensional Intergroup Trust Model to capture five trust types.

## Intergroup Trust Model

One approach for capturing the elusive construct of intergroup trust is the Intergroup Trust Model (IGT-Model). In an effort to construct a comprehensive

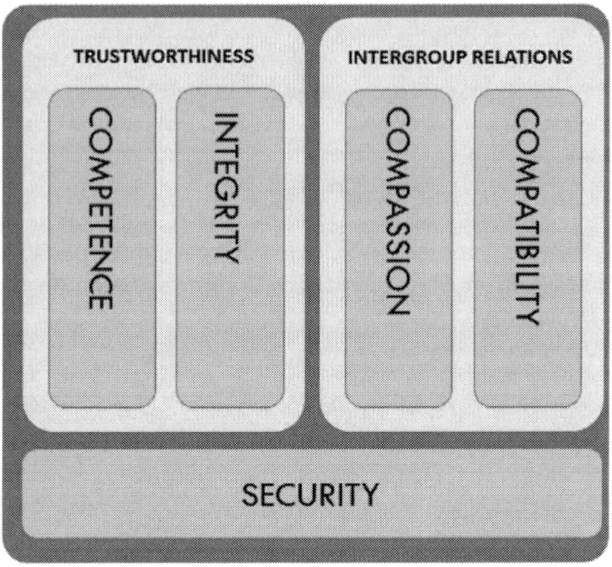


*Figure 7.1* The Intergroup Trust Model and its five dimensions.

and parsimonious model, it conceptualises intergroup trust as five types of trust, each of them a dimension that measures intergroup trust (see Figure 7.1): Competence, Integrity, Compassion, Compatibility and Security (Kappmeier 2016; Kappmeier et al. 2019; Kappmeier and Guenoun, under review).

There are three important features about the IGT-Model. First, because it captures intergroup trust, the model takes into account the particular relationships between groups and the particular perceptions of their counterparts and the perceptions of how trustworthy their counterparts are.

The first two dimensions of the IGT-Model can be clustered into dimensions attributed to the trustworthiness of the other: Competence and Integrity. Competence-based trust refers to an evaluation of the other's capacity and effectiveness. Integrity captures how the other's intentions are perceived, including to what degree their behaviour is attributed to a moral code. Together these two dimensions answer the questions of whether a party is confident the other will be able to negotiate a peace agreement and be willing to comply with that agreement.

The next two dimensions capture how the relationship between the parties is perceived: Compassion and Compatibility. Compassion describes perceived intentions concerning care and consideration towards one's own group. Compatibility encompasses the degree to which groups can relate to each other, such as through shared traditions, values and language. In terms of the reconciliation process, these elements address whether a group believes their counterparts will take their own needs and fears into account, and what common ground they share for coexistence.

Relating to perceived trustworthiness and the specific relations is the final dimension of Security – the sense of risk of harm from the other group, physically or psychologically. While Security is its own dimension, it underlies the other four (see Figure 7.1). For example, if the others are perceived to lack integrity, that they don't have a moral compass, the lack would also justify committing an atrocity against one's own group – thus eroding security-based trust.

This brings us to the other two features of the IGT-Model. The second is that the five dimensions are not independent of each other. While each captures a distinct type of trust, they are also part of a larger construct of intergroup trust, making them partly interdependent on each other (Kappmeier et al. 2019; Kappmeier and Guenoun, under review).

The third feature of this model, which makes it particularly suitable for assessing trust in intergroup conflict, is that the dimensions are not treated as a binary conglomeration: Trust or not-trust. Instead, it is possible for groups to develop, for example, Compatibility-based trust while still facing a weakness in their Integrity-based trust. Thus, the IGT-Model not only distinguishes between particular types of trust, but also to what level the types are existing or deficient. With other words: In our chapter, we are distinguishing between types of trust (the five dimensions) and level of trust – is there a deficit for each dimension or is trust developed for part of the dimensions.

## Conflict assessment

The complexity of large-scale, intergroup conflict often demands a methodical framework to guide the planning and implementation of reconciliation and peacebuilding interventions. To aid in this process, it has become common practice to carry out a conflict assessment – a systematic gathering and analysis of data concerning various aspects of the conflict. The goal is not to capture every detail of the conflict setting (Barrena 2002); instead, it should help "identify who and what are important factors driving or mitigating conflict" (Schirch 2013: 14). While there have been different approaches to developing conflict assessment tools over the last several decades (e.g. Wehr 2006; Susskind et al. 1999; Thurston 2008; Freeman and Fisher 2012; Levinger 2013), overall the topic has received little academic attention, with governmental and intergovernmental organisations filling the vacuum with a plethora of conflict assessment tools (e.g. UNICEF 2012; USAID 2012; SIDA 2006; SDC 2005). Most of the assessments have in common that they help inform interventions by enabling practitioners to understand the key stakeholders, interests and needs (Barrena 2002; Susskind and Thomas-Larmer 1999; Susskind et al. 1999; Schirch 2013).

However, across these many tools, these elements are still examined mechanically, emphasising aspects such as key actors and issues. On the other hand, social psychological dimensions, such as relationships and trust, remain neglected because they are intangible and elusive. While some scholars, such as Coleman (2003), have attempted to address this by producing a meta-framework for engaging with intergroup and relational dynamics in intractable conflict, the practice of conflict mapping and assessment has failed to develop effective methods to account, in particular, for the trust relationship between parties. This means, at best, that trust building efforts scrabble blindly to address the specific dynamics involved and, at worst, that interventions fail as they largely neglect the relational needs of the parties.

## The Trust and Conflict Map

We do not aspire to replace other assessment tools with the Trust and Conflict Map, but to provide a complementary approach that can help improve existing methods. By assessing multiple dimensions of trust alongside the relational and structural elements of conflict, more nuanced and effective interventions can be developed that address not only these aspects but how they interact and reinforce each other.

The TCM begins with a more conventional conflict map, consisting of three areas: 1) The Pillars of Conflict, 2) Relational Factors Sustaining the Conflict and 3) Structural Factors Sustaining the Conflict. This is supplemented by the addition of an intergroup trust map, which assesses trust using the five dimensions of the IGT Model: Competence, Integrity, Compassion, Compatibility and Security. This multidimensional approach to trust provides a more nuanced understanding of the relationship between conflicting parties and how to effectively facilitate reconciliation.

Although they are presented separately, it should not be forgotten that the conflict and trust components of our mapping tool are deeply intertwined. As visualised in Figure 7.2, intergroup trust interacts with the second and third areas of the conflict map through a feedback loop, each impacting the other in turn. By coupling these components in this way, the Trust Map can help us understand how conflict dynamics are intertwined with trust and trust deficits. Together, these can be employed to create a "Trust and Conflict DNA" visualisation that provides a systematic method for patterns to be more easily identified and to approach the reconciliation process from new angles.

## Utilising the TCM: The frozen conflict of Moldova-Transdniestria[1]

To illustrate how this works, we examine the case of the Moldova-Transdniestria conflict. The Moldova-Transdniestria conflict, often referred to as the Transdniestria conflict, is a frozen conflict in dire need of reconciliation that centres around the secession of the Transdniestria region from Moldova. Moldova is a landlocked country and former Soviet republic located between Romania and Ukraine. In the turmoil of following the collapse of the Soviet Union, Moldova strove towards independence, seeking closer ties with its western neighbour Romania. The eastern region of Transdniestria rejected this move, seeing it as highly threatening. Transdniestria is separated from western Moldova by the river Dniester, and prides itself on its close cultural and economic ties to Russia. The strains between these regions grew until Transdniestria declared its

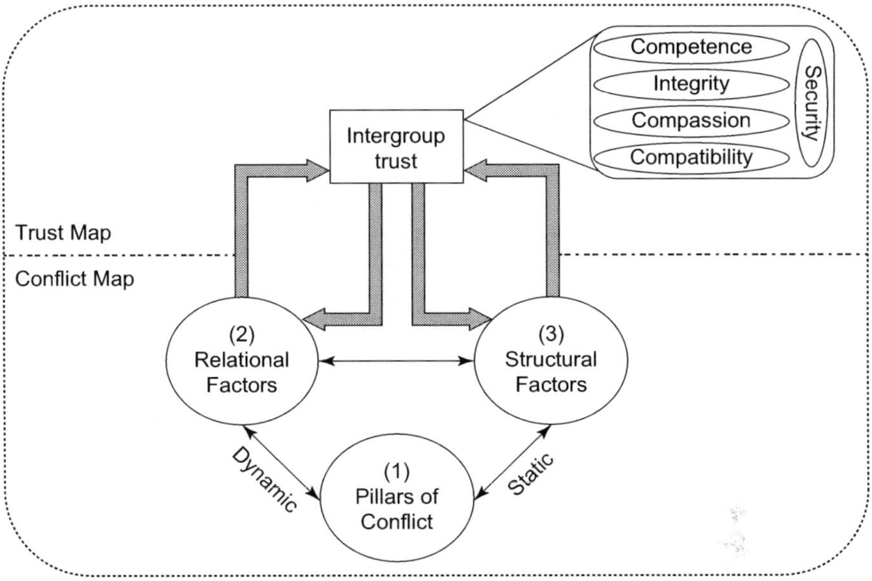


*Figure 7.2* Trust and Conflict Map.

independence unilaterally in August of 1991 as the Pridnestrovian Moldavian Republic (PMR). This was mirrored by Moldova, which also declared its independence from the Soviet Union, while including Transdniestria in its borders. Transdniestria rejected this inclusion, leading to escalation between both sides into an armed conflict in 1992, when Moldovan forces crossing the Dniester and engaging in combat. The Russian 14th Army intervened on behalf of Transdniestria and continues to be based there (International Crisis Group 2003).

On 21 July 1992, a formal ceasefire was signed between Russia and Moldova. However, since that time, all attempts to settle the conflict have failed. The situation is now considered a "frozen conflict," manifesting in a separation of land and civil society, among other aspects. Transdniestria has developed into a *de facto* state, with its own currency and governmental structure, but is unrecognised by the international community (Kappmeier et al. 2012). In the past three decades, the frozen conflict was omnipresent in all sectors of Moldovan and Transdniestrian society, shaping their relations and the barriers towards reconciliation. Unfortunately, there is also a lack of political will on both sides to solve the conflict, as both political and economic elites benefit from the stalemate (International Crisis Group 2003). However, while the pathway towards a peace agreement remains blocked at the political level, civil society provides an opportunity for peaceful engagement and creating spaces for multiple reconciliation processes. Applying the TCM at the community and civil society level of Track III diplomacy helps to map out areas in which tensions remain high and trust low, as well how to strengthen these with targeted interventions.

Within the context of this conflict, the TCM was inductively developed based upon qualitative research. A total of 41 interviews were conducted (20 representatives from Moldovan civil society, 17 from Transdniestrian civil society and 4 external experts). Twenty-one of the interviewees also filled out a questionnaire which explicitly captured their trust of the other side, using the five dimensions of the IGT-Model. All interviewees fulfilled the following three inclusion criteria: First, they came from a wide range of civil society sectors, including academia, politics, and economics; second, they had an influential professional position that gave them nuanced insight into how the conflict affected their sector; third, they had to cover the diversity of opinions and positions within Moldovan and Transdniestrian society to capture a comprehensive perception of trust between the two sides. To build the TCM, we strove for a heterogeneous, but representative representation for both societies. Table 7.1 displays the different sectors our participants represented, with a slight gender bias towards men.

*Table 7.1* Professional background of interview sample, differentiating by large-group and gender

| *Moldovan (n = 20)* | *Male* | *Female* | *Total* |
|---|---|---|---|
| Academic | 2 | 2 | 4 |
| Analyst | 1 | 0 | 1 |
| Politician | 2 | 0 | 2 |
| NGO | 2 | 1 | 3 |
| Municipal | 2 | 0 | 2 |
| Economist | 0 | 1 | 1 |
| Journalist | 1 | 1 | 2 |
| Other | 4 | 1 | 5 |
| Total Moldovan | 14 | 6 | 20 |
| Transdniestrian (*n = 17*) | | | |
| Academic | 0 | 3 | 3 |
| Analyst | 2 | 1 | 3 |
| Politician | 3 | 0 | 3 |
| NGO | 3 | 3 | 6 |
| Municipal | 0 | 0 | 0 |
| Economist | 0 | 0 | 0 |
| Journalist | 1 | 0 | 1 |
| Other | 1 | 0 | 1 |
| Total Transdniestrian | 10 | 7 | 17 |
| Experts (*n = 5*) | | | |
| Political Advisor | 2 | 0 | 2 |
| Analyst | 1 | 0 | 1 |
| International Observer (EUBAM) | 0 | 1 | 1 |
| Total | 3 | 1 | 4 |

## Trust Map: The Intergroup Trust models

### *Perceived trustworthiness*

The first area of the Trust Map aims to understand how each group perceives the other conflict party by uncovering the first two trust dimensions – the perception that members of the other group are *competent* and have *integrity*.

1) Competence

Competence-based trust refers to the perception that the other party is competent – that they have the correct knowledge, as well as the skill, to perform their roles well (e.g. for reconciliation). In the context of Moldova, civil society overwhelmingly reported a lack of trust in this dimension, particularly linked to a lack of knowledge as participants commented upon the other group as being ill-informed about the conflict. The lack of knowledge accuracy is closely connected to the conflict factor of structures influencing public opinion, which we will return to in the third area of the conflict map. For example, one Moldovan explicitly linked lack of knowledge accuracy to the role of the media, explaining that Transdniestrians based their lack of trust in Moldova on inaccurate media coverage, "Because mass-media talks about it every day. When you hear every day that Moldova is the enemy, you begin to believe it, and when people keep living with that mentality it is very hard to change" (Interview September 2009).

2) Integrity

Integrity-based trust denotes the perception that the other group has a moral code that guides their intentions and behaviour, is honest and is not driven solely by self-interest. This is one of the more eroded trust dimensions, with both Moldovans and Transdniestrians perceiving each other as an aggressive and suppressive counterpart – a perception that undermines Integrity-based trust on both sides. For example, Transdniestrians see the Moldovan preference for unification as a move to dominate Transdniestria. Moldovan regulations are seen as harassment, with the objective of hurting Transdniestria, "And after those (MD-imposed) regulations, our population (TD) suffered more. Some factories were closed. And more people had to emigrate after that. The last eight years show that it was used as a method of negative treatment with Transdniestrians" (Interview October 2009). There is a perception that these regulations were not passed with good intentions, but were instead intended to worsen living conditions in Transdniestria to force them to agree to unification by making the stalemate too burdensome. From the Moldovan point of view, however, part of the drive towards unification is believed to be based on compassion and should create Compassion-based trust, leading into the impacts this has on trust relations, which we address in the next section.

### *Perceived intergroup relations*

While the previous category focused on the trustworthiness attributed to the other party, the next area of the Trust Map examines the perception each side has of the relationship between them. To understand this, the next two trust dimensions of Compassion and Compatibility are needed.

3) Compassion

Compassion-based trust is the perception that the other conflict party cares for one's own group, including consideration of one's needs and fears. Engaging with another group who is believed to have no compassion towards one's own is, at best, extremely challenging.

Interestingly, while Transdniestrians often associated negative motives with Moldova's stance towards unification, within Moldova there persists the perception that Transdniestrians cannot be left behind in their oppressive situation. As this Moldovan NGO representative states,

> I would never want Transdniestria to gain its independence because it will mean that it keeps going with their oppressive system. And it is not fair to those people, those are our people, they are Moldovans just like we are.
>
> (Interview September 2009)

Thus, from a Moldovan point of view, not giving up on unification also includes a compassion-based component, though the Transdniestrians mainly see it as self-interest. A space in which Compassion-based trust could be built upon is missed since the motives are not understood by each other to be driven by genuine compassion.

4) Compatibility

Compatibility-based trust encompasses the perception that the other party has some degree of commonality with one's own group. This can be based upon a shared language, culture or customs, but also emotional accessibility and the perception that groups can relate to one another. As discussed above, Moldovans still believe that Transdniestrians were part of "their people," and even Transdniestrians have noted a certain commonality. As one Transdniestrian participants said, "No matter what kind of holiday we have, we would remember the traditions. For example, if it is a Moldovan holiday, we would prepare Moldovan food, we would sing Moldovan songs" (Interview October 2009). Furthermore, interviewees on both sides often felt it was important to share that they had friends, sometimes even family, on the other side of the conflict.

5) Security

Security refers to whether the other group is seen as threatening to one's own group, including both physical threats, such as armed violence, and psychological threats, such as erasure of one's identity. Among the Transdniestrian interviewees in particular, there was no shortage of security-related concerns, both

MD TD

| | | | | | | | | | | | | | |
|---|---|---|---|---|---|---|---|---|---|---|---|---|---|
| Competence | (1) | 1.5 | (2) | 2.5 | (3) | 3.5 | (4) | 4.5 | (5) | 5.5 | (6) | 6.5 | (7) |
| Integrity | (1) | 1.5 | (2) | 2.5 | (3) | 3.5 | (4) | 4.5 | (5) | 5.5 | (6) | 6.5 | (7) |
| Compassion | (1) | 1.5 | (2) | 2.5 | (3) | 3.5 | (4) | 4.5 | (5) | 5.5 | (6) | 6.5 | (7) |
| Compatibility | (1) | 1.5 | (2) | 2.5 | (3) | 3.5 | (4) | 4.5 | (5) | 5.5 | (6) | 6.5 | (7) |
| Security | (1) | 1.5 | (2) | 2.5 | (3) | 3.5 | (4) | 4.5 | (5) | 5.5 | (6) | 6.5 | (7) |

MD n = 13
TD n = 8

*Figure 7.3* The IGT-Profile for Moldovan and Transdniestrian interviewees.

physical and psychological. Indeed, they felt so insecure that they were insistent on demanding that the Russian Army be allowed to stay on Transdniestrian soil under any agreement ending the conflict. One interviewee proclaimed that, of all the proposed steps towards reconciliation, removing the Russian Army was the only one to which Transdniestria could not agree. The Moldovans, on the other hand, felt the constant presence of the Russian Army was a threat towards the independent status of the country, fearing re-annexation reminiscent of the Soviet Union. Additionally, the perception that the Russian Army could cross over to the Moldovan side of the Dniester river at any time poses a physical threat. Interestingly enough, both sides dismiss each other's fears as unfounded and inspired by propaganda.

The qualitative data gathered through interview can be complemented through quantitative data deriving from the questionnaires, which captured the Moldovans and Transdniestrians' trust of the other side, using the five dimensions of the IGT-Model. This tool allows the creation of a trust profile (IGT-Profile), which can give an indication which trust dimensions are positively developed and can be possible resources, which conditions are negatively pronounced and therefore can be a strain for possible reconciliation intervention. The IGT-Profile also displays symmetries and asymmetries between the two groups regarding the prevalence of each trust dimension. Figure 7.3 displays the trust profile based on the 21 Moldovans and Transdniestrians who filled out the questionnaire:

While the reported sample for the questionnaire is small, it still reveals important tendencies: First, it shows that the trust profiles between Moldovans and Transdniestrians are largely symmetric. The biggest gap is for security-based trust, where Moldovans expressed a lower security-based trust than the Transdniestrian. From the qualitative interview we learned that the lowered security-based trust is mostly linked to the presence of the Russian Army, which is still stationed in Transdniestria. Second, the questionnaire indicate that integrity-based trust is the most eroded trust dimension, something that was matched in the interviews as well.

The IGT-Profile can be used for a large sample to get a more representative presentation of the trust relations, but it also can be used for smaller samples, such in this case. In this case, the IGT-Profiles still provide conflict parties and potential interveners with useful graphic data about the often implicit and hard to grasp construct of trust. The TMQ-Profiles can be handed back to the participants as an illustration of the group perception of each, as well as the individual response, which can be a base for explicit work on trust with the participants.

In summary, the IGT-Model provides a parsimonious framework that captures the complexity of trust without getting overwhelmed by its vastness. It allows the creation of Trust Profiles, which identify dimensions with trust deficits and dimensions where the parties trust each other. In particular, better-developed dimensions, such as compatibility-based trust in the Moldovan-Transdniestrian case, offer potential pathways for community-based reconciliation projects, even in times when conflict has severely undermined others trust dimensions.

However, as the example from those interviewed showed, the trust dimension is interwoven with different conflict domains, such as the roles of the Russian Army, the representation in the media and education of each other etc. To get a full picture of how trust is embedded in the intergroup relations, it cannot be treated in a vacuum but needs to be embedded in the conflict dynamic – which are captured through the Conflict Map, the second component of our tool.

## The Conflict Map

As previously explained, the Conflict Map portion of the TCM can help organise and improve upon traditional methods of conflict analysis. This map is divided into three areas, with each bringing a different layer of understanding to the conflict: 1) Pillars of the Conflict, 2) Relational Factors Sustaining the Conflict and 3) Structural Factors Sustaining the Conflict. The first area, Pillars of the Conflict, represents a descriptive cornerstone of the conflict by defining the principal stakeholders, as well as the language and terminology used to frame the conflict and its roots. The second, Relational Factors Sustaining the Conflict, captures those elements, negative and positive, which describe the relationship between the conflict parties. Finally, Structural Factors Sustaining the Conflict include the more static systems that perpetuate the conflict, such as propaganda and media restrictions, bias within the education system, or language barriers.

1) *Pillars of the conflict*

The first area of the Conflict Map captures the backbone of the conflict and addresses traditional conflict analysis themes. This section does not readily overlap with the Trust Map, as it assesses more static and descriptive aspects of the conflict's background, including key actors, their preferred terminology and the issues that these parties identify as the roots of the conflict. This begins by identifying the key actors and stakeholders, then the accepted terminology employed by each of these groups. There may be important differences in how these parties label aspects of the conflict based upon their group's narrative and by understanding these tensions we can grasp some of the subtle dynamics of the conflict to better tailor interventions for specific groups. This can also help us understand how our own use of language may introduce biases into our work. For example, Moldovans refer to the conflict as the "Transdniestrian conflict," a term shared by the international community, while the Transdniestrians prefer the "Moldovan-Transdniestrian Conflict," since it emphasises the role of both groups. From here, this section dives into the typically contested roots of the conflict, identifying what each group views as the core issues of the conflict.

Examination of the Moldovan and Transdniestrian interviews provided a useful picture of these Pillars. As expected, Moldova and Transdniestria were shown to be the primary stakeholders, with Romania and Russia as the international power players. Interestingly, the roots of the conflict were mainly attributed to the influence of these external players or the self-interest of political leaders on each side. This suggests a strong belief on both sides that the people of each group are not necessarily at conflict with one another, with hostilities being sustained by outside forces, such as Romania and Russia, and the leaders of Moldova and Transdniestria.

2) *Relational factors sustaining the conflict*

In this area of the Conflict Map, we move from a descriptive understanding to a more interpretive one. By centring the relational issues perpetuating the conflict, we begin to see the specific dynamics that form a feedback loop with the five dimensions of trust enumerated earlier, impacting reconciliation both positively and negatively. Therefore, this second area consists of two themes: *Factors Suggesting Relational Weaknesses* and *Factors Suggesting Relational Strengths*. Relational weaknesses are examined through: 1) Misalignments in the groups' perceptions of interests, and 2) the alignment of fears. Then, in an effort to also understand the potential relational strengths between the parties, the map explores perceived similarities between groups and existing peaceful, or even friendly, contact between groups, though these will only be briefly discussed here.

The factors belonging to this second area of the Conflict Map are naturally interlinked with the dimensions of intergroup trust, as they undermine or empower different aspects of trust between the parties. Thanks to the Trust Profiles previously introduced, practitioners can anticipate which factors in a relationship are capable of damaging specific aspects of intergroup trust, whereas other factors are expected to contribute to conserving or protecting it. In the case of the Moldova-Transdniestria conflict, the Trust Profiles lead us to expect detrimental relational factors in the second area of the Conflict Map that compromise Integrity- and Compassion-based trust. On the other hand, it also suggests relational strength factors will probably emerge in the more promising levels of Compatibility-, Competence- and Security-based trust. As we will see later on, the interwoven relation between conflict aspects and trust dimensions is the basis for generating another tool which can help practitioners to visualise the particular post-conflict situation they face: The Trust-Conflict DNA model.

### *Factors suggesting relational weaknesses*

#### *Misalignment in perceptions of interests*

Moldovan and Transdniestrian interviewees brought up five to six interests as the ones that their respective groups sought to protect through the conflict or desire to satisfy in a settlement. Table 7.2 illustrates that while some of the interests overlap (striving for a good life and economic development for the region), there are major areas of misalignment, signalled by a lightning bolt symbol.

While this analysis indicates where the points of overlap are, these are insufficient to advance peace if the parties themselves do not have an accurate understanding of the other group's interests. For example, Transdniestrian interviewees were able to correctly identify some of the Moldovan interests, seeing the Moldovan interest in reunification as being motivated by a desire for economic gain. Yet Moldovan interviewees claimed to desire reunification not only for economic reasons, but also because they believed Transdniestrians and Moldovans were one people. Likewise, while Moldovan interviewees correctly understood most of the interests of the Transdniestrians, they failed to understand just how important independence was to Transdniestrians. While the Moldovan interviewees recognised that Transdniestrians wanted independence and a better economic future, they typically assumed that the Transdniestrians cared much more about economic improvement than independence.

If the two sides do not accurately understand one another's interests, they are bound to struggle in efforts to resolve the conflict. The Moldovans may assume, for instance, that the Transdniestrians would give up on independence if the appropriate economic bargain could be struck, while the Transdniestrians may

*Table 7.2* Comparison of Moldovan and Transdniestrian interests

| | *Moldovan interest* | | *Transdniestrian interest* |
|---|---|---|---|
| 1 | Reunification with Moldova | ⚡ | Independence and recognition |
| 2 | A good life – economic stability | | A good life – economic stability |
| 3 | Economic development of the region | | Economic development of the region |
| 4 | European integration | ⚡ | Unity with Russia |
| 5 | Ending the suppression of Transdniestrian society by unification | ⚡ | Self-determination |
| 6 | | | Being an equal partner |

assume that the Moldovans would give up on reunification if it weren't sufficiently profitable. Yet these assumptions, based on an incomplete understanding of each side's interests, may lead to offering the wrong incentives, and frustration may grow when both sides feel that ulterior moral motives are not met. By correctly understanding each side's interests, it may be possible to better incentivise peace and encourage building trust. Thus, this area of the Conflict Map measures how each group perceives the interests that the other group is protecting, as well as how members of each group perceive their own group's interests, to uncover the misunderstandings that typically exist.

### *Alignment of fears*

In the case of Transdniestria and Moldova, it may be significant that Moldovan interviewees frequently brought up the Transdniestrians' fears, such as fear of Romanification, suggesting they were able to identify them, and it perhaps gave them an understanding of how to alleviate those fears. Among Transdniestrian interviewees, on the other hand, there was only a single mention of Moldovan fears, suggesting that they may not be as attuned to these matters.

The map seeks therefore to explain how each group understands the fears of the other group. Fear can be a powerful motivator, particularly when the fear is a threat to a group's identity or even survival. Agreements will not be reached if the conflicting parties do not believe there are sufficient guarantees that their fears will not become reality. Yet if opposing sides do not fully and accurately understand the fears of their opponents, their own actions may serve not to allay those fears, but may even heighten them. Importantly, understanding the extent to which there is an alignment or misunderstanding can help inform strategies for intervention.

## ***Factors suggesting strengths in the relationship***

Despite the wide variety of potential weaknesses in the relationship between conflicting parties, there may be some potential strengths in the relationship, even in some of the most difficult conflict settings. However, these positive aspects may not be noted equally across conflicting parties and it might not be clear how they are related to some of the other aspects of the relational issues sustaining the conflict, such as its power dynamics. An important contribution of the TCM is that it helps account for such potential resources, like perceived similarities between groups. For example, instances in which interviewees note similarities in their values and religions, similar challenges faced by the lower-classes of each group or having friends or family members on the other side of the conflict. Furthermore, regardless of the differences between Moldovans and Transdniestrians, it seems significant that members of both societies were readily willing to point out, without prompting, positive elements in their relations with the other group, suggesting that there is some base of common friendly contact that can be a point of entry for improving relations.

3) *Structural factors sustaining the conflict*

While the second area of the Conflict Map examines relational issues, the third area of the Conflict Map assesses the structural issues that sustain the conflict. In the Moldavan-Transdniestrian conflict, four themes emerged as particularly prevalent: 1) Leadership, 2) language, 3) education and 4) mass media.

### *Leadership*

Leadership accounts for different subfactors, including perceived corruption or criticism of elites. Interviewees on both sides claimed that political elites lack the will to solve the conflict and, closely connected to this, elites refuse to engage unless it benefits their own economic or power interests. This reinforces the notion that the root of the conflict is not a clash between people but between their leaders. There was a strong perception on both sides that the political elites benefit from the status quo and therefore have an interest in maintaining the conflict, whether for economic reasons, personal political interests or an interest in maintaining their own governmental organisations. This indicates, that in the Moldova-Transdniestria context, reconciliation might be more successful by targeting the community level.

### *Language*

Language, as well, is an important factor to consider. Differences in language between Moldovans and Transdniestrians stood out as a clear point of contention and a sustaining factor of the conflict. This was pointed to as proof that the two groups had truly separate identities, and thus were not compatible as the single, unified society that the Moldovans wanted. Transdniestrians were afraid that Moldovans would take away their Russian language and identity. For the Moldovans, however, the issue of language concerned compassion: they noted that, in Transdniestria, the Romanian language was looked down upon and seen as inferior to Russian. One Moldovan interviewee articulated, "People from [Transdniestria] are afraid not to speak in Russian because they might be treated with inferiority" (Interview September 2009).

### *Education*

Closely related to language is education as a divisive issue. On both sides the questions arise: Is education accessible in the Romanian or Russian language, what content is taught, do the schools follow the Russian or European curriculum more closely, how is history and the role of the different countries presented, is Russia presented as a peacekeeper or an aggressor? Both Moldovans and Transdniestrians recognise the potential a shared education has to strengthen an interdependent future for Moldova and Transdniestria, but they also recognise that it currently undermines the relationship. By following different curricula, Compatibility-based trust slowly erodes from generation to generation. Also, by comparing and contrasting each other's education system, Competence-based trust is undermined, as both sides believe that the other has not received a good education, both in regard to their joint history or in building important skills to be an independent country.

### *Influence of mass media*

Of the structures influencing public opinion, the media, and more specifically, propaganda, was the most significant factor for both Moldovan and Transdniestrian interviewees. Moldovan interviewees were upset at the propaganda they believed was prevalent in Transdniestria. They noted that Moldova was presented as Transdniestria's enemy, and that this was a major barrier to a resolution of the conflict. Participants readily pointed out that this propaganda was based on erroneous or outdated beliefs that Moldova was very closely tied to Romania, and that these two groups would team up against Transdniestria, and thus undermining Transdniestrians' Security-based trust.

## Putting together the pieces: The Trust-Conflict DNA helix model

In reviewing the Conflict Map, it became evident that this conflict, like most, is multifaceted and there is a need to not only identify the different dynamics at play, but also how they connect and interact. Although presented separately, the trust and conflict sections of the mapping tool interlace. Indeed, the second and third areas are intertwined with intergroup trust in a triangle that embodies the trust relationship. By combining the Conflict Map and the Trust Map into a single analysis tool, practitioners can gain deep and structured insight into the dynamics of the conflict with which they are working, aiding reconciliation goals. However, the connections between the Trust Map and these two areas of the Conflict Map are complex, and can present a chicken-or-the-egg dilemma: Which came first, the relational and structural factors perpetuating the conflict, or the deficits in the trust relationship between the conflict parties. By structuring the data in such a systematic way, it can be analysed from different angles, allowing patterns to be more easily identified, especially between elements of the conflict and the trust relationship, "the glue that holds relationships together" (Lewicki and Wiethoff 2000: 86). Those trust dimensions or conflict factors that come up most often in interviews point to the key issues of the conflict, and may signal particularly fruitful points of entry for targeted interventions. The Trust-Conflict DNA is a tool to visualise how the types of trust that shape intergroup relations manifest across the different relational and structural conflict themes in just this way.

### *Trust-Conflict DNA for relational factors*

The second area of the Conflict Map captures the relationship between conflict groups, including categories that can create or undermine the context for

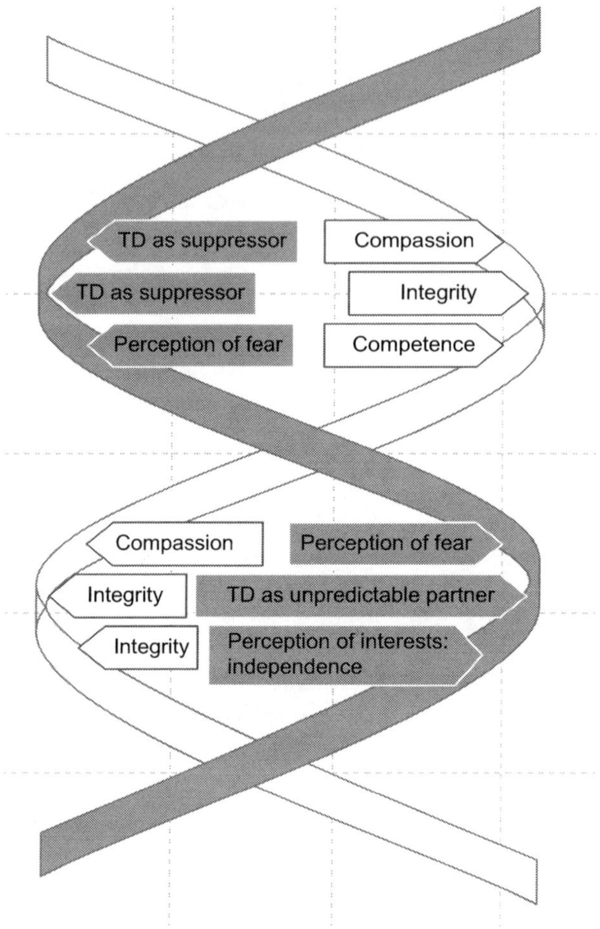


*Figure 7.4* The Moldovan Trust-Conflict DNA for relational factors.[2]

developing trust. As we can see in the images below (see Figures 7.3 and 7.4), the interwoven relation between trust dimensions (in green) and relational conflict factors (in red) can be represented as a unique DNA helix specific to the Moldova-Transdniestria conflict. Below, a Trust-Conflict DNA has been generated from the map of each party's perceptions of the relational factors of the conflict and the impacted trust dimensions.

As illustrated in the picture, the elements from both the Trust and Conflict Map are inextricably entangled with each other, but their connections differ for the two parties. For example, the Moldovans perceive the other party's interest in being independent as a nation as being linked to a lack of Integrity (Figure 7.4), as found in the following quotation: "[Transdniestrians] are becoming parasites,

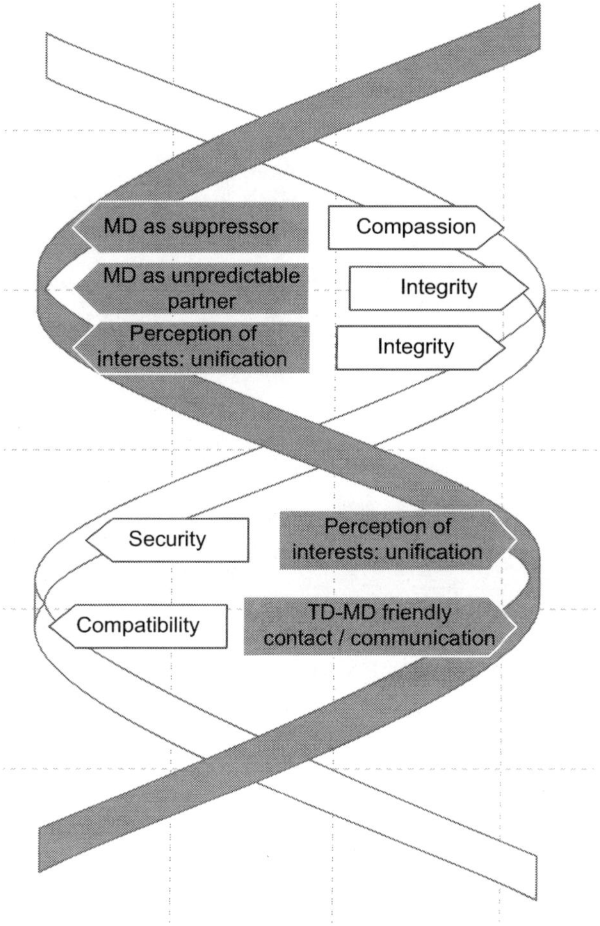


*Figure 7.5* The Transdniestrian Trust-Conflict DNA.

and they have a profit from being unrecognised, because if they are unrecognized everyone is sorry for them and give them opportunities, more than Moldova has" (Interview September 2009). On the other hand, for Transdniestrians, it is not only a lack of Integrity but also a fear for their own Security that is associated with the Moldovan interest in unification (Figure 7.5), "There are some parties that want to expand the territory of Moldova and reunite the left and the right part of the Dniester River … Moldova wants to take control over Transdniestria's economic potential" (Interview October 2010).

However, a more promising finding is that Transdniestrians and Moldovans both recognise the compatibility between them at the societal level – and express their Compatibility-based trust towards each other: "It helps [to trust each other] because in the most part there are the same traditions among people on the both sides and they also have relatives and friends on the both sides of the river" (Interview October 2010).

Employing the tool in this manner provides a unique way for each party to inform tailored interventions that recognise and welcome the viewpoints of principal stakeholders. Understanding how relational characteristics of the conflict are interwoven with dimensions of trust can help untangle the weak knots – and leverage the strengths – of the relationship to move in the direction of a fruitful reconciliation.

### *Trust-Conflict DNA for structural factors*

Once more, the Trust-Conflict DNA in Figures 7.5 and 7.6 illustrates how conflict elements connect to trust dimensions, this time focusing upon the structural factors identified in the third area of the Conflict Map. As we can see, for the Moldovans, language is a point of contention associated with Compassion and Security (Figure 7.6), "In Transdniestria, you can very strongly feel the difference between Russian people and Romanian people. People from there are afraid not to speak in Russian because they might be treated with inferiority and without respect" (Interview October 2010). However, for Transdniestrians, language issues are interlinked with a perceived lack of Compatibility between the two parties (Figure 7.7), "As in Transdniestria, most people speak only Russian, but in Moldova, only Romanian, so it is still separated. As someone said, soon young people will not speak in Romanian, not in Russian, but in English" (Interview October 2010). Using this visualisation organises the structural factors of the conflict, and connects the ways they are interrelated to different dimensions of trust for the two parties.

The Trust-Conflict DNA also highlights contradictory themes, such as the ambiguous role of compatibility-based trust. When it comes to the relational factors of the conflict maps, the shared traditions, language and values were brought up consistently by Moldovans and Transdniestrians alike. However, when reflecting on the structural factors, such as education and language, the disappearing compatibility between both sides becomes apparent, particular for the Transdniestrian side. It also became apparent that compatibility-based trust as resource will be harder to maintain and use for the younger generation of Moldovans and Transdniestrians who have only experienced the frozen conflict. As a take-away, the Trust and Conflict Map, with its accompanying Trust-Conflict DNA, further visualises in a systematic and structured way the different dynamics at play in the conflict.

## Conclusion

A society that is truly on the path to reconciliation following direct violence is one where groups involved in a conflict move beyond perceiving their counterparts as hostile enemies that are incapable of change and to a point where their painful history doesn't define the future and towards seeing their shared humanity

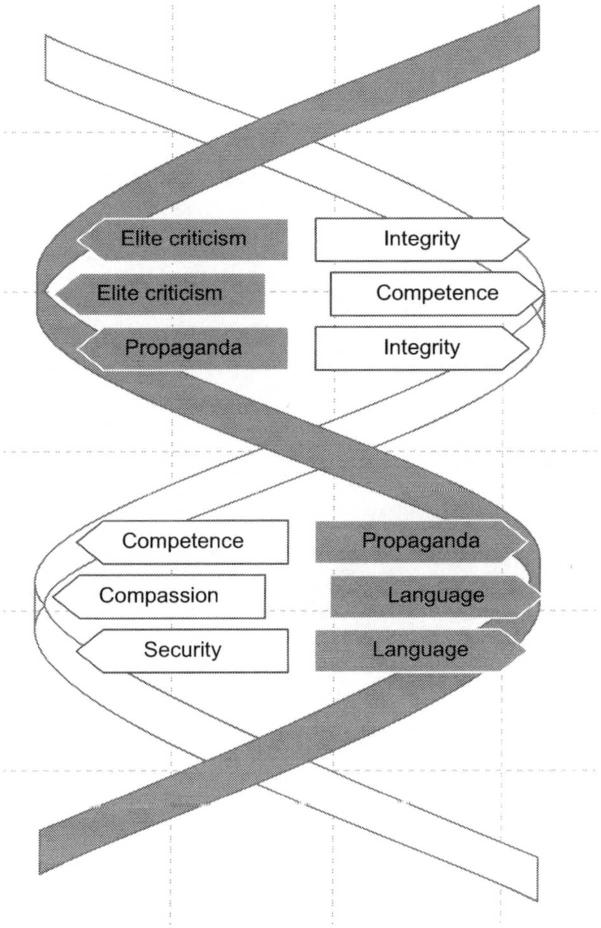


*Figure 7.6* Moldovan Trust-Conflict DNA for structural factors.

(Staub 2006). For potential peacebuilders to support people towards envisioning a shared future, they must find a way to make sense of the conflict, as well the relational and structural dynamics that continue to feed the division. As we have argued, the key to unlocking these changes, especially in a frozen conflict, comes from addressing the role of trust, or the lack thereof, in facilitating or obstructing reconciliation.

In the past, despite the consensus around the importance of trust in reconciliation, trust has either been neglected or treated as a binary question when analysing conflicts (e.g. UNICEF 2012; USAID 2012; SIDA 2006; SDC 2005). Even when trust is not completely neglected (like it is instead in some tools, e.g. SIDA 2006), available tools only broadly measure intergroup trust (often through two

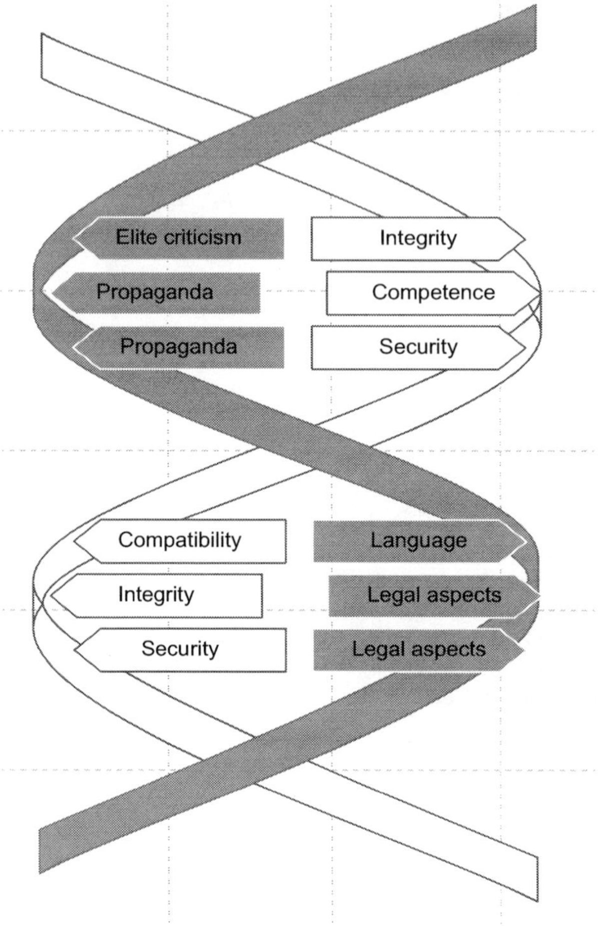


*Figure 7.7* Transdniestrian Trust-Conflict DNA for structural factors.

or three items), and therefore their evaluation falls short on identifying the shades and complex dynamics of this elusive concept and its relation with the conflict. Additionally, the conventional approach to conflict assessment often isolates the static and structural aspects of a conflict using a mechanical, check-list approach. This further leaves practitioners grasping after the social and relational processes that interact with trust to impede reconciliation.

This is why we have proposed the Trust and Conflict Map as a tool for distilling richer and more useful knowledge to inform practitioners in identifying pathways towards the needed improvement in trust and cooperation. This tool allows peacebuilders to employ a flexible coding scheme and booklet to develop a tailored map for a specific conflict,[3] evaluating intergroup relations along five dimensions of intergroup trust, as well as mapping the pillars and the structural and relational factors of a conflict. Furthermore, the TCM can be employed to organise the raw data in a way that reduces its complexity while also highlighting important findings through the Trust-Conflict DNA visualisation tool. By visualising the results of both the trust mapping and conflict mapping as linked strands of a DNA double-helix, it makes it simple to recognise the interconnectedness of different conflict factors and intergroup trust dimensions.

With all of this considered, the TCM and Trust-Conflict DNA tools represent three important steps forward for the field of conflict analysis and reconciliation. First, this system allows researchers to both structure their inquiries and organise information in a way that helps manage large amounts of raw data without losing their richness, all while keeping an eye on the purpose of designing reconciliation processes. Second, although the coding scheme can be very detailed, the tool is sufficiently flexible that practitioners can adapt its implementation to the specific context; by dropping fine-tuned sub-categories of the tool and employing more general categories, the coding schemes can be adjusted to fit the objectives of a specific conflict assessment. Third, these tools illustrate how conflict mapping approaches can expand to encompass socio-psychological dimensions of intergroup relations, such as trust, through the inclusion of a systematic trust assessment that maps interconnections with conflict dynamics.

Further research is needed to elaborate how best to tailor interventions to address specific deficits in intergroup trust dimensions. Even so, the TCM already hints at how this more nuanced understanding can lend itself to improved interventions. For example, the initial analysis of the Moldova-Transdniestria Conflict has identified a widespread perception on both sides that the leaders of both groups gain from existing divisions. With trust in leadership lacking, but shared perceptions of high compatibility-based trust, the assessment suggests that people from both groups may be more amenable to reconciliation efforts bringing people together at the community level, such as approaches taken from Track II and Track III diplomacy. This would allow practitioners to move beyond the strategic arm-wrestling that leads to a stalemate at the level of elite reconciliation efforts, while helping identify concrete spaces for the otherwise elusive community level trust-building and reconciliation to take place within. Crucially, the TCM analysis also has the advantage of helping peacebuilders detect delicate spaces in intergroup relations that need to be protected to prevent the relationship from deteriorating further, while shedding light on these potential points of entry.

Kelman was astute in identifying that while trust is vital for building peace, peace is also crucial in building trust; there exists a feedback loop between trust and the dynamical factors of conflict that continue to divide societies long after open violence has come to an end. If practitioners and researchers better understand how shortcomings in specific dimensions of trust impact and are impacted by relational and structural factors of a given conflict, it begins to seem feasible to arrest this cycle to create the soil out of which robust reconciliation can grow.

## Acknowledgement

We would like to thank Ati Waldman for her contribution to an earlier draft of this chapter.

## Notes

1 In Russian, Transdniestria is called Pridnestrovie. In its English translation, numerous spellings exist. For ease of reading it is often spelled as Transniestria. Here, we use the form "Transdniestria" as an appropriate hybrid between the Romanian and Russian spellings, and one which has also been used in numerous international publications. For an extended explanation of the problems in translating the word Pridnestrovie from Russian to English, see Troebst 2003.
2 MD = Moldova; TD = Transdniestria
3 The coding booklets, semi-structured interview guidelines and other materials are available upon request. Researchers and practitioners are encouraged to employ these associated materials to more easily generate salient data.

## References

Barrena, I. (2002). *Conflict analysis. Conflict-sensitive approaches to development, humanitarian assistance and peace building: Tools for peace and conflict impact assessment.* Retrieved from United States Institute of Peace website: http://www.usip.org/files/file/chapter_2__266.pdf

Bar-Tal, D., & Alon, I. (2016). Sociopsychological approaches to trust (or distrust): Concluding comments. In I. Alon & D. Bar-Tal (Eds.), *The role of trust in conflict resolution: The Israeli-Palestinian case and beyond* (pp. 311–334). Cham, Switzerland: Springer International Publishing.

Cakal, H., & Petrovic, N. (2017). InterGroup contact and ingroup identification as predictors of intergroup attitudes and forgiveness in the Serbian context: The moderating role of exposure to positive information. *Primenjena Psihologija, 10*(4), 477–497. doi: 10.19090/pp.2017.4.477-497

Coleman, P. T. (2003). Characteristics of protracted, intractable conflict: Towards the development of a metaframework-I. *Peace and Conflict: Journal of Peace Psychology, 9*(1), 1–37. doi: 10.1207/S15327949PAC0901_01

Connelly, B. L., Crook, T. R., Combs, J. G., Ketchen, D. J., & Aguinis, H. (2015). Competence- and integrity-based trust in interorganizational relationships: Which matters more? *Journal of Management, 44*(3), 919–945. doi: 10.1177/0149206315596813

Freeman, L. J., & Fisher, R. J. (2012). Comparing a problem-solving workshop to a conflict assessment framework: Conflict analysis versus conflict assessment in practice. *Journal of Peacebuilding and Development, 7*(1), 66–80. doi: 10.1080/15423166.2012.719358

International Crisis Group. (2003). *Moldova - No quick fix ICG Europe report* (Vol. 147). Retrieved from International Crisis Group website.

Kappmeier, M. (2016). Trusting the enemy - Towards a comprehensive understanding of trust in intergroup conflict. *Peace and Conflict: Journal of Peace Psychology, 22*(2), 134–144. doi: 10.1037/pac0000159

Kappmeier, M., & Guenoun, B. (under review). Conceptualizing trust between groups: An empirical validation of the five-dimensional intergroup trust model. *Peace and Conflict: Journal of Peace Psychology.*

Kappmeier, M., Guenoun, B., & Campbell, R. (2019). They are us? The mediating effects of compatibility-based trust on the relationship between discrimination and overall trust. *New Zealand Journal of Psychology*, *48*(1), 97–105.

Kappmeier, M., & Mercy, A. (2019). The long road from cold war to warm peace: Building shared collective memory through trust. *Journal of Social and Political Psychology*, *7*(1), 525–555. doi: 10.5964/jspp.v7i1.328

Kappmeier, M., Redlich, A., & Knyazev, E. (2012). Building local capacity in the region of Moldova – Transdniestria. In J. Rothman (Ed.), *From identity-based conflict to identity-based cooperation* (pp. 99–124). New York: Springer.

Kelman, H. C. (2005). Building trust among enemies: The central challenge for international conflict resolution. *International Journal of Intercultural Relations*, *29*(6), 639–650. doi: 10.1016/j.ijintrel.2005.07.011

Lederach, J. P. (2001). Civil society and reconciliation. In C. A. Crocker, F. O. Hampson & P. All (Eds.), *Turbulent peace: The challenges of managing international conflict* (pp. 189–208). Washington, DC: United States Institute of Peace Press.

Levine, E. E., & Schweitzer, M. E. (2015). Prosocial lies: When deception breeds trust. *Organizational Behavior and Human Decision Processes*, *126*, 88–106. doi: 10.1016/j.obhdp.2014.10.007

Levinger, M. (2013). *Conflict analysis: Understanding causes, unlocking solutions.* Washington, DC: US Institute of Peace Press.

Lewicki, R. J., & Wiethoff, C. (2000). Trust, trust development, and trust repair. In M. Deutsch & P. T. Coleman (Eds.), *The handbook of conflict resolution: Theory and practice* (pp. 86–107). San Francisco, CA: Jossey-Bass.

Schirch, L. (2013). *Conflict assessment and peacebuilding planning: Toward a participatory approach to human security*. Boulder, CO: Kumarian Press.

SDC. (2005). *Conflict analysis tools tip sheet*. Retrieved from ETH Zurich, Department of Humanities, Social and Political Sciences website: https://css.ethz.ch/en/services/digital-library/publications/publication.html/15416

SIDA. (2006). *Manual for conflict analysis*. Retrieved from Conflict Sensitivity website. http://local.conflictsensitivity.org/wp-content/uploads/2015/05/Manual_for_Conflict_Analysis.pdf

Staub, E. (2006). Reconciliation after genocide, mass killing or intractable conflict: Understanding the roots of violence, psychological recovery and steps toward a general theory. *Political Psychology*, *27*(6), 867–895. doi: 10.1111/j.1467-9221.2006.00541.x

Susskind, L., McKearnan, S., & Thomas-Larmer, J. (1999). *The consensus building handbook: A comprehensive guide to reaching agreement*. London: Sage Publications.

Susskind, L., & Thomas-Larmer, J. (1999). Conducting a conflict assessment. In L. Susskind, S. McKearnan & J. Thomas-Larmer (Eds.), *The consensus building handbook: A comprehensive guide to reaching agreement* (pp. 99–136). London: Sage Publication.

Thurston, C. Q. (2008). *Developing a comprehensive framework for conflict analysis: Sources, situation, attitudes, group maintenance, escalation (SSAGE)*. Paper presented at the International Study Association (ISA), San Francisco, CA.

Troebst, S. (2003). "We are transnistrians!" Post-soviet identity management in the Dniester valley. *Ab Imperio*, *1*(1), 437–466. doi: 10.1353/imp.2003.0056

UNICEF. (2012). *Conflict sensitivity and peacebuilding in UNICEF technical note*. Retrieved from UNICEF website: http://www.unicefinemergencies.com/downloads/eresource/docs/conflict%20sensitivity/UNICEF%20Technical%20Note%20on%20Conflict%20Sensitivity%20and%20Peacebuilding[1].pdf

USAID. (2012). *Conflict assessment framework version 2.0*. Retrieved from USAID website: https://www.google.com/url?sa=t&rct=j&q=&esrc=s&source=web&cd=2&ved=2ahUKEwjI85aGzbTnAhUG4XMBHUWNDdgQFjABegQIBhAB&url=https%3A%2F%2Fpdf.usaid.gov%2Fpdf_docs%2Fpnady739.pdf&usg=AOvVaw1k1KwglE54Iy-SDYC0wyU_
Vollhardt, J. K., & Bilali, R. (2008). Social psychology's contribution to the psychological study of peace: A review. *Social Psychology*, *39*(1), 12–25.
Wehr, P. (2006). Conflict mapping. Retrieved from http://www.beyondintractability.org/essay/conflict_mapping/?nid=6793

# Part II

# Reconciliation in practice

# 8 The humanity of the dead

## Rethinking national reconciliation in contemporary Timor-Leste

*Damian Grenfell*

### Introduction

Lolotoe is a mountainous sub-municipality of Bobonaro in Timor-Leste, a Bunak-speaking area whose western border runs contiguously with that of Indonesian West Timor. As with so many communities across Timor-Leste, the effects of the Indonesian occupation from late 1975 through to September 1999 continue to reverberate in Lolotoe to this day. The long-term consequences of the occupation – killings and deaths caused by the conflict, human rights abuses, forced displacement and resettlement, destruction of infrastructure – have resulted in impoverishment, acute shortages of food, community division, disrupted education and a lack of access to basic health and services, as well as an inability to fulfil important ritual obligations. Over the two decades since, there has been a slow but gradual recovery; some new houses have taken the place of burnt out ones, schools have opened, a police station and health clinic provide basic services, there are a couple of general supply shops, the church has been reconstructed and there is electricity much of the time.

While the development of infrastructure provides one obvious sense of recovery, small acts of peace-making and reconciliation have been occurring in important, though less immediately obvious, ways. There has been the return of pro-independence militia from over the border, some sorting through of political divisions, the reconstruction of sacred houses and the renewal of familial networks that provide forms of reciprocated care. An important part of recovery has also been the fulfilment of ritual as it relates to the dead, including the provision of a proper grave. Discussed in more detail through this chapter will be the rehabilitation of 33 graves in one *suku* (a village-level administrative unit) in Lolotoe across 2019. While not all the graves were for those who died directly because of war, the inability to provide a proper burial in these 33 cases was a direct consequence of the Indonesian occupation. The numbers of dead and the lack of resources, as well as the risk of further violence, meant that the building of a proper grave was often impossible. The consequence of this is an inability to follow ritual, important given the profound and widely shared belief that the spirits of the dead are actants with powers that can significantly impact the well-being of the still-living (including death). Ritual fulfilment, including the long-delayed construction of a "home for the dead," is a way of restoring an equilibrium between the living and the *beiala-sira* (ancestral spirits) and is approached in this chapter as an act of reconciliation.

To speak of reconciling the living and the dead requires some adaptation on what might be considered more conventional approaches to reconciliation. In Timor-Leste, major efforts at reconciliation have focused on nationally scaled institutional interventions in the form of commissions. A typical definition would be that reconciliation marks the "mutual acceptance by groups of each other. It means that victims and perpetrator do not see the past as defining the future, but that they see the humanity of one another and see the possibility of a constructive relationship" (Staub 2006: 868; Kappmeier et al. 2021 – Chapter 7 of this volume). This definition incorporates a number of elements common in reconciliation: The emphasis on re-humanising relationships between people in the aftermath of conflict and that such acts are done with the purpose of sustaining peaceful relations. However, drawing from the rehabilitation of graves in Lolotoe and other associated research, the arguments in this chapter mean pushing analytical consideration beyond the secular and humanist approaches that often dominate institution-led reconciliation efforts. Addressing the main question of this collection – "What happens with the everyday lives of the community residents outside of elite level institutional mechanisms for social reconciliation?" – requires approaching reconciliation via a "multi-level" lens that considers the interplay between the scales of the local and national as well as between the living and the dead.

In order to investigate these claims, the chapter is divided into four main sections. In the first section, it is argued that formal reconciliation efforts in Timor-Leste – such as the Commission for Reception, Truth and Reconciliation (CAVR) – emerged out of an elite consensus as part of a consolidation of a new nation and state. The second section then argues that reconciliation was conceived of as being national in scale, focused on current and future life and in turn secular in its constitution. The third section then focuses on alternative forms of reconciliation that continue to occur in Timor-Leste today, tracing the rehabilitation of graves in Lolotoe as one example of the enduring needs of people at the everyday. The last section then maps how these localised forms of reconciliation have little traction with elite-driven forms, even while they remain vitally important to the well-being of people in the aftermath of conflict. Each of these arguments serves in turn to demonstrate the main claim of this chapter that the social significance of the dead means that dominant approaches to reconciliation should be adapted to account for the everyday needs of people as they recover from conflict.

## Peace and national reconciliation

The Indonesian invasion of the former colonial territory of "Portuguese Timor" in December 1975 resulted in a 24-year occupation that is estimated to have led to the deaths of between 102,800 (CAVR 2013: 488) and 183,000 people (CAVR 2013: 491). This would mean the death of between approximately one-fifth and one-third of the pre-invasion population. In an effort to bring the conflict to an end, in 1999 the United Nations Mission in East Timor (UNAMET) oversaw a ballot that would allow a political settlement. The result saw an overwhelming 78.5% vote for independence and the conditions set for Timor-Leste to become an internationally recognised nation-state.

Following an intervention by the International Force East Timor (INTERFET), on 25 October 1999 the United Nations Transitional Authority for East Timor (UNTAET) subsequently assumed full sovereign control over the territory. The potential of new cycles of violence was considered high, not only from militias based in West Timor or the Indonesian armed forces, but also from within the existing population of the territory. Prior to the 1975 Indonesian invasion, there had been violent conflict between emerging political parties which resulted in between 1,500 and 3,000 people being killed and significant human rights abuses (CAVR 2013: 186).[1] The political rivalries of this conflict continued over the Indonesian occupation with claims and counterclaims of abuse, with the concern that independence might see such rivalries being the cause of new violence. A second and very significant potential source of conflict resided between pro-independence and pro-Indonesian East Timorese. During the Indonesian occupation, many East Timorese fought as part of the Indonesian military, collaborated, provided intelligence and participated in the militia-led violence in 1999. While many of these militia had relocated to Indonesia following the vote, many others continued to live on in the territory. The concern then was the risk of violence erupting between rival sides in a newly independent state, including revenge attacks against pro-Indonesian supporters.

In such instances as Timor-Leste, UN missions tend to promote a range of strategies that assist in legitimating a new political order (Feijó 2016): Elections (USAID 2008), civilian oversight, transparency and anti-corruption measures, the legal recognition of human rights (Ingram 2012: 6; Ingram 2018: 366), overhauled systems of policing (Lemay-Hébert 2009), new constitutions (Wallis 2014), civil society strengthening, the creation of and recruitment to a professional military (Hood 2006), the formation of an independent judiciary (Strohmeyer 2001), social services, educational curriculums, cultural policies and so on are all in different ways aimed at creating the conditions for a legitimate state. Yet each of these strategies deals with legitimising a new state while often doing little to address past grievances. As such, transitional justice efforts towards reconciling former adversaries have often been seen as an important layer in the broader efforts at ensuring peace, particularly the case where victim and perpetrator continue to live in close proximity to one another.

While there were local efforts at reconciliation that largely existed beyond the formalised and institutionalised processes (Babo-Soares 2004), desires for reconciliation influenced by the role of Truth and Reconciliation Commissions elsewhere emerged from within UNTAET and associated UN agencies (Larke 2009: 655–656). Beyond the UN, there was strong support for reconciliation within an emergent civil society, as well as top East Timorese bodies such as the National Council for Timorese Reconstruction (CNRT). At that point an umbrella organisation representing the diverse political views of East Timorese groups, CNRT argued that a Truth and Reconciliation Commission would produce "political stability," "national unity" while "reconstructing and generating peace within the society" (Outcomes of the CNRT National Congress: 21–30 August 2000, Dili 2000: 15). For all the political differences between an emerging East Timorese elite and the UN mission, both groups saw merit in the creation of a national commission as a way to prevent further cycles of violence.

The CAVR was formally established through UNTAET Regulation 2001/11 with the Commission undertaking its work between 2003 until 2005. It was organised nationally with headquarters in the capital Dili, with its activities structured by district and sub-district down to local communities. CAVR's remit saw it focus on two key areas: First, via truth-seeking exercises to determine a factual basis regarding human rights abuses from April 1974 until October 1999; and second, the Community Reconciliation Program (CRP) which had the aim of reintegrating perpetrators of "less serious" human rights crimes committed in 1999 back into the community.[2]

In some respects, the death of those that occurred during the occupation became a central dimension of CAVR's work, with killings and fatalities a key dimension in the Commission's work. However, the argument that will be discussed in the following section is that reconciliation was imagined by both groups as national in scale, focused on the living and primarily secular in form. Rather than being grounded in the needs and beliefs of people within localised communities, reconciliation was part of a nationalist project and imagined in terms of securing future life rather than comprehending the importance of the relationship between the living and the dead.

## Truth and Reconciliation Commissions and national life

To argue that a form of reconciliation emerges from an elite consensus between national leadership (Ottendörfer 2013: 25–27) and the agendas of international organisations is not to diminish the effort, the intent nor necessarily the full effect of such initiatives. It does, however, mean that reconciliation can be understood and justified in a way that reflects the assumptions of that elite consensus (Kent 2015). These assumptions may be various, though it is argued here that in Timor-Leste three in particular reduced the likelihood of possible traction with regard to the everyday needs of people. These three assumptions included that reconciliation needed to be scaled to the nation, that it was envisaged as occurring between the still-living and that it was essentially a secular process. Each of these assumptions was concentrically related and understood as essential in securing an emergent political community.

In many respects, it makes sense that in Timor-Leste the nation should be the framing point for how reconciliation is scaled; it was a nationalist conflict and the social division and violence had been caused by competing imaginings of that territory. That said, the nation appears to have been pervasive in terms of how reconciliation was justified and organised to the extent that it has been shaped by a kind of "methodological nationalism," namely, the assumption that the nation has primacy as the container from which social activity is organised, interpreted and reproduced.[3] In other words, it was not as if reconciliation was centred at the level of the nation while other possibilities emerged, but rather, that the *raison d'être* for reconciliation was the nation. This was particularly evident, for instance, in terms of how CAVR justified itself.

> We need to build a solid foundation for our new nation. If we ignore the suffering and violations of our past, we run the risk that they will continue to have a damaging effect on our community and nation. The first ingredient of this foundation must be facing the truth—as individuals, communities and as a nation. To acknowledge what has happened in our country is the first step to ensuring that such violations are never repeated.
>
> (CAVR Pamphlet, May 2002)

Here, "individuals" and "communities" are understood to exist. Rather than having their own unique qualities, values and needs in their own right, here they are treated as subsidiary elements to the overall nation, where for CAVR establishing the "truth" would secure "our country."

As part of the truth-seeking dimensions of CAVR's work, the Commission undertook national hearings, an extensive collection of testimonies across the country as well as a survey of graves to ascertain the mortality rate. Such programmatic interventions can be understood as contributing to reconciliation in various ways, including the clarification of who was responsible for certain actions, an opportunity for East Timorese to listen to different accounts and providing recognition to victims. In each of these cases, the information was gathered and compiled based on a national logic; estimates of the dead were tallied up in national terms, human rights abuses compiled district-by-district to present the sum parts of the national whole and even the numbers of testimonies gathered were determined by the aim of sampling 1% of the national population. In other words, what information was gathered was significantly determined by its value to the nation. The final report of CAVR, titled *Chega!*, drew the intimate and localised experiences of a people – occurring in different sites and times – into a common narrative that shapes their experiences necessarily towards the formation of the nation.

While truth-seeking was justified in securing "our country," the CRP provided a different mechanism, albeit to a similar end. Local hearings were organised throughout the territory where victim's claims were recognised, validated and recorded, while by confessing to abuses the perpetrator avoided possible future state prosecution (Pigou 2004). As such, it brought victim and perpetrator together so as to "see the humanity of one another and see the possibility of a constructive relationship" (Staub 2006: 868). Yet this form of reconciliation, even at the level of individuals and communities, was lifted into the nation, as local hearings were replicated, coordinated and regulated at the national level, again making sense of what might have been intimate and localised experiences of conflict that occurred in sites and at times distant from and unknown to others, and correlating them with other like experiences to form into a singular narrative.

This methodological nationalism intersects with a second key assumption that framed the work of CAVR, namely, that reconciliation was something that necessarily occurred between the still-living. The dead were not part of this form of reconciliation in an immediate sense, as this was about securing current and future life as a way of underpinning the legitimacy of the new state and nation. This might sound counter-intuitive to the extent that so much of CAVR's work is replete with stories of death, from recounting massacres, mass starvation, political killings and military operations through to the anonymised statistical tallies of fatalities. The point here, however, is that these past deaths are important in terms of reconciling the still-living by providing the basis for a common narrative in the formation of a national community. The dead themselves have no intrinsic value in the process of reconciliation or role in social life per se, as in these terms, death means that the relevance of the embodied mortal form and any spirit conclude simultaneously. The dead no longer participate in the political community, and hence their presence in efforts such as truth-seeking persists only to serve a social purpose for the still-living.

The fact that reconciliation focused on the still-living was one possible reflection of a third dimension, namely that reconciliation efforts were encased in a secular logic. The Commission was authorised via a UN transitional authority for the purposes of reconciling the still-living so as "to promote national reconciliation and healing following the years of political conflict in East Timor and, in particular following the atrocities committed in 1999" (UNTAET Regulation 2001/10). Thus, its authority structures, mandate, objectives and operating methods were situated within an approach that did not incorporate or engage with religious or spiritual dimensions of reconciliation. It is not that national reconciliation is antagonistic to faith and spirituality, as it is not uncommon to see religion used for instance as part of mobilising the participation of community members, in the leadership of TRCs, and the said benefits of speaking the "truth" as they resonate with Christian notions of confession (Philpott 2007: 97). Such engagement however tends to occur when religion is of instrumental value to a TRC, or where its presence is tolerated via the distinction between personal beliefs and institutional objectives of a commission (the only time the UNTAET Regulation 2001/10 refers to religion, for instance, is in ensuring that appointed commissioners do not discriminate based on faith). Even in terms of the CRPs that were held in local communities, customary leaders known as *lia nain* (the holder of the word) were present to provide customary witness. Again, however, this was significantly understood in terms of legitimising the CRPs process within local communities rather than as part of a systematic approach to drawing spiritual dimensions into thinking on reconciliation *per se*.

To provide a summary of the argument to this point, as the first major institutionalised effort at reconciliation in Timor-Leste, CAVR emerged via a political consensus that saw reconciliation as important in terms of consolidating the new nation. Human rights and justice were critical as well, but these did not shape the operational and legitimising practices of the commission in the same way as its role in nation-building did. Not only was reconciliation operationalised on a national scale, it was also part of reproducing the nation via the creation of common narratives. Death in such circumstances was significant in terms of its value to the new nation rather than because it was seen to carry any inherent value in and of itself. As such, the second claim has been that the focus has been on present and future life as part of sustaining that national community, rather than drawing in the potential relationships between the living and dead. Lastly, the focus on life is a reflection of a third dimension, namely, that just as the logic of reconciliation was anchored in national logic, so too was it secular. Reconciliation was effectively independent of, rather than adaptive to, spiritual needs. None of these three dimensions is necessarily problematic in and of themselves, though when these are taken to be representative of reconciliation per se, it can mean that the needs of people in the everyday are missed. In order to begin considering this claim, the next section will consider ways in which reconciliation occurs at a local level by returning to and examining the rehabilitation of the graves in Lolotoe.

## Everyday reconciliation and the humanity of the dead

The built environment in Lolotoe (which in Bunak means "encircled by mountains") is woven into the steep hills and deep forests that characterise the sub-municipality. Roads weave along sharp cliff-faces, houses are built on land carved out from hills and trails run along crests linking one site of human activity to another. Rather than being concentrated in one cemetery, graves appear variously in small pockets on the side of pathways, in the yards of people's homes and in a variety of graveyards that are situated between villages.

As discussed briefly in the introduction, across 2019 there was a rehabilitation of 33 graves in Lolotoe. This rehabilitation, it is argued here, presents a very different way of understanding reconciliation that shows how more elite-led efforts that are nestled in the logic of both the national and the secular are at times unable to respond to the everyday needs of people. Before this argument is examined more fully in the next section, it is important first to explain how the rehabilitation of graves and other like activities can be considered an act of reconciliation.

Up until recently, the 33 graves discussed here had remained extremely simple, mostly comprised of circles of stones in dirt and barely distinct amongst other larger, more established graves. Several of the graves were for people who had died prior to the 1975 invasion and several others for those who had passed soon after independence. For the most part, however, the graves were for those who had died during the Indonesian occupation; some had been killed by strafing from Indonesian military aircraft, some had been beaten to death, while many others had died from starvation and disease. Three had been buried together in one site, while the remaining 30 were located either in one graveyard that had existed at least since Portuguese colonialism or in another that had grown exponentially in the aftermath of the Indonesian occupation.

The rehabilitation of the graves saw the construction of raised cement structures of various sizes, though it did not require the exhumation and reburial of remains. Names were added by those who could identify whose grave was whose (on many occasions having buried them themselves), Catholic crosses added and all 33 graves were painted pink to signify that they were from the same extended families from within one particular *uma lulik* (sacred house). Many family members participated in the making of the new graves, whether by making the grave itself or by preparing and cooking food, as well as by undertaking rituals. Significant store was placed on people's attendance, both as a way of sharing labour and costs, but also following the idea that the living need to be present so that the spirits of the dead are aware of each person's contribution.

All of this has multiple significance in terms of rethinking reconciliation. First, in ideal circumstances, a proper grave is built at the actual time of burial so that their spirit is safe in the after-life, and yet here discord had entered the relationship because a proper grave had to date not been possible. That the graves could not be built at the time of burial did not mean that the living were somehow exempt from their responsibilities, even if this was to take decades to fulfil. Here reconciliation is achieved when the new graves replaces the original and inadequate markings that identified a grave. Second, by building the graves as they should have been built in the first instance, this was an act of "making right" that is deeply social across both levels of the living and the dead; 33 graves are built at one time for reasons of resource (labour, and so that family can come one time), but also to ensure that any spirits are not left feeling neglected. Spirits, after all, have a humanity to them and to reconcile properly means ensuring that none are left feeling excluded or envious of the others.

The argument here is such an act of rehabilitation represents a form of reconciliation that is constituted in local relations and encompasses a social act across the levels of the living and the dead. This is reconciliation without the written laws and mandates, regulations, record-keeping, timeframes or the institutional presence of appointed staff, and one that gives significance to the dead in ways that extend beyond the secular instrumentalism discussed above.[4] This case in Lolotoe is not untypical of that which continues to occur across Timor-Leste; the searching for remains, secondary burials, "calling of the spirits" and the rehabilitation of graves. In such acts, war between the living (the war with Indonesia) has led to a rupturing of the relations between the living and their dead, a circumstance where the fulfilment of ritual obligation falls to the still-living relatives (and not the political elite, or the state, on either side of the conflict).

That two decades had elapsed between the end of the war and the rehabilitation of the graves, and that nearly 50 years had passed from when the earliest grave had been made, did not indicate a lack of care by the still-living. The building of graves can represent a significant financial undertaking in the context of subsistence agriculture, more so where the effects of war – deaths of family members, looting and burning of a house, killing of livestock, displacement, disruption of income-generating activities – have been the cause of acute economic precariarity. It was not that building new graves was unimportant, but rather, a result of "*economia la to'o*" (literally this translates to "there was not enough economy," meaning in this instance that there were not the resources available to fulfil the material and the ritual needs for burial).[5] War had not only been the cause of many of the 33 deaths but had also triggered a breakdown in the mutual care typically reciprocated between the living and the spirits of the dead. So many people had died unnaturally in a narrow timeframe while the resources required to bury the dead had been severely diminished (often resulting in the simplest of burials, which can remain a point of shame to the still-living). However, by 2019 gradual economic recovery within the community, in combination with state-initiated veterans payments and compensation for development projects, as well as an increasingly mobile workforce earning cash incomes, meant that there was enough additional wealth being generated to allow 23 families to pool funds in order to finance the rehabilitation.

The need to attend to ritual does not lapse over time nor is it allayed by circumstances, and thus by 2019 the necessity of rehabilitating graves was not only undertaken because there was an economic capacity for doing so, but also as spirits were expressing their power. In Timor-Leste, spirits of the dead are not simply passive, but rather demonstrate agency through their interventions into the lives of the still-living. While an ancestral spirit can provide care, protection and oversight for a still-living family member, a slighted spirit can cause all kinds of harm. Across Timor-Leste, it is extremely common to believe that a lack of a proper burial, the absence of or a poorly constructed grave, a lack of visitation, sustenance to the spirits not being provided (for instance, offerings at the grave-site), graves being left unkept or a failure to follow ritual adequately all risk the wrath of ancestral spirits. As such, the focus on graves here is only one manifestation in a range of practices that are required to keep the relation between the living and the dead in equilibrium. When the relationship falters, illness can be caused by ancestral spirits, as can accidents and sudden deaths, as well as broader calamities such as crop failure or events such as damaging winds and rain, flooding and so forth (Trindade and Barnes 2018).

In Lolotoe, that children in the family continued to become sick was attributed to ancestral malfeasance as a response to their neglect. That illness was felt most acutely at night was taken as additional confirmation, given that spirits are understood to live in temporal inversion to the living; day is night, dusk is dawn and thus effects felt at night are a result of spirits at their most punishingly active during their day. In addition, spirits are often understood as communicating their intentions or demands via the dreams of the living where, in this instance, these were interpreted as spirits demanding a new "home." As one woman in Lolotoe explained "the dead act like this when people (still-living) have made their own houses, however when their houses are not yet completed then they enter our dreams to remind us … ."

In this context, while a war had led to the deaths of many people, it was the inability to give them a proper grave that was seen as leading to a breakdown in relations between the living and the dead. As such, grave-making in this example represents an act that re-establishes mutuality, though this is a mutuality of interdependent care rather than an acceptance of mutual difference. On the making of the new graves in Lolotoe, the *lia nain* implored the spirits to be calm, to protect the living, especially now that they have a new "home" built for them. Like CAVR, this form of reconciliation is about securing a relationship, though it is not the nation's future but that of the living and the dead within their own immediate community. And yet while definitions of reconciliation can be amended and parallels drawn, reconciliation approached from a multi-level lens begins to extend definitions in ways that challenge the basic assumptions that guide formal transitional justice approaches. The concept of "humanity," for instance, in Staub's aforementioned definition cannot be contained only to the living, but needs to be extended to include those who have passed. In turn, the value given to reconciliation linking otherwise distinct sites needs to be loosened to accommodate the regeneration of what constitutes a good life at a local level, with the significance of both of these points explored in the following and final section of this chapter.

## Rethinking national reconciliation

To mark the handover of *Chega!*, the massive final report by CAVR, a formal event was held at a newly restored Portuguese colonial building (also in a garish pink) that had in turn been used by the Indonesian military before being burnt out in 1999. With a view looking down on the capital Dili, armed personnel checked the embossed invitations of East Timorese state elite, CAVR Commissioners and staff and a mix of non-East Timorese. The handover of the report effectively marked the end of CAVR's work, though this was not because reconciliation had been fully achieved or justice attained. Rather, limits are required, given the combination of finite resources and political imperatives, and because transitional justice mechanisms rest on the assumption that a shift can occur, and thus Commissions such as CAVR must by the nature of their purpose have an end date.

An approach that affirms hard close dates, however, misses out on many crucial aspects in terms of what is required by reconciliation, not least the sheer complexity of attempting to venerate the dead in a post-conflict context. The rehabilitation of graves in Lolotoe is just one example of acts that are occurring all across Timor-Leste, not just of grave-building, or mourning on key dates, but the search for remains, of secondary burials, and the still occurring ceremonies—often involving many hundreds of people—to 'call' the spirits of the dead where their bodies have never been retrieved. There are other ways to reimagine reconciliation, however, and one obvious one here is to have far more open-ended processes that are geared to the needs of people in local communities. However, to do this in Timor-Leste would require a shift in the three dimensions that were argued above to be key with regard to CAVR – notably the emphasis on the still-living, the secular nature of that approach to reconciliation and how the nation is scaled – with why this is important discussed in turn here.

The first dimension returned to here is the way reconciliation is assumed to focus only on the relations between the still-living. To argue for the dead to be included as actants may appear a radical departure from the norm and to be a demand that distracts too far from international human rights regimes and the practicalities of limited resources. Nevertheless, such a move does not require a shift in terms of understanding the importance of the dead, as both elite and local approaches to reconciliation outlined here share this. Rather, the requirement is for a shift in understanding that for many people spirits are understood as having an ongoing role as part of a community; they are actants, have will and agency and as such carry their "humanity" with them into the spiritual domain. The shift that needs to occur then is away from the instrumentalisation of the dead and for them to be seen as having a part in a political community in their own right. For all the concern with new cycles of violence, of threats from militia and the need for justice, 20 years on from independence it is spirits who are posing the most significant threat to the lives of the living through their malicious acts of retribution (Sakti 2013: 243).[6] It matters little that international workers may not believe this to be the case, as East Timorese continue to allocate scarce resources towards such acts of reconciliation and often prior to fulfilling other needs, such as their own homes.

The second dimension that requires a significant shift is in an ability to accommodate spirituality into reconciliation approaches where it is relevant to do so.[7] Beliefs in spirits are pervasive in Timor-Leste, though as discussed above in terms of CAVR this rarely surfaced other than as part of CRP process. In terms of reconciling with the dead, both religion and custom combine to provide the parameters for the appropriate interpretation of death and the rituals required in order to maintain the mutual care between the living and the spirits of the dead (Viegas and Feijó 2017). *Lisan*, which refers to customary regulations, will typically guide processes for determining the reason for death, the animals that need to be killed at a funeral and who has what role and responsibility. In Lolotoe, to make amends for its absence at the time of burial, a piece of *Tais* (a piece woven cloth) was laid under the concrete graves as a way of locating and dressing the dead. A hen was killed at the grave of a woman and a rooster for each man. As this was done, the *lia nain* would repeat the phrase "*ene tara le tara*" (Bunak for "you know day, you know night") as the chicken's death would communicate to the spirits their new homes were ready (Fieldwork, Lolotoe April and November 2019).

To speak of spirituality, however, is not only to speak of custom, but to also speak of religion. One consequence of Timor-Leste's former status as a colony of the Portuguese Empire has been that Catholicism has become pervasive and most clearly manifest in the use of crosses, tiled images and small statues of saints and angels that typically adorn graves. Funerals will typically incorporate a Mass and blessings. *Loron Matebian* (All Souls' Day) sees people en masse return to their origin villages, clean graves, pray and attend Mass. Before embarking on the rehabilitation of the graves in Lolotoe US $2 was given to the church so that the names of those in the 33 graves were read at Mass, a way of compensating for the lack of Catholic blessing at the time of the original burial.

Allowing for spiritual needs to be recognised as important to reconciliation does not necessarily mean giving a Commission "over" to either the Church or custom. Rather it is a matter of altering both the programmes and also the approach to those programmes that allows for a greater plurality in how needs might be met. For instance, for all the focus given to reintegrating the still-living into their respective communities by CAVR, there was little provision that allocated resources to the location of remains, of missing people and of family reunion. What if, for instance, an open-ended commission had enabled a programme for the relocation of remains, helping provide resources (logistical, customary knowledge, modern forensics) in a coordinated way and in the aftermath of the independence vote and building up local knowledge, infrastructure to do so over the longer-term. Rather than leaving forensic investigations to occur on a piece-meal and ad hoc basis (Kinsella and Blau 2013: 4) or for the state preferring of the retrieval and burial of veterans over civilians (Roll 2018), institutionalising the pursuit of the missing may have enabled and supported people to undertake their own customary and religious practices towards reconciliation.

While the influence of Catholicism draws the experience of death into a broader community of faith as institutionalised via the Church, the belief in custom anchors the relations between the living and the dead in a discrete form of customary community. This brings us to the third dimension discussed above, and the question of the relationship between reconciliation and political community. Institutions such as CAVR undertake interventions that are designed so that otherwise distinct groups of people experience reconciliation with some levels of equivalence between them. That is what "national reconciliation" is. It is not just that reconciliation on these terms needs to make sense within a group, but it also needs to make sense across groups of those who largely remain unknown to each other. This is in part based in demands for efficiency as per the repetition of interventions across sites, as well as a way of ensuring protection for human rights based on uniform rules. But this sameness is also essential for the nation-building project, as the experiences of people are recorded in a way that allows for a mutual legibility that is the foundation for the creation of a national narrative. This is what "truth-telling" in effect ends up doing; disaggregating the comparable points of narrated trauma between people in order to bring them into comparison and, in effect, a singular narrative that retrospectively names them as part of the formation of the nation.

Here, then, a third shift needs to occur in terms of pluralising the scales on which reconciliation is undertaken, notably a shift away from identifying the national as the assumed scale on which this should occur. To be multi-level is not to argue for one scale over the other – for instance, the local over the national – but to allow a recognition that both scales (and others) might be important to people at different moments and in different ways, and equally may allow for more space for other important forms of reconciliation to come to the fore. Such an approach will not appeal to nationalists of course (especially of the methodological variety); however, this would enable a greater diversity and depth in terms of how reconciliation might be important to people across different levels and over the longer-term.

## Conclusion

At the end of 2019, and to coincide with *Loron Matebian* (All Souls' Day), members of the family from Lolotoe returned home from all over Timor-Leste and even overseas to participate in a ritual referred to as "*fase liman*" (literally to "wash hands," though in effect to cleanse those who had been involved in the rehabilitation of the graves, the tools that had been used to do so and to pay respects as an extended family for the work that had been done). Animals were killed for the consumption of their meat and a large amount of food and drink was consumed. Such a ritual marks an important moment in a process of reconciliation where there has been a rectification in the relationship, where a proper grave for the dead should in turn ensure the protection of still-living children in the family. That such a ritual is occurring so long after independence, and while modest in comparable terms, represents a very significant commitment of resources (food, money, animals, labour), suggests a need for an opening up of reconciliation commissions, not just in terms of time, but also in the ways in which reconciliation itself might be imagined.

To reframe this claim in analytical terms, the main arguments in this chapter have claimed that organisations such as CAVR originated out of an elite consensus at the intersection of international workers and East Timorese leadership, and that such an approach is framed by assumptions that reconciliation should occur as a secular act between the still-living and be scaled at the national level. In turn, the chapter has shown how such an approach can miss important opportunities to connect to local needs for reconciliation, arguing that the continuing focus on retrieving and reburying the dead of war, and rehabilitating new graves as per the examples here in Lolotoe, represent a kind of reconciliation by the living so as to redress inadequate expressions of veneration that occurred at the point of original burial and as a result of the war with Indonesia.

Putting these more analytically framed arguments back into a more grounded context, institutions such as CAVR approach reconciliation in ways that are significantly narrowed by sets of assumptions that in turn reduce their relevance to people at the everyday level. Such processes may play important roles in containing the potential for future violence, or act as forms of recognition, though questions of efficacy are different to the arguments that are being made here. Rather, the argument here is not a judgement on whether reconciliation processes work to fulfil their own objectives, but rather that their objectives are too narrowly conceived in order to address, adapt to and incorporate the needs of everyday people. That the search for the remains of those lost in war, rituals calling their spirits and the rehabilitation of graves continues to occur across the country some 20 years after the conflict, and 15 years after CAVRs closure, and that people are putting their own often limited resources to this, speaks to an enduring need for reconciliation in ways that cannot be captured or adequately addressed by national reconciliation processes. A key to this, in Timor-Leste at least, is not just to shift away from a preoccupation with the nation, but to understand the humanity of the dead.

## Notes

1 For a more detailed overview of the political rivalries in the lead up to the Indonesian invasion, see, for instance, Carneiro de Sousa (2001) or Rees (2004).

2 Running concurrently with CAVR was the Serious Crimes Unit followed by the Serious Crimes Investigation Team (SCIT). As their names suggests, these focused on crimes such as murder, and were, with CAVR, integral to the early transitional justice mechanisms in Timor-Leste.

3 A methodological nationalism is extremely common in the social sciences and humanities and at times simply frames even the conventional ways of expressing ideas. See, for instance, how in the introduction of this chapter the writing moves from Lolotoe to Timor-Leste without hesitation (as if it is natural to do so), and how the statistics for the dead at the outset of the first section are presented as national, as is the norm.
4 Reconciliation here is focused on the interaction between the living and the spirit, but is not the only way to understand this set of dynamics. For instance, it is possible to speak of the security that is gained for the living when the anger of a spirit is quelled (Winch 2017; Grenfell in press), or as the attainment of a kind of peace where the pursuit of a burial or the creation of graves creates the conditions for the living to "live" a good life and for the dead not be left to wander as vagrant spirits (Grenfell in press).
5 In this instance, the killing of animals, as well the food required for *fase liman* (literally "washing of the hands," a form of ritual cleansing of the extended family to mark the completion of the rehabilitation), also require a significant commitment of resources.
6 See Quiñones-Reyes and Ávila's (2018) article for more detail on processes of ritual sacrifice to "silence" the spirits of victims of violent deaths ("*mate mean*").
7 This first and second dimension are held as separate, as while a belief in ancestors is enabled by faith and spirituality, in some scenarios it may be the case that reconciliation requires a focus on spirituality but in a way that does not require a reconciliation specifically with the dead.

## References


Babo-Soares, D. (2004). *Nahe biti*: The philosophy & process of grassroots reconciliation (& justice) in East Timor. *The Asia Pacific Journal of Anthropology*, *5*(1), 15–33.

Carneiro de Sousa, I. (2001). The Portuguese colonisation and the problem of east Timorese nationalism. *Lusotopie*, *8*, 183–194.

*CAVR: Commission for Reception Truth and Reconciliation in East Timor*, Pamphlet, May 2002 (English and Portuguese version).

Comissão de Acolhimento, Verdade e Reconciliação Timor-Leste (CAVR). (2013). *Chega! The final report of the Timor- Leste Commission for Reception, & Reconciliation.* Jakarta: KPG in cooperation with STP-CAVR.

Feijó, R. G.. (2016). *Dynamics of democracy in Timor-Leste: The birth of a democratic nation, 1999-2012.* Amsterdam: Amsterdam University Press.

Grenfell, D. (in press). Death, emplaced security & space in contemporary Timor-Leste. *Cooperation and Conflict.*

Hood, L. (2006). Missed opportunities: The United Nations, police service & defence force development in Timor-Leste, 1999—2004. *Civil Wars*, *8*(2), 143–162.

Ingram, S. (2012). Building the wrong peace: Reviewing the United Nations Transitional Administration in East Timor (UNTAET) through a political settlement lens. *Political Science*, *64*(1), 3–20.

Ingram, S. (2018). Parties, personalities & political power: Legacies of Liberal peacebuilding in Timor-Leste. *Conflict, Security and Development*, *18*(5), 365–386.

Kappmeier, M., Venanzetti, C., & Inton-Campbell, J. M. (2021). No peace without trust: The trust and conflict map as a tool for reconciliation. In K. Clements & S. Lee (Eds.), *Multi-level reconciliation and peacebuilding* (pp. 110–134). London: Routledge.

Kent, L. (2015). *Remembering the past, shaping the future: Memory frictions & nation-making in Timor-Leste*, SSGM Discussion Paper 2015/1. Canberra: Australian National University.

Kinsella, N., & Blau, S. (2013). Searching for conflict-related missing persons in Timor-Leste: Technical, political and cultural considerations. *Stability*, *2*(1), 1–14.

Larke, B. (2009). '…And the truth shall set you free': Confessional trade-off's and community reconciliation in East Timor. *Asian Journal of Social Science*, *37*(4), 646–676.

Lemay-Hébert, N. (2009). UNPOL & police reform in Timor-Leste: Accomplishments & setbacks. *International Peacekeeping*, *16*(3), 393–406.

Ottendörfer, E. (2013). Contesting international norms of transitional justice: The case of Timor-Leste. *International Journal of Conflict and Violence*, *7*(1), 23–35.

Philpott, D. (2007). What religion brings to the politics of transitional justice. *Journal of International Affairs*, *61*(1), 93–111.

Pigou, P. (2004). *The community reconciliation process of the commission for reception, truth & reconciliation*. Dili: UNDP Timor-Leste.

Quiñones-Reyes, E., & Ávila, S. (2018). Animal sacrifices: A mechanism to silence the spirits of victims of violent deaths: *Mate mean* or Red Death in East Timor. *Janga Pana: Revista de Ciencias Sociales y Humanidades*, *17*(1), 117–133.

Rees, E. (2004). *Under pressure: Falintil—Forças de defesa de Timor-Leste: Three decades of defence force development in Timor-Leste 1975–2004*, Working Paper No. 139. Geneva: Geneva Centre for the Democratic Control of Armed Forces.

Roll, K. (2018). Reconsidering reintegration: Veterans' benefits as statebuilding in. In J. Bovensiepen (Ed.), *The promise of prosperity: Visions of the future in Timor-Leste* (pp. 139–153). Canberra: ANU Press.

Sakti, V. (2013). 'Thinking too much': Tracing local patterns of emotional distress after mass violence in Timor-Leste. *The Asia Pacific Journal of Anthropology*, *14*(5), 438–454.

Staub, E. (2006). Reconciliation after genocide, mass killing, or intractable conflict: Understanding the roots of violence, psychological recovery & steps toward a general theory. *Political Psychology*, *27*(6), 867–894.

Strohmeyer, H. (2001). Policing the peace: Post-conflict judicial system reconstruction in East Timor. *University of New South Wales Law Journal*, *24*(1), 171–182.

Trindade, J., & Barnes, S. (2018). Expressions of the 'good life' & visions of the future: Reflections from Dili & Uatolari. In J. Bovensiepen (Ed.), *The promise of prosperity: Visions of the future in Timor-Leste* (pp. 157–172). Canberra: ANU Press.

UNTAET. (2001). *Regulation no. 2001/10 on the establishment of a commission for reception, truth & reconciliation in East Timor*. Dili: UNTAET.

USAID. (2008). *Elections & political processes program in Timor-Leste: Evaluation report*. Dili: USAID Timor-Leste.

Viegas, S. M., & Feijó, R. G. (2017). Territorialities of the fallen heroes. In S. M. Viegas & R. G. Feijó (Eds.), *Transformations in independent Timor-Leste: Dynamics of social & cultural cohabitations* (pp. 94–110). London: Routledge.

Wallis, J. (2014). *Constitution making during state-building*. Cambridge: Cambridge University Press.

Winch, B. (2017). *'La iha fiar, la iha seguransa'*: The spiritual landscape & feeling secure in Timor-Leste. *Third World Thematics: A TWQ Journal*, *2*(2–3), 197–210.

# 9 Tales of progress

## Creating inclusive reconciliation narratives post-conflict

*Caitlin Mollica*

### Introduction

Truth and reconciliation commissions (TRC) have been instrumental in facilitating the heightened engagement of individuals traditionally excluded from retributive justice approaches. By providing demographics such as youth with a public forum to tell their stories, TRCs are well-placed to empower young people by providing opportunities for them to claim ownership over the way their relationships within the post-conflict community are represented and rebuilt. These practices have the capacity to expose the silences often experienced by individuals whose stories operate on the fringes of society, and thus can produce a more inclusive and meaningful reconciliation process.

Increasingly, TRCs have offered those traditionally denied opportunities to exert ownership over their conflict narratives a platform to claim agency and display citizenship through participation. This is evident in the case of the Solomon Islands TRC, where the unique contributions and voices of youth were acknowledged from its inception, particularly during the implementation process. Established through an Act of Parliament in 2008, the Solomon Islands TRC was mandated to promote reconciliation and community restoration by investigating and reporting on the experiences of the community during the civil conflict, known as "The Tensions."[1] Where youth were concerned, the physical, socio-economic and structural consequences of the tensions were far-reaching, as the closure of schools, the abandonment of the *National Youth Policy* and a lack of employment opportunities resulted in youth pursing "collective solutions to their marginalisation," including active engagement in the fighting (Braithwaite et al. 2010). In addition, youth participation in the violence and instability during the Tensions informed public beliefs about youth, perpetuating deep-rooted cultural notions of youth as *Masta Liu*.[2] Cultural sentiment that casts the youth of the Solomon Islands as *Masta Liu* emphasised their delinquency and positioned them as subordinates to the "big men" during the conflict, placing a strain on their relationships with the broader community (Allen 2013: 5). Given this, recognition of the impact of "the Tensions" on Solomon Islands' youth through the TRC was instrumental for ensuring that the process met the aims of reconciliation and community unity.

As this chapter demonstrates, youth's active participation in the TRC process denotes a significant shift in the way their agency is conceptualised in reconciliation contexts and reflects broader trends toward the implementation of inclusive, formal reconciliation practices. Yet the quality of this inclusion still presents a significant challenge for the reconciliation discourse, as substantive inclusion involves ensuring that the voices of traditionally silenced individuals are not only heard, but respected throughout all stages of the transitional justice process. Despite the significant gains made for youth engagement during the Solomon Islands TRC, the formal reporting process suggests that tensions between the interpersonal and political goals of reconciliation practices remain, most notably when the stories of those traditionally excluded do not "fit" with the dominant political discourse.

Broadly speaking, the participation of youth throughout these consultation processes, provides important insights about the character of "successful" reconciliation. This chapter therefore argues that a greater emphasis on the TRC *process* is needed when conceptualising the contributions of TRCs to the goal of reconciliation. Previous studies of success prioritise outcome-based assessments where the final report and the implementation of recommendations inform our perceptions of the efficacy of the TRC, rather than considering how the process as a whole can facilitate a form of reconciliation that is both lasting *and* meaningful (Guthrey and Brounéus 2017; Jeffery and Mollica 2017). This chapter suggests that TRCs need to find a way to balance the political goals of producing a cohesive conflict narrative with the often divergent, dynamic and unique perspectives of marginalised communities, including youth. Where TRCs are concerned, a move away from political reconciliation towards the interpersonal approach provides a more inclusive space for the voices of these individuals. TRCs that emphasise interpersonal reconciliation when engaging with the voices of marginalised individuals are more capable of acknowledging and addressing their interests and experiences. Claims that TRCs are inclusive and representative have proven to be largely conceptual, as, in practice, the voices of youth, women and children often fail to break through international and local normative frameworks that emphasise vulnerability (manifested either through deviance or innocence). This chapter concludes that it is not sufficient to simply make these groups more visible in the reconciliation process; agents also need to take on board the content of their stories and include them in the decision-making and implementation process.

## Interpersonal reconciliation: Prioritising stories and relationships

As approaches to transitional justice have evolved to allow for the substantive inclusion of marginalised individuals, acknowledgement of their unique conflict experiences has become an increasingly prominent focus within the design and implementation of justice practices, most notably TRCs. Through the public retelling of their stories, the practice of acknowledgement offers traditionally silenced individuals "knowledge and recognition and communities' opportunities to confer this knowledge and recognition" (Philpott 2008: 128). The production, receipt and adoption of their unique narratives, therefore, which occurs through the process of acknowledgement, legitimises their voices within the formal reconciliation structures. Acknowledgement offers visibility to historically excluded individuals, and thus contributes to their integration in the broader community, as the practice encourages community empathy, restoration and the naming of their experiences (Quinn 2011; Philpott 2008). Where youth are concerned, the rebuilding of interpersonal relationships is essential for challenging the persistence of narrow binary classifications often used to describe their conflict experiences (Berents and Mollica 2020).

While there are many definitions, the central theme of the literature suggests that the process of reconciliation is fundamentally "about building relationships of trust and cohesion" by "addressing conflictual and fractured relationships" (Quinn 2009: 5). Notions of reconciliation in these contexts as such emphasise the importance of interpersonal relationships to the production of meaningful and lasting peace and stability. As John Paul Lederach observes, reconciliation is an "adaptive" series of practices, the purpose of which is to "build" and "heal relationships and societies and ultimately, achieve … a positive peace" (Lederach 2001: 842). In addition, Susan Dwyer suggests that reconciliation in practice requires "bringing apparently incompatible descriptions of events into narrative equilibrium" to create a public record of the conflict that reflects a series of often competing stories through a shared platform (Dwyer 1999: 89). TRCs, therefore, have the capacity to represent the varied and often contentious interpretations of the roles youth occupy during conflict, as well as the range of youth representations which evolve throughout the reconciliation process.

The TRC process provides a forum for a diverse range of voices, however, tensions between individual and political narratives often reproduce marginalising conditions, particularly in the reporting phase. As Daniel Philpott concludes, political reconciliation seeks to "restore an entire political community, or a relationship between political communities, to a condition of respected citizenship, the rule of law, legitimacy, and trust" (Philpott 2008: 126). The aim is to restore relationships within communities, and thus create conditions for sustainable peace. Political reconciliation also looks to ensures that post-conflict communities "are not haunted by the conflicts and hatreds of yesterday" by encouraging an open forum for communities to confront a wide variety of harms, in order to prevent a relapse into violence (Hayner 2003: 161; Wallis, et al. 2016: 159). Often however, the restoration of political relationships reproduces hierarchies that privilege the collective voice, reproduced within formal governing structures, and in doing so silences traditionally marginalised individuals, in particular women and youth.

While political and interpersonal reconciliation share the same broad goal of restoring relationships, the types of connections they prioritise differ. Political reconciliation is predominantly a "top-down, 'structural' process" that derives legitimacy by prioritising the restoration of the community and institutions through formally derived processes, most notably TRCs (Waldorf and Shaw 2010: 4). Moreover, Murphy suggests that this approach seeks to expose the "presence of pervasive and widespread negative attitudes" in order to "rebuild trust within the polity by reinforcing normative expectations, or to reconstitute [the] political community" (Murphy 2010: 10). Political reconciliation as such, pursues a reframing of the collective relationships and structures, which produced the violence and instability. In contrast, interpersonal reconciliation, which preferences "bottom-up 'cultural' ... processes," typically performed on a "small[er]-scale and/or [at the] grassroots level," acknowledges the broad range of public and private harms that individuals experience during conflict (Waldorf and Shaw 2010: 4). This approach seeks to restore the "right relationship between the perpetrator and victim of a non-political harm – for example, a simple act of theft or domestic harm" (Wallis et al. 2016: 161; Murphy 2010: 10). Unlike political reconciliation, therefore, the interpersonal approach conceives of harm through an expansive lens which prioritises and seeks to address the experiences of the individual. Given this, reconciliation practices that emphasise an interpersonal approach are better equipped to fulfil the inclusive peace mandate.

When employed together, these two approaches have the capacity to produce an inclusive post-conflict environment in which the institutions, structures and community relationship are meaningfully rebuilt. However, when political reconciliation is prioritised over the restoration of interpersonal relationships, structural barriers emerge, which constrain the capacity of these reconciliation practices to hear and take seriously historically marginalised individuals. Including the voices of individuals whose perceptions of what constitutes reconciliation diverge from institutionalised discourses lends legitimacy to these practices, and encourages widespread ownership over the outcome of reconciliation. Recent scholarship on the effectiveness of reconciliation echoes this claim highlighting the relationship between political will, local buy-in and sustainable peace (Jeffery and Mollica 2017; Fortna 2018). Moreover, recent empirical examinations of peace processes demonstrate that quality of inclusion is a key indicator for determining the overall durability of peace (Paffenholz 2015: 242; Donais and McCandless 2017: 304). The more post-conflict practices are grounded in substantive dialogue that extends beyond "inter-elite bargaining and pact-making," the more potential there is to elicit wide-spread, local ownership, which encourages meaningful peace (Paffenholz 2015: 242).

## Solomon Island youth: Engaged stakeholders in reconciliation

Young people are increasingly visible within the reconciliation practices of post-conflict communities. Their stories and experiences are often employed to represent the changing character and potential of transitional states to be inclusive. In particular, youth's heightened participation and representation in reconciliation reflects the "positioning of youth as a social metaphor" for inclusive and transformative transitions (Kwon 2019: 926). Yet, the engagement of youth with practices such as TRCs is more complex than this linear narrative of inclusion suggests. While this broad homogenous representation of youth as a metaphor for inclusion has emerged in recent years dominant deviance classifications, which suggest that youth are both "a risk" and "at-risk" persists (Berents and Mollica 2020). Moreover, due to the advocacy of youth activists, there is growing recognition that young people are politically engaged stakeholders with diverse experiences who occupy multiple shifting roles that cannot be narrowly characterised (Sukarieh and Tannock 2018; Mollica 2017). As the case of Solomon Islands demonstrates, reconciliation practices which rely on homogenous representations of youth's stories perpetuate stereotypes that are problematic for the pursuit of substantive, interpersonal reconciliation.

The participation of youth during the Solomon Island's TRC process reflected their prominence in the community, as well as a broader trend towards political ownership amongst the youth demographic that started to emerge prior to conflict. This is evident in language employed in *The National Youth Policy of the Solomon Islands 2010–2015*, which characterised the Solomon Islands as "a youthful nation … that demands action" and explicitly acknowledged the capacity of youth to act as political actors (National Youth Policy 2010–2015). The acknowledgement in government policy that youth were central to the national identity and that they had the capacity to engage as stakeholders laid the foundation for their substantive participation in the formal reconciliation process. During the Tensions, youth constituted 32% of the population, and therefore their voices were essential for the development of an inclusive record of the conflict. Indeed, the 1999 census (conducted a year into the Tensions) found that 131,231 Solomon Islanders were between the ages of 14 and 29 (Solomon Islands National Statistics Office 2009). Youth as such, were a pervasive presence whose stories were an essential part of the national reconciliation conversation, as they had a unique investment in the production of an inclusive reconciliation narrative that accurately portrayed their experiences.

Where Solomon Islander youth are concerned, the development of an inclusive reconciliation narrative echoes historical attempts to develop meaningful relationships with the broader community and to enable substantive engagement with the institutional structures. Since the 1980s, the political participation of the youth has evolved through a series of policies and programmes which sought to empower youth to take ownership over their stories and experiences. For example, both the *National Youth Development Plan* and *National Youth Congress*, which have been key focal points of the broader development agenda of the Solomon Islands, highlight youth's agency and emphasise their capacity to positively contribute to the political landscape of the Solomon Islands (Hassall 2003: 46). Furthermore, in recognition of the diverse cultural identities that youth possess, a series of provincial policies were developed to complement the priorities outlined in the *National Youth Policy*. These provincial policies reveal the wide-ranging needs and experiences of youth across the Solomon Islands and demonstrate institutional acknowledgement that youth are not a homogenous entity. Through the development of these provincially targeted policies the government has sought to respond to the diverse and unique interests of Solomon Islander youth and to capture their distinct voices by creating responsive policy objectives. For example, while the national youth policy focuses on macro issues, such as "career pathways …

governance … wellbeing and development," the policies of the Central Island and Guadalcanal emphasise community challenges, such as "youth enterprises … young parents … sex workers in the Central Islands" and "communication and music" in Guadalcanal (National Youth Policy 2010: 6; Central Islands Provincial Youth Policy 2009; Guadalcanal Provincial Youth Policy 2010). These policies are central to youth's engagement with the TRC as they informed the character of their experiences, most notably their participation as witnesses, counsellors, researchers and transcribers, as well as the nature of the Commissioners' recommendations in the final report. Yet, as demonstrated below, unlike these provincial policies, which emphasised the building of interpersonal relationship between youth and their local communities, the reconciliation process, in particular the final report, often failed to meaningfully engage with youth's unique stories. This is due in part to the existence of competing and contradictory political objectives.

The youth policies of the Solomon Islands, which were created through direct consultation with young people are indicative of recent trends in post-conflict justice and peacebuilding globally. For example, Jeff Helsing et al. observed that youth's peace and justice activism in Bosnia was essential for "getting politicians … to view youth development as an integral element of reconstructions, rehabilitation and reconciliation," as it demonstrated their capacity and political will (2006: 197). This suggests that when youth are heard and their participation is taken seriously, reconciliation practices are more likely to succeed, as the process will be perceived as more relevant and legitimate by young people. Broadly speaking, the engagement of youth in the development of inclusive reconciliation, development and peacebuilding practices highlights the importance of ownership and buy-in to sustainable peace and meaningful reconciliation.

The development of the 2010–2015 Youth Policy in the Solomon Islands demonstrated the government's renewed commitment to youth engagement, which was stalled by the violence and instability associated with the Tensions. As the final report of the TRC noted, the government's failure to implement the previous *National Youth Policy* was the result of the instability brought about by the Tension and not a lack of commitment to the meaningful political inclusion of youth (TRC Final Report 2012: 64). This new policy not only renewed the Solomon Islands' commitment to substantively engage with youth politically, it also included specific provision to empower their participation in reconciliation practices. In particular, amongst the priorities of the new youth policy was a pledge to "increase" the "number of young people participating in activities that promote peace building and conflict prevention," including the TRC (National Youth Policy 2010: 8). This policy objective, sought to meaningfully engage youth "at all levels" in the decision-making and programme development essential for sustainable peace and community reconciliation.

Furthermore, the policy acknowledged that substantive engagement, which "address[es] the challenges' youth face requires activities that [would] do more than just skills training and helping youth to do things" (National Youth Policy 2010: 8). Embedded in the post-conflict mandate outlined within this youth policy as such, is the recognition that they are political agents with the ability to be transformative and to participate in decision-making. This provision within the youth policy institutionalised the Solomon Islands commitment to recognising youth's agency and their voices and thus provided further formal acknowledgement of the importance of youth to the development of inclusive reconciliation. Broadly speaking, the institutionalised commitment made by the Solomon Islands to engage with youth in decision-making processes, supports emerging claims in both scholarship and practice that "youth have the capability to effect change independent of outside actors" (McEvoy-Levy 2006: 168; Lee-Koo 2015). For example, in Mozambique, Kosovo and the Democratic Republic of Congo, Schwartz observed that when youth's agency is acknowledged during peacebuilding and justice processes they reveal the "complex reality" of youth's experiences, which are often blurred when youth are excluded or represented through narrow external representations (Schwartz 2010). This has implications for how we understand and engage with youth in reconciliation processes, as it suggests that they have the ability to participate in the development of TRC mandates, to engage in restorative story-telling that rebuilds relationships and to take ownership over their role in conflicts. When the voices of youth and their stories are prioritised therefore, reconciliation practices such as TRCs are better able to represent their needs, interests and experiences.

As the National Youth Policies outlined above suggest, the voices of youth have historically received institutional consideration in the Solomon Islands. Given this, the government was perfectly positioned to recognise the value of substantive youth engagement in the reconciliation process. Yet, the TRC process in the Solomon Islands reveals the complexity associated with balancing political and interpersonal reconciliation agendas. While the recommendations and process demonstrate inclusivity, the institutional narrative in the final report reveals an absence of diverse representation.

## Revealing substantive participation

Restoring fractured relationships following conflict requires the creation of inclusive forums that enable the involvement of a broad cross section of the community. This form of participation requires the pursuit of practices that respect the voices of these individuals during decision-making and implementation. Often, however, attempts to balance political and structural demands with the needs of the broader community results in the implementation of reconciliation practices that fail to consider the character and extent of the inclusion mandated. Where youth are concerned, substantive forms of participation are informed by the notion that youth's stories are innately valuable and thus contribute substantively to the development of knowledge and the restoration of relationships (Lee-Koo 2015; Oswell 2013: 6).

An examination of the mandate of the Solomon Islands TRC and the recommendations reveals evidence of youth's agency, as well as efforts to enable their substantive participation. Most notably, the inclusion of youth as thematic stakeholders, alongside women, ex-combatants and children fulfils the broader reconciliation agenda of inclusion and acknowledgement, and thus aims to elicit a more accurate representation of their experiences. By placing the interests of youth at the centre of reconciliation concerns, the Solomon Islands TRC mandate sought to enable youth's active participation in the process and to rebuild social trust between youth and the broader community. The listing of youth as a "thematic stakeholder," and the inclusion of youth-focused recommendations in the final report heightened youth's visibility and revealed their agency to the broader community. In doing so, the TRC mandate enabled a process of acknowledgement, which, as Quinn observes, "is responsible for the creation of the bonds of social capital and social trust," and thus the implementation of a successful reconciliation process (Quinn 2011: 5). Enabling substantive participation that reveals youth's interest indicates an attempt to facilitate a more inclusive reconciliation process.

While the chapter in the final report represents young peoples' experiences by combining the stories of children and youth, thus silencing youth's unique voices; the recommendations section demonstrates the importance of youth and their distinct experiences to the reconciliation dialogue. Most notably, the recommendations indicate that youth agency was visible, as the Commissioners described them as "productive citizens of th[e] nation" (Solomon Islands TRC Commission 2012: 722). Although problems of labelling persist within this section of the report, in particular the use of the "child soldier" rhetoric to describe youth, the substantive discussion acknowledges the distinction between children and youth. In addition, it explores how youth's experiences were informed by their status *as* youth, and their occupation of this constantly evolving transitional life phase (Furlong et al. 2003; Durham 2004: 593). For example, the recommendations section highlights the on-the-ground realities of youth's conflict experience, most notably the issue of "youth unemployment" by providing a table of unemployment statistic for individuals aged between 15 and 29. Moreover, it is noted throughout these recommendations that "address[ing] feelings of marginalisation in the youth population of the country" was a key reform priority (Solomon Islands TRC Commission 2012: 768). The contrasting framings evident in the recommendations section reveal a key barrier to inclusive reconciliation. While the substantive discussion emphasised the distinct interests of youth, the rhetorical classifications framed their experiences alongside those of children, thus blurring the line of representation and inclusion.

The recommendations chapter acknowledged explicitly the importance of youth's substantive inclusion in the Solomon Islands reconciliation process. Specifically, there was a general consensus that the "leaders of tomorrow [youth] should be heard by all," as their political will and support was a necessary condition for sustainable peace (Interview November 2015). This sentiment was echoed by the Commissioners who recommended that:

> The government promote and encourage maximum youth participation in decision-making and leadership at all levels of government, that is real and meaningful, as a means to take seriously the concerns, aspirations, and wishes of the youth.
>
> (Solomon Islands TRC Commission 2012: 796)

At the core of the recommendations is an acknowledgement that youth have the capacity to influence the social structures of the community through participation. To that end, the Solomon Islands TRC process demonstrates the importance of visibility and meaningful engagement, which extends beyond tokenism. This is further highlighted by the recommendation that youth should be included in "community decision making" (Solomon Islands TRC Commission 2012: 767). Reflecting on the importance of this recommendation, youth explained that their heightened visibility as statement-takers, researchers and transcribers enabled them to "show the community what [they] could do and to help relationships heal by changing beliefs about who youth are" (Interview November 2015). This belief echoes scholarly claims within the peacebuilding literature, which suggest that youth's substantive participation challenges narrow stereotypes that cast youth as vulnerable or deviant, and thus helps to rebuild meaningful relationships between youth and the broader community (McEvoy-Levy 2011: 41–42; Özerdem and Podder 2015; Lee-Koo 2015: 203). Moreover, the emphasis on participation and opportunity in these recommendations aligns with the agency-centric empowerment discourses evident in the *National Youth Policies* of the Solomon Islands.

Despite a commitment to inclusion in the recommendations, structural and political conditions diminished the sense of ownership young people displayed in the reconciliation process. Most notably, the persistence of traditional power structures perpetuated hierarchies, which prioritised the voices of elites over youth. This is evident throughout the submission's youth made to the TRC. For example, as one youth leader describes:

> **Generosity:** One of the biggest problems after the ethnic tension is the *wantok* system.[3] We did not learn to appreciate each other after the ethnic tensions.
>
> (Solomon Islands TRC Commission 2012: 1022)

Furthermore, transcripts from youth's participation in the reconciliation process also indicate a need to prioritise the broader relationships within the country beyond the traditional *wantok* system. As they conclude:

> I should see a brother from Guadalcanal as a Solomon Islander; I should see a brother from Western Province as a Solomon Islander. What I can see now there is no sense of appreciating each other.
>
> (Solomon Islands TRC Commission 2012: 1022)

These submissions by youth indicate that an overreliance on kinship-like bonds silences youth's voices, and as thus limits opportunities for substantive participation. This sentiment is further supported by the work of Matthew Allen who observed that the relationship between youth and "governments, media and think tanks" was heavily impacted by the *Masta Liu* classification (Allen 2013). A reliance on the *Masta Liu* classification and cultural structures renders invisible instances of meaningful, positive participation where youth seek to rebuild their communities by prioritising programs that foster development through collaboration (Mollica 2017: 188–192). Overreliance on the deviant classifications, therefore, obscures the voices and stories of empowered young people. Moreover, this representation creates inaccurate normative assumptions about why individuals engage with conflict and reconciliation. As Allen's work with ex-combatants in the Solomon Islands demonstrates the motivations of youth extended beyond feelings of helpless and aimlessness, to a belief that they were "fighting for something" (Allen 2013: 6). Taken together, the reconciliation narratives of youth evident in the Solomon Islands TRC's final report, as well as in the Commission transcripts and interviews, reveal a complex story about the experiences of youth that is neither linear or one-dimensional.

Youth present a unique challenge for institutions pursuing reconciliation, particularly when their stories challenge the dominant discourse supported by local governments or the international community. While post-conflict reconciliation practices are constantly evolving to reflect beliefs about what constitutes "best-practice" regarding inclusivity and acknowledgement, the underlying norms that produce these practices remain highly contested. TRCs that prioritise the development of linear conflict narratives often valorise "a particular kind of memory practice-truth-telling" which perpetuates narrow victim and perpetrator archetypes (D'Costa 2015: 214). This echoes broader trends within the peace and conflict field, which suggest that traditional power structures act as significant barriers to substantive participation. Most notably, the continued reliance on technocratically developed TRC narratives, which are underpinned by notions of "neutrality and efficiency" gives prominence to the voices of elites and perpetuate structural barriers for historically marginalised groups (Mac Ginty 2012). Where youth are concerned, Kwon suggests that "institutionalised spaces of power" are dominated by the "politics of consensus" which privileges certain types of knowledge, rather than reflecting of the reality of individuals experiences (Kwon 2019: 930). In the context of reconciliation, traditional power structures inform how youth's stories are conceptualised.

## Youth agency in the TRC process

Efforts to create an inclusive reconciliation narrative in the Solomon Islands began in 2006 with the formulation of a Truth and Reconciliation Steering Committee, which sought participation from a wide range of stakeholders, amongst them youth. The steering committee was responsible for consulting with key stakeholders about the design and implementation of a potential TRC. It was "directed to explore and plan the structure, functions and powers of a Commission" (Solomon Islands TRC Commission 2012: 1102). In this respect, the purpose of the committee was to ensure that the potential TRC reflected the experiences of the Solomon Islands community and was mindful of the cultural and social dynamics that informed the relationships between individuals and groups prior to, during and after the Tensions. To fulfil this inclusive, consultative mandate, membership for this committee was sought from across key organisations in the Solomon Islands, as well as from those groups identified as having a significant stake in the outcome of the reconciliation process, namely women, ex-combatants and youth.

The youth representative of this committee was responsible for gathering the opinions of youth and ensuring that these were represented in the decision-making and implementation of the proposed TRC. To capture the voices of youth, the representative conducted focus groups and town halls across the Provinces for the youth demographic, which facilitated comprehensive engagement, as well as providing information about the proposed reconciliation process (Solomon Islands TRC Commission 2012: 1102). Central to the responsibilities of the youth representative was the implementation of forums that would engage youth from all provinces in fact-finding sessions to assess their interest in participating in the proposed formal reconciliation process (Solomon Islands TRC Commission 2012: 1102). This consultative process, which sought to capture the diverse range of youth voices that exist throughout the Solomon Islands, demonstrates early attempts at facilitating substantive participation.

The leadership potential that the steering committee of the Solomon Islands TRC aimed to harness echoes broader community perceptions, particularly amongst individuals who engaged first-hand with young people following the Tensions. As one TRC counsellor described "the youth were fast learners … they will integrate very well into the community" (Interview October 2015). Similarly, another TRC counsellor concluded that:

> Unity and youth programs that build relationships were a big concern … [the youth] are young ambassadors for peace who everyday raise issues on social media … and when the leaders are not connected to their issues … they establish forums between themselves.
>
> (Interview November 2015)

As these quotations and youth's participation in the steering committee consultations demonstrate, youth possess the leadership potential, capacity and agency to contribute meaningfully to restoring community relationships following violence and instability. Yet the tension evident in the above quotation between leaders and youth highlights a key challenge associated with inclusive reconciliation, namely, the balancing of competing interests. This tension is further acknowledged in the submissions of youth to the Commission which call for interpersonal relationships to be prioritised. For example, one youth leader used his testimony to the TRC to "appeal to [his] fellow youths and citizens of this nation" to acknowledge their capacity to contribute productively to reconciliation (Solomon Islands TRC Commission 2012: 1023). Furthermore, during his submission he sought to challenge community perceptions of youth explaining that "we are not who we are, we are defined [by] how well we rise after this problem that we went through … We are stronger than what we have been labelled as before, yesterday and today" (Solomon Islands TRC Commission 2012: 1023).

The presence of these tensions often results in the implementation of reconciliation mechanisms that pay lip-service to notions of inclusivity, while falling short of their capacity to substantively engage with historically marginalised groups. As Lee-Koo suggests, meaningful participation pursues engagement that is "politically transformative" and extends beyond notions of "presence, inclusion and involvement" by taking up their ideas at both the decision-making and implementation stages (2015: 203). Given this, maintaining this level of engagement throughout the Solomon Islands TRC process proved to be a significant challenge. The contrast between youth's engagement in the development process of the TRC and their institutionalised stories reveals the impact of political agendas on the creation of formalised reconciliation narratives. The tension between these two representations suggests that the external beliefs and the political will of powerful actors and institutions often act as significant barriers to the production of inclusive conflict narratives that acknowledge the voices of youth.

## Where are the youth? Conflict participation and hearing their voices in reconciliation

The conflict in the Solomon Islands was a low-level, ethnic conflict waged between the Malaitan Eagle Force and the Isatabu (Guadalcanal) Freedom Movement in their provinces and the capital city of Honiara. By the time the conflict in the Solomon Islands reached its peak in June 2000, young men, particularly those from Malaita, needed little convincing to join the resistance. Motivated by a desire to "defend and protect their people," these youths were ready for change (Braithwaite et al. 2010). Driven from their villages and their jobs by Guale militants (most of whom were also young men), Malaitan youth sought refuge with their families in temporary shelters around Honiara. Compelled to act, due to forced evictions, as well as a wide range of human rights abuses committed by both sides, "Malaitan men form[ed] vigilante groups to 'secure' the outskirts of Honiara" and to protect themselves and their families (Allen 2013: 124–125). In contrast, the youth of Guadalcanal played a key role in the Tensions from the beginning. Young Guals' participation in the violence was born largely out of frustration that their voices and the voices of their community were not being acknowledged (Allen 2013: 124–125). In particular, many young Guals joined the Isatabu Freedom Movement (IFM) to voice their dissatisfaction, following a lack of institutional action on a 1999 submission to the central government titled "Demands by the Bona Fide and Indigenous People of Guadalcanal," which detailed claims for compensations with respect to land and other grievances (Fraenkel 2004: 197–203).

The stories of these young men demonstrate the central role that youth played in the tensions as active and informed stakeholders. They reveal a complex and diverse range of motivations , as political and cultural factors informed the decisions by both groups of young men to actively engage in the violence associated with the Tensions. Central to their reasoning was the perception that participation in the conflict was a necessary act of resistance against a corrupt and unjust system. As such, the meaningful inclusion of their stories throughout the TRC process provided opportunities for the reconciliation narrative to reflect the realities of conflict participants. As one participant explained, the "TRC process was very important for youth's identity, as it validated their experiences and place in the community" (Interview October 2015). Broadly speaking, acknowledging youth's agency facilitates interpersonal reconciliation by strengthening community bonds through trust and recognition (Quinn 2011). In the Solomon Islands context, the restoration of relationships between youth and the broader community was essential for ensuring the widespread success of reconciliation, as the Commissioners noted in the conclusion to the final report:

> Youth no longer have a sense of belonging … most … especially those affected by the tensions, feel that they are not part of the social and economic activities of the country, as their age and status have put them apart.
>
> (Solomon Islands TRC Commission 2012: 768)

Reconciliation practices which fail to meaningfully engage with youth and their stated motivations for participation in violence and instability or to trust their contributions perpetuate structural barriers to inclusive reconciliation. Indeed, as demonstrated below, the cultural and structural factors that drove youth to participate in the Tensions acted as a catalyst for action rather than, as the final report suggested, a means of coercion. Yet, rather than hearing and believing youth when they exerted agency over their decision to participate in the conflict, the final report drew on policy research to highlight the victim narrative, which assigned narrow normative assumptions about young people to their experiences (Berents and Mollica 2020).

The institutional narrative of young people published in the final report of the Solomon Islands TRC prioritised information and data collected by organisations with a specific mandate, rather than hearing and taking on board the perceptions of youth. While policy reports are valuable as they have the capacity to make youth visible within the formal institutions of peace and justice; their work is largely underpinned by a protectionist lens that represents the experiences of children and youth together to further the political cause (Brocklehurst 2006: 55). Scholars suggest that this framing represent all young people regardless of their experience or positioning as "isolat[ed], victimised and vulnerable" individuals in order to evoke an emotional response amongst the global community (Jacob 2013: 32–34). In the Solomon Islands context, the chapter on children employed characterisations of young peoples' conflict experiences from the *Global Report on Child Soldiers* to highlight the vulnerability of young people, which prioritised their status as victims. In doing so, the Solomon Islands reconciliation narrative reproduced homogenous, and marginalising stereotypes to describe young peoples' participation in the Tensions, rather than prioritising their first-hand stories. For example, the final report contended that:

> The line between free will and coercion is quite flimsy … voluntary recruitment is often a choice not exercised freely; it is rarely based exclusively on the volition of the child but tends to be conditioned by factors beyond his/her control.
>
> (Coalition to Stop the Use of Child Soldiers 1998)

While the coercive framework described above explained the participation of Solomon Islander youth in some instances, it also relied on a one-dimensional and linear understanding of *why young people fight*, which perpetuates institutional bias. The stories included in the chapter on children emphasised only the behaviours of those that fit the narrow classifications of young people as either trouble-makers or innocent and vulnerable victims (McEvoy-Levy 2011; Berents and Mollica 2020). For example, the report observed that:

> The ethnic tension pushed a lot of young people out from their normal activities. Most got involved in drinking, smoking, and all sorts of criminal activities even today.
>
> (Solomon Islands TRC Commission 2012: 636)

Similarly, it emphasised the stories of "youth gangs, some ethnically based" who

> appeared in areas of the town such as Burns Creek and Fulisango Zion and started to fight each other to establish territories. Marijuana and kwaso, the home brewed distilled alcohol made with yeast, became readily available at prices that were lower than that of beer.
>
> (Solomon Islands TRC Commission 2012: 637)

Finally, the report focused on the material motivations of youth fighters, emphasising the possessions and opportunities available to young militants. As one militant's submission included in the final report explained, "during the tensions, everyone had a car" (Solomon Islands TRC Commission 2012: 637). While these stories are an important component of the conflict experiences of youth, the institutionalised narrative of the TRC seemed to suggest that they were the only experiences. Yet, as this chapter demonstrates, this is only part of youth's conflict narrative in the Solomon Islands. By prioritising these stories, and by failing to acknowledge displays of agency and ownership by youth that were also evident in the TRC process, the reconciliation narrative in the final report reproduces the normative and structural barriers that often render youth invisible in retributive forms of transitional justice.

A reliance on the coercion narrative to question young people's claims about their participation furthered the political agenda of elites and the international community, while silencing the first-hand stories of youth. The challenge inherent in this coercive representation is evident in the report itself, which after applying this narrative to five submissions from young people goes on to demonstrate that "Malaitans were emphatic in claiming they joined voluntarily" (Solomon Islands TRC Commission 2012: 639). That is, the authors of the final report appeared to grapple with the complexity of the stories of youth and the inherent normative tension associated with the development of inclusive reconciliation narratives. While the institutional narrative prioritised a homogenous representation of young people, embedded in stories of vulnerability, intermittent displays of ownership are included throughout the chapter. For example, the willingness of children and youth to fight to protect their rights and to publicly and "emphatic[ally]" expose their grievances, demonstrated their capacity to act as political stakeholders (Solomon Islands TRC Commission 2012: 656). In addition, their heightened engagement with the Guadalcanal Revolutionary Army (GRA) and later the IFM challenged dominant understandings of youth in the Solomon Islands, which framed their public identity as subordinate to the "big men" in the community. Displays of agency, responsibility and choice were prominent features of the conflict narratives of Malaitan and Guadalcanal youth. While the final report sporadically acknowledged that young soldiers "insist[ed] that their involvement was voluntary," it added the caveat that "the adult members of their respective militant groups failed in their responsibility to protect them" (Solomon Islands TRC Commission 2012: 646). That is, when the choices and agency of youth were recognised they were displayed within a broader protectionist narrative, which placed the final ownership of their voices in the hands of adults.

The chapter on children employed the term "child soldiers' to represent all "young people caught up in a militant group" (Solomon Islands TRC Commission 2012: 646). The lack of differentiation between children and youth displayed within the final report produced a homogenous representation of why and how youth participated in the violence and instability. The inclusion that the Solomon Islands TRC sought initially through the establishment of the Steering Committee did not extend to the institutional narrative which minimised or rendered invisible displays of agency and responsibility. The characterisation of all young militant fighters as child soldiers denotes a passivity and vulnerability which obscured the diversity evident in their actual stories. As a result, the final report of the Solomon Islands TRC perpetuated the common assumptions from the literature that young people, in particular child soldiers, are either "dangerous and disorderly" or in this case the "hapless victim" (Denov 2012: 6–9). To that end, rather than amplifying youth's voices and prioritising inclusion, the institutionalisation of conflict narratives through a final report often perpetuate an environment where the perceptions of external actors are framed as legitimate surrogates for youth voices.

## Conclusion

The Solomon Islands TRC sought to prioritise interpersonal reconciliation, while remaining mindful of the importance of political reconciliation within the international architecture and to donor states (most notably the Regional Assistance Mission to the Solomon Islands (RAMSI)). It revealed the tension between the goals of interpersonal and political approaches and highlighted their impact on the overall success of formalised reconciliation practices as a mechanism for inclusive peace. The emphasis on structural restoration, citizenship and the rule of law which underpins attempts for political reconciliation creates barriers of exclusion and inauthentic processes that constrain the limits of peace and healing, particularly amongst traditionally marginalised groups such as young people (Philpott 2008: 128). In contrast, interpersonal reconciliation, which prioritises the rebuilding of community relationships and the healing of trauma produces inclusive processes that are mindful of the experiences of a diverse range of voices (Wallis et al. 2016: 161). Yet attempts to balance these two goals are often constrained by traditional structural hierarchies where the participation of marginalised individuals is performative rather than substantive. Creating inclusive reconciliation processes, therefore, requires a commitment to representing the on-the-ground realities of youth's experiences. In doing so, reconciliation processes can ensure that youth are not only visible, they are also taken seriously as empowered political agents.

The Solomon Islands TRC process highlights the capacity of historically excluded individuals, specifically youth, to contribute meaningfully to the development of inclusive reconciliation. As demonstrated throughout this chapter, the interactions of youth with the TRC denote a more interpersonal notion of reconciliation, which focuses attention on the needs of individuals. This approach to reconciliation allowed youth to engage extensively with the process of reconciliation and to reframe their position within the broader Solomon Islands community. By actively participating in the decision-making and implementation process of the TRC, Solomon Islander youth were able to demonstrate political will and agency and to position themselves as leaders. At the same time, despite these well-intentioned efforts to create an inclusive and responsive reconciliation process, the final report of the TRC often rendered meaningless their substantive participation due to the pervasiveness of external voices.

## Notes

1 The civil conflict that occurred between 1998–2003 in the Solomon Islands is commonly referred to as "The Tensions." It is estimated that 200 people died during this period, 11,000 were displaced from their homes and thousands of individuals were the victims of a wide range of human rights violations, including torture, arbitrary detention and sexual violence. For more see: Mollica and Jeffery 2017; Allen 2013.

2 *Masta Liu* is a term used to describe people, usually young men, as deviant due to their tendency to loiter, hang around or wander aimlessly (Jourdan 1995: 202). Introduced into Solomon Islands Pijin by the Malaitans, the term took on greater significance in the 1970s when the *Masta Liu Project* was established to provide training to unemployed youth in Honiara (Wulff and Amit-Talai 1995).

3 The term wantok refers to a group who shares mutual social obligations. Literally translated as "speaking the same language," it is often used to denote a kinship-like relationship (Braithwaite et al. 2010: 3).

## References

Allen, Matthew G. (2013). *Greed and grievance: Ex-militants' perspectives on the conflict in Solomon Islands, 1998–2003*. Honolulu: University of Hawai'i Press.

Berents, H., & Mollica, C. (2020). Youth and peacebuilding. In *The Palgrave encyclopedia of peace and conflict studies*. United Kingdom: Palgrave Macmillan.

Braithwaite, J., Dinnen, S., Allen, M., Braithwaite, V., & Charlesworth, H. (2010). *Pillars and shadows: Statebuilding as peacebuilding in Solomon Islands*. Canberra: ANU E Press.

Brocklehurst, H. (2006). *Who's afraid of children? Children, conflict and international relations*. Farnham: Ashgate Publishing Ltd.

Central Islands provincial youth policy (2009). *Central Island Provincial Youth*. Honiara: Solomon Islands: Policy.

D'Costa, B. (2015). Children and justice: Past crimes, healing and the future. In K. Huynh, B. D'Costa & K. Lee-Koo (Eds.) *Children and global conflict* (pp. 212–248). Cambridge: Cambridge University Press.

Denov, M. (2012). Child soldiers and iconography: Portrayals and (mis)representations. *Children and Society*, *26*(4), 280–292.

Donais, T., & McCandless, E. (2017). International peace building and the emerging inclusivity norm. *Third World Quarterly*, *38*(2), 291–310.

Durham, D. (2004). Disappearing youth: Youth as a social shifter in Botswana. *American Ethnologist*, *31*(4), 589–605.

Dwyer, S. (1999). Reconciliation for realists. *Ethics and International Affairs*, *13*, 81–98.

Fortna, V. P. (2018). *Peace time: Cease-fire agreements and the durability of peace*. Princeton: Princeton University Press.

Fraenkel, J. (2004). *The manipulation of custom: From uprising to intervention in the Solomon Islands*. Victoria University Press.

Furlong, A., Cartmel, F., Biggart, A., Sweeting, H., & West, P. (2003). *Youth transitions: Patterns of vulnerability and processes of social inclusion*. Edinburgh: Scottish Executive Social Research.

Guadalcanal Provincial Government (2010). *Guadalcanal provincial youth policy*. Honiara: Solomon Islands.

Guthrey, H. L., & Brounéus, K. (2017). Peering into the 'Black Box' of TRC success: Exploring local perceptions of reconciliation in the Solomon Islands. In R. Jeffery (Ed.) *Transitional justice in practice* (pp. 85–111). New York: Palgrave Macmillan.

Hassall & Associates and AUSAID. (2003). *Youth in Solomon Islands: A participatory study of issues, needs and priorities*. Honiara: Solomon Islands.

Hayner, P. (2003). *Unspeakable truths: Facing the challenge of truth commissions*. New York: Routledge.

Jacob, C. (2013). *Child security in Asia: The impact of armed conflict in Cambodia and Myanmar*. New York: Routledge.

Jeffery, R. (2015). The foregiveness dilemma: Emotions and Justice at the Khmer Rouge Tribunal. *Australian Journal of International Affairs*, *69*(1), 35–52.

Jeffery, R., & Mollica, C. (2017). The unfinished business of the Solomon Islands TRC: Closing the implementation gap. *The Pacific Review*, *30*(4), 531–548.

Jourdan, C. (1995). Stepping stones to national consciousness: The Solomon Islands case. *Nation Making: Emergent Identities in Postcolonial Melanesia*, *127*, 127–150.

Kwon, S. A. (2019). The politics of global youth participation. *Journal of Youth Studies*, *22*(7), 926–940.

Lederach, J. P. (2001). Civil society and reconciliation. In C. Crocker, F.O. Hampson & P. Aall (Eds.), *Turbulent peace: The challenges of managing international conflict* (pp. 841–854). Washington, DC: United States Institute of Peace.

Lee Koo, K. (2015). Children and peace building: Propagating peace. In K. Huynh, B. D'Costa, & K. Lee Koo (Eds.), *Children and global conflict* (pp. 185–209). Cambridge: Cambridge University Press.

Mac Ginty, R. (2012). Routine peace: Technocracy and peacebuilding. *Cooperation and Conflict*, *47*(3), 287–308.

McEvoy-Levy, S. (Ed.) (2006). *Troublemakers or peacemakers? Youth and post-accord peace building*. South Bend: University of Notre Dame Press.

McEvoy-Levy, S. (2011). Children, youth and peacebuilding. In T. Matyok, J. Senehi & S. Byrne (Eds.), *Critical issue in peace and conflict studies: Theory, practice and pedagogy* (pp. 159–176). United Kingdom: Lexington Books.

Mollica, C. (2017). The diversity of identity: Youth participation at the Solomon Islands truth and reconciliation commission. *Australian Journal of International Affairs*, *71*(4), 371–388.

Murphy, C. (2010). *A moral theory of political reconciliation*. Cambridge: Cambridge University Press.

Oswell, D. (2013). *The agency of children: From family to global human rights*. Cambridge: Cambridge University Press.

Özerdem, A., & Podder, S. (2015). *Youth in conflict and peacebuilding: Mobilization, reintegration and reconciliation*. Basingstoke: Palgrave Macmillan.

Paffenholz, T. (2015). Unpacking the local turn in peacebuilding: A critical assessment towards an agenda for future research. *Third World Quarterly*, *36*(5), 857–874.

Philpott, D. (2008). Reconciliation: An ethic for responding to evil in global politics. In R. Jeffery (Ed.), *Confronting evil in international relations: Ethical responses to problems of moral agency* (pp. 115–150). New York: Palgrave Macmillan.

Quinn, J. (2009). Introduction. In J. Quinn (Ed.). *Reconciliation(s): Transitional justice in post conflict societies* (pp. 3–17). Montreal: McGill-Queen University Press.

Quinn, J. R. (2011). *The politics of acknowledgement: Truth commissions in Uganda and Haiti*. UBC Press.

Schwartz, S. (2010). *Youth in post-conflict reconstruction: Agents of change*. Washington, DC: United States Institute of Peace.

Solomon Islands National Statistics Office (2009). *Solomon Islands population and housing census: National report* (Volume Two). Honiara: Solomon Islands.

Solomon Islands TRC Commission (2012). *Solomon Islands truth and reconciliation commission final report: Confronting the truth for a better Solomon Islands*. Honiara: Solomon Islands.

Sukarieh, M., & Tannock, S. (2018). The global securitisation of youth. *Third World Quarterly*, *39*(5), 854–870.

Waldorf, L., & Shaw, R. (2010). Introduction: Localizing transitional justice. In *Localizing transitional justice. Interventions and priorities after mass violence* (pp. 3–27). Palo Alto: Stanford University Press.

Wallis, J., Jeffery, R., & Kent, L. (2016). Political reconciliation in Timor Leste, Solomon Islands and Bougainville: The darker side of hybridity. *Australian Journal of International Affairs*, *70*(2), 159–178.

Wulff, H., & Amit-Talai, V. (1995). *Youth cultures*. London: Routledge.

# 10 Between forgiveness and revenge

## The reconstruction of social relationships in post-Khmer Rouge Cambodia

*SungYong Lee*

### Introduction

How are victims and harm-doers in local communities developed and transformed after mass violence? This topic has been extensively examined in the contemporary peacebuilding discourse under the broad theme of reconciliation. Nevertheless, despite the rapid increase in the number of studies, the promotion of reconciliation in contemporary peacebuilding programmes has focused on a limited range of state-centric institutional arrangements for truth-telling, trial and compensation. A large number of studies have examined key features of these institutions, criticised their limitations and proposed ways for further improvements. Their insights and empirical findings have made significant contributions in both theoretical and empirical aspects (just a few examples include Boraine 2001; Hamber and Wilson 2003; Breen Smyth 2007; Miller and Bunnell 2011; Williams and Scharf 2002).

A problem is, however, that these studies do not explain what is happening to the people who are outside such institutional support. According to the PAM Implementation dataset, just over half of the peace processes actively incorporate any type of mechanisms for social reconciliation, while the remaining processes either do not have any plan or achieved limited implementation (PAM Implementation Dataset 2015). Moreover, even in cases where such institutional arrangements were promoted, due to the limited scope and capacity, such arrangements usually include only a small percentage of victims in their operations. This means that a majority of the victims and population in conflict-affected societies have had to handle the past atrocities without any institutional support. What is happening then to these victims and local communities who are outside of such institutional mechanisms? A lack of empirical studies on this question is a significant knowledge gap.

This chapter aims to take a modest step to address this gap by examining the reconstruction of the relationship between the perpetrators and victims occurring in people's daily lives in Cambodia. Specifically, it looks at the forms of the victim–harm-doers' relations in the post-Khmer Rouge (KR)[1] period. Since the end of 1978, when the KR regime was ousted from power, local communities in Cambodia have developed various types of actions individually and collectively in order to redefine and develop their relations with former KR leaders. Due to the subtlety, however, the significance of such actions has often been neglected in academic studies.

As a framework to examine these forms, this chapter proposes a typology of post-war relationship-building at community levels on a scale between revenge and re-humanised relationships, which consist of revenge, concealed antagonism, efforts to "move on," tolerance of coexistence and re-humanised relationships. It then examines the complex motivations of victims to develop each type of relationship-building. Finally, it will highlight the forms of agency that community residents develop and utilise for developing "everyday peace." For this purpose, the author conducted 22 interviews with direct victims of the Khmer Rouge violence and community residents in January and December 2019. The interview participants were recruited in Svay Rieng, Battambang and Phnom Penh in Cambodia, in order to capture different dynamics of social reconciliation.[2]

Victims are difficult to identify in Cambodia, as most people who survived the KR period had multiple identities as victims, bystanders, harm-doers and their collaborators over time. In this chapter, "victim" denotes people who lost their direct families or were physically wounded by KR leaders or soldiers. All interviews were conducted with the victims; however, some of the interactions described in this chapter are collective actions of the wider community members.

## Handling the legacy of the Khmer Rouge

During interviews, many victims and community residents repeated "three years and eight months" to denote the radical social *revolution* of the KR. When I mentioned somewhat unclear words like "approximately four years," some immediately corrected this, reconfirming the exact period. Some interviewees remembered the dates when the KR first came into their villages, when the KR captured Phnom Penh and when the Vietnam-backed new ruling group expelled the KR in their areas. Despite, or due to, its relatively short period of dominant power (1976–1979), the impact that its rule left on Cambodian society is deep and devastating. Even after 40 years, the KR rule is still taken seriously by many victims.

The socialist projects imposed by the KR, such as a collective agricultural system, depopulation of cities and prohibition of markets arguably caused the deaths of approximately 1.6 million people (Manning 2017: 38). An absolute majority of the population who survived the KR regime had psychological trauma from previous hardships like the deaths of close family members, having their lives threatened, lack of food, separation of family members and forced labour (Field and Chhim 2008). Moreover, KR rule destroyed the cultural and religious institutions central to the society (Harris 2005) and divided communities with deep distrust and mistrust (Zucker 2013).

The process to promote justice and reconciliation in relation to the KR started immediately after the new political authority – the People's Republic of Kampuchea (PRK) – was established in early 1979. In the 1980s, such programmes were highly politicised in order to strengthen the legitimacy of the PRK regime that wanted to identify itself as "the liberator" from the anti-humanitarian KR cadres. For instance, in 1979 the new government set up the Revolutionary People's Court to deal with the KR leaders, especially Pol Pot and Ieng Sary. After a five-day-long judicial process, the court pronounced death penalties for the two people *in absentia*. Moreover, in 1983, a Genocide Research Committee was set to collect victims' testimonials and identify mass graves and detention facilities. The committee produced approximately 10,000 documents that were apparently approved by a million people (Chandler 2008; Guillou 2012).

In addition, the most symbolic places that demonstrated the Khmer Rouge's brutal policies were preserved and restored to show the past anti-humanitarian action. The two most well-known sites are the Killing Fields in Cheong-Ek and S-21 in Toul Sleng. S-21 was the biggest of the security prisons operated across the country during the KR period and an estimated 14,000–20,000 people were tortured and killed at the site. The Killing Fields in Cheong-Ek is one of the sites used for mass execution. Multiple investigations have found approximately 8,800 bodies. When these sites were found soon after the purge of the KR regime, the PRK leaders deliberately maintained them in the way to "prove" the cruelty of the KR. The government then invited foreign journalists and international delegates to these sites (Manning 2017).

More importantly for local communities, the PRK government created boneyards and memorials where the scattered skulls and bones were collected and placed. Approximately 80 memorial places were built across the country in the 1980s. These projects were primarily undertaken by local authorities and the quality and forms of the memorials vary depending on the authorities' financial capacity. While some were in sophisticated forms of stupa made of bricks or wood, others looked more like simple graves (Guillou 2012).

In 1984, the government declared 20 May as the Day of Anger (*tivea chang komheung*) to acknowledge the crimes of the KR and to communally mourn the victims.[3] Ceremonies were hosted by local authorities every year, usually at the sites of mass killings or open places. These events normally consisted of the testimonials of the victims, speeches from political figures, art performances and Buddhist prayers, in which the KR's anti-humanitarian actions were condemned and prayers for the victims were conveyed. In addition, the government supported the publication and dissemination of the survivors' memories of their victimisation under the KR (Chandler 2008).

The directions for handling the KR issues significantly shifted in the early 1990s when the Paris Peace Agreements "officially" terminated the civil war in the country. After a short period of a coalition government, the central political power fell back to the former PRK leadership. However, the government's approaches to the KR-related issues significantly changed. Primarily, the government wants to let the past be forgotten. Seeing that the KR would not be a political threat any longer, Prime Minister Hun Sen wanted to "dig a hole and bury the past" in order to promote national reconciliation (Hun Sen 1998, cited in Chandler 2008: 356). He offered to "pardon" core KR leaders in 1996, and accepted them to keep their influence in the stronghold areas of KR. Some senior leaders of the KR were accepted into the government ranks or the ruling Cambodian People's Party. The national curricula barely explained the history related to the KR and the mass media under government control seldom covered the relevant issues (Chandler 2008).

Transitional justice vis-à-vis KR leaders was pursued through the Extraordinary Chambers in the Courts of Cambodia (ECCC). ECCC is an outcome of a lengthy negotiation between the Cambodian government and international actors like the UN, NGOs and foreign governments. While the Cambodian government officially requested the UN to set up the tribunal in 1997, the government continued to present a resistant or ambivalent posture to its formation until the court finally began to function in 2006. The tribunal limited the target to the five most senior leaders who had ordered the serious crimes against humanity (Manning 2017).

To sum up, the state-led programmes for social reconciliation have been inappropriate and insufficient to address the dire anxiety between the harm-doers and victims. While the PRK regime during the 1980s was mostly interested in strengthening its legitimacy by condemning the KR's wrongdoings, the new governments since the Paris Peace Accords in 1991 did not take any substantial action to deal with the past. While the ECCC was conducted with international support, the slow court process was only briefly covered in the mass media and a majority of the people could not relate to the process. For instance, a report confirmed that 85% of the population had little knowledge of the ongoing tribunal until 2009 (Pham et al. 2009).

Such a lack of support for reconciliation was partially supplemented by the roles of non-state actors who undertook various programmes at individual and collective levels. At individual levels, for example, some NGOs offered victims the opportunities to speak up about their victimhood through individual dialogues, group workshops or via radio broadcasting. Probably the most well-known examples are the Documentary Center of Cambodia (DC-Cam) and the International Center for Conciliation (ICFC) that have played central roles in collecting, analysing and disseminating the stories relevant to the KR regime; Trans-cultural Psychological Organization (TPO) in mental support and clinical interventions for the victims of violence; Youth for Peace (YFP) and the Centre for Social Development organised workshops and public fora to nurture mutual understanding between different groups regarding the KR history (McGrew 2011; McGrew 2018; Interview II). At the collective level, attempts have been made to develop alternative historical narratives about the Khmer Rouge period. For instance, DC-Cam has set memorial sites in many primary schools across the country. The same organisation also recently developed the first textbook on the KR history, which has now been adopted by the government as the supplementary material for official education. However, compared to the number of victims, the people who are part of these initiatives are less significant.

## Conceptual framework: Reconciliation as a process and everyday peace

To reiterate, this study explores how victims and harm-doers have developed their relationships in post-KR period Cambodia. It pays particular attention to and unpacks the differences between actions that may look identical at the superficial level. It will argue that local communities' varied actions that may look similar in form in fact represent very distinct motivations of victims and community residents, and thus should be dealt with as different types of actions. Moreover, it will explain that the subtlety itself reflects local actors' strategies to express their views while protecting themselves from any unnecessary life challenges in the given social, structural and cultural restrictions. Seeking a suitable framework to examine social relationship building in the local communities, the analysis in this chapter will rely on two sets of theoretical discussions.

First, the studies that understand reconciliation as a *process* offer a good conceptual ground to capture the differing states of the mutual relationship between former harm-doers and victims. Although the detailed arguments vary, this group of studies commonly acknowledges that reconciliation involves a slow, long-term process rather than an (ideal) outcome (Etcheson 2005; Lederach 1997; Rigby 2006). In this process, the people develop and transform different types of mutual engagement and the nature of the engagement evolves, reflecting the actors' beliefs, attitudes, emotions and goals. To clarify such complexity, some studies propose typologies that conceptualise different "levels" of reconciliation. These typologies usually put the levels of reconciliation on linear scales from shallow coexistence to deep reconciliation. For instance, Rigby (2006) proposes three levels of reconciliation – surface coexistence, shallow coexistence and deep reconciliation – while Crocker (2002) describes the amount of reconciliation by using the terms thick and thin. Similar types of conceptualisations have been proposed in Bar-Siman-Tov (2004), Bloomfield et al. (2003), Sampson (2003), Fletcher and Winstein (2002), Brounéus (2007) and Strupinskiene (2017). Based on the typologies, studies tend to propose ways to encourage social actors in divided societies to move from shallow to deep reconciliation.

Second, this study adopts the *everyday peace* concept to identify and examine the local communities' agency and reconciliatory elements embedded in Cambodian people's daily practice for living. This section will not repeat the detailed introduction to the academic debates on everyday peacebuilding which has already appeared in the introductory chapter of this volume. However, it is worth reiterating that these studies by and large highlight that the avenues of people's livelihood such as local agency, rights, needs, custom and kinship provide an important context for decision-making, and promote active peacebuilding (Richmond 2010; Chandler 2015; Brāuchler 2015; Richmond and Mitchell 2012; Mac Ginty 2014; Berents and McEvoy-Levy 2015; Felix da Costa and Karlsrud 2012; Tadjbakhsh 2011). In these studies, everyday denotes "a set of micro-processes of practices in a constant interaction driven by the agency of ordinary people in concrete circumstances" (Chandler 2015: 43). The framework of everyday

*Table 10.1* Patterns of victim–perpetrator interaction in Cambodia

| *Revenge* | *Concealed antagonism* | *Efforts to "move on"* | | *Tolerance of coexistence* | *Re-humanised relationship* |
|---|---|---|---|---|---|
| | | *Healing and commemoration* | *Forgetting* | | |
| Physical violence | Segregation, social shunning | Minimal engagement | | Minimal engagement, sympathising | Befriend |

is particularly relevant to the studies examining the local process and strategies for post-war reconciliation and local actors' agency within it.

Based on the theoretical frameworks, this chapter proposes a typology of victim–perpetrator interaction (see Table 10.1). For each type of interaction, this study will investigate the motivations of victims and perpetrators to develop and maintain such relationships and the detailed forms of mutual interactions. This typology has been conceptualised based on the author's pilot research conducted in January 2019. Interview participants (victims and wider community members) referred to various actions upon the author's request to describe how they manage their relations with former KR leaders. These actions were categorised into five rough patterns based on the underlying motivations: Revenge, concealed antagonism, efforts to "move on," tolerance of coexistence and re-humanised relationship.

## Reconstruction of social relationships in post-war Cambodia

(Re)development of social relationship in a post-conflict society is a complex process in which various actors engage in various forms of interaction based on dissimilar motivations. Cambodia is no exception. This section will examine a few types of interactions that are more prevalent in the local communities in north-eastern and south-western provinces of Cambodia as of the late 2010s. For each type of interaction, this section will investigate the motivations of victims to develop and maintain such relationships, the main narratives adopted for this purpose and the detailed forms of actions taken by the victims. Out of the five conceptual categories introduced above, examples of **revenge** are rare. A few research participants reported episodes of revenge against the former Khmer Rouge soldiers, either doing physical harm or reporting the perpetrators to the Vietnamese army as spies serving the Khmer Rouge guerrilla groups (Interview XI). However, these victims tend to repeat a small number of the same episodes and they remembered the cases because they were examples of rather unusual and extreme behaviour. All of these occasions occurred immediately after the Khmer Rouge regime collapsed.

**Concealed antagonism** denotes the cases where people harbour antagonism and mistrust against former KR leaders although they do not express it in violent actions. A significant number of interview participants said that they still have a high level of anger. Some suffered from post-traumatic stress and still wondered why they had to face such horrific events. One interview participant said that some victims including himself would commit to revenge if there were triggers like perpetrators' open denial of responsibility (Interview III). For these victims, in this sense, antagonism is constrained and not expressed in visible actions.

A few cultural and social factors were raised as key deterrents to physical violence. Particularly significant was their fear of the consequences. The sources of fear vary depending on geographical locations. In the north-western provinces, for instance, the combat between the KR and the new government continued until the last phase of the civil war. The authorities that controlled certain areas changed many times. Since there was a possibility that the KR could return to their areas, local residents did not want to stand out as aggressors out of fear of any potential revenge (Interview I). In contrast, in the south-eastern provinces, the new regime quickly controlled the area and banned unauthorised violence soon after the KR regime collapsed. Moreover, to stabilise the security in the areas, the new authority applied strong restrictions on the use of violence against former KR leaders. Community leaders had repeated the message that anyone who does physical violence against the KR leaders would be convicted (Interview IV). In some cases, former KR soldiers and collaborators collectively lived in villages and, although they were outnumbered, other people could not challenge the former KR associates (McGrew 2011: 94).

In addition, the Buddhist concepts of *karma* formed an important narrative that prevented many people from committing to physical violence, especially killing. Based on the concept of "cause and effect" of a certain phenomenon, Buddhism teaches that the native action will without fail bring about negative consequence. From this standpoint, no killing and no stealing are two of the Five Precepts, which many Cambodian Buddhist uphold as crucial elements of practice. This prevention of violence convinced many people not to "pay back" what they had received from KR leaders. For instance, one victim who lost his father mentioned:

> Actually, I wanted to see him, thinking of doing revenge because he killed my father. But my mother said 'don't do that. It will create a bad karma again. In the previous life, your father must have done something bad to him.' … When Vietnamese soldiers came to my village, I reported about him (a KR leader). But, when the soldiers were about to arrest him, my mom did not want another killing. She said 'No, no. He is not (a KR leader).' So the Vietnamese soldiers let him survive.
>
> (Interview III)

With less likelihood of violently expressing their anger, people explored alternative methods to express their anxiety. Although the details of the methods vary, as will be explained below, they can be broadly conceptualised as social shunning.

In some cases, former KR leaders have found shelter somewhere far from local villages, hiding themselves from people's sight. When they encounter local residents, according to interviewees, these people usually attempt to avoid interaction (Interview IV, also see McGrew 2011). In other cases, KR leaders and their families are allowed to live in local villages. They are also allowed to shop and often work within the communities. However, the direct interaction with other members of the population was kept to a minimum. These people are excluded from major local events and activities including most important ones like weddings, funerals or Buddhist festivals (Interviews III and IV). The stories of the leaders' cruelty were transmitted to the next generations within each family, from parents' mouths to their children. Accordingly, the sense of antagonism was also inherited by the next generation (Interview III).

**Efforts to move on** denotes varied types of victims' actions that aim not to be affected by the previous pain and the presence of the perpetrators. When focusing on the forms of actions, the actions in this type may look similar to the "tolerance of coexistence" that will be discussed in the following section. The victims and wider community do not express their anxiety against former KR associates. Often, the former KR associates and their families are requested to be involved in economic and social activities as well. As a result, it is observable that victims and perpetrators live in the same community, without significant attempts at mutual harm or mutual interaction. McGrew (2011) conceptualises it as the *state of surface coexistence* or *shallow coexistence* in which victims and perpetrators achieve a non-lethal détente.

When looking into what lies behind the motivations, nevertheless, victims' attention is not given to the reconstruction of the relationship with the harm-doers. In the author's interviews, there were participants who did not want to talk so much about their pain or their feelings about the harm-doers. Instead, they hoped to concentrate on how to make their current life more comfortable and to prevent past memories affecting it so much. A statement made by an interview was "No, they didn't want to forgive. But they didn't want to get bothered by that any more" (Interview V). Such efforts to "move on" were often expressed in two distinct ways.

*Healing and commemoration*: Healing and commemoration are related to the victims' internal process for recovering from the past pain. Many victims had suffered a sense of guilt as survivors/bystanders who could not take any actions to protect their families. While they observed how the families were captured, tortured and never allowed to return, they had to turn blind eyes and deaf ears so that they did not become the next targets of the KR (McGrew 2011). Moreover, in the Cambodian tradition, proper burial or cremation of dead bodies is culturally important. It is believed that the dead who cannot be buried or cremated are likely to become nasty spirits. The spirits frequently do harm to living people. During the KR period, however, people have observed thousands of cases where people were killed and collectively dumped in open areas (Bennett 2018). Hence, for many victims and community residents, cultural healing and commemoration were their priority in three ways. First, they needed a decent opportunity to send off the killed and to pray for good fortunes in their next lives. Second, they needed to wash out their sense of guilt and avoid any negative *karma* caused by their action (or inaction) during the KR period. Third, they wanted to calm down and prevent any bad actions from the thousands of bad spirits that could move around their communities.

For this purpose, people conduct mock funerals and commemorative services. Although the bodies of those killed cannot be discovered, the families perform Buddhist rituals in the places where the killing was believed to have taken place or at local monasteries (Interviews I and IV). During the interviewees, community members often brought me to a place in a field and pointed out sites where most killing was done. There was no particular sign for remembering, but most community members, including children, seem well aware of the history of the place. The specific forms, sizes and procedures of the rituals vary depending on the host family's financial capacity. For poorer families who do not have money to host commemorative rituals, *Pchum Ben* – a Buddhist day when people provide offerings to the dead – is a time that they can send prayers.

As an opportunity for collective mourning, the annual ceremony on the Day of Anger/Remembrance (20 May) offered one of the few opportunities for victims to openly express their emotion, especially anger, under cultural conditions that discourage the expression of anxiety (Bockers and Knaevelsrud 2011). These events primarily focused on condemning the brutal and inhumane actions of the KR, and hence, were unsuitable to "bring a nation together as one in remembering shared trauma and loss" (Etcheson 2004). Nevertheless, the theatrical performances and emotional speeches as well as religious rituals played important roles in acknowledging the pain of the victims (Ly 2017). In the 1980s, such commemorations took place across the country at province or district levels. While the detailed programmes vary, on many occasions, these events concluded with the prayers and blessings (*bangskol*) of prominent Buddhist monks and most participants collectively joined the recitations of Buddhist teachings (Guillou 2012; Interview IV).

*Forget*: Another type of motivation is to forget the previous pain or devalue the significance of the past and the perpetrators. Many victims often feel that the past trauma is simply too difficult to cope with, especially when their everyday life is surrounded by many challenges like insecurity and economic hardships. To avoid misunderstanding, *forgetting* in this study is different from *putting the past unquestioned* or *collective amnesia* that are deliberately adopted as part of social reconciliation (Rigby 2001; Uvin 2009; Etcheson 2005) or attempts to eliminate the memory shameful to the community (Zucker 2009). In fact, the research participants who expressed the above responses did not hope that the past would be forgotten. Some of them had repeated their stories to their children for decades (Interviews IV and V). However, they worried that to talk openly about their pain or to talk with former KR leaders would require the processing of too much of an emotional burden and too many complicated procedures.

Accordingly, these people chose to ignore the issues which occurred during the KR period. A group of research participants, for example, mentioned that their current lives are too busy and they did not have time to think so much about the past, although they still felt sad and angry when they recalled the difficult time under the KR, such as the below quotation.

> During the Khmer Rouge, I lost one of my uncles. But my mother never asked who killed him. She just came back to life and then worked hard to get rice. Reconciliation at individual person's life was like that. When they were hungry, it was difficult for them to discuss who killed who.
>
> (Interview VI)

In some cases, people attempt to undervalue the significance of the past experience or the former harm-doers. One interview participant, for instance, said "I don't take him human and don't care whether he is there. When a cockroach bites you, do you spend so much time to bite back?" (Interview VII).

The practical consequence of these actions is to open slightly more space for former KR leaders to be involved in social activities, as the people who concentrate on their own issues do not take any deliberate actions. One villager in Svay Rieng said that he knew that a KR leader was living close to him but he would not want to do anything about this. Another interview participant said that he did not mind that the grandchildren of a former KR leader attend the same school with his grandchildren (Interview XI). In this regard, such actions or inactions as these people present seem rather tolerant; this does not necessarily represent their acceptance of the harm-doers. Nevertheless, when focusing on the "relations" between victims and harm-doers, the actions/non-actions are not motivated by any desire to build relationships with the former harm-doers. While the types of actions described above are distinct, they are common in that they primarily focus on sorting out their own pain.

**Tolerance of coexistence** denotes a range of actions that are similar to the conditions conceptualised in the conventional studies as "thin reconciliation," "partial acceptance," "shallow coexistence," "nonviolent coexistence" (Borneman 2002; Bloomfield et al. 2003 Kriesberg 1998; McGrew 2011; Kumar 1999; Fischer 2011). Victims are willing to accept former KR leaders as part of their human network and to engage with them for pragmatic economic cooperation and mutually beneficial social projects. The former harm-doers and their families are informed about public events and social activities including major religious/family activities that take place within their local villages. These actors are allowed to engage in most economic activities (e.g., operating shops, offering services) without being subject to significant discrimination. When asked their opinions about former KR leaders, the respondents often acknowledge the positive contributions that they make, although they might not be prepared to be friends again. For instance, one respondent said "He (a former KR associate) is skilful in making fences. So I ask for his help when I need to fix my fences. He is by far more effective than others." (Interview VIII).

Following Staub and Pearlman (2001), coexistence in this study means the condition where people (individually or collectively) live together, trade and may share the same vision for the future as the members of the same community, but do not necessary build mutual trust or understanding. Respondents highlighted three factors when responding to the question of why they (and their fellow villagers) were able to accept them as part of the communities and move beyond the anxiety with former perpetrators. First, victims often differentiated the level of "cruelty" that the former KR leaders/soldiers demonstrated and were sympathetic to the people with more moderate behaviour. Many interview respondents made a statement like "The people who came back are usually the people who has not done particularly cruel actions. The really bad people were killed soon after Vietnam came in" (Interview IV). Moreover, victims were often sympathetic to the situation in which KR leaders were placed. Two narratives were particularly highlighted: (1) The harm-doers themselves were "forced to commit" to violence, and (2) they were the young and least educated in the communities and the KR utilised their ignorance. (Similar findings are also reported in McGrew 2011).

Second, pre-established relationship is an important factor. Some victims had maintained family relationships or friendships with KR leaders that had been established in the pre-KR period. While the victims do not forgive them, they feel it difficult to deny such pre-established relationships. For example, one research participant said "There was only one villager who still see him (a KR leader). But he was his (the KR leader's) nephew. So, what can he do?" (Interview I). Another respondent said "Some of them were the people that I had known before. We didn't know whether these people had committed any bad things. So we could feel good with each other" (Interview III).

Third, people often accepted former KR leaders based on the behaviour that they showed when they returned after the KR period. When former perpetrators look "scared," "apologetic," and "silent," community members felt sympathetic to them. Once the interaction begins, victims and community residents have more opportunities to build (re)humanised relationships with the former harm-doers. Some former KR leaders took more proactive actions in order to be treated as trustworthy, actively joining the collective labour for communities and taking more roles for social service. A good example appears in Zucker (2009)'s study on a former KR agent who later became an *achar wat*, lay functionaries who deal with the management of monasteries. After having committed to the role, which is usually respected by local communities, for decades, the former agent established a decent reputation in areas surrounding the town where he had committed violent actions.

Although indirect, harm-doers occasionally acknowledged their wrongdoings, which strengthened the relationships. For instance, one village leader mentioned

> Yes, I had asked questions about why they did that, often when we drank together. Rather than in a serious manner, I tried to make the conversation light. They usually said that they felt bad with their previous actions. Also,

> they looked sad when they explained that they were ordered to do that. If they hadn't followed the order, they would have been killed as well.
>
> (Interview IV)

The attitudes of victims/community members are influenced by the combined impact of the above factors. While the first two factors determine the possibility of "acceptance" by the community, the third factor opens the opportunities for expanding mutual understanding. One short statement from a victim, in this regard, shows such an example:

> When they came back, the former Khmer Rouge soldiers behaved modest. Also, we used to know each other and I remembered him as honest person. … He said, 'Yes I committed to that … higher officers commanded to do so.' But he did not have knowledge, he just followed orders. I understand that. … So I treat him as a normal person. However, I could not develop deep relationship with him. He knew what he had committed and he did not attempt to be closer. (Interview XI)

The category of *rehumanised relationship* denotes the types of relationship identified as "deep reconciliation" in many previous studies. In this type of relationship, both victims and harm-doers reach the point of recognising their counterparts as valued human beings and engage in mutual trust-building actions. Harm-doers' acknowledgement of their previous wrongdoing and victims' forgiveness are often expressed in this process, according to their cultural contexts (Kriesberg 1998; Theidon 2007). Although the examples relevant to this category were reported during the author's field studies, the number is less significant than the previous categories. It is noteworthy that this small number of examples emphasise personal experiences that convinced the victims to be openminded to the KR leaders. For instance, one victim who lost his leg due to actions of the KR soldiers mentioned his experience of seeing the humanistic actions of some KR soldiers during combat (Interview XI). Moreover, these interview participants' attitudes were not backed up by other community members. Although further study is required to identify to what extent these examples represent the overall situation in Cambodia, this means that re-humanised relationships are more an individual choice, while the types of interactions stated above are more collectively conducted. It is beyond the scope of this chapter to investigate why and how the attempts at more positive relationships fail to mobilise collective action. However, this demonstrates that the promotion of deep reconciliation in people's everyday lives faces many challenges even four decades after the end of the KR regime.

## Concluding discussion

Thus far, this chapter has examined how the victims of the KR regime and other community members have re-developed their relationships with the former harm-doers in Cambodia. First, the overall state of social reconciliation in the

Cambodian local communities achieves "non-violent coexistence" between the former harm-doers and their victims. Among the five categories of the victim–perpetrator relationships proposed in this chapter, the examples that represent extreme resentment (revenge) or deep reconciliation (re-humanised relationship) were rare. Physical violence was adopted for a short while in the aftermath of the KR ruling; however, most interview participants recall them as abnormal occasions occurring against particular persons. While some evidence of re-humanised relationship was reported during the interviews, the number is too small to be identified as a pattern. Instead, most cases present varied conditions in between surface coexistence and shallow reconciliation.

Second, the conditions relevant to non-violent coexistence reflect distinct motivations of the victims. This chapter presented three types of actions that may look similar in form but are based on different motivations: Concealed antagonism, efforts to "move on," and tolerance of coexistence. Many people still harboured strong anxiety towards the harm-doers but did not find the right ways to express the emotion and anger, which is conceptualised as concealed antagonism. Efforts to "move on" denote victims' attempts not to be trapped by their previous pain and includes two major types of actions: Healing/commemorating and forgetting. While victims do not do any harm to the former perpetrators, their primary motivation is the desire not to be swayed by the past. Tolerance of coexistence presents the conditions where victims and harm-doers acknowledge their counterparts and the members of the communities.

It is important to note that multiple levels of reconciliation can coexist within the same community. Victims (and wider communities) engage in different types of relationships with former KR leaders, frequently depending on the level of victimisation, victims' pre-established relationships and the attitudes of the former harm-doers. For example, the actions for commemoration or social acceptance are taken to be parts of other activities, such as annual Buddhist ceremonies or major development projects. Hence, they are difficult to distinguish as actions taken for victim–perpetrator relationship-building.

Another point of discussion is that the choices of communities frequently look inactive, subtle or episodic, as seen in the actions for social shunning, the creation of boundaries and minimal engagement. People who spend a short period of time in communities may not notice if such action is ongoing or may take it as happening coincidentally. However, in most cases, these subtle actions are deliberately chosen as a systematic social punishment.[4] While many of the actions undertaken for such relationship-building are collectively mobilised and approved (e.g. collective participation in social shunning), there are individuals who engage in significantly more aggressive or accommodating relations. Moreover, the people who engage in certain types of relationship tend not to switch their attitudes. While the research participants expressed that their anxiety against the KR gradually weakened, few of them mentioned that their attitudes radically jumped to another category. In other words, the complexities in the reconciliation states within a community should be considered as a constant factor that will affect the dynamics of peacebuilding in the area.

From a theoretical perspective, the above findings are particularly relevant to the ongoing academic debates on "silence" in peacebuilding and reconciliation. In the conventional studies on post-war reconciliation, silence has frequently been understood as lack of acknowledgement and as detrimental to victims' healing, harmful to social reconciliation, risky when utilised for political marginalisation and causing a second wound to the victims, making them feel ignored, forgotten and incapable (Govier and Verwoerd 2002; Cohen 2001; Eastmond and Selimovic 2012). Nevertheless, more recent studies adopting an "everyday" framework began to adopt silence as "cultural ways of dealing with personal pain, local post-war realities and quotidian social interactions" (Eastmond and Selimovic 2012: 504) and to "promote pragmatic ways of mending relations." While appreciating the values of the new approaches to silence, the examples in this study call for more careful empirical examination of the cases previously conceptualised as silence. Many occasions that may look like "silence" to outsiders may in fact present many subtle actions of local communities that have a real impact in relationship-building. Otherwise, we are likely to neglect the significance of the *devils* in the details.

## Interview list

Interview I – A victim of the KR violence living in Battambaing (January 2019)
Interview II – An NGO practitioner living in Phnom Penh (December 2019)
Interview III – A victim of the KR violence living in Battambaing (January 2019)
Interview IV– A village leader living in Svay Rieng (January 2019)
Interview V – A former commune leader living in Battambang (January 2019)
Interview VI – A victim of the KR violence living in Svay Rieng (January 2019)
Interview VII – A victim of the KR violence living in Svay Rieng (January 2019)
Interview VIII – A victim of the KR violence living in Svay Rieng (January 2019)
Interview IX – An NGO practitioner living in Phnom Penh (March 2018 and January 2019)
Interview X – A former NGO practitioner involved in social reconciliation (October 2019)
Interview XI - A victim of the KR violence from Battambang (Phnom Penh, December 2019)

## Notes

1 The group's self-claimed official name is the Party of Democratic Kampuchea and it is often called *Khmer Krohom* ("Red Khmer" in the Cambodian language) within local communities. However, this chapter uses the Khmer Rouge (French for "Red Khmer"), which is most widely used in the academic studies.

2 Svay Rieng is one of the first places that were under the control of the anti-KR alliance, whereas Battambang was where the civil conflicts continued until the last moment. The capital city Phnom Penh had been "emptied" during the KR regime, and the entire population was re-migrated after its collapse.

3 The name was changed to the Day of Commemoration in 2001.
4 In terms of social shunning, community members often considered that the former KR leaders do not exist until the author explicitly asked questions about them. Similar observations were reported in Zucker (2009) and McGrew (2011).

## References

Bar-Siman-Tov, Y. (Ed.). (2004). *From conflict resolution to reconciliation.* Oxford: Oxford University Press.

Bennett, C. (2018) Karma after democratic kampuchea: justice outside the khmer rouge tribunal. *Genocide Studies and Prevention: An International Journal, 12*(3), 68–82.

Berents, H., & McEvoy-Levy, S. (2015). Theorising youth and everyday peace (building). *Peacebuilding, 3*(2), 115–125.

Bloomfield, D., Barnes, T., & Huyse, L. (Eds.). (2003). *Reconciliation after violent conflict: A handbook.* Stockholm: IDEA.

Bockers, E., & Knaevelsrud, C. (2011). Reconciliation in Cambodia: Thirty years after the terror of the Khmer Rouge regime. *Torture, 21*(2), 71–83.

Boraine, A. (2001). *A country unmasked: Inside South Africa's truth and reconciliation commission.* Oxford: Oxford University Press.

Borneman, J. (2002). Reconciliation after ethnic cleansing: Listening, retribution, affiliation. *Public Culture, 14*(2), 281–304.

Brāuchler, B. (2015). *The cultural dimension of peace: Decentralization and reconciliation in Indonesia.* Basingstoke: Palgrave Macmillan.

Breen Smyth, M. (2007). *Truth recovery and justice after conflict: Managing violent pasts.* London: Routledge.

Brounéus, K. (2007). *Reconciliation and development, dialogue on globalization.* Occasional Papers 36, Berlin: Friedrich-Ebert-Stiftung.

Chandler, D. (2008). Cambodia deals with its past: Collective memory, demonisation and induced amnesia. *Totalitarian Movements and Political Religions, 9*(2–3), 355–369.

Chandler, D. (2015). Resilience and the 'everyday': Beyond the paradox of 'liberal peace.' *Review of International Studies, 41*(1), 27–48.

Cohen, S. (2001). *States of denial: Knowing about atrocities and suffering.* Cambridge: Polity Press.

Crocker, D. (2002). Punishment, reconciliation, and democratic deliberation. *Buffalo Criminal Law Review, 5*(2), 509–549.

Eastmond, M., & Selimovic, J. M. (2012). Silence as possibility in postwar everyday life. *The International Journal of Transitional Justice, 6*(3), 502–524.

Etcheson, C. (2004). *Reconciliation in Cambodia: Theory and practice.* Study guide accompanying the 2004 Reconciliation Workshop series. Washington, DC: Johns Hopkins University.

Etcheson, C. (2005). The limits of reconciliation in Cambodia's communes. In E. Skaar, S. Gloppen, & A. Suhrke (Eds.), *Roads to reconciliation* (pp. 201–224). Lanham, MD: Lexington Books.

Felix da Costa, D., & Karlsrud, J. (2012). Contextualising liberal peacebuilding for local circumstances: UNMISS and local peacebuilding in South Sudan. *Journal of Peacebuilding and Development, 7*(2), 53–66.

Field, N., & Chhim, S. (2008). Desire for revenge and attitudes toward the Khmer Rouge tribunal among Cambodians. *Journal of Loss and Trauma, 13*(4), 352–372.

Fischer, M. (2011). Transitional justice and reconciliation: Theory and practice. In B. Austin, M. Fischer, & H. J. Giessmann (Eds.), *Advancing conflict transformation* (pp. 405–430), The Berghof Handbook II. Opladen, Germany: Barbara Budrich Publishers.

Fletcher, L., & Winstein, H. (2002). Violence and social repair: Rethinking the contribution of justice to reconciliation. *Human Rights Quarterly*, *24*(3), 573–679.

Govier, T., & Verwoerd, W. (2002). The promise and pitfalls of apology. *Journal of Social Philosophy*, *33*(1), 67–82.

Guillou, A. Y. (2012). An alternative memory of the Khmer Rouge genocide: The dead of the mass graves and the land guardian spirits [neak ta]. *South East Asia Research*, *20*(2), 207–226.

Hamber, B., & Wilson, R. (Eds.). (2003). *Recognition and reckoning: The way ahead on victims' issues*. Belfast: Democratic Dialogue.

Harris, I. (2005). *Cambodian Buddhism: History and practice*. Honolulu, HI. University of Hawai'i Press.

Kriesberg, L. (1998). Coexistence and the reconciliation of communal conflicts. In E. Weiner (Ed.), *The handbook of interethnic coexistence* (pp. 182–198). New York: The Continuum Publishing Company.

Kumar, K. (1999). *Promoting social reconciliation in postconflict societies: Selected lessons from USAID's experience*. Washington, DC: Center for Development Information and Evaluation, U.S. Agency for International Development.

Lederach, J. P. (1997). *Building peace*. Washington, DC: United States Institute of Peace.

Ly, S. (2017). *Reconciliation process in Cambodia: 1979–2007 before the Khmer Rouge tribunal*. Phnom Penh: Documentation Center of Cambodia.

Mac Ginty, R. (2014). Everyday peace: Bottom-up and local agency in conflict-affected societies. *Security Dialogue*, *45*(6), 548–564.

Manning, P. (2017). *Transitional justice and memory in Cambodia: Beyond the extraordinary chambers*. London: Routledge.

McGrew, L. (2011). *Reconciliation in Cambodia: Victims and perpetrators living together, apart*. PhD Thesis, Coventry: Coventry University.

McGrew, L. (2018). Victims and perpetrators in Cambodia: Communities moving towards reconciliation on a Rocky Road. In B. Jenkins, D. B. Subedi & K. Jenkins (Eds.), *Reconciliation in conflict-affected communities* (pp. 21–39). Singapore: Springer Nature.

Miller, M. A., & Bunnell, T. (2011). *Post-disaster urban renewal: Memories of trauma and transformation in an Indonesian city*. ARI Working Paper No. 154. Singapore: Asia Research Institute.

Peace Accords Matrix (PAM) Implementation Dataset V.1.5 (2015, 29 July). Retrieved from https://peaceaccords.nd.edu/research.

Pham, P., Vinck, P., Balthazard, M., Hean, S., & Stover, E. (2009) *So we will never forget: A population-based survey on attitudes about social reconstruction and the extraordinary chambers in the Courts of Cambodia*. Berkeley, CA: University of California, Berkeley, Human Rights Center.

Richmond, O. (2010). Resistance and the post-liberal peace. *Millennium: Journal of International Studies*, *38*(3), 665–692.

Richmond, O., & Mitchell, A. (2012). *Hybrid forms of peace: From everyday agency to post-liberalism*. Basingstoke: Palgrave Macmillan.

Rigby, A. (2001). *Justice and reconciliation: After the violence*. Boulder, CO: Lynne Rienner Publishers.

Rigby, A. (2006). Reflections on reconciliation. *Committee for Conflict Transformation Support (CCTS). Newsletter, 29* (December 2005), 1–4.

Sampson, S. (2003). From reconciliation to coexistence. *Public Culture, 15*(1), 181–186.

Staub, E., & Pearlman, L. A. (2001). Healing, reconciliation, and forgiving after genocide and other collective violence. In R. G. Helmick & R. L. Peterson (Eds.), *Forgiveness and reconciliation: Religion, public policy and conflict transformation* (pp. 205–227). Philadelphia, PA: Templeton Foundation Press.

Strupinskiene, L. (2017). "What is reconciliation and are we there yet?" Different types and levels of reconciliation. *Journal of Human Rights, 16*(4), 452–472.

Tadjbakhsh, S. (2011). Introduction: Liberal peace in dispute. In S. Tadjbakhsh (Ed.), *Rethinking the liberal peace: External models and local alternatives* (pp. 1–16). London: Routledge.

Theidon, K. (2007). Gender in transition: Common sense, women, and war. *Journal of Human Rights, 6*(4), 453–478.

Uvin, P. (2009). *Life after violence: A people's story of Burundi*. London: Zed Books.

Williams, P., & Scharf, M. (2002). *Peace with justice?: War crimes and accountability in the former Yugoslavia*. Lanham, MD: Rowman & Littlefield.

Zucker, E. M. (2009). Matters of morality: The case of a former Khmer Rouge village chief. *Anthropology and Humanism, 34*(1), 31–40.

Zucker, E. M. (2013). *Forest of struggle: Moralities of remembrance in Upland Cambodia*. Honolulu, HI: University of Hawai'i Press.

# 11 Competitive victimhood, reconciliation and intergenerational responsibility

*Ria Shibata*

## Introduction

One thing that characterises groups that are engaged in intractable conflict is that they often develop polarised interpretations of the same past, especially if that history involves a violent injustice. Competing narratives of the same historical trauma between the victims and the perpetrator can become one of the most challenging obstacles to the process of reconciliation (Noor et al. 2012; Bilali and Ross 2012). How both the perpetrator and victims deal with the past is critical to a lasting reconciliation and successful resolution of intractable conflicts (Staub 2006; Lederach 1997; Minow 2002). Whether it be colonial occupation, genocide or war, if the injustice is left unaddressed, feelings of humiliation and victimisation may often lead to prolonging of the conflict (Nadler and Shnabel 2008).

Intractable conflicts are interstate or intergroup conflicts that continue over a long time, even across generations, because they are often complex, and deeply rooted in identity-driven needs (Lederach 1997). Theorists who have studied intractable conflicts stress that identity-related conflicts resist traditional conflict resolution strategies such as negotiations or mediation, are persistent and extremely difficult to reconcile (Burton 1990; Azar 1983, 1990; Bar-Tal 2007). Even after the implementation of peace agreements and conflict settlements, reconciliation can become a long and arduous process. Unresolved violent trauma, identity-driven needs and the way in which that historical memory is passed on across generations can become a major hindrance to peacemaking. The main obstacles to reconciliation often involve victims' deep humiliation and emotional wounds that are rooted in unaddressed historical injustices. When past misdeeds are not acknowledged and dealt with properly, they can lead to the derailing of the peace process and become a major hindrance to reconciliation (Noor et al. 2008). For this reason, the perpetrator's acknowledgement of responsibility for the harms committed becomes an important pre-requisite in promoting reconciliation (Minow 2002; Kelman 2008).

Accepting collective intergenerational responsibility for the injustices of the past is a crucial component in advancing reconciliation between the transgressor and the transgressed. Collective memory of violent trauma can be transmitted via narratives in official textbooks, mass media, rituals and commemorations, popular cultural products and through individual sharing of stories. Japan has often been criticised for downplaying information about its wartime atrocities like the Nanjing Massacre and coercion of "comfort women" in its official discourse.

This chapter examines how current generations of Japanese "remember" the past war and how exposure to narratives focusing on Japanese people's wartime victimisation may affect their willingness to accept the nation's responsibility to redress past mistakes and thus become an obstacle to Japan's reconciliation with its neighbours in East Asia – namely South Korea. More specifically, the key aim of this study is to examine the role of competitive victimhood in affecting the willingness of today's Japanese people to assume intergenerational responsibility for the nation's harm-doing in the colonial era before and during the Second World War. The study examined in depth the phenomenon of Japanese victimhood – the sources, dynamics and social processes that shape contemporary Japanese generations' victim consciousness and the memory of the war. The design of the mixed methods study used a survey to assess to what extent competitive victimhood exists within the Japanese mentality and how it affects the respondents' willingness to assume responsibility for the nation's past injustices. This was followed by in-depth interviews that explored how salient the victim trope is in shaping Japanese understanding of the war history.

## Reconciliation, intergenerational responsibility and competitive victimhood

Reconciliation has been described as the culminating point of a long and arduous process of conflict resolution. In order to understand the important components required to promote reconciliation, it may be useful to draw on peace and conflict theories that distinguish between conflict settlement, conflict resolution and reconciliation (Kelman 2008). Herbert Kelman (2008) defines conflict settlement as a negotiated agreement which aims to meet the interests of both parties. On the other hand, conflict resolution explores beyond tangible interests and seeks to analyse the causes of conflict in which basic needs for identity, security, recognition, autonomy and justice are threatened (Burton 1990). A peace agreement may receive public endorsement but may not necessarily lead to changes in people's perception and attitudes toward the former enemy. Conflict resolution can lead to transforming an adversarial relationship into a pragmatic partnership in which parties can cooperate and co-exist; however, this type of instrumental relationship could be fragile and vulnerable to change depending on the circumstances, such as changing interests of the political leadership (Kelman 2008).

Kelman further argues that in order for reconciliation to advance, changes in the identities of the conflicting parties become critical. In other words, negative public perception of the "Other" has to be transformed. In this regard, squarely facing the past and acknowledging harms committed to the other, and a re-examination of dominant historical narratives and national myths – on both sides of the conflict – become critical components of the process of reconciliation (Kelman 2008; Lazare 2004; Tavuchis 1991). It may be unrealistic to establish a single, objective truth. However, it is nonetheless vital to recognise and accept that the different narratives will exist and that they will reflect different historical experiences (Kelman 2008). Perpetrators' apology and collective acknowledgement of past wrongdoing is a necessary element in the victims' healing (Govier 2003; Shibata 2018). The foremost purpose of apologising for wrongdoing is to address the victims' grievance, and to validate their self-worth (Brooks 1999; Minow 2002). For the perpetrator group to accept responsibility for past wrongdoing accords the victims the dignity and respect they need in order to restore damaged relationships.

Having stressed the importance of acceptance of responsibility for past harm, it is also essential to understand how identity-related needs culminating in collective victimhood can become major barriers to reconciliation. Needs theorists state that the need for recognition, prestige and respect from others is a critical component of an individual's security (Burton 1990; Nudler 1980). A positive personal and collective identity constitutes an integral part of an individual's well-being. Social Identity Theory reinforces this thinking by stressing that individuals derive a sense of positive esteem from their association with an important social group or ingroup (Tajfel and Turner 1986). Individuals strive to heighten their self-worth by identifying themselves with their dominant social group's positive image and status . This generates the ingroup versus outgroup, or "us" versus "them" dynamic. Research has shown that when the "us" versus "them" dynamic escalates and becomes utilised as a means for political mobilisation, it can provoke intense popular emotion that can become the basis for political violence and conflict (Staub 1998).

Studies have shown how threats to a group's positive identity can exacerbate conflicts between groups (Roccas and Elster 2012; Bar-Tal 2003). When a group's identity is threatened, collective memory will be glorified and reinforced to restore the group's collective esteem. Collective memory can be defined as a group's shared understanding of the past that may not have been personally experienced but has been socially constructed, transferred and remembered by members of the society through formal and non-formal channels (Paez and Liu 2011). Collective memory of the past is an essential construct in the formation of national identity and can escalate conflicts between nations that have experienced histories of violent conflict (Liu and Hilton 2005; Bar-Tal 2003).

Furthermore, victims' accusations that one's ingroup has committed immoral wrongdoings against them undermines and threatens that group's sense of positive identity. Because historical memory constitutes the fundamental core of a group's identity, perpetrator groups may choose to "forget," erase or revise any past that threatens the group's moral status and places its people in shame (Buckley-Zistel 2006; Shibata 2017). Extreme nationalists who identify strongly with their ingroup are prone to defend the pride of the nation by instrumentally rewriting and distorting historical narratives (Hammack 2008). Such are the dynamics that lead groups in conflict to have inconsistent interpretations of the same history and distinct narratives attached to those histories. Collective amnesia of an immoral past can be seen as the perpetrator group's tactical decision to defend its group's pride and dignity (Volpato and Licata 2010). As such, threatened identity and conflicting memories of past violence between the transgressor and the transgressed can perpetuate a memory war, and become an enormous hindrance to the process of reconciliation.

This identity dynamic leads groups in prolonged conflict to compete over their victim status (Bar-Tal et al. 2009; Noor et al. 2008). Competitive victimhood emerges when groups in conflict perceive and strive to establish that one has suffered more than its adversary (Noor et al. 2008, 2012). In order to protect their group's moral status and reputation, the perpetrator group may choose to downplay their acts of violence and highlight their own history of victimisation, emphasising how much they have suffered. According to studies conducted by Bar-Tal and colleagues (2009), collective victimisation arises when individuals believe that 1) they were harmed; 2) they were not responsible for the occurrence of the harmful act; 3) they could not prevent the harm; and 4) they deserve sympathy. These scholars emphasise that in order for individuals to experience collective victimhood, the group needs to perceive the harm to be immoral, unjust and undeserved (Bar-Tal et al. 2009). Even if the individuals have not personally experienced the violence, history of victimisation becomes part of the group's core identity which then is passed on as narratives from one generation to another (Volkan 2001).

## The case of the South Korea and Japan conflict

More than seven decades have passed since the end of the Second World War, and yet memories of the war and colonial history continue to aggravate the relations between Japan and South Korea. As mentioned earlier, studies demonstrate that conflicts can be prolonged and parties are unable to reconcile because of divided memories of the same historical trauma between the transgressor and the transgressed. This is particularly true in the case of South Korea and Japan where geopolitical conflicts over territorial claims become easily exacerbated when historical issues are revisited. What emerges as a significant obstacle in obstructing reconciliation between Japan and South Korea is the unresolved historical grievances (Clements 2018; Kwak and Nobles 2013; Dudden 2008).

The 2019 polling data based on a joint survey by Yomiuri Shimbun, Japan, and Hankook Ilbo Dailies, South Korea, show that one of the primary sources causing distrust between South Korea and Japan is Japan's lack of remorse and apology for injustices committed in its colonial and wartime past. Distrust between Japan and South Korea remained escalated, with a high proportion of 75% of South Koreans feeling that Japan cannot be trusted and 73% of Japanese feeling the same towards South Koreans. This is the highest level of distrust towards South Koreans observed among Japanese in 14 surveys since 1996. As for possible factors that may be driving these negative sentiments, 87% of South Koreans felt that Japan has not shown enough remorse and needs to apologise for the colonial injustices which occurred between 1910 and 1945. On the contrary, 80% of the Japanese public is experiencing a so-called "apology fatigue," claiming that their government has done enough to atone for its wartime past and feel that additional apologies are not necessary. Furthermore, unaddressed historical grievances can not only create distrust, but position the Other as a source of threat to the nation. In a similar poll in 2015, 60% of South Koreans felt that Japan was a security threat to their nation, second to North Korea.

In order to understand the driving force behind identity politics in both countries, it is imperative to understand how a need to defend the nation's moral status shapes Japanese conservatives' behaviour. Various social psychological studies cited earlier reveal that threats to a group's identity and esteem occurs when its collective morality and reputation are questioned (Branscombe et al. 1999). When confronted with accusations of the ingroup's immoral act, individuals who identify strongly with the ingroup would attempt to protect the group's reputation by averting collective guilt and denying responsibility for the harms committed in the past (Sullivan et al. 2012). This behaviour is clearly demonstrated by Prime Minister Abe and the conservative allies' attempt to put Korean "comfort women's" accusations to rest by attempting to strike a deal that would silence the Korean government on this issue for eternity. Driven by a need to maintain the nation's pride, Japanese conservative leaders want to ensure that the shameful, "masochistic" historical legacy is not passed on to the successive generations. This intent was expressed in Japanese Prime Minister Shinzo Abe's commemorative war message (Abe 2015) in which he stressed, "We must not let our children, grandchildren, and even further generations to come, who have nothing to do with the war, be predestined to apologize." The question remains, with the nation's leader feeling that present and future Japanese should not have to apologise, how are these societal narratives about the war affecting these individuals' willingness to accept intergenerational responsibility for the past atrocities?

## Disputes over the 2015 landmark comfort women agreement

Disputes over the "comfort women," a euphemism used to refer to women who provided sexual services, including those who did so against their will, at Japanese military brothels before and during the Second World War, has been the source of an unending row between South Korea and Japan. As studies in reconciliation reveal, victims will continue to demand the perpetrator's genuine contrition before the two parties can reconcile. Since 2011, comfort women memorial statues, also known as the "Peace Statue," were erected one after another by Korean civil society groups in more than 50 parks and public places in South Korea and in the diasporas like the United States and Australia since the first one was unveiled in front of the Japanese Embassy in Seoul. These statues become an ongoing reminder of the past injustices committed by military Japan and the victims' incessant demand for apology and contrition. Abe, who has continuously denied this shameful past including negating the Kono statement and removing any mention of the comfort women from all Junior High School textbooks, took action to propose a deal that would put this issue to rest. A deal was struck in 2015 with the Park Geun-hye administration whereby Japan offered to contribute 1 billion yen ($8.3 million) to a foundation set up by South Korea to help former comfort women as part of a "final and irreversible resolution" of the controversy. This was Abe's proposal for a final settlement to permanently put this divisive issue to rest. This landmark agreement between Shinzo Abe and Park Geun-hye was signed in 2015, only to be nullified three years later by Park's successor, Moon Jae-in. Under the negotiated deal, which failed to involve the victims in the discussion, Japan was to put 1 billion yen to a South Korean foundation to support the Korean victims, and in response to this, South Korean government agreed to "make efforts" to remove a statue symbolising the comfort women. Tokyo's proposal appeared insincere to many Koreans as it required the removal of the comfort woman statue in front of the Japanese Embassy in Seoul as well as a silencing of this issue which would never be raised internationally by the Korean government. In 2018, Moon Jae-in announced that Korea would dissolve the foundation which was set up between the two governments to compensate the comfort women – the centrepiece of the 2015 agreement with Japan. Moon stated that the emotional damage sustained by victims cannot be resolved through simple exchange between the two governments and that both countries must continue to make efforts to heal the victims' wounds. The 2015 agreement designed to "finally and irreversibly" resolve the comfort women issue failed to not only receive traction as an expression of sincere remorse, but was condemned by the Korean public as a "disgraceful act" which must be reversed.

To understand the source of ongoing tension between the two countries, it is vital to understand the divided official narratives of the two countries surrounding the comfort women and colonial reparation. According to the 2019 poll by Yomiuri, 78% of Japanese felt that the Korean government's claims are a violation of international law. Japan's colonial rule of Korea ended in 1945 after its defeat in the war. Twenty years later, in 1965, the relations between South Korea and Japan were normalised in exchange for more than 800 million dollars in loans and grants from Japan which went toward Korea's economic development. The Japanese official argument is that the 1965 treaty that restored diplomatic ties between the two countries together with the huge financial assistance had already settled the historical issue. Unfortunately, President Park Chung-hee's dictatorship used Japan's rapprochement fund for the country's economic development and failed to put it towards compensating the victims.

This position was expressed by the Japanese government when Moon Jae-in announced the dissolution of the comfort women fund. When the bilateral agreement was signed in 2015, Abe demanded that South Korea remove all the statues of comfort women that had been installed in different countries around the world. For Abe and the conservatives in Japan, the statues of the comfort women were not a symbol for peace, but an irksome reminder of what they interpreted as a shameful part of nation's history that did not really happen. Over the years, Abe has made several attempts to deny that these women were forced to provide sexual services to the Japanese Imperial Army. The Korean public, no matter how many times the Japanese leaders have offered official apologies, do not trust Abe and his conservative cohorts because their past words and actions have not been genuine. For the majority of the Koreans, the 2015 bilateral agreement on the comfort women is nothing but a flawed agreement that blatantly dishonours and ignores the suffering of the wartime victims. This sentiment was expressed by President Moon Jae-in who criticised the accord as "lacking compassion" and failing to acknowledge Japan's responsibility.

## Analysis of Japanese victimhood and intergenerational responsibility

An empirical study was designed to examine to what extent contemporary Japanese people remember the Second World War mainly as a history of their own victimisation and if such narratives affect their acceptance of intergenerational responsibility for the nation's wartime injustices. To develop a comprehensive understanding of these factors, mixed methods were employed to integrate both quantitative and qualitative data. During the first phase in April 2017, quantitative data was obtained from a survey of 147 Japanese university students in Tokyo and Osaka who were solicited to test a range of variables that may predict Japanese intergenerational war responsibility, one of them being competitive victimhood. The age of the respondents ranged from 18 to 30. During the second phase of the study in November and December 2017, 20 survey participants were selected for semi-structured in-depth interviews in order to gain a comprehensive understanding of the perceptions and experience of contemporary Japanese youth about their war history. Use of both quantitative and qualitative methods enabled a more nuanced insight into the behaviour and attitudes of present-day Japanese who were not directly involved in the nation's wartime atrocities. The study attempted to address the following research questions: 1) How do the current generations of Japanese "remember" the Asia-Pacific War; 2) To what extent are the current generations willing to accept intergenerational responsibility for the historical misdeeds committed by their forebears during the Asia-Pacific War; 3) To what extent are the war narratives they are exposed to about the victimisation of the Japanese people; 4) How does exposure to narratives that focus primarily on the history of their own people's victimisation impact their willingness to accept responsibility for the injustices committed by their forebears?

## Findings

### *Competitive victimhood*

Past social–psychological studies using other cases have identified that competitive victimhood could be a significant negative mediator of collective guilt. In order to understand the degree of competitive victimhood amongst contemporary Japanese, participants were asked in the survey to what extent they agreed or disagreed with the five items in the competitive victimhood scale (see Table 11.1) on a 7-point scale (1=strongly disagree and 7=strongly agree). As the data in Table 11.1 suggests, on average 74% of survey participants agreed that the atomic bombing of Hiroshima was the most tragic event in war history, and that the Japanese were

*Table 11.1* Competitive victimhood scale *Cronbach's α = .96*

| | *Strongly agree/ Agree/Somewhat agree (%)* | *Neither agree nor disagree (%)* | *Strongly disagree/ Disagree/Somewhat disagree (%)* | *Mean/Standard Deviation* |
|---|---|---|---|---|
| 1. Atomic bombing of Hiroshima and Nagasaki was the most inhumane and immoral act in history. | 77.8 | 9.3 | 12.9 | M=5.50 SD=1.45 |
| 2. The dropping of the atomic bomb was the most horrendous act perpetrated in human history. | 70.4 | 8.6 | 21.0 | M=5.30 SD=1.66 |
| 3. Japanese people suffered as victims of the war. | 75.4 | 9.9 | 14.8 | M=5.38 SD=1.45 |
| 4. As the only country in the world that has ever suffered from a nuclear bomb, we must never forget this history. | 75.3 | 9.3 | 15.4 | M=5.67 SD=1.60 |
| 5. The magnitude of the destruction wrought by the atomic bombing of Hiroshima cannot be compared to any other tragic event of war. | 71.0 | 13.6 | 15.4 | M=5.31 SD=1.48 |

Note: Items are scored from 1 (strongly disagree) to 7 (strongly agree). Higher scale scores denote greater competitive victimhood. (N = 147)

the victims of this inhumane catastrophe. A strong majority of the survey participants indicated the atomic victimhood and the suffering of the Japanese people were extremely salient in their consciousness when thinking about the last war.

The survey results presented in Table 11.1 show an important learning – participants' responses to the following key items of the competitive victimhood scale: "atomic bombing of Hiroshima and Nagasaki was the most inhumane and immoral act in history"; and "the magnitude of the destruction wrought by the atomic bombing of Hiroshima cannot be compared to any other tragic event of war." The findings indicate that that more than 70% of the Japanese participants felt that the horrific suffering wrought by the atomic bombs was a victimising experience unique to Japan which should not be compared to any other event in human history. This learning reveals that Japanese competitive victimhood is not about comparing its own people's suffering with those of the Koreans, Chinese or other Asian victims stressing that the "Japanese suffered more than the outgroups," but a belief that Japan being the only country in the world that has ever suffered from a nuclear bomb, this unprecedented tragedy should never be forgotten.

## Remembering the Asia-Pacific War

The technique of spontaneous association, which entails eliciting words or thoughts inspired by a stimulus, was employed during the in-depth interviews when discussing what interviewees "remember" about the Asia-Pacific War. Interviewees were asked to share what came to mind when they first thought of "the Pacific War," including words, thoughts and images. The salience of the victimhood trope in Japanese educational and political institutions (Yoshida 2005; Seaton 2017; Orr 2001) makes it unsurprising that most interviewees first thought of the atomic bombings:

*Seijiro*: I think of the atomic bombing of Hiroshima and Nagasaki. A horrifying image of people suffering.

*Hiromi*: I associate the war with the suffering of Japanese civilians and images of the atomic bombing of Hiroshima and air raids. I have watched different television programmes on the war, but what really influenced my understanding was what teachers taught me in elementary and junior high school during history class. The history of the Pacific War was all about Japan's war history. That's why, to me, the Pacific War is about the suffering of the Japanese people. That image is deeply embedded in my mind. Only after I entered college did I learn that the Pacific War was not just about Japan's suffering.

Interview respondents were then asked who they perceived as victim and victimiser in the Pacific War. Most interviewees who reported low levels of intergenerational responsibility answered that ordinary Japanese people were the victims. For these respondents, the war was automatically associated with scenes of civilian suffering. Some interviewees found the identity of the victimiser more difficult to determine; they believed the Japanese public had little choice regarding mobilisation into the war, and that only a handful of military leaders were culpable.

Emiko: The majority of those who supported Japan's war efforts were forced to. Absolute obedience to the Emperor was demanded. Who was responsible for the war? The top political and military leaders of Imperial Japan created the mood of the times.

Toshiyuki: It was just like Germany under the Nazis. The top leaders mobilised the people to believe that the war was sacred and just. Japanese soldiers were influenced by wartime propaganda and went to China, massacred the Chinese and raped the women or used them as 'comfort women.' It was a top-down decision and the public was forced to obey the military regime. The soldiers were victims of the war, too (Figure 11.1).

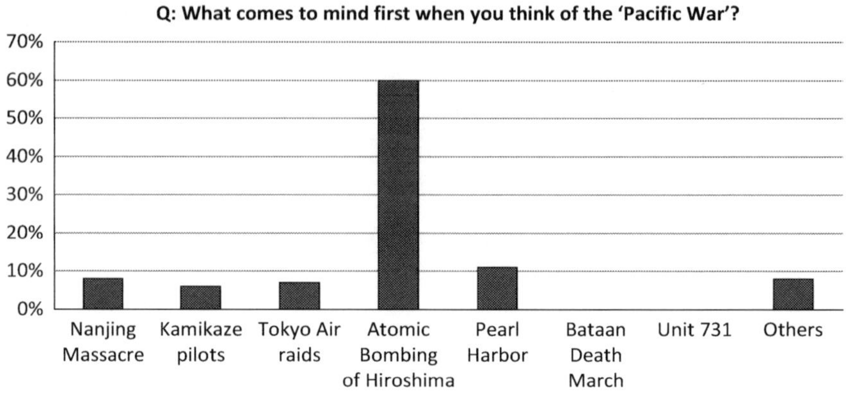


*Figure 11.1* Association with the Asia-Pacific War.

## Intergenerational responsibility

The survey was also designed to understand whether today's Japanese people feel responsibility and even remorse for the past harm committed by their nation. Japan's lack of repentance for past injustices is, after all, at the heart of the ongoing dispute between South Korea and Japan. Participants were asked to what extent they agreed or disagreed with the five items in the intergenerational responsibility scale (see Table 11.2) on a 7-point scale (1=strongly disagree and 7=strongly agree). The intergenerational responsibility scale in the survey was adapted from the widely-accepted Collective Guilt Scale developed by Branscombe et al. (2004). The intergenerational responsibility scale included questions that examined whether today's Japanese were willing to apologise for harms that they were not even part of – such as "our generation should not be held responsible for Japan's military actions during the last war" and "we shouldn't have to feel responsible for the actions of our forebears."

As Table 11.2 suggests, survey results showed that 64% of respondents felt that they did not and should not have to bear any responsibility for what their forebears did during the war, while 36% felt that the current generation should assume some ongoing guilt and responsibility for the nation's past actions.

A dominant argument that emerged in the in-depth interviews among those respondents who scored low on intergenerational responsibility is the unreasonableness of demanding that today's Japanese feel contrition for war crimes committed more than seven decades ago. These young descendants of the perpetrator group, represented below by comments from Tatsuya and Kuniko, wish to distance themselves from the Imperial Military Japan that colonised its Asian neighbours. Their comments demonstrate the attitudes of a post-war generation that clearly cannot see how they should be held responsible for the "sins" of their ancestors. They feel that modern Japan is a far cry from the military regime that committed cruel atrocities during the Asia-Pacific War.

Furthermore, they believe that they should not be held accountable for the crimes committed by a generation of Japanese, and in particular the Japanese military responsible for the war, with whom they cannot and would not wish to be identified. Their emotional distance from the perpetrators of war crimes and human rights abuses leads them to question whether further apology – made after nearly three generations have passed – would even be disingenuous, insincere and even absurd.

*Tatsuya*: I don't feel responsible for what happened during the war. I don't see myself as part of the group of militarists who committed these horrible crimes. We're from entirely different generations. I can't feel responsible for something I never took part in. I wasn't even born then. And most of the people who committed the atrocities are dead.

*Kuniko*: If the victims asked me to apologise, I probably would … but in my heart, I'd wonder if the apology has any meaning. I acknowledge that the Japanese committed brutal acts in the past, but I can't feel personal guilt or remorse for what these people did. I wasn't directly involved. That's why I wonder if my apology would have any significance. Would it be considered sincere?

Some interviewees like Satoko were annoyed with what they perceive as endless demands from South Koreans for apology and felt that Japan has apologised enough regarding the "comfort women." Her comments echo the "apology fatigue" that the majority of the Japanese public is currently experiencing. They also reflect the Japanese government's official position regarding the "comfort women" issue – that Japan has already apologised countless times and expressed remorse by offering reparations. The Japanese government believed that the 2015 bilateral agreement on the "comfort women" resolved the issue "finally and irreversibly." These comments also reflect the public's thinking that no matter what Japan does, South Korea and other victimised nations in Asia will never be satisfied.

*Satoko*: How long do we have to continue apologising? Are the victims ever going to be satisfied? I accept that Japan has committed terrible crimes in the past. However, Japan has already apologised often, and even offered a lot of money to the 'comfort women' victims. Why do the Koreans keep asking for compensation? I heard that leaders in Korea use the public's anti-Japanese sentiments for their own political agendas.

The survey data also demonstrated a strong negative correlation between Japanese competitive victimhood and their willingness to accept intergenerational responsibility with $r\ r = -\ 78$ and significant at the 0.01 level when two-tailed. This data implies an important finding that those who scored high on victim mentality demonstrated diminished levels of willingness to accept responsibility for the nation's historical injustices.

*Table 11.2* Intergenerational responsibility scale Cronbach's α = .94

| | *Strongly agree/ Agree/Somewhat agree (%)* | *Neither agree nor disagree (%)* | *Strongly disagree/ Disagree/Somewhat disagree (%)* | *Mean/Standard Deviation* |
|---|---|---|---|---|
| 1. Our generation should not be held responsible for Japan's military actions during the last war. [Reverse coded] | 63.6 | 0.6 | 35.8 | M=3.43 SD=2.0 |
| 2. As Japanese, we should feel remorse for Japan's military actions during the war. | 40.8 | 1.9 | 57.4 | M=3.96 SD=1.88 |
| 3. We shouldn't have to feel responsible for the actions of our forebears. [Reverse coded] | 66.0 | 0.6 | 33.4 | M=3.4 SD=1.95 |
| 4. As Japanese, we should accept responsibility for Japan's injustices in the last war. | 56.8 | 0 | 43.2 | M=4.2 SD=1.89 |
| 5. I think as Japanese, we are accountable for what the other Japanese did in the past. | 47.5 | 0.6 | 51.9 | M=3.92 SD=1.97 |

Note: Items are scored from 1 (strongly disagree) to 7 (strongly agree). Items 1 and 3 were reverse scored, so that higher scale scores denote greater acceptance of collective responsibility. (N = 147)

## Historical awareness of outgroup's victimisation

Part of the main reason why the majority of the Japanese respondents feel such diminished empathy and responsibility towards the outgroup's victimisation is because of lack of knowledge and awareness about what happened in history. Survey respondents were asked to indicate the extent of their awareness regarding Japan's colonial history and wartime aggression. A majority of respondents (59%) answered that they were somewhat aware of Japan's history of colonisation and wartime atrocities, while a combined 32% stated that they were "not really aware" or "unaware"; 9% regarded themselves as "fully aware" of the historical circumstances. The majority response of "somewhat aware" suggests that most Japanese have at least partial knowledge of Japanese conduct during the colonial era and the Second World War (Figure 11.2).

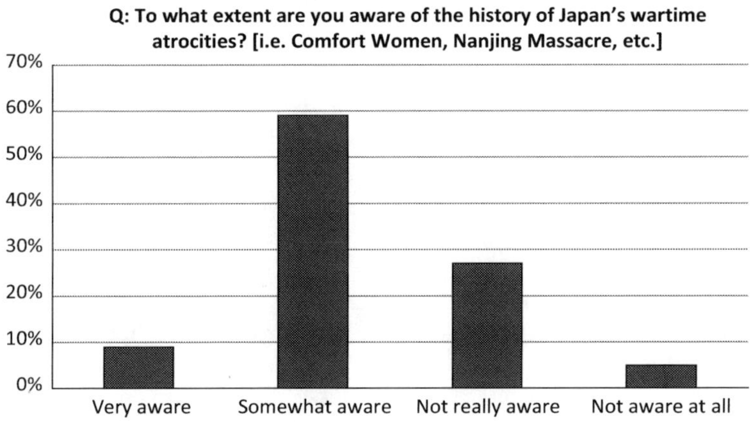


*Figure 11.2* Historical awareness of Japan's wartime atrocities.

## Erasing the past

Personal in-depth interviews attempted to understand the process with which the participants came to learn about Japan's history of colonisation. As Kayoko and Tatsuya's comments imply, respondents felt that classes only hastily touched upon or entirely ignored discussing Japan's history of colonial occupation. Both Kayoko and Tatsuya commented that teachers generally glossed over the topic, and neither the Nanjing Massacre nor "comfort women" were addressed in any depth in classrooms. Kayoko points out that it may be because modern Japanese history is not a central piece of information that would be covered in the high school or university entrance exams.

*Kayoko*: My knowledge of Japan's history of colonisation and the things that the Japanese soldiers committed during the war is very limited. I had never heard of the 'comfort women' issue and it was never discussed in our history class in junior high or high school. Normally, the teacher breezed through modern Japanese history because it is not that important for our entrance exams [high school/university].

*Tatsuya*: I answered, 'somewhat aware.' I first learned about what the Japanese military did in history class in junior high and high school. In all my history classes, the teacher only briefly mentioned incidents that occurred and never discussed the matter in depth. So, to this day, I don't really know much about what actually happened.

When it came to awareness about the history of victimisation of the outgroup represented by the "comfort women issue," most respondents answered that they hardly remember seeing any information on it in their history textbooks. This is not surprising as it is assumed that these respondents were in junior high or high school from roughly 2010–2016. Due to the persistent efforts of Prime Minister Shinzo Abe and his conservative allies, by 2006 the term "comfort women" was removed from the main text of Japanese junior high school textbooks. Furthermore, by 2012 reference to "comfort women" disappeared completely from all junior high school textbooks, including footnotes. For many of the young Japanese, the issue surrounding the "comfort women" only became known after wide coverage in the domestic media of the dispute between South Korea and Japan over the 2015 bilateral agreement on "comfort women."

*Yoko*: I had never heard about the 'comfort women issue' until I entered college. I was watching the evening news program on Nippon Television with my mother and grandmother. I don't recall reading or learning about this issue in school textbooks. I had the impression that Japanese television was defending Japan's position and seemed to be introducing only one side, Japan's perspective. So, based on what I learned from TV, many Japanese would feel that South Korea's actions were unfair and not abiding by the agreement and rules of international law. The program emphasised the fact that South Korea accepted compensation from Japan and signed the agreement, and questions why 'comfort women' statues are still around.

Kyoko said she was compelled to do further research on the internet because she could not quite understand why Koreans were so upset. She felt that their reaction seemed a little "extreme" and was curious to delve deeper. Kyoko and Satoko are both perplexed and taken back by the virulent anger that the Korean public express. With limited knowledge, both felt that the Koreans were overplaying the "comfort women" dispute.

*Kyoko*: When I heard about the Koreans' furious reactions on television, I wondered what 'comfort women' are. So, I googled the term. I think I was able to cover most of the facts, although what I found was, after all, information on the internet …. I read the Wikipedia entry on the 'comfort women' and several other online sources but most denied the accuracy of Korea's accusations, or even stressed that they were fabricated. I was surprised that our high school teacher didn't mention the issue in class.

*Satoko*: The first time I even heard about the 'comfort women' issue was on television news. All I remember is the rising tensions between Korean and Japan surrounding this issue. I cannot remember any of the details. I couldn't understand why the Koreans were so overzealous when it comes to this problem. Why were they so angry? … To me, they seem to be exaggerating the whole thing.

The above quotes support the survey findings on respondents' information sources about Japan's colonial history: 77% of respondents had learned about the "comfort women" through Japanese news programmes, followed by 70% who learned

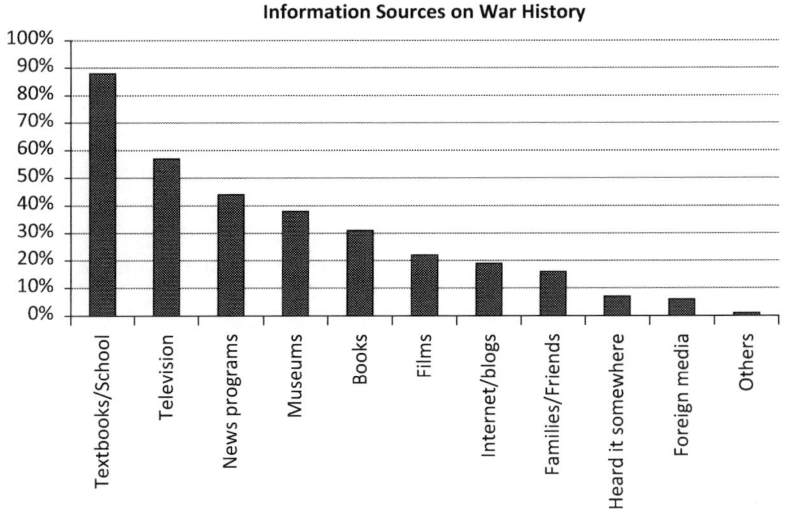


*Figure 11.3* Information sources on war history.

through Japanese information programmes (TV), and 44% who cited internet blogs. Only 23% answered that they had been informed by school textbooks. In contrast, 84% of respondents cited that they first learned about the Nanjing Massacre through history textbooks. These findings reflect the efforts of Prime Minister Abe and Japanese historical revisionists to deny state-driven coercion and recruitment of women as sex slaves during the war and completely remove reference to it from school textbooks.

## Information sources shaping Japanese war memories

To gain a better understanding of the social processes by which the collective memory of the current-day Japanese is shaped by the nation's narratives, survey participants were asked to choose three sources that they considered to be most important and influential in shaping their views of the Asia-Pacific War. 88% of respondents selected textbooks and school education (teachers) as most prominent; 57% chose television (information programmes, dramas and documentaries); and 44% selected news programmes (Figure 11.3).

## Conclusion

One of the greatest hurdles for achieving reconciliation in Northeast Asia is addressing the disparate memories of historical injustices between South Korea and Japan. How the perpetrator acknowledges responsibility and makes an effort to redress that past has been found to be critical in healing the victims' wounds and sense of humiliation and in advancing the process of reconciliation. Both countries continue to propagate divisive narratives attached to those histories. Studies have shown that, in the face of a shameful past, perpetrator groups may defend their reputation and positive identity by deleting or altering accounts of injustices from their master narratives (Bar-Tal 2003; Hammack 2008; Volpato and Licata 2010). Desire to defend collective esteem has been frequently found to drive "forgetting" of past injustices, together with an emphasis on the perpetrator group's history of victimhood. Volpato and Licata (2010) argue that "collective amnesia" is therefore a common phenomenon and a part of nation-building in many post-colonial societies.

This chapter has examined the impact of competitive victimhood on the perpetrator group's sense of war responsibility and how that could become an impediment to reconciliation in East Asia. It explored how present-day younger Japanese understand and "remember" the Asia-Pacific War, and the role of victimhood in their historical consciousness. Findings of this research indicate that Japanese collective war memory is shaped by a discourse in which Japanese civilians are treated as the war's true victims. Consistent with Orr's analysis (2001: 6), the research presented in this chapter found that the most salient victimhood narrative for the Japanese invokes the atomic bombing of Hiroshima and Nagasaki. The images of civilian suffering are deeply entrenched in the Japanese consciousness and enhance a sense of victimisation. Staub (1998) warns that a victim mentality makes it difficult for a perpetrator group to view things from the victimised group's perspective, empathise with its suffering and accept responsibility for the harm inflicted by its own group. Importantly, the survey data reveals that those Japanese respondents who scored high on victim mentality demonstrated lower levels of willingness to accept responsibility for the nation's wartime injustices. This finding revealed the salience of victim consciousness in the public narratives of Japanese society, making it difficult for them to accept the victims' accusations to redress the past.

A dominant opinion that emerges in interviews is the perceived unreasonableness of demands that today's Japanese feel contrition for colonial and wartime misdeeds. A majority of 21st-century descendants wish to distance themselves from wartime's imperial, militarised Japan. Their emotional distance from perpetrators of war crimes has led them to question whether further apology – made after nearly three generations have passed – is truly necessary and even sincere.

Past studies have shown that when two societies are engaged in an intractable conflict, it is extremely challenging to create a common historical narrative between the perpetrators and the victims (Bilali and Ross 2012). In the light of this, what would be recommended for South Korea and Japan to do is to jointly develop programmes that would foster mutual empathy and an "inclusive victim mentality" which acknowledges that others have also suffered (Vollhardt 2012). Efforts should be made to introduce educational content, whether it be museum exhibitions or popular cultural products like films and manga, that highlight and acknowledge the suffering of all sides. Showing films about the traumatic experiences of the "comfort women" that can help Japanese post-war descendants humanise the "other" and empathise with the victims' suffering may be one way to counter the "exclusive victimhood" narrative in Japanese society. In summary, peace education that addresses the deep psychological identity needs of both perpetrator and victim group may be considered as one possible way to generate mutual empathy and help the conflicting groups to reconcile.

## References

Abe, S. (2015). *70th anniversary statement by Prime Minister Shinzo Abe*. Retrieved from https://japan.kantei.go.jp/97_abe/statement/201508/0814statement.html

Azar, E. E. (1983). The theory of protracted social conflict and the challenge of transforming conflict situations. *Monograph Series in World Affairs*, *20*(2), 81–99.

Azar, E. E. (1990). *The management of protracted social conflict*. Hampshire: Dartmouth Publishing.

Bar-Tal, D. (2003). Collective memory of physical violence: Its contribution to the culture of violence. In E. Cairns & M. D. Roe (Eds.), *The role of memory in ethnic conflict* (pp. 77–93). Houndmills: Palgrave Macmillan.

Bar-Tal, D. (2007). Sociopsychological foundations of intractable conflicts. *American Behavioral Scientist*, *50*(11), 1430–1453.

Bar-Tal, D., Chernyak-Hai, L., Schori, N., & Gundar, A. (2009). A sense of self-perceived collective victimhood in intractable conflicts. *International Review of the Red Cross*, *91*(874), 229–258.

Bilali, R., & Ross, M. A. (2012). Remembering intergroup conflict. In L. R. Tropp (Ed.), *The Oxford handbook of intergroup conflict* (pp. 123–135). New York: Oxford University Press.

Branscombe, N. R., Ellemers, N., Spears, R., & Doosje, B. (1999). The context and content of social identity threat. In N. Ellemers, R. Spears, & B. Doosje (Eds.), *Social identity: Context, commitment, content* (pp. 35–38). Oxford: Blackwell Publishing.

Branscombe, N. R., Slugoski, B., & Kappen, D. M. (2004). The measurement of collective guilt: What it is and what it is not. In N. R. Branscombe & B. Doosje (Eds.), *Collective guilt: International perspectives* (pp. 16–34). Cambridge: Cambridge University Press.

Brooks, R. L. (1999). *When sorry isn't enough: The controversy over apologies and reparations for human injustice*. New York: New York University Press.

Buckley-Zistel, S. (2006). Remembering to forget: Chosen amnesia as a strategy for local coexistence in post-genocide Rwanda. *Africa: The Journal of the International African Institute*, *76*(2), 131–150.

Burton, J. W. (1990). *Conflict: Human needs theory*. New York: St. Martin's Press.

Clements, K. P. (2018). *Identity, trust, and reconciliation in East Asia: Dealing with painful history to create a peaceful present*. Cham: Palgrave Macmillan.

Dudden, A. (2008). *Troubled apologies among Japan, Korea and the United States*. New York: Columbia University Press.

Govier, T. (2003). What is acknowledgement and why is it important. In C. A. L. Praeger & T. Govier (Eds.), *Dilemmas of reconciliation: Cases and concepts*. Waterloo: Wilfrid Laurier University Press.

Hammack, P. L. (2008). Narrative and the cultural psychology of identity. *Personality and Social Psychology Review*, *12*(3), 222–247.

Kelman, H. C. (2008). Reconciliation from a social-psychological perspective. In A. Nadler, T. E. Malloy, & J. D. Fisher (Eds.), *The social psychology of intergroup reconciliation* (pp. 15–32). New York: Oxford University Press.

Kwak, J. H., & Nobles, M. (2013). "Inherited" responsibility and historical reconciliation. In J. H., Kwak & M. Nobles (Eds.), *Inherited responsibility and historical reconciliation in East Asia* (pp. 3–19). New York: Routledge.

Lazare, A. (2004). *On apology*. New York: Oxford University Press.

Lederach, J. P. (1997). *Building peace: Sustainable reconciliation in divided societies*. Washington: United States Institute of Peace Press.

Liu, J. H., & Hilton, D. J. (2005). How the past weighs on the present: Social representations of history and their role in identity politics. *British Journal of Social Psychology*, *44*(4), 537–556.

Minow, M. (2002). *Breaking the cycles of hatred: Memory, law, and repair*. Princeton: Princeton University Press.

Nadler, A., & Shnabel, N. (2008). Instrumental and socioemotional paths to intergroup reconciliation and the needs-based model of socioemotional reconciliation. In A. Nadler, T. E. Malloy, & J. D. Fisher (Eds.), *The social psychology of intergroup reconciliation* (pp. 37–56). New York: Oxford University Press.

Noor, M., Brown, R., & Prentice, G. (2008). Precursors and mediators of intergroup reconciliation in Northern Ireland: A new model. *British Journal of Social Psychology*, *47*(3), 481–495.

Noor, M., Nurit, S., Halabi, S., & Nadler, A. (2012). When suffering begets suffering: The psychology of competitive victimhood between adversarial groups in violent conflicts. *Personality and Social Psychology Review*, *16*(4), 351–374.

Nudler, O. (1980). Human needs: A sophisticated holistic approach. In K. Lederer, J. Galtung, & D. Antal (Eds.), *Basic needs* (pp. 131–150). Cambridge: Oelgeschlager, Gunn and Hain Publishers, Inc.

Orr, J. J. (2001). *The victim as hero: Ideologies of peace and national identity in postwar Japan*. Honolulu: University of Hawai'i Press.

Paez, D., & Liu, J. H. (2011). Collective memory of conflicts. In D. Bar-Tal (Ed.), *Intergroup conflicts and their resolution: A social psychological perspective* (pp. 105–124). New York: Psychology Press.

Roccas, S., & Elster, A. (2012). Group identities. In L. R. Tropp (Ed.), *The Oxford handbook of intergroup conflict*. Oxford: Oxford University Press.

Shibata, R. (2017). Memories of war and Japanese "historical amnesia." *Education and Society*, *35*(1), 5–25.

Shibata, R. (2018). Apology and forgiveness in East Asia. In K. P. Clements (Ed.), *Identity, trust, and reconciliation in East Asia: Dealing with painful history to create a peaceful present* (pp. 271–297). Cham: Palgrave Macmillan.

Staub, E. (1998). Breaking the cycle of genocidal violence: Healing and reconciliation. In J. Harvey (Ed.), *Perspectives on loss* (pp. 231–241). Washington: Taylor and Francis.

Staub, E. (2006). Reconciliation after genocide, mass killing, or intractable conflict: Understanding the roots of violence, psychological recovery, and steps toward a general theory. *Political Psychology*, *27*(6), 867–894.

Sullivan, D., Landau, M. J., Branscombe, N. R., & Rothschild, Z. K. (2012). Competitive victimhood as a response to accusations of ingroup harm doing. *Journal of Personality and Social Psychology*, *102*(4), 778–795.

Tajfel, H., & Turner, J. C. (1986). The social identity theory of intergroup behavior. In S. Worchel & W. G. Austin (Eds.), *Psychology of intergroup relations* (pp.7–24). Chicago: Nelson-Hall.

Tavuchis, N. (1991). *Mea Culpa: A sociology of apology and reconciliation*. Stanford: Stanford University Press.

Volkan, V. D. (2001). Transgenerational transmissions and chosen traumas: An aspect of large-group identity. *Group Analysis*, *34*(1), 79–97.

Vollhardt, J. R. (2012). Collective victimization. In L. R. Tropp (Ed.), *The Oxford handbook of intergroup conflict* (pp. 136–157). Oxford: Oxford University Press.

Volpato, C., & Licata, L. (2010). Introduction: Collective memories of colonial violence. *International Journal of Conflict and Violence*, *4*, 4–10.

Yoshida, Y. (2005). *Nihonjin no sensōkan: Sengoshi no naka no henyō. [Japanese perception of the war: Changes within postwar history*]. Tokyo: Iwanami Gendai Bunko.

# 12 Legitimising peace

## Representations of victimhood and reconciliation in the narratives of local peacebuilders in Northern Ireland

*Rachel Rafferty*

### Introduction

Societies that have experienced violent interethnic conflict often fail to transition into a sustainable peace. Reconciliation, particularly in its "thick" sense of developing more collaborative and empathetic relationships between groups, requires much more than institutional peacebuilding; it entails widespread willingness among ordinary citizens to make changes in how they interact with out-group members in their everyday lives (Lederach 1997; Strupinskienė 2017). However, international peacebuilding efforts often fail to achieve widespread local engagement in working towards a fully reconciled society (see Lemay-Hébert and Kappler 2016). Instead, in post-conflict societies, reconciliation can be viewed as a "dirty word" (see McEvoy et al. 2006: 81), and groups often voluntarily maintain patterns of segregation and hostility long after the official end to a violent conflict (Strupinskienė 2017; Brewer 2010; Höglund and Kovacs, 2010).

The lack of enthusiasm for pursuing reconciliation raises important questions about why local populations do not see reconciliation as a legitimate social goal, and how this perception might change. Many scholars believe post-conflict populations view peacebuilding efforts as lacking legitimacy because they follow a one-size-fits-all approach that is imposed by international agencies without regard for local needs or local culture (Autesserre 2014; Lemay-Hébert and Kappler 2016; Richmond 2013). While this may be true in many cases, these critiques tend to ignore the socio-psychological barriers that can also prevent post-conflict populations from viewing reconciliation as a legitimate goal (Bar-Tal and Cehajic-Clancy 2014; Rafferty 2019). These socio-psychological barriers need to be overcome as part of developing a sustainable peace; if this is not achieved, empowering local communities to take ownership of peacebuilding may fail to result in meaningful moves towards reconciliation. Instead, resources intended to support peacebuilding may be misdirected into deepening bonds within identity groups while opportunities for creating bridging relationships and cooperative working between groups are avoided (see Morrow 2012).

From a socio-psychological perspective, legitimacy involves a cognitive process of categorising a social object as morally acceptable (Kelman 2001). This process, however, does not occur in a vacuum; what individuals view as moral is influenced by socialisation experiences such as exposure to narratives that circulate in a society. Narratives offer explanations for events that convey judgements about who and what is moral (Murray 2017). In conflict-affected societies, ethnic or religious groups often adhere to biased collective narratives that legitimise intergroup violence by conveying a dehumanised image of the out-group and by representing the in-group as morally superior and entitled to use violence to pursue their goals (Bar-Tal 2007).

As a result, the continued circulation of biased conflict narratives in a post-conflict society can be a major impediment to the development of sustainable peace (Bar-Tal and Cehajic-Clancy 2014; Rafferty 2017b). A conflict narrative is an account of the past, present and expected future trajectory of a conflict that often conveys an interpretation of the causes of the conflict and attributes motivations and characteristics to the parties involved (Rafferty 2019). Collective conflict narratives are often highly biased in post-conflict societies; they tend to focus on in-group victimhood while ignoring in-group harmdoing and often delegitimise the out-group's claims to victimhood while portraying out-group harmdoing as motivated by evil intentions (Bar-Tal and Cehajic-Clancy 2014; Bar-Tal and Hammack 2012). Widespread adherence to such biased perspectives deters participation in important aspects of reconciliation processes such as publicly acknowledging in-group harmdoing and extending trust to out-group members (Kappmeier and Mercy 2019; Noor et al. 2017).

The challenge for peacebuilders in post-conflict societies, then, is how to successfully confront and transform the collective narratives that legitimated the recent intergroup violence, while also developing and disseminating a narrative that legitimises reconciliation as a social goal. If biased conflict narratives are not addressed, institutional peacebuilding efforts that aim to promote reconciled relationships between parties to the conflict will likely fail to achieve legitimacy in the eyes of many individuals living in post-conflict societies, regardless of whether they are championed by international agencies or local actors. Yet, while the role of biased collective narratives in underpinning support for violent conflict is well-recognised, and while the potential for alternative narratives to build support for peace has been theorised (see Bar-Tal et al. 2014), to date there has been little empirical investigation of the particular narrative content that can enable individuals to frame reconciliation as a legitimate social goal in the aftermath of violent intergroup conflict.

This chapter addresses this gap by examining how local peacebuilders in Northern Ireland interpret the violent past in ways that support them to frame reconciliation as a legitimate and important goal for their society. These peacebuilding activists are unusual in the context of post-conflict Northern Ireland, in that they are highly committed to working towards reconciliation, despite living in a society where social separation, polarisation of political attitudes and intergroup mistrust are the norm. Hence, identifying common themes in how they interpret the past violent conflict can offer important insights into the types of narrative content that support an individual to perceive reconciliation as a legitimate social goal, even within the fraught atmosphere of a post-conflict society.

The chapter begins by examining how narratives can alternatively legitimise or delegitimise social change in general. It then outlines the socio-psychological barriers to sustainable peace provided by collective conflict narratives, and in particular how biased representations of collective victimhood call into question the legitimacy of reconciliation processes. It goes on to explore the counterfactual case of local peacebuilders in Northern Ireland who view reconciliation as a highly desirable goal. The findings presented identify common themes in how these local peacebuilders interpret victimhood and reconciliation in their conflict narratives, and the chapter concludes by discussing how these particular representations support their motivations to work towards reconciliation.

## Narratives, legitimacy and social change

In social psychology, legitimacy is understood as the categorisation of a social object as morally acceptable (Zelditch 2001). Perceptions of legitimacy, however, are rarely unique to individuals, but rather are strongly influenced by narratives that circulate in a society. Narratives are a cognitive tool that individuals use to construct coherent meanings out of sequences of events, making them a central mechanism through which individuals engage with their social world (Murray 2017). At the group level, collective narratives about a group's historical experience provide group members with a shared sense of identity and support cohesion and collective action (Bar-Tal et al. 2014). Both individual and collective narratives often convey implications about what is and isn't morally acceptable behaviour (Murray 2017). In this way, the narratives that circulate in a particular society, or among a particular group of individuals, have an important influence on what people perceive as a legitimate or illegitimate course of action.

In the aftermath of years of violent conflict, peace represents a profound social change. Whether a social change is perceived as legitimate has an important influence on whether that change will be supported or resisted (Ford et al. 2008; Hirsh-Hoefler et al. 2019). Processes of legitimisation and delegitimisation are, therefore, an important aspect of achieving social change (Kelman 2001). Delegitimising existing social arrangements and asserting that new arrangements would be more legitimate is often the starting point for societal transformation. From a socio-psychological perspective, legitimisation is a process of re-categorising as morally acceptable a social object that was perceived as immoral. When social objects are perceived as binary, legitimisation of one object often results in delegitimisation of the other (Kelman 2001). Hence, for example, if engaging in violent conflict is categorised as a legitimate endeavour, peace-making becomes delegitimised, and vice versa.

Processes of legitimisation and delegitimisation require changes to narratives. Social change often begins with changes to collective narratives that result in delegitimisation of the status quo, concurrently making a case for the legitimacy of a new vision for society (Kelman 2001). Hence, the content of the dominant collective narratives in a society, and the degree to which individuals are willing to question those narratives, can be expected to influence whether a particular social change, such as transition from violent conflict to reconciliation, will be widely viewed as legitimate.

Understanding how narratives shape perceptions of legitimacy has, therefore, particular relevance for peacebuilding initiatives that aim to persuade post-conflict populations to categorise reconciliation as a legitimate social goal. This is no easy task, as the collective narratives that legitimised engagement in violent conflict often become routinised into patterns of separation and hostility that shape everyday life (Bar-Tal et al. 2014). In particular, as explored in the next section, the biased ways in which collective conflict narratives often represent conflict-related victimhood can provide a significant barrier to individuals developing motivations to pursue reconciliation.

## Representations of victimhood and the (de)legitimisation of reconciliation

In post-conflict societies, there are often fierce debates over whose victimhood is recognised, by whom, and in what ways (Ferguson et al. 2010). Victimhood carries a certain implication of moral superiority; the term implies that someone has suffered through no fault of their own, and that they can make moral claims on the perpetrators of an act that harmed them, and on society as a whole (Brewer 2010). Due to the group-based nature of interethnic violence, concepts of victimhood often extend beyond those individuals most directly affected by the violence to encompass all members of an identity group (Brewer 2010). Collective victimhood refers to a psychological phenomenon where individual members of an identity group hold a perception that they have been victimised as a group, regardless of their personal experiences of violence (Noor et al. 2017). It often results when targets for violence are selected solely on the basis of their ethnic or religious identity, and in turn a sense of collective victimhood can be used to justify retaliatory violence. Groups involved in a violent conflict often engage in "competitive victimhood" where each group asserts that its own collective victimhood is greater and less deserved than that of the out-group (Bar-Tal et al., 2009). This phenomenon has also been termed "exclusive victimhood" and is associated with more hostile attitudes towards the out-group, and reduced willingness to accept responsibility for in-group harmdoing (Vollhardt and Bilali 2015).

Collective conflict narratives that convey an exclusive representation of the in-group's victimhood present a serious challenge to achieving sustainable peace. Reconciliation involves recognising in-group harmdoing, extending forgiveness to the out-group and re-establishing more trusting and collaborative patterns of interaction with out-group members (Lederach 1997; Strupinskienė 2017). Conversely, a sense of exclusive victimhood legitimises continued hostility towards out-group members (Brewer 2010). Hence, conflict narratives that represent victimhood as exclusive to the in-group help to maintain a sense of collective grievance regarding the past victimisation of in-group members, and can fuel fears that the out-group cannot be trusted and will attack the in-group again in future (Bar-Tal et al. 2009; Breen-Smyth 2018). Meanwhile, the requirement in a reconciliation process to acknowledge in-group harmdoing can be viewed as incompatible with the group's narrative that it is the primary victim of the conflict (Brewer 2010). Moreover, individuals socialised to adhere loyally to their in-group's conflict narrative may find that questioning that narrative as part of a reconciliation process feels like an act of disloyalty (Ross 2014). Representations of exclusive victimhood then, when disseminated by collective conflict narratives, provide a significant psychological barrier to post-conflict populations viewing reconciliation as a legitimate social goal. Instead, these narratives support perceptions that reconciliation is an immoral compromise with an evil enemy, and a threat to the group's moral self-image as innocent victims of the conflict (see Bar-Tal and Cehajic-Clancy 2014; Lawther 2013).

However, not all representations of victimhood lead to the delegitimisation of reconciliation as a social goal. Socio-psychological research has also identified a phenomenon termed "inclusive victimhood consciousness" (Volhardt and Bilali 2015). When individuals exhibit this belief that suffering is shared equally by groups engaged in a violent conflict, they hold more tolerant attitudes towards the out-group and are more motivated to engage in helping all the victims of violence. Inclusive victimhood consciousness is also associated with greater willingness to extend forgiveness to the outgroup and to develop collaborative relationships with out-group members. These are key aspects of any reconciliation process.

Moreover, research also indicates that local peacebuilders hold an alternative conflict narrative from that of their wider identity group, and this supports their motivations to engage in efforts to achieve reconciliation (Rafferty 2019). In particular, these local peacebuilders have been noted to acknowledge both out-group suffering and in-group harmdoing in their narratives. Although these individuals typically represent a small minority of the population in conflict-affected societies, they do demonstrate that it is possible for individuals living in these societies to develop an inclusive and balanced interpretation of the conflict. Moreover, while some local peacebuilders in Northern Ireland have explained their activism as resulting from the early influence of parents, others have recounted experiencing a profound change in their perspective on the conflict as adults (Rafferty 2017a). This suggests that individuals can change from adhering to a biased collective conflict narrative, and develop a more balanced interpretation of the conflict that supports their motivations to work towards reconciliation.

It seems, then, that there is potential for alternative, more inclusive, conflict narratives to support individuals to frame reconciliation as a legitimate social goal. However, to date, the specific conflict narrative content that supports the legitimisation of reconciliation has received little attention from researchers. In particular, detailed qualitative exploration of the inter-relationships between representations of conflict-related victimhood and the legitimisation of reconciliation as a social goal is currently lacking. This chapter aims to contribute insights in this area by analysing the conflict narratives of local peacebuilders in post-conflict Northern Ireland and exploring the interplay between how they represent conflict-related victimhood and their framing of reconciliation as a desirable and important goal for their society.

## Post-conflict Northern Ireland

Two decades after the peace agreement, thick reconciliation between the Catholic and Protestant communities remains elusive in Northern Ireland. Between 1969 and 1998, over 3,700 people were killed and over 40,000 were injured as a result of the violence known as "the Troubles" (McKeown 2009). The conflict was primarily fuelled by a combination of Catholic resentment over discrimination and political exclusion, and by Protestant fears that Catholics wanted to force them to join the Republic of Ireland where they believed they would lose their distinct British identity (Cairns and Darby 1998). Violence was committed by Irish Republican paramilitaries from the Catholic community who aimed to unite Northern Ireland politically with the rest of the island, and by Loyalist paramilitaries from the Protestant community who aimed to maintain Northern Ireland as part of the United Kingdom. Both local armed police and soldiers in the British Army were tasked with defeating these paramilitaries, and at times their members committed human rights abuses against non-combatants as well as paramilitaries, including indefinite detention, unlawful injury and unlawful killing.

Despite the signing of a peace agreement in 1998, separation and hostility remain embedded in Northern Irish politics and society (Hall 2018). Ethnonationalist political leaders continue to draw on communal conflict narratives to justify their pursuit of zero-sum political goals (Leahy 2018). Debates about how the legacies of the Troubles should be addressed are highly contentious, and fierce contestation over the nature of the conflict, and by extension who should be considered a victim or a perpetrator, continues to shape Northern Irish political debate (Jankowitz 2017). In particular, each of the two main communities asserts a conflict narrative that portrays in-group members as the most innocent victims, while delegitimising the claim to victimhood of at least some out-group members. This means that there is little agreement between the two main communities around how the legacies of the violent past should be addressed, nor around what a legitimate reconciliation process should involve (Jankowitz 2017; Little 2012).

The Protestant community's collective conflict narrative asserts the violence was primarily driven by terrorists pursuing the nationalistic goal of a united Ireland (Rafferty 2017b). In this narrative, British state forces are understood as defenders of law and order and protectors of innocent civilians. Meanwhile, those killed by paramilitary groups are represented as the most innocent victims, while harmdoing by members of state forces is largely ignored or perceived as justified (Hancock 2014). Protestants in Northern Ireland tend to oppose public inquiries and legal prosecutions directed at members of state forces (Brewer and Hayes 2015; Lawther 2013). They also tend to express discontent with provisions in the peace agreement that gave paramilitaries early release from prison (Hancock 2014).

Meanwhile, the Catholic community's collective narrative represents the Troubles as the inevitable response of a community prevented from achieving their civil rights, and forced to defend themselves against repression (Rafferty 2017b). Within this narrative, state forces are understood as discriminatory and repressive, while members of Irish Republican paramilitary organisations are viewed as defenders of their community in at least some quarters. Meanwhile, killings committed by members of state forces are seen as the most important to address while violence committed by Irish Republican is represented as a justified reaction against oppression, meaning that members of paramilitaries can be viewed as victims of the conflict. Moreover, while Northern Irish Catholics tend to be broadly supportive of the 1998 peace agreement, as it contains many measures to prevent discrimination (see MacGinty and DuToit 2007), some articulate concerns that the peace process has framed the conflict as a case of ethnic hatred between the two communities and hence ignores wrongdoing by the British government and by state forces (McEvoy et al. 2006). Moreover, there is substantial support among this community for legal prosecutions against members of state forces, without perceiving any double standards in their concomitant support for paramilitaries to be viewed as victims of the conflict and given early release from prison (Brewer and Hayes 2015; Jankowitz 2017).

There are, then, clear difficulties for constructing an agreed definition of a conflict "victim" in Northern Ireland. While the Belfast Agreement of 1998 affirmed that its signatories "believe that it is essential to acknowledge and address the suffering of the victims of violence as a necessary element of reconciliation" (Northern Ireland Office 1998: 22), the document does not define a "victim" and does not made any prescription for how reconciliation should be achieved. In the years since, multiple attempts have been made to reach an agreement on how to address the legacies of the Troubles, but none have yet been effectively implemented (Jankowitz 2017). Instead, both communities in Northern Ireland continue to avoid explicitly acknowledging responsibility for the suffering experienced by the out-group during the conflict, while simultaneously calling for the suffering of in-group members to be better recognised within the peace process. Hence, the persistence of biased collective conflict narratives in public discourse and political debate drives a situation where each community is arguing for a version of "reconciliation" that favours their own interpretation of the conflict and that the other community finds illegitimate (Little 2012).

Nonetheless, amid this context of ongoing division, a committed minority of local peacebuilding activists in Northern Ireland have developed collaborative approaches to dealing with the legacies of violent conflict (Rafferty 2017a). Initiatives include a shared day of reflection to acknowledge the loss of life on all sides during the conflict, facilitated dialogues between victims and ex-combatants, support for individuals and communities most directly affected by the violence and promoting efforts to teach a balanced interpretation of the conflict in history classrooms. While various civil society organisations associated with a particular community lobby to achieve support for in-group victims of violence, or to see particular injustices addressed, locally run peacebuilding organisations place an emphasis on supporting all victims of conflict-related violence and on the need to heal relationships between the two communities (Hallman 2017).

Given the tendency in Northern Ireland, and in post-conflict societies in general, for individuals to adhere to biased collective narratives that delegitimise a vision of reconciliation that includes out-group concerns, these local peacebuilders present an important counter-factual case. We can learn from how they interpret conflict-related victimhood in ways that support them to frame mutual reconciliation as a legitimate goal. Such insights have the potential to inform the development of new peacebuilding initiatives in post-conflict societies that could effectively promote interpretations of the past violent conflict that increase motivations among local actors to work towards achieving an inclusive vision of reconciliation.

## Northern Irish peacebuilders' representations of victimhood and reconciliation

This chapter is based on qualitative fieldwork conducted in Northern Ireland in 2014. The goal of the overall study was to understand how motivations to engage in intergroup peacebuilding emerge, and are sustained, in a protracted conflict (see Rafferty 2017a). As part of this study I conducted in-depth narrative interviews with 15 individuals who have spent at least five years working to improve relations between Protestants and Catholics, who are termed here "local peacebuilders." The interviews were semi-structured, covering topics such as personal philosophy, vision of peace and experiences of family life and education.

For this chapter, I created two subsets of data; a "representations of victimhood" subset was created from instances in the transcripts when respondents referred to suffering or harm resulting from the conflict in Northern Ireland, and a "representations of reconciliation" subset was created instances in the transcripts when respondents referred to reconciliation or peace. I then subjected each of these two datasets to inductive thematic analysis based on the principles outlined by Braun and Clarke (2006). I identified the most prevalent themes in how the peacebuilders represented victimhood and reconciliation and these are presented below. These findings are followed by discussion of the inter-relationship between the peacebuilders' particular representations of victimhood and their framing of reconciliation as a legitimate goal for Northern Irish society.

## Representations of victimhood

There were two prevalent themes in how the local peacebuilders represented victimhood resulting from the conflict. First, almost all of them articulated an inclusive understanding of victimhood as a shared experience, asserting that members of both main communities suffered in equal measure, and making no claims that their in-group's suffering was greater or less deserved. Second, many of the peacebuilders also represented victimhood as a complex concept, not necessarily mutually exclusive with having perpetrated violence.

### *Victimhood as a shared experience*

The local peacebuilders' inclusive interpretation of victimhood involved representing the suffering of members of both communities as equal in magnitude, and rejecting any idea that one community can claim greater victimhood than the other. As a result, all of them expressed concern for suffering experienced by members of the out-group. For example, a Catholic peacebuilder who grew up in an area of Belfast that experienced heavy military presence during the Troubles, expressed her concern that ex-members of the security forces have not had their suffering adequately addressed:

> I feel really sorry for a lot of the people I work with .... It's because the Troubles are still very real for most of the men I see .... Many of them are ex-UDR. I think there hasn't been enough done about (supporting) ex-UDR people through the Troubles. (LP-1)

Clearly, this is quite distinct from the typical Catholic conflict narrative that represents members of state forces as repressive agents rather than potential victims of the conflict.

Overall, the local peacebuilders did not represent the conflict as an experience of exclusive in-group collective victimhood. Instead, a strong majority of them displayed concern for the suffering of all those most directly affected by the violence, regardless of their background or the circumstances of their trauma and/or bereavement. For example, a Protestant peacebuilder related how her work is a response to the conflict-related suffering of people from all backgrounds:

> It goes back to violence, and the reality of what violence does .... It's one of the driving factors of why I work with victims. I don't care who they are, what their background is, what their story is. What I do care about is that the consequences of violence makes them a victim ....
>
> (LP-2)

This peacebuilder's concern with human suffering, distinct from social identities or political considerations, was reflected across the local peacebuilders' narratives.

Hence, these local peacebuilders displayed a strong tendency to represent conflict-related victimhood in inclusive terms, acknowledging that both Catholics and Protestants suffered during the conflict. This was illustrated by their tendency to avoid discussing victimhood in terms of groups' experiences and, instead, to repeatedly articulate concern for all those individuals who were directly harmed by the violence, regardless of their communal affiliation.

### *Victimhood as a complex concept, not separate from harmdoing*

The Northern Irish peacebuilders also tended to represent victimhood as a complex phenomenon that could overlap with harmdoing. This was part of their tendency to portray the conflict as a mutually destructive cycle of violence, rather than an experience of in-group suffering caused by the out-group.

Hence, peacebuilders from both Protestant and Catholic backgrounds rejected a binary view of victims and perpetrators as mutually exclusive categories. As a Catholic peacebuilder working in a majority-Protestant region recounted:

> I was reading [the local paper] yesterday, and there was a job advertisement for a person to support the 'genuine' or 'real' victims of the Troubles .... And I just think to myself, 'what [are they thinking]?' .... I mean, my view is, going back to the wee fella [I told you about earlier] who was so badly injured [by the British Army] with the plastic bullet, all his brothers joined the IRA .... And they probably committed terrible atrocities. And then two of them got killed and are down in with the IRA volunteers [in the cemetery]. So that whole hierarchy of victimhood, to me, is [misleading] .... I don't really see how you can have a 'genuine' victim of the Troubles or an 'innocent' victim, [and say at the same time] like 'see him there, no [he's not a victim].'
>
> (LP-1)

Similar representations of the complexity of victimhood and its inter-relation with harmdoing were articulated by most of the local peacebuilders. Most of them tended to represent victimhood and harmdoing as categories that could overlap and most of them were willing to extend a degree of understanding and support to individuals who had perpetrated violence during the conflict.

At the same time, almost all the peacebuilders represented the conflict as a mutually destructive cycle of harm, and this was associated with representing perpetrators of violence as ordinary people caught up in extraordinary times. For example, a Protestant peacebuilder ascribed the end of the Troubles to a growing recognition among paramilitaries that violence was a harmful cycle that could not achieve any political goals;

> It was actually the prisoners in jail who were having the conversations .... who were then looking at the fact that people were being slaughtered in the streets – and what was going happen? Because there was a realisation here that they were going to be no winners, only losers, that no one was going to outdo each other here. So that's how the ceasefires came about.
>
> (LP-7)

This same peacebuilder also explained her view that perpetrators of the violence can be considered victims of the conflict:

> So [reconciliation work] it's a passion for me, it's a passion because of my own involvement [in the conflict] and the people that I knew being slaughtered, and the wonderful people I know who have gone to prison, who have done things that they would never have done if they had been brought up in another place ....
>
> (LP-7)

This lack of distinction between different forms of conflict-related suffering was a recurring theme in the narratives of all the local peacebuilders.

Overall then, these inclusive and complex representations of victimhood were associated with interviewees articulating a conflict narrative where the responsibility and the suffering of both groups is acknowledged. Of particular note, they strongly tended to disassociate victimhood from communal identities. Instead, they often expressed concern for the suffering of individuals regardless of their group membership, and at the same time represented people from all backgrounds in Northern Ireland, including perpetrators of violence, as victims of a destructive cycle of conflict.

## Legitimising reconciliation as an appropriate response to violent conflict

Alongside displaying an inclusive understanding of victimhood, the Northern Irish peacebuilders all represented reconciliation as a legitimate response to the suffering caused by violent conflict. There were two prevalent themes in how they represented reconciliation as a desirable social goal. First, they legitimate reconciliation by representing it as a process that can heal harms caused by violence. And second, they further legitimate reconciliation by representing it as an essential pre-requisite to developing a future society that can meet the needs of all its citizens.

### *Reconciliation as a process that heals the harms of violence*

Most of the peacebuilders represented reconciliation as a process that can, at least partly, heal trauma through a process of restoring broken relationships. At the same time, none of them expressed any idea that revenge or punitive justice against perpetrators could be beneficial for victims of violence.

The local peacebuilders displayed a strong awareness of the multiple ways in which violence had harmed individuals who lived through the conflict, and a strong commitment to supporting them. For example, a peacebuilder from a Catholic background who had himself almost been killed during the Troubles, described the importance he saw in Protestants and Catholic victims of violence mutually supporting one another to cope with the legacies of violence:

> One of the pieces of work that I am proudest of was with a group called 'survivors of trauma' … and what they all had in common was that they had all lost people …. They were just captives of their past, if you know what I mean. It was like a cage that they lived in. And the way they supported each other was so good, like at anniversaries [of the death of a loved one] and all this kind of thing – it was so good.
>
> (LP-9)

This view that intergroup contact and mutual support among victims of violence is an appropriate and positive response to the harms caused by violent conflict, was expressed by a strong majority of the respondents.

At the same time, a number of the peacebuilders expressed a belief that individuals can heal from conflict-related trauma by restoring broken intergroup relationships, as part of a mutually reinforcing process. For example, a peacebuilder from a Catholic background described his conviction that reconciliation work can heal individuals and relationships at the same time;

> [In reconciliation work] You're going on a journey and you may pick up some understanding and you may pick up some healing .... And the vehicle for the journey is a story .... Part of what needs to happen for healing here is that people hear each other – so you need to create a climate where people can come together to do that .... And sometimes in our work that is what happens. It happened when we were on (a) residential [intergroup reconciliation activity] on the weekend. Two women [from different backgrounds] in front of the group spoke to each other. They didn't realise what they have in common [as victims of the conflict], and as they spoke it became manifest. It wasn't just that they spoke it, but you could feel it .... And I was one of the people who became quite tearful as a result ....
>
> (LP-10)

This sentiment, that building relationships across identity divisions can help individuals to acknowledge and heal personal trauma associated with the conflict, was expressed explicitly or implicitly by a many of the peacebuilders, particularly those who work directly with victims of violence.

Overall, then, most of the peacebuilders represented reconciliation as a positive process that can heal the hurts of individual victims in ways that cannot be achieved through punitive legal justice or violent acts of revenge. They also tended to represent reconciliation initiatives that heal intergroup relationships as having positive emotional benefits for healing individuals from conflict-related trauma, meaning that, in their eyes, there is no need to choose between meeting the psychological needs of victims of violence and building collaborative intergroup relationships that can support sustainable peace.

### *Reconciliation as the pathway to a society that works for everyone*

All the local peacebuilders represented reconciliation as the only viable means to create a society in Northern Ireland that can meet the needs of all its citizens. This theme included representing reconciliation as the means to ensure the identity of both main communities is respected, and representing reconciliation as essential to the development of a new form of politics focused on social justice.

All the peacebuilders expressed, either explicitly or implicitly, a belief that in order for each community to have its identity and culture respected, everyone needs to become more tolerant of difference. For example, a peacebuilder who grew up in a Protestant enclave in a Catholic-dominated area of Belfast described how he is motivated by a vision of a future Northern Ireland where minority identities are protected and valued:

> [in my vision of future peace] people would be living together more, we'd have more integrated areas. It'd be ok to be the minority in a village that's traditionally majority one side or the other, that's alright, you're cherished .... I think that would be great, a sense that you can live wherever you want really, and it's ok. No-one's going to bother you because you're a minority, it's the opposite, they think it's great that you're there.
>
> (LP-4)

Similarly, but going further, a peacebuilder from a Catholic background related his hope for a future society where national identities would no longer be framed as mutually exclusive binaries, but could be recognised as interdependent and overlapping within each individual;

> I would like to see ... a future where ... we find a way for people to say that they're Irish while at the same time acknowledge that they're British, that we could even live with that .... I think that is the only way that we would get to somewhere that I feel happy with – otherwise a whole load of people will feel that they have lost ....
>
> (LP-9)

This sentiment was a prevalent theme among the peacebuilders, that in order for members of each community to have their identity respected there needs to be a widespread shift towards a more inclusive society where all identities are accommodated.

Many of the peacebuilders also articulated a belief that reconciliation is needed to establish a new form of politics that can better meet the material needs of all those struggling with poverty and social exclusion. For example, a Protestant peacebuilder described her belief that sectarian divisions must be overcome to achieve a more socialist-orientated politics in Northern Ireland;

> I think that, for me, peace is a new generation of politicians who don't have the legacy of the past ... to haunt them, or to keep informing their politics in the future. So for me peace will look like a whole range of new politicians, fighting for ... the [ordinary] man and woman on the street rather than doing party politics [based on sectarian identities].

Many of the peacebuilders expressed similar ideas, that the lack of intergroup collaboration in Northern Ireland is damaging to the material interests of all those struggling with poverty and/or social exclusion, and that reconciliation can be an effective pathway to developing a new form of politics that could reduce material inequalities regardless of ethno-national identities.

Overall, then, the peacebuilders represent reconciliation as a legitimate social goal that can bring benefits to individual victims harmed by the conflict and that can, through greater tolerance of diversity and a new form of politics, bring about a future society that meets the needs of all its citizens. This seems to be related with their representation of victimhood as an experience shared across identity groups and across non-combatants and combatants, and with their representation of the violent conflict as a destructive cycle that inflicted a collective harm on the whole society. The particular nature of this inter-relationship between representations of victimhood and the legitimisation of reconciliation are discussed now below.

## Discussion

Despite being born into a deeply divided society as members of either the Protestant or Catholic community, these peacebuilders represented victimhood in ways that are distinct from the collective conflict narratives of both main communities in Northern Ireland. In turn this was associated with articulating a strong conviction that intergroup reconciliation is a legitimate response to the harms of violent conflict, a position that remains rare in Northern Irish political debate to this day. Their conviction that reconciliation is a legitimate goal seems to be strongly informed by their representation of victimhood as a category disassociated from ethno-national identity or status as a combatant or non-combatant. Effectively, no one is excluded from their sphere of moral concern, not even perpetrators of violence, and all must be included equitably in any future social arrangements.

Moreover, the peacebuilders frame reconciliation as an effective response to individual-level and societal-level harm caused by the conflict. None of the interviewees advocated punitive responses to the past violence. Instead, they spoke enthusiastically of the benefits of improving intergroup relationships, both for individuals suffering from trauma and for society as a whole. As such, their representation of victimhood as shared and complex seems to delegitimise punitive responses to the past violence, and instead provides a rationale for focusing on healing individuals and relationships and building a more inclusive future society that can benefit all its citizens. From this perspective, reconciliation becomes not only legitimate, but urgently needed in the aftermath of such a destructive conflict.

When compared with the norm in post-conflict societies, these local peacebuilders present an unusual case. Typically, individuals living in post-conflict societies tend to continue to adhere to biased collective narratives that provide a cognitive barrier to acknowledging in-group harmdoing and out-group suffering (Bar-Tal and Cehajic-Clancy 2014; Rafferty 2019). Moreover, individuals often view victimhood and guilt as mutually exclusive categories, leading individuals strongly focused on in-group victimhood to avoid acknowledging in-group guilt (Noor et al. 2017). Overcoming such psychological barriers can be challenging, but the local peacebuilders featured in this chapter demonstrate that this can be achieved.

Viewed in light of the aforementioned research, the peacebuilders' cognitive balancing act between acknowledging the harms suffered by all victims of violence, and concurrently humanising all the perpetrators of violence is a significant achievement. Typically, post-conflict populations in societies that have witnessed two-sided violence tend to humanise in-group perpetrators and acknowledge the suffering of in-group victims only, while simultaneously ignoring or delegitimising in-group suffering and advocating punishment of out-group perpetrators (Bar-Tal and Cehajic-Clancy 2014). Instead, from the peacebuilders' perspective, no one identity group is the source of suffering, but rather the conflict itself is the true enemy. As a result, they frame reconciliation as a highly desirable goal as they believe it can reduce the harmful impacts of the conflict, helping individual victims and improving social structures in the process.

While research to date has pointed to the role of biased collective conflict narratives in supporting continued hostility and violence between groups (see Bar-Tal and Cehajic-Clancy 2014; Psaltis 2016; Ulug and Cohrs 2017), this study demonstrates that individuals living in a post-conflict society can, and do, develop counter-narratives that support their motivations to work towards reconciliation. While prior research has shown that a sense of inclusive victimhood can support more tolerant attitudes towards out-group members and greater willingness to extend forgiveness to out-group perpetrators (Noor et al. 2017; Vollhardt and Bilali 2015), this study goes further to suggest developing an inclusive and complex understanding of conflict-related victimhood is key to enabling individuals to frame reconciliation as a goal that can bring healing and greater well-being to the whole society. This insight has important implications for peacebuilding practices in post-conflict societies.

## Conclusions and recommendations

The findings presented in this chapter can help to inform more effective peacebuilding practices in post-conflict societies, particularly those where violence has been two-sided and victimhood is a contested concept. In particular, these findings call attention to the need to go beyond local–international binaries when seeking to explain why post-conflict populations often view institutional peacebuilding efforts as illegitimate. Instead, this chapter points to how collective conflict narratives that continue to circulate widely in post-conflict societies often disseminate exclusive representations of conflict-related victimhood, deterring members of that identity group from viewing reconciliation as a legitimate goal. Hence, we can expect that while biased conflict narratives that promote an exclusive understanding of victimhood remain unaddressed, there will be little motivation to work towards reconciliation among post-conflict populations, regardless of the geographical origin of those leading the peacebuilding initiatives. As a result, efforts to ensure greater local ownership of peacebuilding efforts are unlikely to result in sustainable peace unless they simultaneously address the impact of collective conflict narratives that legitimise continued hostility and mistrust between identity groups.

This study suggests that in order to achieve widespread legitimisation of reconciliation as a social goal it is particularly important to develop and disseminate conflict narratives that represent victimhood in inclusive terms, framing the conflict, rather than the "other side," as the true enemy. This chapter has provided an illustration of how an inclusive and balanced interpretation of the recent conflict supports categorisation of reconciliation as a legitimate social goal among individuals in Northern Ireland. While many existing psychosocial peacebuilding interventions, such as intergroup dialogues, aim to encourage participants to acknowledge the legitimacy of the out-group's narrative, this study indicates that it could be important to support individuals to recognise in-group harmdoing as well as out-group suffering. Reconciliation initiatives may also benefit from directly encouraging participants to become aware of biases in their in-group's conflict narrative, particularly the tendency to represent victimhood as exclusive to the in-group. It may also be effective to expose participants to individuals who share their group identity but who are convinced that reconciliation is a legitimate goal that can achieve positive benefits for members of all identity groups. This may require local peacebuilders, who often facilitate such interventions in a role of "neutral third party," to re-envision their role and become vocal advocates for the cause of reconciliation.

Past research, and the findings presented in this chapter, suggest that we can expect initiatives that effectively support individuals to develop an inclusive and balanced interpretation of conflict-related victimhood to make an important contribution to developing a groundswell of support for reconciliation in post-conflict societies. Such a process would involve challenging the conflict narratives that legitimated engagement in intergroup violence and developing more inclusive interpretations of the conflict that acknowledge out-group suffering and in-group harmdoing. Such narrative content is likely to support individuals to re-categorise reconciliation from an illegitimate compromise with an evil enemy to an important social change that can benefit everyone in society by breaking the mutually destructive cycle of violence. With reconciliation widely viewed as a legitimate goal for society, we would expect to see increased motivations among local actors to accept the compromises and self-reflection required in a reconciliation process that can lead to sustainable peace.

While the findings in this chapter are subject to the limitations of a small-scale study conducted within the particular context of post-conflict Northern Ireland, they do indicate the importance of understanding how individuals in post-conflict societies construct narratives to make sense of the violent past, and how these narratives shape their present-day attitudes and their motivations to work towards a particular future. Further research is needed across a variety of post-conflict societies, in order to more fully explore the relationship between inclusive representations of victimhood and the legitimisation of reconciliation as a social goal. Such research can provide an empirical basis for more effective initiatives to address the contribution of biased collective conflict narratives to continued intergroup hostility in post-conflict societies. It can also lead to the identification of specific narrative content that supports individuals to categorise reconciliation as a legitimate goal for their society, according to the particular context of the conflict in their society. Moreover, further research is required, across a variety of contexts, to better understand under what conditions individuals develop their conflict narratives, and into the nature of the processes whereby individuals change their perspective on a conflict and develop a more balanced and inclusive interpretation.

Ultimately, this chapter indicates that there is an important link between how conflict-related victimhood is represented and whether reconciliation is framed positively or negatively. While the legacies of violent conflict will always be painful, it seems that how a past conflict is interpreted is key to whether motivations emerge to ensure that such violence will never be repeated in future.

## References

Autesserre, S. (2014). *Peaceland: Conflict resolution and the everyday politics of international intervention*. Cambridge: Cambridge University Press.

Bar-Tal, D. (2007). Sociopsychological foundations of intractable conflicts. *American Behavioral Scientist, 50*(11), 1430–1453.

Bar-Tal, D., Abutbul-Selinger, G., & Raviv, A. (2014). The culture of conflict and its routinisation. In C. Kinvall, T. Capelos, & P. Nesbitt-Larking (Eds.), *The Palgrave handbook of global political psychology* (pp. 369–387). London: Palgrave Macmillan.

Bar-Tal, D., & Cehajic-Clancy, S. (2014). From collective victimhood to social reconciliation: Outlining a conceptual framework. In D. Spini, G. Elcharoth, & D. Corkalo Biruski (Eds.), *War, community, and social* change: Collective experiences in the former Yugoslavia (pp. 125–136). New York: Springer.

Bar-Tal, D., Chernyak-Hai, L., Schori, N., & Gundar, A. (2009). A sense of self-perceived collective victimhood in intractable conflicts. *International Review of the Red Cross, 91*(874), 229–258.

Bar-Tal, D., & Hammack, P. L. (2012). Conflict, delegitimization, and violence. In L. R. Tropp (Ed.), *The Oxford handbook of intergroup conflict* (pp. 29–52). Oxford: Oxford University Press.

Bar-Tal, D., Oren, N., & Nets-Zehngut, R. (2014). Sociopsychological analysis of conflict-supporting narratives: A general framework. *Journal of Peace Research, 51*(5), 662–675.

Braun, V., & Clarke, V. (2006). Using thematic analysis in psychology. *Qualitative Research in Psychology, 3*(2), 77–101.

Breen-Smyth, M. (2018). The uses of suffering: Victims as moral beacons or icons of grievance. In V. Druliolle & R. Brett (Eds.), *The politics of victimhood in post-conflict societies* (pp. 211–236). Cham: Palgrave Macmillan.

Brewer, J. D. (2010). *Peace processes: a sociological approach*. Cambridge: Polity Press.

Brewer, J. D., & Hayes, B. C. (2015). Victimhood and attitudes towards dealing with the legacy of a violent past: Northern Ireland as a case study. *The British Journal of Politics and International Relations, 17*(3), 512–530.

Cairns, E., & Darby, J. (1998). The conflict in Northern Ireland: Causes, consequences, and controls. *American Psychologist, 53*(7), 754–760.

Ferguson, N., Burgess, M., & Hollywood, I. (2010). Who are the victims? Victimhood experiences in postagreement Northern Ireland. *Political Psychology*, *31*(6), 857–886.
Ford, J. D., Ford, L. W., & D'Amelio, A. (2008). Resistance to change: The rest of the story. *Academy of Management Review*, *33*(2), 362–377.
Hall, A. (2018). Incomplete peace and social stagnation: Shortcomings of the Good Friday agreement. *Open Library of Humanities*, *4*(2), 7.
Hallman, C. (2017). Hope and temporality in the Irish long peace. *Journal for Peace and Justice Studies*, *27*(1), 3–23.
Hirsch-Hoefler, S., Kahn, D. T., & Hirschberger, G. (2019). Reactions to imposed political change: A prospective experimental investigation of Jewish settlers' resistance to state contraction. *Peace and Conflict: Journal of Peace Psychology*, *25*(1), 13–23.
Höglund, K., & Kovacs, M. S. (2010). Beyond the absence of war: The diversity of peace in post-settlement societies. *Review of International Studies*, *36*(2), 367–390.
Jankowitz, S. (2017). Sociopolitical implications of exclusive, intergroup perceptions of victims in societies emerging from conflict. *Peacebuilding*, *5*(3), 289–304.
Kappmeier, M., & Mercy, A. (2019). The long road from cold war to warm peace: Building shared collective memory through trust. *Journal of Social and Political Psychology*, *7*(1), 525–555.
Kelman, H. C. (2001). Reflections on social and psychological processes of legitimization and delegitimization. In Jost, J. T. & Major, B. (Eds.). *The psychology of legitimacy: Emerging perspectives on ideology, justice, and intergroup relations* (pp. 54–75). Cambridge: Cambridge University Press.
Lawther, C. (2013). Denial, silence and the politics of the past: Unpicking the opposition to truth recovery in Northern Ireland. *International Journal of Transitional Justice*, *7*(1), 157–177.
Leahy, T. (2018). The politics of troubles memories in Northern Ireland and the Republic of Ireland, 1998 to 2018. *Innovation: The European Journal of Social Science Research*, 1–22.
Lederach, J. P. (1997). *Sustainable reconciliation in divided societies*. Washington, D.C.: United States Institute of Peace.
Lemay-Hébert, N., & Kappler, S. (2016). What attachment to peace? Exploring the normative and material dimensions of local ownership in peacebuilding. *Review of International Studies*, *42*(5), 895–914.
Little, A. (2012). Disjunctured narratives: Rethinking reconciliation and conflict transformation. *International Political Science Review*, *33*(1), 82–98.
Mac Ginty, R., & Du Toit, P. (2007). A disparity of esteem: Relative group status in Northern Ireland after the Belfast agreement. *Political Psychology*, *28*(1), 13–31.
McEvoy, L., McEvoy, K., & McConnachie, K. (2006). Reconciliation as a dirty word: Conflict, community relations and education in Northern Ireland. *Journal of International Affairs*, *60*(1), 81–106.
McKeown, M. (2009). *Post-mortem: An examination of the patterns of politically associated violence in Northern Ireland during the years 1969–2001 as reflected in the fatality figures for those years*. Retrieved from http://cain.ulst.ac.uk/victims/mckeown/mckeown01.pdf
Morrow, D. (2012). The rise (and fall?) of reconciliation in Northern Ireland. *Peace Research*, *44*(1), 5–35.
Murray, M. (2017). Narrative social psychology. In B. Gough (Ed.), *The Palgrave handbook of critical social psychology* (pp. 185–204). London: Palgrave Macmillan.
Noor, M., Vollhardt, J. R., Mari, S., & Nadler, A. (2017). The social psychology of collective victimhood. *European Journal of Social Psychology*, *47*(2), 121–134.

Northern Ireland Office (1998). *The Belfast agreement.* Retrieved from https://www.gov.uk/government/publications/the-belfast-agreement

Psaltis, C. (2016). Collective memory, social representations of intercommunal relations, and conflict transformation in divided Cyprus. *Peace and Conflict: Journal of Peace Psychology*, *22*(1), 19–27.

Rafferty, R. (2017a). *Civil society activists in a protracted conflict: Explaining differences in motivation to engage in intergroup peacebuilding in Northern Ireland* (Doctoral Dissertation). Otago: University of Otago Retrieved from https://ourarchive.otago.ac.nz/handle/10523/7158

Rafferty, R. (2017b). Engaging with the violent past to motivate and direct conflict resolution practice in Northern Ireland: Engaging with the violent past in conflict resolution practice. *Conflict Resolution Quarterly*, *35*(2), 197–221.

Rafferty, R. (2019). Conflict narratives, action frames and engagement in reconciliation efforts among community activists in Northern Ireland. *Peace and Conflict: Journal of Peace Psychology*, *26*(1), 9–21.

Richmond, O. P. (2013). Failed statebuilding versus peace formation. *Cooperation and Conflict*, *48*(3), 378–400.

Ross, K. (2014). Narratives of belonging (and not): Inter-group contact in Israel and the formation of ethno-national identity claims. *International Journal of Intercultural Relations*, *42*, 38–52.

Strupinskienė, L. (2017). "What is reconciliation and are we there yet?" Different types and levels of reconciliation: A case study of Bosnia and Herzegovina. *Journal of Human Rights*, *16*(4), 452–472.

Uluğ, Ö. M., & Cohrs, J. C. (2017). "If we become friends, maybe I can change my perspective:" Intergroup contact, endorsement of conflict narratives, and peace-related attitudes in Turkey. *Peace and Conflict: Journal of Peace Psychology*, *23*(3), 278–287.

Vollhardt, J. R., & Bilali, R. (2015). The role of inclusive and exclusive victim consciousness in predicting intergroup attitudes: Findings from Rwanda, Burundi, and DRC. *Political Psychology*, *36*(5), 489–506.

Zelditch, M. (2001). Theories of legitimacy. In J. T. Jost & B. Major (Eds.), *The psychology of legitimacy: Emerging perspectives on ideology, justice, and intergroup relations* (pp. 33–53). Cambridge: Cambridge University Press.

# 13 Modelling reconciliation and peace processes

## Lessons from Syrian war refugees and World War II

*Raymond F. Paloutzian, Zeynep Sagir and F. LeRon Shults*

## Introduction

Humans have searched for peace as long as there have been humans. But the database left from human history is dire: It has not come. Lofty ideals and assumptions of human goodness express hope of peaceful, loving companionship of all people. Our intellectual disciplines compel us to think that if our strategies are based on knowledge, positive outcomes will happen. But there are barriers, conditions and limits. This chapter unpacks the fundamental issues that undergird such efforts and describes a model of key elements of processes that regulate reconciling and peacebuilding. Uniquely, the starting point is people perhaps most qualified to address the concerns – whose feelings about the issues are most grievous and deeply felt – refugees from the war in Syria, 2011–2020. The following five steps help unpack our argument:

1. Quantitative and qualitative findings from a large database on Syrian refugees (Sagir 2018) give a close-up, comprehensive look at a severe "refugee problem" in one locality. This case study constitutes a snapshot of refugees globally and raises questions that a model of reconciling and peacebuilding must address. Small interdependent reconciliatory steps may nevertheless signal a process of reconciliation to begin and continue.
2. A theoretical argument is made for the personal, social psychological and cultural issues to be included in a successful approach to reconciliation and peace – individual, local or global. The focus is on processes of collaborating in reconciling, not static states or end goals. The key is to collaborate in small, reciprocal, trust-inducing steps under a common superordinate value and goal not achievable by either party alone, not to initially state ultimate ends.
3. The above principles can lead to computational modelling of the process of reconciling in which success depends on taking steps of an acceptable size, small enough not to violate the expectations of the adversary, while all sides share the same superordinate values and confront a common enemy – whether

a human or non-human existential threat. Given these conditions, the probability of each adversary taking a cooperative step and it being reciprocated is increased. They may jointly accomplish something that otherwise cannot be done, fostering near-term reconciliation and long-term peace. If functional and adaptable in a multilevel sense, a model can be extrapolated to apply to various contexts, populations and combinations of variables. Its input variables can be manipulable and testable at different parametric levels and combinations over varying time spans. Computer simulations can test hypotheses about variables that may predict reconciliation and peacebuilding. A validated model could be used to make forecasts – probabilistic predictions of reconciliation and peaceful outcomes.

4. This kind of information can be provided to individuals, agencies, or governments who make decisions that affect reconciling and peace – between individuals, groups, and countries – so their decisions are based on knowledge, not the latest opinion poll (Richer and Haslam 2016). The principles underpinning the argument and model are applicable to any challenge that confronts opposing parties, whether it is an intergroup or international conflict or a nonmilitary existential threat. The Covid-19 virus constitutes such a threat. If all parties respond to it collaboratively, they may not only save lives, but begin a reciprocal sequence of reconciliatory steps toward each other as well.

## Refugees close-up: The Syrian example

The world's biggest example of a "refugee problem" at the beginning of the 21st century is the 5,000,000+ Syrians, refugees of the civil war that is ten years old as of the year 2020. It began in 2011 after three middle-school-aged boys wrote an anti-government note on the side of a building in a small farming town, Dara, in southern Syria (Alpert and Marrouch 2012). This simple act prompted violent government responses. Counter actions by opposition groups were met by the government with lethal violence. The so-called *Islamic State of Iraq and Syria or the Greater Levant* (IS, ISIS or ISIL; Daesh in Arabic) entered and by force, threats to life and killing occupied large swaths of Syrian land. Its leader proclaimed that Allah made him the new Caliph – a seat empty for about 90 years. For partially overlapping reasons (considering refugees from Syria and elsewhere, mostly the Middle East), the scope of the problem became greater than at any time since the end of World War II (United Nations 2015).

Our initial concern is on how refugees respond to the idea of reconciling with their perpetrators. A snapshot of refugees globally appears in the following section of this chapter. Those fleeing Syria went to several countries, but about 3.5 million are in Turkey (UNHCR 2018), because southern Turkey borders northern Syria where much of the fighting occurred. Fleeing to Turkey was the shortest route by which to escape hostilities. In this context, Sagir (2014, 2016, 2018, 2020), supplemented by Paloutzian and Sagir (2019), between 2014 and 2017 collected quantitative data on over 2,500 refugees, plus qualitative data via 100 in-depth interviews. Before presenting these findings, let us look at their war experiences, losses and traumatic events.

### *What did Syrian refugees face?*

There were few safe border-crossings. The Turkish town of Kilis, 90 km from Aleppo in Syria, is one of them. Its southern boundary is the international border. Before the war its population was approximately 100,000. By 2013–2014 it hosted about 10,000 refugees; this number swelled to 100,000. Kilis is now home to 200,000 people, approximately evenly split between Turks and Syrians. At the height of refugee traffic, it was a transfer point for Syrians to go elsewhere in Turkey.

Upon crossing the border, refugees walked about 1 km to a fenced rectangular asphalt-covered area about the size of a soccer field. Along one length of it, containers were set end to end. At first, refugees slept in them. But as the number of refugees increased, living and sleeping areas were created elsewhere, so the containers stored clothing, children's toys, and other supplies. A middle school, approximately 50 meters away, was in view of it. At times, ISIS fighters came to the border with shoulder-mounted rocket launchers and fired shells into the town. Several students and an adult died at the school because a shell hit them and blew them up. Photos depicting this were on a bulletin board in the container field. The refugees understood that they were still at risk.

The Syrians were not ordinary migrants. Their basic need was not income; it was security – to save their lives (UNHCR 2016). Almost 100% of the research participants said their most important reason for going to Turkey was "to be safe" (Sagir 2018). The citizens of Kilis provided this and helped them, with help added by non-governmental organisations (NGOs). Kilis underwent rapid change as both shipping container ("container") and tent cities were built. Temporary housing areas were equipped with facilities or services such as a school, worship centre, health centre, children's playgrounds, psychologist, art centres and a small toilet and bathroom for each family. Temporary housing spread throughout Turkey and included containers, empty buildings in poor sections of towns, garages, alleyways, tents and parks. It continues as of 2020.

The refugees' biggest challenge was the language barrier. They spoke Arabic; the Turks spoke Turkish. Both countries are culturally Muslim, but some clothing and other customs differed between the two peoples. For example, how a woman wore a hijab (head scarf) could identify her as Syrian, i.e., as an "other." Approximately two-thirds of the refugees were women, one-third men. The men tended to be older because the young men were either engaged in combat in Syria, or dead. Approximately 50% were children. They mostly viewed ISIS/ISIL/Daesh and Syrian President Assad as the perpetrators.

### *War trauma*

To understand Syrian refugees' feelings about forgiveness, reconciliation and revenge, we must first understand that the traumatic events they endured were of a magnitude far greater in number and in kind than those typical in life without combat. Sagir (2014, 2018) collected data during the height of the war relevant to these issues.

Sagir (2014, 2016) surveyed 553 refugees in Kilis. The percentage who reported being victims of war-caused traumas are as follows: Being bombed (48%), assaulted (35%), tortured (24%), shot (24%), having to use guns, knives or other weapons to defend self and family (21%), living in squalid camps (20%), being held hostage (11%), raped (3%) and attempting suicide (8%).

Sagir (2018, 2020) later surveyed 2018 participants in four cities in Turkey. All suffered war-caused traumas: 67% were bombed; 55% forced to evacuate their homes and in all cases before crossing the international border were internally displaced persons (IDPs); 46% were shelled. Others were assaulted (40.4%), shot (31.1%), tortured (30.9%), imprisoned (37.1%), sniper-attacked (39.8%), forced into squalid camps (20.3%), faced suicide bomber attack (19.8%), had to use weapons to defend self and family (16.1%), kidnapped (13.3%) and raped (4.7%). All faced at least one traumatic event. The maximum number experienced by a refugee was 11; the mean number per person was 4.45.

The data reported above are part of the refugees' war histories. Even so, such information may have been received as a nuisance, not as a problem for all to solve collectively, like the present global Covid-19 threat (Cascella et al. 2020). People far from the action may have responded as if war refugees had nothing to do with them. But as we write this, we face the worldwide Covid-19 pandemic. It shows that every traumatic event, whether suffered by Syrian refugees or the pandemic of today, may be relevant to all.

Let us examine whether these refugees might be inclined or at least open to reconciling with those who harmed them. If so, what needs to unfold for a process of reconciling to begin? Do they first need to forgive, as is often assumed (Kalayjian and Paloutzian 2010; Rutayisire 2010; Tutu 1999)? The larger concern is whether processes of reconciliation can be extrapolated and successfully applied to other military conflicts or to nonmilitary existential threats.

## Syrian refugee views on forgiveness, reconciliation and revenge[1]

Most war refugees do not want to reconcile with the enemies who killed, bombed or shot them or their loved ones. Even so, we gain knowledge and theorise to create strategies to foster peace. In particular, refugees may be uniquely able to provide insights into what should go into a successful process of reconciliation. Two forms of data from 100 Syrian refugees in Istanbul who had been in Turkey from 1 to 6 years provide insight into their feelings and opinions about those who had hurt them in Syria (Paloutzian and Sagir 2019).

### *Quantitative data*

The participants answered several questions on a 6-point Likert scale with no neutral point: (1 = "not at all"; 6 = "a great deal"). Three questions are of direct concern here.

(1) To what degree would you feel capable of *forgiving* those who did harm to you or your loved ones?
(2) If the decision was left up to you, to what degree would you want to *reconcile* with those who did harm to you or your loved ones?
(3) To what degree would you like to see *revenge* taken against those who did harm to you or your loved ones?

The answers to all three questions were significantly non-uniform across the six answer options ($\chi^2$, $p < .001$). For present purposes it is sufficient to split the response range at the theoretical neutral point, 3.5, such that the total frequency of responses below and above it reflects being more inclined to reject (1+2+3) versus favour (4+5+6), respectively, what the question asks.

In response to question #1 on *forgiving*, 81%[2] felt not capable of doing so (49% selected "not at all"); 19% felt capable (13% selected "a great deal"). In response to question #2 on *reconciling*, 75% said they would not want to do so (51% selected "not at all"); 25% said they would want to do so (7% selected "a great deal"). In response to #3 on *revenge*, 43% said they would not like to see it done (22% selected "not at all"); 57% said they would like to see it (37% selected "great deal"). These ratings of the refugees' inclinations toward the perpetrators make clear two important things: (1) One model of the "refugee mind" does not fit all, and (2) refugees' inclinations do not default to the positive side of neutral. For severely harmed people, the desire to reconcile is low.

### *Qualitative data*

The participants also provided qualitative data by giving written answers to the following two open-ended stem questions:

1) Regardless of how you feel, what, if anything, might enable you to reconcile behaviourally with those who harmed you or your loved ones in the war in Syria?
2) Regardless of what you do, what, if anything, might make you feel forgiving toward those who harmed you or your loved ones in the war in Syria?

This kind of information adds "active voice" to the refugees to help us understand what they went through and what the issues they faced meant to them. At least 49 participants emphatically did not want to "reconcile behaviorally with those who harmed you or your loved ones." They said: "The wound is too deep," "No," "I won't ever," "Don't want to" and "No no, because of the blood." Seventeen percent said forgiveness was important, but they saw it as a wish or a hope. Many said too much damage was done, so that "nothing can fix it." As to forgiving perpetrators, 12 said "yes." Supernatural agency was invoked by many: "God will judge them," "God forgives everyone," "I will complain my situation to almighty God … ," "Forgiving … is hard, … they are criminals, and only almighty God can forgive them, if they confessed … ." Their need for justice was clear: "Only if they are first brought to trial and brought to justice." Participants' responses were also coded and submitted to analysis by NVIVO11. Reconciling was disconfirmed by 57%, affirmed by 28%; 11% said something else ($\chi^2$, $p < .001$). Forgiving was rejected by 60%, accepted by 22%; 13% said something else ($\chi^2$, $p < .001$). Neither gender nor years as a refugee was related to the above pattern of responses.

### *Acculturation strategy*

It is crucial to distinguish between the near- and long-term. This is because how a refugee responds to questions about forgiving and reconciling is related their strategy for how to acculturate to their new country. The important acculturation strategies for present purposes are assimilation and integration, which, like any manner of acculturating, can take a great many years. But because the refugees were not permanent citizens but temporary residents of Turkey, whether they felt "fully assimilated" could not be assessed. They were instead asked about their intention, or strategy, for relating to their original and host cultures.

Thus, if one intends to acculturate by assimilating, one aims to exchange the old culture for the new, adopting the new as one's own. If he or she adopts an integration approach, one keeps the old and holds the new cultures simultaneously (Berry 2006). Paloutzian and Sagir (2019) found that Syrian refugees who intended to assimilate into Turkish culture valued forgiveness significantly more than those who wanted to integrate the Syrian and Turkish cultures ($p < .03$). This difference suggests that assimilators are more able to leave the past behind and feel more free of their wounds, and forgive sooner and to a greater degree. In contrast, the integrators may hold on to the past – culture and wounds – and be less able to forgive.

Interestingly and in contrast to the above findings on forgiveness, assimilators and integrators valued reconciliation to about the same degree. This suggests that they distinguish these two values in their minds and do not necessarily see one leading to the other. As one participant said, "I can forgive but not reconcile." It remains to be understood what happens if two enemies are brought together.

### *Refugees and reconciling*

The above snapshot of data paints a stark picture. The findings make it difficult to link knowledge of refugees to a model of processes toward reconciliation. But a small window remains open for some possibility to begin a process with perpetrators that could evolve, perhaps in small ways, to become reconciliatory. If carefully done, it might evolve to be a model of transactional "dialogue" between victim and perpetrator (Abu-Nimer 1999, 2020; Tint 2010).

The place to begin might be illustrated by the verbal, small group dialogues reported by Busse et al. (2010) between descendants of Holocaust survivors and descendants of Nazi perpetrators. Each verbal exchange signalled openness and trust in the other, who reciprocated, and it repeated again. Thus, the subset of refugees more inclined to forgive or reconcile might, with adequate safety and guidance, take one positive step toward the adversary, openly stated as an intended peace-making gesture. Signals of trustworthiness would be essential. Such steps could eventually lead to reciprocal steps by the adversary, additional steps by refugees not initially so inclined and further gradual and reciprocated steps. In general, beginning with those few most inclined and capable, small initial steps could result in accomplishing a big vision for peacefulness. Importantly, and as argued below, this becomes more likely when the two sides want the same higher values and goals, and when they must collaborate to reach them (Kappmeier, Guenoun, & Campbell, 2019).

### *Refugees globally*

Space constraints do not allow for a full picture of refugees worldwide. Suffice it to say that it is strikingly similar to that of the Syrian refugees in Turkey, multiplied. There are 70.8 million forcibly displaced people worldwide (UNHCR 2019; United Nations 2015). If they were one country, it would be the 24th largest on earth. The traumas they suffered parallel those faced by the Syrians: Forced displacement, torture, abduction, imprisonment, poverty, women raped, death of loved ones, loss of livelihood and property (Fiddian-Qasmiyeh et al. 2016). Their general well-being was affected accordingly, not only in circumstantial ways – unemployed, desperate, disoriented, acculturation stress, social isolation, language barriers – but also in psychological difficulties such as depression, anxiety, PTSD, painful levels of loneliness, somatic symptoms and suicidal thoughts (see Riley et al. 2017; Rintoul 2010; and Tay et al. 2019, for examples).

The refugee/IDP problem is not a local problem; it is a global problem. We the people, citizens of the world, are in this together – whether we want to be or know it or not. Local governments, schools, NGOs and individuals need to prepare, ready to respond and care for people who need it – analogous to preparing to respond to the onset of a deadly disease such as Covid-19.

Almost all refugee research focuses on their sufferings, traumas, treatment by host countries and health variables. A literature review found no study beyond Paloutzian and Sagir (2019) that specifically examined their inclinations toward forgiveness, reconciliation or revenge. Because of the direct similarity between the Syrian and global refugees on all circumstantial, mental health, host country and war experience variables, it seems reasonable to proceed on the basis that they are also similar in the degree to which they tend towards forgiving, reconciling with or revenge against those who harmed them. The suffering of all refugees seems unpleasantly similar.

## Theory on processes of reconciliation

Two important sources may provide essential information for theoretical arguments to help make a strategy to facilitate reconciliation. These are (1) psychological research on the relative roles of forgiving and reconciling as instances of attitude and behaviour change, integrated with research on the roles of superordinate goals and social identity in opponents collaborating, and (2) a lesson from history showing how direct adversaries cooperated to defeat a powerful common enemy. Arguments about reconciling typically have roots in context of conflicts, enemies and war. But at the time of writing, the whole world faces the COVID-19 virus, which no country alone can erase, but which may be overcome if all parties collaborate. The superordinate value? Life. The goal? Maximum control with minimum deaths at the earliest time.

### *Forgiveness, reconciliation and trust*

Forgiveness is typically understood as an affect; reconciliation is a behaviour (see Kalayjian and Paloutzian, 2010, for illustrations). The difference matters greatly. The two concepts at the heart of this book – reconciliation and peacebuilding – refer not to what people feel or think, but what they do. Behaviour is the bottom line, the acid test of whether humans "get along," or fight. Let us unpack these concepts in order to facilitate reconciliation and help subdue the common existential threat, Covid-19.

A model of steps toward reconciling sufficiently realistic to be implemented in the midst or aftermath of real-world hostilities (Paloutzian and Sagir, 2019) listed the following essential elements:

(1) Both sides of a conflict must *want* hostilities to stop
(2) All parties must *display* truth, honesty and transparency
(3) The circumstances must be interpersonal, intergroup and safe
(4) *Behaviours* in the common interest must be *performed*, reinforced and reciprocated; interdependent trust and mutual forgiving between opposing parties may thereby be gradually built, increasing in small steps as reciprocal reconciliatory behaviours are performed and reinforced in an ever-widening circle.

Notice that in the above steps, neither forgiveness nor trust as affects are mentioned as prerequisites. They are in an incremental sequence of consequences that increases in stepwise fashion within each party to a conflict – having performed a reconciliatory behaviour. Thus, unlike much writing that assumes forgiving precedes reconciling (Rutayisire 2010; Satha-Anand, Chapter 5, this volume; Tutu 1999; see Kalayjian and Paloutzian, 2010, for further examples), we argue that the reverse sequence has greater success, and is more realistic in the short-run and more promising in the long-run.

It is well known that behaviour change can yield affect change (Albarracin et al. 2005). Therefore, the forgiveness affect is better understood to follow reconciliatory behaviour than to first develop independent of it (Paloutzian and Sagir 2019). Extending this argument and following the four steps outlined in the above model, behaving well towards an enemy, although counter-intuitive, may constitute a small signal of trust (Kappmeier 2016, 2020) which, if reciprocated, may in stepwise fashion continue in a healthy direction.

We are not suggesting that forgiveness and trust are not part of peacebuilding. Trust is essential (Alon and Bar-Tal, 2016; Kappmeier and Mercy 2019; Kelman 2005), and forgiveness is highly desirable. But we cannot expect the process to begin with them because, as the refugee data show, their default probability for victims is very low. They are better understood as consequences or desired byproducts of initial steps that signal trust (Kappmeier 2016, 2020). If such steps begin and these effects result, even to a small degree, they may trigger a sequence of back and forth steps that help enemies collaborate to mutual and individual benefit (Kappmeier et al., 2019).

### *Reconciling: Process of doing*

Reconciliation is best understood not as an end state that opposing parties reach and "just stay there." We should understand it as a graded sequence of behaving a certain way interactively that can spiral upward. It is not about a goal as a fixed outcome, but about what we are doing when we are reconciling that differs from what we are doing when we are not reconciling (see Paloutzian 2010, for similar arguments about forgiving), thus best approached as a process, not a goal (Bar-Tal and Bennink 2004; Rafferty 2020).

This puts the emphasis on what people are doing instead of what they did – on violating people instead of violence as a category, trusting instead of trust as a do or don't binary and being transparent instead of transparency as a condition. Once begun, the sequence of steps in the process of reconciling can continue and increase via reinforced feedback loops so that opposing parties begin trusting (Kappmeier et al., Chapter 7 of this volume) in degrees that prompt either conscious awareness or unconscious recognition sufficient to remain in long-term memory, available for retrieval in re-evaluating and adjusting tendencies toward the adversary (Charbonneau and Parent 2012). If continued, they may help decrease systemic and episodic violence, and increase systemic and episodic peacebuilding (Christie and Montiel 2013; Christie et al. 2008).

What factors should be in place for initial steps to signal trust and prompt beneficial counter-responses from the adversary? Two social psychological principles are of great importance. The first documents how people define themselves as members of a group and its power to define their identity. The second makes clear how important superordinate values and goals are in reducing intergroup conflict. These two processes may need to fuse into one for humans to win a war, or win against Covid-19.

### *Social identity and group biases*

The power of social identity in groups has been demonstrated in that belonging to a group, any group, including those formed randomly, by flip of a coin, fosters in-group bias. This phenomenon is the *minimal group effect* and has been replicated across cultures, ages, group tasks and gender (Tajfel 1981; Tajfel and Turner 1979). The present concern is that if merely being in a group (even a randomly formed group) sets one up for identity with that group and in-group bias, it is no wonder that real world groups (ethnic, religious, sexual, countries) dominate people's minds and lives – especially separate from and compared to "the others" – while individuals imagine they are independent and freely choose what they value, think and work for. Social identity with one's group fosters in-group favouritism and out-group prejudice. Those biases should be replaced with *identification with all humanity* (McFarland et al. 2013; de Rivera 2018; de Rivera and Carson 2015; Paloutzian et al. 2014). How can humans become citizens of the world?

### *Superordinate values and a lesson from World War II*

One of the most important concepts in social psychology relevant to reconciliation and peacebuilding concerns the role of superordinate values and goals in the reduction of intergroup conflict. Such values and goals often cannot be fulfilled by oneself. Reconciling and establishing peace are among them. For reconciling to begin and lead to peaceable engagements between opposing parties, both sides are required. They must collaborate, or reconciliatory behaviours will not occur and there will be no peace.

When combined with insights on social identity and in-group bias, foundational research on groups (Sherif 1966; Sherif et al. 1961) provides principles demonstrated in laboratory and field experiments to aid our understanding. In Sharif's *Robber's Cave* experiment, two groups of teenage boys at a summer camp were opponents but given a task that neither could do alone. Initially, group biases were manifest. But the assignment required the boys to work together. They did. The opponents became collaborators and did something neither could do alone. From 1941 to 1945, the world saw those principles in operation at the heart of the greatest military confrontation in history. We are fortunate that its residual effects helped save the world from annihilation for a generation. Let us now step out of our "ivory tower" of academic social psychology and grasp this lesson from the most compelling of all examples of the application of the above argument to the real world.

The most catastrophic war of all time was World War II. Fifty million people, military and civilian, died. Starting with Hitler's invasion of Poland in 1939, it expanded to involve most regions of the earth. As is well known, the chief combatants were, on one side, Hitler's military apparatus, and on the other, the Allies (the UK, Soviet Union and US). Our present focus is on the formation and collaboration of the Allies.

The Western democracies (UK and US) and the Soviet Union were bitter adversaries. They despised each other (Hamilton 2019). In addition, following Stalin's total surprise at Hitler's attack on Mother Russia in June 1941, Churchill wrote, "so far as strategy, policy, foresight, competence are arbiters, Stalin and his commissars showed themselves at this moment the most completely outwitted bunglers of the Second World War" (Churchill 1950). Nevertheless, upon the eve of Hitler's invasion of Russia, Churchill, when questioned on whether he, "the arch anti-communist," in collaborating with Stalin and the Soviets, "was [not] bowing down in the House of Rimmon," replied: "Not at all. I have only one purpose, the destruction of Hitler, and my life is much simplified thereby. If Hitler invaded Hell I would make at least a favourable reference to the Devil in the House of Commons" (Churchill 1950: 370). Sometimes one's enemy's enemy is one's friend.

At the meetings between Roosevelt, Churchill and Stalin in Tehran, 1943, the Roosevelt–Churchill duo and Stalin disagreed about particulars of strategy, but agreed fully on overriding concerns. Their singular purpose was to defeat Hitler. They well knew their differences, but deliberately set them aside for the common purpose. They cooperated, shared information and met their commitments to each other and the cause; the US even shipped equipment and weapons to Russia. During the Tehran meeting, Stalin remarked that the war was won by machines – that that the US built (Hamilton 2019). The collaboration of these adversaries is a model for us.

Their alliance set in motion a trend in global affairs that lasted for approximately 70 years. It was that the nations of the world unite and be so governed that it would no longer be possible for any nation to again attempt what Hitler's regime did – if not forever, then at least during the remainder of their lifetimes (Roosevelt 1943, noted in Hamilton 2019). So, even during the Cold War, during which the US and the Soviets were confrontational and "enemies," and each built thousands of nuclear weapons, they knew that neither side had the slightest intention of ever using them against the other.[3]

People, as well as governments, even though they differ, can collaborate so long as they share important "higher" values and want them bad enough to set the issues over which they differ aside in order to accomplish a higher purpose. We hope that now, a generation later with leaders unfamiliar with the intimacies of that past, all citizens, leaders and countries understand the important lessons from the past, and guard any pressures or tendencies that might repeat the errors that made cold conflicts become hot ones. One fears that governments are showing signs of decay – lack of awareness of, or care about, the lessons of the past, as if a new generation came along to disregard wisdom gained by blood. But the world now faces another common enemy – not a military dictator who invades other countries and kills its people. It is a strand of RNA (Cascella et al. 2020).

## Modeling reconciliation and peace processes

These processes are complex and informed by many scientific disciplines. How might we render them more tractable? Computational modelling and simulation (CMS) offers a promising option. These methodologies are designed to study complex systems, and have been used in the psychological and social sciences in recent years (Alvarez 2016; Sun 2012). Given their explanatory and forecasting power, it is not surprising that scholars have already used CMS techniques to address questions related to conflict and cooperation (e.g., Axelrod 1997). While many earlier agent-based models had relatively simple agent architectures, often presupposing rational choice theory, the field is rapidly developing more psychologically realistic agents in more realistic social networks. Here we briefly outline the next steps in the development of such a model that might help us discover some of the key conditions under which – and mechanisms by which – reconciliation and peace processes occur in diverse human populations.

The easiest procedure would be to adapt a model that has already been successfully calibrated and validated. One candidate would be the *mutually escalating religious violence* (MERV) model, whose causal architecture is informed by social psychological theories such as terror management theory, social identity theory and identity fusion theory (Shults et al. 2018a; cf. Shults et al. 2018b). MERV was validated at two levels: (1) At the micro-level (agent behaviours and interactions) in relation to data from social psychological experiments; (2) at the macro-level (emergent phenomena such as mutually escalating conflict between two groups) in relation to data from the Christchurch earthquake in New Zealand and the escalation of conflict in Northern Ireland during "The Troubles," where the dependent variable was the mutual escalation of anxiety and conflict.

In the current case, the concern is in the mutual escalation of reconciliatory behaviours that promote peaceful coexistence and cooperation between diverse groups, especially under threatening conditions such as those surrounding refugee crises. What would it take to adapt MERV so that we could provide a computational model that tests hypotheses proposed in, e.g., Paloutzian and Sagir (2019), briefly summarised above? The "virtual minds" of the simulated agents in the model would need to be informed by the insights from the social psychological literature described above, and the environment of the "artificial society" would need to designed with parameters whose alteration would be relevant for simulating the emergence of the sort of historical cooperation described above. In other words, it would require the construction of a model in which we could "grow" reconciliation and peace between two or more diverse groups from the micro-level behaviours and interactions of agents within those simulated societies.

Each of the four elements of the theoretical model outlined above would need to be carefully operationalised and implemented within the computational architecture. For example, a variable such as "wanting" hostilities to stop should be differentially distributed within the artificial population, as would variables related to "displaying" truth, honesty and transparency. The agents would also need to have the capacity to interact in ways that allowed the "performance" of reconciliatory behaviours at different levels of intensity. The element of the theoretical model dealing with "safety" could also be implemented as an agent-level variable, such that agents felt more or less safe depending on their interpersonal and intergroup interactions. Another option would be to implement this variable as an environment level parameter, which we might call "existential security" and validate it using datasets such as the Human Development Index (see Gore et al. 2018, for illustration of such an approach). In dialogue with the relevant subject-matter experts, we would identify ways of measuring each variable or find convincing proxies, such as questionnaire responses or answers in qualitative interviews.

In order to develop and run simulations that could test the hypotheses outlined above, we would need to incorporate at least two additional elements into the model: The "superordinate value" of life and the presence of various levels of threat in the environment such as Covid-19. The former could be implemented as a (potentially) shared norm, indicating the extent to which the simulated agents have the same or similar ranking of the valuation of human "life" in relation to other values, such as the protection or survival of a particular in-group. Our research teams have already used "shared norms" in other computational models designed to simulate interactions between immigrant and host populations (Shults et al. 2020). We could incorporate the threat of Covid-19 (or other pandemics) as an environmental parameter, whose intensity (perhaps operationalised as frequency of contact with potentially contagious persons) could be altered in simulation experiments in order to explore how various levels of threat, combined with other distributions of independent variables, such as number and size of "reconciliatory behaviours," affect the dependent variable. The good news is that the MERV causal architecture already includes contagion threats as part of its simulated environment. The next step would be working with subject-matter experts to adapt the model to adequately simulate the impact of a pandemic (construed as a common enemy) on the attitudes and behaviours of the agents within an artificial society.

Once appropriately validated, we could explore the parameter space of the model to discover the relations among the relevant variables and the distributions and conditions under which reconciliation and peace processes are likely to occur (or not). We emphasise that the use of CMS techniques is far more complicated than explained in this chapter section, and, like all research methods, it has limitations and should not be embraced as a panacea. However, one advantage of M&S techniques is that they require their creators to be explicit about the assumptions built into the architecture and purpose of the simulation experiments. In this way, the ethical dimensions and ramifications of the research are brought front and centre for ethical consideration, making it less likely that they will be used for malevolence or manipulation (Shults and Wildman 2019, 2020). Also, and importantly, there is a growing consensus among scholars working in this field that, given the availability of these tools for addressing societal challenges, in some cases it might be unethical *not* to use them – especially when those challenges are exceedingly complex and the implications of policy decisions are so serious (Gilbert et al. 2018).

## Challenges

### *To refugees and empires*

Our arguments identify specific steps people (e.g., a traumatised refugee or head of state) can take to confront an existential threat. Governments want to continue; so do people. Countries want to keep their land; refugees want to keep their homes. Any party can take a first step to trigger even slight trust by the "other."

***Decisions***

Know your values and decide what you genuinely want. Many individuals and governmental officials seem not to know. If it is to establish peace, proceed; if it is to get re-elected, resign. Ask for criticism. Have a dialogue with opponents who clearly articulate what they want, and with experts who supply accurate information, knowledge of relevant facts and wisdom to guide decisions. Know the processes at work, lessons from history and research-based evidence that must underpin good decisions.

***Big vision, small steps***

A conflict at any level matters. This is so whether it is between two individuals or between mighty nation-states. The latter is infinitely more complicated than the former, but known fundamental social psychological principles operate in both. This book has argued that behaviour, not attitudes or feelings or words, is the bottom line in all transactions. However, processes of trusting, forgiving and believing matter, because humans make attributions about these properties and respond accordingly. And problems between parties arise when there is inconsistency between what one says and what one does, when verbal behaviour and overt actions are discrepant. Thus trust, which is built when positive pronouncements are backed up with positive actions, is an essential mediating process. Nonviolence without it is mere compliance with rules or submission under pressure. Freedom requires mutual reciprocal trusting – built in graded fashion openly, transparently and behaviourally. Reconciling and building peace at multiple levels is a big vision. It can be accomplished by sustained, reciprocal small steps.

***From war to virus***

I (RFP) have been alive since 1945, while the Allies were still in World War II collaboration, up to today when Covid-19 is killing people worldwide. These are two global existential threats from which, when combined, the line of argument in this chapter extends. But the argument is research-based, not mere opinion. The hopes it leaves for mediating trust and reconciliatory actions are relevant to conflicts small and large, and to collaborating and trusting in order to subdue medical threats; for the highest value, subduing our common enemy.

## Covid-19 as our common enemy

On 1 April 2020 António Guterres, the Secretary General of the United Nations, said,

> The COVID-19 pandemic is one of the most dangerous challenges this world has faced in our lifetime. … Now is the time for unity, for the international

community to work together in solidarity to stop this virus and its shattering consequences.

(United Nations 2020)

Although this virus is not an enemy in the sense of nations engaged in combat, defeating its "death value" reflects a superordinate value (human life in the broad sense) and goal (prevent its spread and subdue its disease properties) that requires the participation, collaboration and cooperation of all, everywhere. In doing so, enemies do not need to be friends. But each must do its part for any "side" to survive. Such is a shared existential threat. Trusting may develop in steps as parties do their part. As adversaries over other disagreements begin to collaborate, steps toward reconciling may be a byproduct. Call it reconciliation-by-force of a superordinate value that sets a common goal that if unmet, kills all as one.

Like climate change, Covid-19 could teach us that there may be no human life on earth if we insist on continuing to perceive each other as members of "other" groups, whether ethnic, country, skin colour, religious or gender. It could teach us that either we all live, or none do. Perhaps this disease affords us a survival test because it is an exceptionally powerful common "enemy." We see trusting as an integral modulating element in a graded stepwise process, and forgiving and reconciling over other issues as correlates and byproducts of adversaries collaborating to fulfil any common purpose, even if is not a military one. We hope it lays the foundation for collaboration worldwide.

## Notes

1 Part of this section is adapted from Paloutzian and Sagir (2019).
2 In this study, because N = 100, the number of responses per answer option also equals the percentage (%).
3 Most subsequent leaders of the two sides understood this, although as time passed it seemed less so in a few cases.

## References

Abu-Nimer, M. (1999). *Dialogue, conflict resolution, and change*. Albany: State University of New York Press.

Albarracin, D., Johnson, B. T., & Zana, M. P. (Eds.) (2005). *The handbook of attitudes*. New York: Psychology Press.

Alon, I., & Bar-Tal, D. (2016). *The role of trust in conflict resolution*. Heidelberg: Springer.

Alpert, E., & Marrouch, R. (2012). How teenagers with a can of paint sparked Syria's uprising. *Los Angeles Times*. Retrieved from https://latimesblogs.latimes.com/world_now/2012/03/dara-teenagers-syria-anniversary.html

Alvarez, R. M. (Ed.) (2016). *Computational social science: Discovery and prediction*. Cambridge: Cambridge University Press.

Axelrod, R. M. (1997). *The complexity of cooperation: Agent-based models of competition and collaboration*. Princeton: Princeton University Press.

Bar-Tal, D., & Bennink, G. H. (2004). The nature of reconciliation as an outcome and as a process. In Y. Bar-Siman-Tov (Ed.), *From conflict resolution to reconciliation* (pp. 11–49). Oxford: Oxford University Press.

Berry, J. W. (2006). Contexts of acculturation. In D. L. Sam & J. W. Berry (Eds.), *The Cambridge handbook of acculturation psychology* (pp. 27–42). Cambridge: Cambridge University Press.

Busse, W. J., Emme, M., & Gerut, R. (2010). Dialogue in action. In A. Kalayjian, R. F. Paloutzian, A. Kalayjian, & R. F. Paloutzian (Eds.), *Forgiveness and reconciliation: Psychological pathways for conflict transformation and peace building* (pp. 278–282). New York: Springer.

Cascella, M., Rajnik, M., Cuomo, A., Dulebohn, S. C., & Di Napoli, R. (2020). *Features, evaluation and treatment coronavirus (COVID-19)*. NCBI, National Institutes of Health. Retrieved from https://www.ncbi.nlm.nih.gov/books/NBK554776/

Charbonneau, B., & Parent, G. (2012). *Peacebuilding, memory and reconciliation: Bridging top-down and bottom-up approaches*. London: Routledge.

Christie, D. J., & Montiel, C. (2013). Contributions of psychology to war and peace. *American Psychologist*, *68*(7), 502–513.

Christie, D. J., Tint, B. S., Wagner, R. V., & Winter, D. D. (2008). Peace psychology for a peaceful world. *American Psychologist*, *63*(6), 540–552.

Churchill, W. S. (1950). *The Second World War: The grand alliance*. Boston: Houghton Mifflin Company.

de Rivera, J. (2018). Themes for the celebration of global community. *Peace and Conflict: Journal of Peace Psychology*, *24*(2), 216–223.

de Rivera, J., & Carson, H. A. (2015). Cultivating a global identity. *Journal of Social and Political Psychology*, *3*(2), 310–330.

Fiddian-Qasmiyeh, E., Loescher, G., Long, K., & Sigona, N. (2016). *The Oxford handbook of refugee and forced migration studies*. Oxford: Oxford University Press.

Gilbert, N., Ahrweiler, P., Barbrook-Johnson, P., Narasimhan, K. P., & Wilkinson, H. (2018). Computational modelling of public policy. *Journal of Artificial Societies and Social Simulation*, *21*(1), 1–19.

Gore, R., Lemos, C., Shults, F. L., & Wildman, W. J. (2018). Forecasting changes in religiosity and existential security with an agent-based model. *Journal of Artificial Societies and Social Simulation*, *21*, 1–31.

Hamilton, N. (2019). *War and peace: FDR's final odyssey D-day to Yalta, 1943–1945*. Boston: Houghton Mifflin Harcourt.

Kalayjian, A., & Paloutzian, R. F. (Eds.) (2010). *Forgiveness and reconciliation: Psychological pathways for conflict transformation and peace building*. New York: Springer.

Kappmeier, M. (2016). Trusting the enemy - towards a comprehensive understanding of trust in intergroup conflict. *Peace and Conflict: Journal of Peace Psychology*, *22*(2), 134–144.

Kappmeier, M., Guenoun, B., & Campbell, R. (2019). They are us? The mediating effects of compatibility-based trust on the relationship between discrimination and overall trust. *New Zealand Journal of Psychology*, *48*(1), 97–105.

Kappmeier, M., & Mercy, A. (2019). The long road from cold war to warm peace: Building shared collective memory through trust. *Journal of Social and Political Psychology*, *7*(1), 525–555.

Kelman, H. C. (2005). Building trust among enemies: The central challenge for international conflict resolution. *International Journal of Intercultural Relations*, *29*(6), 639–650.

McFarland, S., Brown, D., & Webb, M. (2013). Identification with all humanity as a moral concept and psychological construct. *Current Directions in Psychological Science, 22*(3), 194–198.

Paloutzian, R. F. (2010). The bullet and its meaning: Forgiveness, non-forgiveness, and their confrontation. In A. Kalayjian & R. F. Paloutzian (Eds.), *Forgiveness and reconciliation: Psychological pathways for conflict transformation and peace building* (pp. 71–80). New York: Springer.

Paloutzian, R. F., & Sagir, Z. (2019). Forgiving, reconciling, and peace-building in refugee contexts: Theory, research, and data from the war in Syria. In M. G. C. Njoku, L. A. Jason, & B. Johnson (Eds.), *The psychology of Peace promotion* (pp. 181–200). New York: Springer.

Paloutzian, R. F., Shankar, U., & Luyten, P. (2014). Forgiveness and Gandhian nonviolence: Their confrontation in light of psychological research. *Gandhi Marg, 35*(4), 631–654.

Reicher, S. D., & Haslam, S. A. (2016). Fueling terror: How extremists are made. *Scientific American Mind, 27*(3), 34–39.

Riley, A., Varner, A., Ventevogel, P., Taimur Hasan, M. M., & Welton-Mitchell, C. (2017). Daily stressors, trauma exposure, and mental health among stateless Rohingya refugees in Bangladesh. *Transcultural Psychiatry, 54*(3), 304–331.

Rintoul, A. (2010). *Understanding the mental health and wellbeing of Afghan women in South East Melbourne*. Melbourne: Department of Health.

Rutayisire, A. (2010). Rwanda: Repentance and forgiveness – pillars of genuine reconciliation. In A. Kalayjian & R. F. Paloutzian (Eds.), *Forgiveness and reconciliation: Psychological pathways for conflict transformation and peace building* (pp. 171–187). New York: Springer.

Sagir, Z. (2014). *Religious coping and mental health among Syrian refugees*. Paper presented at the meeting of Society for the Scientific Study of Religion and Religious Research Association, 31 October–2 November 2014. Indiana, USA.

Sagir, Z. (2016). *In earshot of bombs: Identity, acculturation, mental health, and coping in Muslim refugees on the Syria-Turkey border*. Paper presented at the Small Group Meeting on Immigration to Major Immigrant-Receiving Countries. Society for the Psychological Study of Social Issues and the Society of Australian Social Psychology, Ottawa. Retrieved from https://spssi-sasp.com/well-being-of-immigrants-and-refugees/

Sagir, Z. (2018). Suriyeli Kadın Mültecilerde Kültürel Uyum, Ruh Sağlığı ve Din.* Yayınlanmamış Doktora Tezi. Unpublished PhD Thesis. İstanbul Üniversitesi SBE, İstanbul. (*Translation of title: Acculturation/Cultural Adaptation, Mental Health, and Religion Among Syrian Woman Refugees).

Sagir, Z. (2020). Spiritual counseling and guidance in healthcare institutions for disabled foreigners with different religious, ethnic and cultural identities. In A. Ayten, N. Tınaz, & M. Zengin (Eds)., *Spiritual Counselling and Care in Health and Prison Services: Diverse Experiences and Practices*. Istanbul: Ensar Publication House.

Sherif, M. (1966). *Group conflict and cooperation*. London: Routledge and Kegan Paul.

Sherif, M., Harvey, O. J., White, B. J., Hood, W. R., & Sherif, C. W. (1961). *Intergroup conflict and cooperation: The Robbers Cave experiment* (vol. 10). Norman: University Book Exchange.

Shults, F. L., Gore, R., Wildman, W. J., Lynch, C., Lane, J. E., & Toft, M. (2018a). A generative model of the mutual escalation of anxiety between religious groups. *Journal of Artificial Societies and Social Simulation, 21*(4), 7.

Shults, F. L., Lane, J. E., Diallo, S., Lynch, C., Wildman, W. J., & Gore, R. (2018b). Modeling terror management theory: Computer simulations of the impact of mortality salience on religiosity. *Religion, Brain and Behavior*, *8*(1), 77–100.

Shults, F. L., & Wildman, W. J. (2019). Ethics, computer simulation, and the future of humanity. In S. Y. Diallo, W. J. Wildman, F. L. Shults, & A. Tolk (Eds.), *Human simulation: Perspectives, insights and applications* (pp. 21–40). Heidelberg: Springer.

Shults, F. L., & Wildman, W. J. (2020, May). Artificial social ethics: Simulating culture, conflict, and cooperation. In *Proceedings of the Spring Simulation Conference* (pp. 1–10). Meeting of the Society for Modeling and Simulation International, Fairfax, VA.

Shults, F. L., Wildman, W. J., Diallo, S., Puga-Gonzalez, I., & Voas, D. (2020). The artificial society analytics platform. In H. Verhagen, M. Borit, G. Bravo, & N. Wijermans, (Eds.), *Advances in social simulation* (pp. 411–426). Cham, Switzerland: Springer.

Sun, R. (2012). *Grounding social sciences in cognitive sciences*. Cambridge: MIT Press.

Tajfel, H. (1981). *Human groups and social categories: Studies in social psychology*. Cambridge: Cambridge University Press.

Tajfel, H., & Turner, J. C. (1979). An integrative theory of intergroup conflict. In W. G. Austin & S. Worchel (Eds.), *The social psychology of intergroup relations* (pp. 33–47). Monterrey: Brooks/Cole.

Tay, A. K., Riley, A., Islam, R., Welton-Mitchell, C., Duchesne, B., Waters, V. (2019). The culture, mental health and psychosocial wellbeing of Rohingya refugees: A systematic review. *Epidemiology and Psychiatric Sciences*, *28*(5), 489–494.

Tint, B. S. (2010). Dialogue, forgiveness, and reconciliation. In A. Kalayjian & R. F. Paloutzian (Eds.), *Forgiveness and reconciliation: Psychological pathways for conflict transformation and peace building* (pp. 269–285). New York: Springer.

Tutu, D. (1999). *No future without forgiveness*. New York: Doubleday Publishing.

United Nations. (2015). *Antonio Guterres (Portugal): 2005–2015*. Retrieved from https://www.unhcr.org/antonio-guterres-portugal-2005-2015.html

United Nations. (2020). *Statement by the secretary-general on COVID-19*. Retrieved from https://www.un.org/sg/en/content/sg/statement/2020-04-08/statement-the-secretary-general-covid-19

United Nations High Commissioner for Refugees. (2016). *UNHCR viewpoint: "Refugee" or "migrant"-which is right?* Retrieved from http://www.unhcr.org/news/latest/2016/7/55df0e556/unhcr-viewpoint-refugee-migrant-right.html

United Nations High Commissioner for Refugees. (2018). *Global trends forced displacement in 2017*. Retrieved from https://www.eutm-somalia.eu/wp-content/uploads/2018/06/UNHCR-Global-Trends-for-Displacement-in-2017.pdf

United Nations High Commissioner for Refugees. (2019). *Refugee facts: What is a refugee?* Retrieved from https://www.unrefugees.org/refugee-facts/what-is-a-refugee/

# 14 Conclusion

*SungYong Lee and Kevin P. Clements*

Residual grievances between different social groups and the experience of past violence offer significant obstacles to the consolidation of peace and sustainable development in the aftermath of dire violence. Hence, social reconciliation has become one of the most crucial issues in post-conflict peacebuilding. Peacebuilding has made a significant contribution, to the re-establishment of "order" in post-conflict environments; however, conventional peacebuilding has mostly been based on state-centric stabilising assumptions. In particular much attention was given to institutional support for three areas of activity: Truth-telling (e.g., truth and reconciliation commissions), trial and persecution (e.g., international tribunals) and compensation and reparation (e.g. government subsidies for reparation). In addition to these practices, peacebuilding actors also paid most attention to the roles of security, political, economic and governance structures in developing pre-conditions for reconciliation. Such approaches tend to develop elite-driven models of reconciliation programmes and to disregard the significance of less visible practices of peacebuilding that are carried out by local populations in their everyday life.

This volume has asked and explored a different central question, "How do people rebuild and define the relations with former harm-doers in their everyday lives?" by incorporating the perspectives and insights from social psychology and "everyday peace" discourse. Extensive academic analysis has clarified the complexity and multidimensionality of reconciliation and called for holistic, contextualised and systematic approaches to reconciliation. Reconciliation requires deep psychological, sociological, theological and philosophical insights and actions at multiple levels: National, societal and communal. However, there has been limited exploration of if and how such theories and knowledge can be applied in the post-war contexts. The chapters included in this volume present a good number of findings and lessons with regard to understanding the complex nature of the factors that affect the dynamics of social reconciliation at individual, group and state levels, problems of conceptual limitations and proposals for better practice for promoting reconciliation. This concluding chapter summarises the discussions presented in these chapters, by integrating them under four concurrent themes.

First, the dynamics of post-conflict reconciliation are primarily about the ways in which individuals, groups and nations deal with suffering, pain and trauma.

Reconciliation has to do with the narratives with which each one of us deals with "theodicy" problems, which include problems about why innocent people suffer, and feel afflicted and disempowered. Identity, memory and identity-based politics play critical roles in coping with why extreme violence and victimisation occur and how the people are put in the atrocity as either harm-doers, victims or bystanders. To promote reconciliation, therefore, we need to acknowledge and examine the psychological, sociological, religious and political questions that lie at different levels. Nevertheless, in the peacebuilding process for promoting reconciliation, the practitioners and local communities in a conflict-affected society face various challenges such as psychological war-trauma, people's lack of confidence in managing public lives, heavy reliance on patron-client relationships and extreme distrust/antagonism between different social groups (Cox 2008; Özerdem and Lee 2016).

Various cognitive, cultural and political factors that have generated the tendencies in human behaviour have been explored in this volume. For instance, Mari Fitzduff in Chapter 3 pays particular attention to the individual level, and attempts to discover the factors within the human brain which affect individuals' positions on and perceptions of outgroups by adopting recent findings in behavioural neuroscience. Specifically, the chapter introduces how some brain functions that are related to people's beliefs and moralities are affected by genetic, social and environmental factors. One example of many insightful findings is that the human brain is like a dual-mode camera with both automatic settings and a manual mode, which function in distinct ways. People's emotional feelings associated with the amygdala tend to emerge beyond the control of the conscious/intellectual side of brain, especially when people's own communities/groups feel under stress. Once such a condition is set, cognitive skills and deliberate engagement have restricted capacity for successful reconciliation. Moreover, the chapter explains that conservatives' support for the status quo is partly attributed to brain patterns that lead them to be more cognisant of impending dangers. In addition, in Chapter 13, Raymond Paloutzian, Zeynep Sagir and F. LeRon Shults provide striking examples of the perceptual and practical challenges that individual refugees may face in relation to reconciliation with former harm-doers. The promotion of actions for reconciliation seems daunting while refugees are under the influence of the experience of mass violence and the challenges in the new host societies, and are experiencing a sense of marginalisation, and suffering the hardship occurring in daily life. Nevertheless, the chapter also presents that, among the people who expressed more willingness for reconciliation, religious principles and philosophy were highlighted as major factors that encourage them to forgive the perceived perpetrators.

Challenging issues underlying reconciliation also exist at community levels. SungYong Lee's Chapter 10 examines how local communities deal with the significance of massive violence and determine the level of social acceptance of former harm-doers. The dynamics of narrative formation are determined by various factors, such as economic hardships, security stability, the proportion of harm-doers' associates, the local power structure and the influence of religious institutions. Due to the combined impact of these factors, the majority of the local communities studied in the chapter have achieved a limited level of reconciliation – shallow co-existence – between victims and former harm-doers. In a similar vein, Rachel Rafferty's Chapter 12 demonstrates that narrative formation can even restrict the scope of practitioners' activities for peacebuilding. The chapter explains that the historical narratives and victimhood frequently prevent local populations in Northern Ireland from seeing reconciliation as a legitimate social goal. In conflict settings, collective conflict narratives tend to highlight in-group victimhood and delegitimise the out-groups' claims and normative positions.

Chapter 7, written by Mariska Kappmeier, Chiara Venanzetti and J. M. Inton-Campbell, highlights the perceptual challenges between two nations in Moldova-Transdniestria, which deter the promotion of effective conflict resolution and trust-building. For instance, the chapter describes that the two nations often fail to understand their counterparts' key interests that have generated the ongoing tensions between them. The risk of misinterpretation of the counterparts' position tends to be higher in the relations between the states/nations, in which the in-group's self-centred narratives have more chances to grow. Ria Shibata's case study of the historical disputes between Japan and South Korea in Chapter 11 explains that such narratives (especially collective victimhood in the case study) can be transmitted to the next generations via narratives in official textbooks, mass media, rituals and commemorations, popular cultural products and through individual sharing of stories.

To deal with the mechanisms for narrative generation and psychological healing requires culturally reflective approaches that take multi-layered issues into consideration. Many conventional programmes for social peacebuilding have ended up with stunted reconciliation due to the lack of such consideration. Some early models implemented in Argentina and Uganda left a deep sense of "unjust silence" as they granted blanket amnesty for former war crimes in pursuit of political peace, while the international tribunals in the former Yugoslavia and Rwanda present the pitfalls of elite-driven punitive judicial mechanisms. The reparation and compensation schemes for victims adopted in South Africa demonstrate the limitations of short-sighted and material-based arrangements. Although some programmes have attempted to generate new national narratives to identify the in-groups and out-groups, many of them were utilised as the opportunity to push forward the new political authorities' propaganda, as was seen in Rwanda (Özerdem and Lee 2016). While each of these examples presents a unique set of lessons, they demonstrate one common underlying issue: Such state-driven mechanisms have failed to acknowledge the various needs of victims and wider community members in dealing with social narratives and psychological challenges.

Second, reconciliation is ultimately a question of how to heal and fix broken relationships, which involves not only the interplay between scales of the local and national but also between even the living and the dead. At the early stages, reconciliation has to do with a shared vision of *good enough* working relationships at individual, interpersonal, group and cultural levels. In Chapter 8, Damian

Grenfell's concern with the spirit world, and whether or not it is in equilibrium, is a good example of this. While building a proper grave, following ritual and demonstrating ongoing care are considered an important way of restoring an equilibrium between the living and the *beiala-sira* (ancestral spirits), the official mechanisms for social reconciliation have failed to address such a spiritual reflection for the Timorese. If the Timorese feel that the spirit world is not in harmony, then they will feel discombobulated, dislocated and unbalanced as well. In the face of suffering and death, therefore, different religious traditions place "banners," which offer explanations that either soothe or aggravate the situation. Similar examples appear in SungYong Lee's chapter on Cambodia. Commemorations, mock funerals and other forms to venerate the dead have been widely conducted across the country, as a form of remembering and moving away from the past for local communities.

As a key requirement for building such a working relationship, the importance of building trust has been emphasised in many chapters in this volume. Mariska Kappmeier, Chiara Venanzetti and J. M. Inton-Campbell in Chapter 7 clarify the roles played by different aspects of trust, which should be considered in the process for promoting reconciliation. Five features of trust, namely, competence, integrity, compassion, compatibility and security, have a significant influence on people's attitudes towards out-groups. Raymond F. Paloutzian, Zeynep Sagir and F. LeRon Shults in Chapter 13 further discuss the essential elements for building the working relationship in the midst or aftermath of real-world hostilities; these are: (1) Both sides of a conflict must *want* hostilities to stop; (2) all parties must *display* truth, honesty and transparency; (3) the circumstances must be interpersonal, inter-group and safe; and (4) *behaviours* in the common interest must be *performed*, reinforced and reciprocated. Mohammed Abu-Nimer (Chapter 4), from a more practical perspective, discusses the notion that people's commitment to develop trust based on honesty and transparency is the first principle for inter-religious dialogue for reconciliation. It can be a daunting task to promote mutual trust between different faith groups in contexts in which religious identities have been manipulated by the various sides to justify violence in the name of protecting one's own faith groups. Religious traditions have all grappled with this problem. It is important, therefore, that we understand the centrality of the different theological/spiritual explanations/narratives about suffering if we are to take the first steps towards reconciliation with self, negative others and those that wish to harm us.

From a long-term perspective, at the same time, questions of reconciliation are, at heart, questions of inclusion into integrated, valued moral communities where those who are broken can find wholeness and where concepts of self and identity can be positive rather than negative. A more inclusive social space should facilitate broader contexts for empathic awareness, equality of opportunity and outcome and social and political security. Among a few components of the new social space discussed by Kevin P. Clements in Chapter 2, a "culture of peace" is noteworthy in this regard. What is interesting about these positive peaceful dynamics is that they all depend on individuals and groups controlling egotism, selfishness and greed. They all vindicate Levinas's concern for personal relationships where there is a commitment to the care of others and the promotion of cultures of peace as opposed to cultures of war, violence and revenge (De Rivera 2008). Cultures of peace flow from experiences of positive informal and formal relationships at the micro- and meso-levels. It is very difficult for rule-based political institutions to legislate for these types of relationships. Their presence enables families, groups and organisations to generate strong, welcoming, inclusive groups and associations, while their absence means that solidarity is much more likely to be achieved by divisions between in-groups and out-groups (Morgan 2007). Sharing the same vision, Chaiwat Satha-Anand (Chapter 5) proposes the concept of a "culture of reconciliation" as a contextual factor that generates further reconciliation. While his analysis particularly focuses on "forgiveness" as its key element, various features and the relations between these features can be discussed under the broad theme of the reconciliation culture.

The key point is, as Ervin Staub argues in Chapter 6, the practice for conflict resolution and reconciliation should address people's tendency to create divisions and generate "otherness" between them. More proactive research is required to explore how such practice can be promoted from within local societies' own resources and how external actors can assist with the process. For instance, long-term peacebuilding in a society can benefit from the practice for developing inclusive caring in children. In this type of caring, a goal should be to extend beyond the boundaries of their in-group and present ways to care about members of other groups in their society. In cases where children are affected by victimisation and trauma, Staub continues, bystanders may endeavour to generate *altruism born of suffering*.

Third, although their positive roles are undeniably important, the limit of the role of elite-level political systems is clear and more bottom-up process for supplementing the limit should be explored. Many previous examples confirm that the state-oriented institutional systems for reconciliation are usually insufficient, if not unsuitable, for building new relationships between different social actors and generating friendship, compassion, empathic awareness and an ethic of responsibility. State systems can focus attention on the recognition of specific perpetrator roles but because of their remoteness and aloofness, states are normally quite bad at dealing with healing processes. This binding-up, healing and attentiveness is better done by civil society actors.

States have difficulty envisioning commonality, unity and wellbeing. Without this, the prospects for deep-rooted and lasting reconciliation in precarious. This is why multi-level approaches are crucial. Moreover, the development of such political arrangements is largely dependent on individuals and groups articulating these values as ideals and making commitments to realise these ideals in practice. The onus is on individual actors who have experienced positive attachments to others in the past to reproduce these relationships in the future. For instance, political leaders in Japan and South Korea attempted to utilise the historical narratives to overcome domestic challenges. Such a political process activated or re-activated deep and painful historic memories and conflicts over past perpetrator–victim roles; spoiled political reputations; and raised deeper questions about collective responsibility for past acts of aggression that were examined in Ria Shibata's Chapter 11. As a result, the levels of people's fear and "negative othering" within the populations in the two countries were intensified through manipulation.

Moreover, institutional mechanisms for reconciliation, such as transitional justice mechanisms and truth and reconciliation commissions, have been challenged in recent times by those in power being willing to trample on truth, engage in and normalise lies and deceit and promote immoral and exclusive communities. These conditions are all inimical to the promotion of peace, justice, compassion and truth. This means that transitional justice mechanisms need to be bolstered by active civil society actors who can speak truth to power; effectively challenge the perpetrators of different kinds of suffering; and engage with painful pasts/histories so that actors are liberated by truthfulness and can become self-motivated, self-actualised and capable of transforming violent relationships into peaceful ones.

One common direction is to make a balance between the political goals of producing a cohesive conflict narrative with the often divergent, dynamic and unique perspectives of various social groups within the society. Their elite representation of individual and collective *suffering history* will never adequately address what people have experienced and it often fails to do justice to the specific memories, remembering and the socio-cultural context within which the suffering was inflicted. Chapters 8 and 9, for instance, describe how the peace processes in Timor-Leste and the Solomon Islands failed to acknowledge and reflect people's different needs related to social reconciliation. In these chapters, a particularly outstanding issue is the state-led institutions' efforts to promote generalised collective narratives/identity. Caitlin Mollica's Chapter 9, in this regard, articulates how interpersonal reconciliation was neglected in the process of reconciliation in Solomon Islands, while the mainstream institution promotes a coherent narrative of the whole society. In particular, it discusses that the institutions failed to recognise the perspectives and needs of youth in the country, which are distinct from the liberal structure of the institutions as well as the traditional social/cultural trends. The author also highlights the various opinions and life-attitudes among the youth, which can generate various dynamics of reconciliation movements in the country. Damian Grenfell's Chapter 8 insightfully points out how the state-led mechanisms for post-conflict reconciliation can neglect the multiple needs of the people. The structure and operation of the Commission for Reception, Truth and Reconciliation (CAVR) in Timor-Leste emerged from an elite consensus between national leadership, and restricted the scope of its mandates. The mandates followed the setting of three aspects of reconciliation: Being scaled to the nation, envisaged as occurring between the still-living, and essentially being a secular process. Accordingly, it presents significant limitations in reflecting many Timorese's approaches to reconciliation and peacebuilding in the post-civil war phases, which concerned reconciliation at the level of individuals and communities, as well as between the survivors and the dead.

Accordingly, to promote effective post-conflict reconciliation, more analytic and political attention should be directed to understanding *bottom-up* strategies for reconciliation at interpersonal or inter-group levels. Social actors like families, kinship groups and religious and economic organisations can play critical roles in this process. In this way, attention is directed toward the ways in which different sectors – such as the family, village, friendship networks, and religious, educational, health, economic and political institutions – intersect with each other, and identifying the positive and negative consequences of such connections.

To do this effectively requires deliberate attention to the many different ways in which individuals and groups imagine peace and a more sensitive appreciation of the ways in which locals see challenges to peace. This step can be quite challenging for internal and external peacebuilders. Rachel Rafferty in Chapter 12 explains the positive roles that external bystanders may play in developing more inclusive ways for understanding conflicts and victimisation rather than intensifying social division. Internal peacebuilders' capacity for this goal is frequently restricted by the in-group's own historical narratives and normative legitimisation of violence. Political leaders, for example, see cultural and social differences in perspectives on peace through the lens of elite politics and national interests. External interveners see these differences (if at all) from the perspective of official or unofficial bilateral or multilateral agencies. All of these actors will be applying very particular models of both change and politics to the locality.

In addition, for this purpose, attention to the connection between, on one hand, the initiatives at individual and interpersonal levels and, on the other hand, the efforts for addressing social and institutional issues is much needed. The effective and collaborative connection of such bottom-up initiatives to the top-down elite-level structure is a crucial element for promoting successful reconciliation. As Mari Fitzduff (Chapter 3) rightly points out, while the attitudes and behaviours of individual actors are influenced and restricted by structural and societal contexts, such structural and societal issues are also subject to the collective actions to address the challenging issues underlying such contexts. In the ideal scenario, multi-track collaboration should incorporate the efforts of all governmental and non-governmental actors with interests in the transformation of violent conflict to join forces in a complementary fashion to ensure that their respective comparative advantages can be turned to positive ends.

A wide range of civil society organisations can work alongside or in conjunction with official level actors to generate awareness of ways in which violence can be prevented, managed or resolved. Thus religious, humanitarian, development, artistic and medical organisations all have roles that they can play in relation to building peaceful relationships. In Chapter 4, Mohammed Abu-Nimer explains how the achievements of individual inter-religious dialogues can be affected by the shifts in institutional priorities. In fact, the rapid increase in the quantity of inter-religious dialogue over the past decades has not been matched by an improvement in their quality. One main reason behind it is that the religious authorities and their institutions have not generated a substantial shift in their structure and priorities in agenda in support of such initiatives. Constructive shifts, for example, in the way to recognise religious pluralism and diversity, require the religious authorities' careful examination of their roles in the conventional structure of the violence and its potential transformation.

Ervin Staub in Chapter 6 pays attention to the cooperation between authorities and "experts." When there is sufficient political motivation, the example demonstrates that local authorities can open a space in which academics and other experts share the information from their previous research and experience. As a practical proposal based on the example, Staub encourages academic associations like American Psychological Association to establish task forces to reach out to political authorities. The media also play a critical role in relation to escalatory dynamics and need to be given more prominence in the designing of processes for dealing with conflict. The private sector can also play a critical role in these processes by mainstreaming conflict sensitivity into its decision-making processes and by ensuring that investment, employment, production and distribution decisions are aimed at enhancing the bottom line but, more importantly, making a contribution towards structural stabilisation. By and large, however, it is the not-for-profit civil society organisations that are committed to working with locals and international actors in analysing, understanding and responding to conflict in constructive and creative ways that are going to play the most important roles in responding to conflict.

Finally, a number of chapters acknowledge the importance of dialogue in promoting reconciliation and present proposals for engaging in more meaningful dialogue. The positive influence of contact and dialogue in generating more empathetic and reconciliatory attitudes has been clarified in Mari Fitzduff's chapter. Through fMRI imaging, it was revealed that well-formulated dialogue can alter the neural circuits concerned with identity differences. Interestingly, the chapter reports that the disempowered groups tend to become more empathetic by having more chances to tell their stories and to be heard, whereas the dominant groups become more empathetic by listening to the counterparts' stories. Moreover, Chapters 2, 4 and 5 point out the cultural, institutional, structural and practical challenges facing the efforts for facilitating the dialogues for reconciliation.

In particular, care should be given in the dialogues at an early stage when the people in conflicts are just beginning their interaction. In such instances, the chapters in this volume highlight a few social-psychological prerequisites that should be taken into consideration by the conflict parties as well as mediating actors.

*A safe catalytic space*: This is a space within which both parties (or all parties if there are more than two) feel comfortable. They should not feel too comfortable though, otherwise nothing catalytic will happen. A safe space, as the name implies, is a place within which actors can vent concerns without fear. It's a space for costing the conflict and it's a space within which impasse-breaking possibilities can be explored. The third party guarantees the personal and relational safety of all the participants. The intervener enables individuals to take risks that they might be otherwise unwilling to take.

*An invitation to the parties to converse with each other*: This invitation can be given by the intervener or by the parties themselves, through conciliatory gestures, signalling a desire to talk or to engage in dialogue in order to transform antagonistic relationships into cooperative ones. As Mohammed Abu-Nimer states in Chapter 4, it is challenging for the groups in conflicts to accept the out-groups as the counterparts for dialogue. Trusting the out-group is a kind of risk-taking. However, meaningful dialogue cannot start without the courage and willingness to take the risk.

*An invitation to collaborative problem solving*: Productive dialogue rests on a willingness to engage in collaborative problem-solving – both with allies and with putative enemies. Thus, interveners have to model the benefits of non-zero-sum decision-making and the costs of the alternatives. With this element, Ervin Staub mentions that such a process can be supported when active, positive bystandership is established by all segments of the population – leaders, the media, community organisations, individual citizens. In this process, Mohammed Abu-Nimer articulates the importance of symmetry in the relationship between the involved actors (Chapter 4).

Collaborative dialogue, however, does not mean that they talk only about the issues that they can agree on. Although acknowledging and cherishing commonalities is important, the dialogue should be directed to develop the participants' critical self-reflection on difference. The respect for differing perspectives can be generated through the process. Due to the sensitivity involved, the process of touching upon difficult issues needs to be done in a gradual and professional way (See Chapter 4 for more details).

*A delight in social encounter for its own sake*: It is important that there be some participants who derive enjoyment from "social encounters" for their own sake, although this is not a quality that can be prescribed or taught to those who have no inclination to see the satisfactions that flow from good relationships.

*Acknowledgment of the "eternal" in the other, a "reverence for life"*: This quality is not one that can be forced on others, but it flows from an enhancement of empathetic awareness. It grows as one's circle of compassion grows and as one becomes more deeply aware of the essential interdependence of life. It also creates very positive dispositions towards collaborative problem-solving. Taking it one step further, Ervin Staub in Chapter 5 explains that humanising the "other" is essential to overcome devaluation and the danger of violence.

*Deep listening skills and a willingness to engage in non-judgemental listening*: This quality is absolutely critical to good dialogue. Without listening to the presenting and underlying problems, it is difficult for individual actors to discern areas of commonality and areas of difference. Without such a capacity it is also difficult to understand what is critical and what is non-critical to hostile parties.

*A reflective capacity that helps the parties understand themselves and each other more deeply and intimately*: This quality is intimately connected to listening qualities. The more one listens to others and attends to their underlying needs and interests, the more one is inclined to adopt a reflective and reflexive stance in relation to them and the more likely it is that antagonistic parties will engage de-escalating dynamics. When such reflective dialogue continues, the chance for promoting mutual understanding, accommodation, and the shared vision of a good society that Ervin Staub highlights in Chapter 5 will grow.

*An option-generating capacity*: This capacity is also vital to effective problem-solving. Having identified the issues at stake, it is always important that there be some actors who are adept and skilled at generating creative options. It is also important that they, and/or others are able to implement the options that are generated. This role should not be underestimated in any conflict transformation process. It is often the creative opportunistic response to what appears to be an impossible impasse which unfreezes stuck relationships.

As a final remark, we would like to summarise two broader messages that flow from peacebuilding research and practice. First, the findings and arguments in this volume call for a more nuanced framework for examining multilayered factors surrounding reconciliation in conflict-affected societies. The utility of conventional peacebuilding models for reconciliation would be unachievable without engaging with political authorities and the transformation of negative dynamics in state institutions. Nevertheless, those who wish to advance reconciliation need to pay more attention to the opportunities it creates for various social actors to participate in reconciliatory processes and to weave their own distinctive contributions into reconciliation design and implementation plans. Second, the findings of this volume should encourage researchers and practitioners in peacebuilding to be more creative and bolder in imagining new visions and directions for reconciliation. While it is important to find "realistic" methods to address various challenges *facing* conflict-affected societies, this should not mean that peacebuilding should remain conventionally driven. As Elise Boulding (2000: 29) wrote,

> [p]eace cultures thrive on and are nourished by visions of how things might be, in a world where sharing and caring are part of the accepted lifeways for everyone. The very ability to imagine something different and better than what currently exists is critical for the possibility of social change.

A critical component of reconciliation, therefore, is to have a shared vision of how to heal broken relationships and to understand how those transformed relationships can guarantee stable peace and harmony between states and peoples emerging from violent conflict.

## References

Boulding, E. (2000). *Cultures of peace: The hidden side of history* (1st ed.). Syracuse: Syracuse University Press.

Cox, M., (Ed.) (2008). *Social capital and peace-building: Creating and resolving conflict with trust and social networks*. Abingdon: Routledge.

De Rivera, J. (2008). *Handbook on building cultures of peace*. New York: Springer.

Levinas, E. (1989). Ethics as first philosophy. In S. Hand (Ed.), *The Levinas reader* (pp. 75–87). Oxford: Blackwell Publishing.
Levinas, E., & Hand, S. (1989). *The Levinas reader*. New York: Blackwell Publishing.
Morgan, M. (2007). *Discovering Levinas*. Cambridge: Cambridge University Press.
Özerdem, A., & Lee, S. (Eds.) (2016). *International peacebuilding: An introduction*. London: Routledge.

# Index

Made in the USA
Las Vegas, NV
24 October 2024

62905129-d2d6-4590-97db-28682c44f8f5R01